Roll over Beethoven

STANLEY ARONOWITZ

Roll over Beethoven

The Return of Cultural Strife

WESLEYAN UNIVERSITY PRESS

Published by University Press of New England / Hanover and London

Wesleyan University Press

Published by University Press of New England,

Hanover, NH 03755

Printed in the United States of America

5   4   3   2   1

CIP data appear at the end of the book

To my daughter Kim,
who told Tchaikovsky the news

Contents

Preface

AS THIS WORK began the short journey from manuscript to book, Americans were witnessing the year-long quadrennial ritual that we call a presidential election campaign. For the most part, the ritual was being enacted according to script: charges and countercharges, warnings from each major party candidate that the election of his rival would plunge the nation into crisis—economic and otherwise—and a pledge to the electorate by the sitting president that if given another chance he would do better. But 1992 was somewhat different from previous exercises. For in this year cultural and social issues seemed to occupy an unusually large place in the proceedings: the vice-president revealed himself to be a poor speller and, at the same time, a born-again cultural populist. In an astounding series of speeches he attacked the television sit-com "Murphy Brown" for glorifying single motherhood, thereby violating "family values," by deciding to have a baby out of wedlock. Quayle lashed out at the "cultural elite," which, in his view, dominates prime-time television with programming "out of step" with the mainstream. In reply, in the opening episode of its 1992–1993 season, "Murphy" stepped out of character to refute the vice-president's contention by praising the "gorgeous mosaic" of cultural diversity.

In fact, the Bush presidency (which, aside from its glorious if indecisive pursuit of Iraq's ruler, Saddam Hussein, may have been rivaled only by the ill-fated administration of James Buchanan for ineptitude) did effect some notable changes. It managed to virtually obliterate federal aid to higher education; to reintroduce, after nearly a decade of conservative activism, benign neglect in welfare and other aspects of social policy; and perhaps most saliently, for the purposes of the present work, to gut federal support to the arts and humanities and introduce overt political criteria to some aspects of science policy. The cases in point, administrative vetoes of peer recommendations for funding—not only for performance artist Karen Finley and other heretics, but also for an academic conference organized with the conservative premise that violence may be genetically based—represented the most overt politicization of the National Endowments of the Arts and Humanities and the Health Institutes in their respective histories. To the extent that many artists, scholars, and scientists rely on federal funding for their work, the Bush administration has succeeded in closing off avenues for dissent, on a non-partisan basis. In the name of fighting political correctness (see Chapter 1) in these fields, it has distinguished itself by simultaneously condemning and imposing political criteria for supporting the intellect in ways that would make its predecessor, the Reagan administration, appear wildly libertarian. It is not that George Bush cares one way or another about these issues. In fact, he is the scion of a well-known Rockefeller Republican and his prior record reveals no propensity to involve himself in social and cultural issues. Rather, as Gary Wills has noted, it appeared that Mr. Bush is a prisoner of his political base, which in the absence of any other, has veered radically to the right—fundamentalist Christians, professional conservative pundits (although not all of them), and, of course, important elements of the military-industrial complex and the private health and pharmaceutical industries. He is, in fact, a bona fide member of the foreign policy and intelligence establishments that have prevailed over American politics for the past fifty years. Based on his performance, we can safely assert that Bush neither knows nor particularly cares about anything domestic, including the arts, the humanities, and the sciences. For this reason he ceded decision-making over these matters to others—usually, but not always, ultraconservatives whose morality is firmly rooted in the nineteenth century. In the case of the NIH's withdrawal of funding to the conference that proposed to explore the genetic basis for violence, the abrupt volte-face by the director of the agency may be explained purely by election year politics. The racist implications of the study made a grant risky. But this ordinary political gesture disguises the more disquieting tendency to subordinate inquiry to the vicissitudes of politics, coming as it does on the heels of the NEA's refusal to fund a group of artists for their sexually explicit performances in theater and photography. These decisions made it clear that, as eminent art critic Senator Jesse Helms declared, government had no obligation to fund art that violated mainstream moral standards. Let dissent find a private market; the government had to reflect majority sentiments. So much for the avant garde!

And, who can deny the salience of the abortion debate for our politics? After years of denial, even the "expert" political spin-doctors—whose role in elections often exceeds that of the candidates—have finally acknowledged the so-called "gender gap." Either the consensus has been broken or women have emerged from the underground to become perhaps the most significant single political constituency. The Democrats have increasingly nominated women for Senate and House berths; there are a record number of elected women mayors; and, perhaps equally important after two Supreme Court decisions affirming the right of states to abridge the provisions of *Roe* v. *Wade,* Congress will more than likely enact a law protecting the right to abortion against Supreme Court and state limitations.

Despite trying circumstances, it is clear that cultural study, once safely relegated to the margins of public discourse, has come of age. While it would be somewhat conceited to attribute, entirely, recent political victories and defeats to candidates' positions on social and cultural issues, it is fairly obvious that economistic contentions that "culture" is a purely secondary sphere are being refuted by events, at least in the United States. Instead of merely churning out standardized products of a culture industry, television and radio have become displacements of an emergent civil society. While the "public" is still an endangered species (less than half the eligible population bothers to vote in the presidential election and even fewer vote in off-year contests, for example), talk radio and television, increasingly provocative situation comedies, and the welter of dramatic series that address social issues attest to a restless, even contentious audience that wants spicy rather than bland. Oprah Winfrey and Phil Donahue have managed to transform the most degraded of TV genres, daytime talk TV, into vociferous sounding boards for discontent.

With more than thirteen million students in colleges and universities the academy has descended from its tower and become a space of intense struggle. The rise of multiculturalism—women's, African-American, Latino, Asian, and cultural studies—has been greeted by cultural conservatives as nothing short of a takeover of the intellectual agenda in American universities. Although this is something of a paranoid reaction (the Bush administration's Humanities Chair argued that the phenomenon known as "political correctness" is rampant in the academy), the present book argues that there is a sea change in the nature of legitimate intellectual knowledge.

For example, the idea that the mission of higher education is to conduct the disinterested pursuit of truth and objectivity, always a controversial notion, is under siege. The left holds that the ideal of value-free scholarship has always been an ideology that masks the fact that intellectual practices are free neither of context nor of standpoints. The right declares the concept of disinterestedness as consensual for all true scholars, universalizing its views as a series of "values" the violation of which constitutes, prima facie, heresy, even conspiracy. Its canon, its methods of evaluation, its judgments are arrived at via unimpeachable scholarship. All others need not apply.

Roll over Beethoven was conceived in the context of these battles and is meant to be an intervention rather than a neutral account of them. In my efforts to delineate the issues in contemporary cultural debates I have been helped by my friends to avoid many inaccuracies and conceptual gaffes. Ellen Willis read the manuscript, but especially Chapter 6. She called my attention to several important omissions in the first draft, which I was happy to correct.

Fredric Jameson, Henry Giroux, and Barbara Martinsons read the entire manuscript and made apposite criticisms and suggestions. If I did not heed all of them, it is probably to the detriment of the final product. I owe a considerable debt to Kim Paice, my research assistant, whose work far exceeded her compensation. She offered careful and intelligent readings of the first three chapters and made available to me material I would not otherwise have known. I owe a special debt to Biodun Inginla who first suggested that I write the book.

I want to thank my students in Cultural Studies courses, study groups, and tutorials at CUNY Graduate Center who over the past five years endured my ruminations and contributed their own. Many of the ideas in the present book were developed in these settings. I want to thank Margaret Yard and Kimberly Flynn for what I have learned from them.

For their collaboration on the theory and practice of television, I thank my colleagues in the media group of CUNY Cultural Studies—Bill DiFazio, Paolo Carpignano, Robin Andersen, Jeff Schmidt, and, later, Elayne Rapping. At many points of the present work, I remember and cherish our often heated discussions with pleasure and gratitude.

S. A.

Roll over Beethoven

Introduction

THE CATEGORY of "culture" once and still endlessly debated by critics and ethnographers in mostly sequestered precincts has, over the past decade, become a major political issue. For example, conservatives do not view "multiculturalism" as a curriculum reform best discussed among those involved in schooling. In the modest proposal to open the curriculum to "represent" the cultures of diverse populations of the United States, many see a frontal assault on the core values of western civilization. Among these values none stands higher than the assumption that America's greatness depends on melting and otherwise obliterating group differences. In their quest for "unity," California voters made English the standard language in schools and other public venues, despite the state's growing Asian and Latino populations who typically retain and actively speak their native tongues; everywhere in universities and colleges a raging dispute continues over the literary canon as women, blacks, and other hitherto excluded groups demand significant alterations in what is taught as representative of tradition; and many gays and lesbians have more recently asserted their cultural autonomy. For them, sexuality is not merely a question of preference, but involves the right to exercise these preferences free of discrimination. "Queer" theory, one of the more bold contemporary academic movements, argues that sexuality can only be comprehended as practices which connote a distinct culture that, even if mediated by the social and historical conditions of its development, amounts to a form of life.

Cultural politics is, in the first place, about group and personal identities beyond that of the traditional affiliation of individuals with the "imagined community" of the nation.[1] Its fundamental presupposition, the celebration of difference as vehicle of "empowerment" in what many subaltern groups perceive is a hostile social environment, is no longer a subterranean pledge of initiates. Difference, sometimes transmuted into the slogan of "diversity" and attached to one of the more progressivist definitions of American nationality, has become the battle cry of what a conservative philosopher once called "unmeltable ethnics."[2] However, ethnicity hardly encompasses the multiplicity of discourses that in recent years has claimed political and cultural space.

Yet, like many struggles for national identity and autonomy in earlier periods, the issues are frequently joined over language. For even as English enjoys the enviable position of a common international language and the United States has emerged from the cold war as perhaps the only global power, Americanism as an identity has suffered considerably in the past two decades. Although the Gulf War of 1991 demonstrated that there remains a sedimented reservoir of patriotism, national patriotic holidays are widely celebrated by consuming leisure: they have become occasions for family gatherings, short vacation trips, or shopping rather than times for public demonstration of national loyalty. Polling data reveal that many cannot name the last three presidents; few know who represents them in various legislative bodies. And, perhaps a more telling sign for the United States, the flood of new immigrants from Latin America and the Caribbean, Asia, and Eastern Europe have, in growing numbers, declined to follow earlier waves in agreeing to relegate their cultural identity to that of the nation state.

This reluctance to "fit in" to what is widely understood as "American" culture is understandable from a number of perspectives. Unlike the three previous periods of large-scale immigration (1500 to 1800, 1840 to 1880, 1880 to 1920, America has been less than welcoming this time. Since the late 1970s, which were years of rapid immigration, economic expansion has slowed to a crawl. In the wake of plant closings and other types of capital flight, technological displacement, and a growth of imports, nativism—never absent in American history—has enjoyed a dramatic revival. Following these developments, many voices have been raised to close the borders to newcomers: this call has been elevated to a legitimate political demand and has been abetted by the rising tide of conservative thought and politics; organized labor, stung by increasing foreign competition from Europe and Japan, has also viewed the large influx of low-wage immigrant labor as a threat to its already eroded living standards; and, of course, the historic shift of immigration from the global north to the south has raised, yet another time, the ever present specter of racism. Indeed, racially motivated incidents have achieved a prominent place in media headlines. Howard Beach, Crown Heights, Bensonhurst, Liberty City, and Central Los Angeles have become emblematic of identity conflicts arising from the conjunction of economic scarcity, race, and immigration.

Perhaps a major source of the growing unmeltability of recent immigrants is that they perceive that the opportunity structure of the United States has become fairly restricted. Certainly, many have chosen to leave their own countries because, relatively speaking, there are more chances for work, income, and education in the United States. And many value the freedoms that, as eventual citizens, they might enjoy. However, immigrants, even when documented, find that they are often obliged to work at low-paying jobs or in the informal economy where wages are often below legal minimums; families survive by working long hours and frequently pressing their own children into labor; housing and health conditions are usually far below what are considered decent; and undocumented immigrants are subject to harassment by police and immigration officials and to superexploitation by employers.[3]

But the politics of cultural difference antedates multiculturalism and immigration. I want to call attention to two aspects of the current cultural conflicts that remain deeply disturbing to those whose vision of a national culture was forged during the cold war era. The first is perhaps more well known than the second: the penchant of the largely native-born generational movement of the 1960s to declare its independence from, if not outright hostility to, precisely those values and beliefs that underlie conventional American identity—the summary judgment of which is that this country, notwithstanding its warts, is the best of all possible worlds. From this position issues the details: America enjoys more democracy, more opportunity (meaning better chances for social mobility), a higher standard of living than most, if not all other nations, and more individual freedom than any other major industrialized country, not to mention Eastern Europe before the fall and the Third World. For the purposes of my argument, it is not necessary to evaluate these claims. More important is the historical validity of the statement that a considerable portion of an entire generation once challenged their efficacy, a shift that has motivated much, if not all of the conservative and neoliberal counterattack of the past two decades. The second dissonance is the product of the emergence of what generally has been labeled postmodernism. For, as I illustrate in the next chapter, aesthetic modernism became the emblem of the new intellectual patriotism of the postwar era, a modernism that was defined by its opposition and disdain of both socialist realism and fascist mysticism. Perhaps it was likely, if not inevitable, that, with the breakup of the modernist consensus in artistic and critical circles after the 1960s, its proponents would identify the new politics of culture with the barbarians at the gates. It is ironic that the politicization of art during the first decades after the war was an unintended consequence of the modernist creed that art, above all, should be exempt from politics. Since the communist left and the right insisted that art could not sustain such a separation, for many intellectuals the ideology of the autonomy of art became a political creed, but it was also a measure of the degree to which individuals and groups were judged from a democratic perspective.

The spread of postmodernism to social sciences, philosophy, and even natural sciences in the recent past has raised the stakes of the postmodern debate, but also deepened the resolve of cultural conservatives to stem its tide. Of course, if J. F. Lyotard is right that postmodernism cannot be understood as an "ideology" in the traditional meaning of the term (i.e., as a system of beliefs that may or may not translate into practices), but is, instead, a "condition" marking a profound paradigm shift in the fundamental assumptions of the production and dissemination of knowledge, not a choice but the ineluctable outcome of a series of historically situated events, then the culturally conservative counterattack can hope only to slow down the shift.[4] Clearly, writers as otherwise politically diverse as Irving Kristol, Irving Howe, Eugene Genovese, and Arthur Schlesinger, Jr., have sensed that, however righteous, they are fighting a rear-guard action.[5] Consequently, their panic grows in proportion to their acute sense that their collective work has, above all, historical, even archaeological interest.

This in no way diminishes the vehemence with which they conduct the campaign to marginalize, if not stamp out, the scourge that is shaking the artistic and intellectual landscape. Since 1989, when it became apparent that the previous conservative policy of benign neglect of cultural radicalism collapsed as, even in the face of a growing conservative hegemony in economic and political life, cultural politics spread especially but not exclusively in colleges and universities, the daily press, no less than intellectual and middlebrow journals, has been filled with polemics: against feminist and black studies, postmodernism, multiculturalism, and one of the major forms these departures have taken in universities—cultural studies. The issues raised during these fulminations bear on those of academic freedom, the role of the university in economic, political, and social life, questions of science and ideology, legitimate and trivial knowledge, as well as perhaps the most historically explosive question, the responsibility of intellectuals for promoting democratic public life.

This book situates itself in these debates. In what follows, I offer an interpretative genealogy of cultural studies that I take as one of the crucial crossroads where the questions of cultural politics are today concentrated and concatenated. However, while *Roll over Beethoven* focuses on the specific history and characteristics of contemporary cultural studies in Great Britain and the United States, one cannot avoid addressing the larger issues of the new configuration of knowledge and the ways in which it intersects with the rise, the decline, and the resurgence of social movements. If knowledge is the underlying object of cultural studies, as well as the real stake in contemporary controversies, then problems of high/low, popular culture and canon do not exhaust its purview. Consequently, I have been obliged, in addition to the specifically literary disputes, to address some of the debates about shifts in historiography and social and natural scientific knowledge, for these areas are closely linked to the new currents in cultural politics.

At the risk of belaboring an already overused term, I want to argue that the brisk, often incendiary debates within American intellectual circles about these questions amount to a "crisis" whose consequences are felt in almost every area of politics and culture. Simply stated, the crisis consists in the breakup of the cultural consensus that emerged from historical conditions of the twentieth century that sustained it: the assimilationist melting pot, modernity and modernism, long-term economic expansion and its concomitants of consumerism, imperialism, and a virtual one-party state that, nevertheless, maintained two or more competing organizations differing chiefly on strategic and tactical questions. The deep fissures that have appeared in intellectual circles take the form of theoretical arguments such as, for example, whether poststructuralism is a fraud or a genuinely new way of seeing; whether modernity is exhausted or merely in need of a transfusion; the "clarity of language" question raised most notably by Dinesh D'Souza and Roger Kimball, prominent battering rams for the conservative counterrevolution; and, most recently, Paul Hollander's charge that many intellectual radicals are really anti-American. Their common root is a desperate effort to reestablish, by invective and other means including repression, the old consensus.

Despite the strides made by cultural conservatives in some quarters, not the least of which is their virtual domination of mainstream media, the outcome is by no means clear. One might reasonably argue that the skeptical, decentered, multifarious cultural politics of the emerging discourses of feminism, race, sexuality, and ethnicity are unpatriotic, primitive, misguided, and misinformed or even dangerous. The problem for the would-be consensus builders is that the fault lines of the conflict may be too deep to repair short of openly stifling dissent—in which case, as with the finger in the dike, the water is likely to find a way to overflow.

As I show below, the defenders of the old faith face formidable obstacles. Even if they may take solace in the collapse of communism, at least for the moment, the decline of many of their own cherished institutions such as universities, "serious" classical music, modernist art, and the so-called legitimate theater—indeed many of the apparatuses of high, western culture—weakens the polemical thrust of those who would declare marginal the minions of postmodern culture. Of course, with the shrinking of professional and technical jobs and, concomitantly, of academic institutions owing both to depressed economic conditions and educational policy, cultural conservatism can impose tradition through executive authorities by putting students' noses to the grindstone and thereby reimpose the conditions of Plato's cave allegory.

Cultural consensus may be achieved even as economic and political systems exhibit considerable flux. But, unlike previous periods of rapid transformation, what the quest to reinstate traditional values lacks now is a widespread perception of progress. While the idea of progress has been subject to severe intellectual scrutiny since the late nineteenth century, American popular culture was, until fairly recently, suffused with hope. One only need consult the

Golden Age of movie musicals (1933 to 1960) to support the contention that the perception of progress prevailed even in the depths of the Depression and the jarring postwar problems of adjustment and reconversion during which millions left their families and communities, either driven from their homes and jobs and forced to migrate in search of work, or discharged from the armed forces to a fairly protracted period of uncertainty.

Musicals such as those of Busby Berkeley, and postwar hits *State Fair, Oklahoma, Singin' in the Rain,* along with the steady stream of pre- and postwar sunny Fred Astaire movies may be seen as vital components of the ideological glue that preserved the consensus perception of America as a land of opportunity and, equally, of reconciliation. Even when the musical addressed social themes as, for example, in *Finian's Rainbow* or *South Pacific,* racial discrimination (or in the contemporaneous vernacular, "prejudice") was depicted as a local phenomenon; Hammerstein's liberal sincerity in the song "You Have to be Taught to Hate" is an appeal to Understanding, directed to the largely middle-class white audiences of the musical theater whose liberalism had, by the end of the war, embraced ideas of racial integration.

It is important to consider that there is no absence of social themes in American popular culture during these halcyon days of American progressivism. Particularly important were the plethora of plays, in the 1940s on and off Broadway, on racial themes prior to the development of the modern civil rights movement. Issues of discrimination were represented *within* and not against the consensus view that race was a giant wart on the face of democracy which was, in most respects, healthy.

Three years before the publication of *The Vital Center* (1950), a book that became a virtual manifesto for anti-communist liberalism in the fifties and the sixties, Arthur Schlesinger, Jr., laid down some of the leading ideas of this era in the *Partisan Review.*

"There seems no inherent obstacle to the gradual advance of [democratic] socialism in the United States through a series of New Deals. . . . The next depression will certainly mean a vast expansion in government ownership and control. The private owners will not only acquiesce in this. In characteristic capitalist panic, they will demand it."[6] Schlesinger identifies two enemies of this reasonable scenario: Soviet communism, which, in his rhetoric, is the embodiment of postfascist evil, and their fellow traveling intellectuals within the United States; and the shortsighted business class that is likely to oppose any enlightened foreign or domestic program on archaic ideological grounds. But, according to Schlesinger, if liberals can overcome these resistances, the time is at hand for the triumph of democracy "step by step, in a way that will not disrupt the fabric of custom, law and mutual confidence, upon which personal rights depend."[7]

Schlesinger's gradualist message has marked his political interventions for forty-five years. Note that political democracy and socialism (here identified wholly with "ownership by the state of all significant means of production")[8] can avoid the pitfalls of totalitarianism only if the "fabric of custom" is not disrupted. Democratic socialism (really a kind of state welfarism) in its liberal, gradualist phase must, in the interest of preserving democracy, accept the cultural system and the rule of law as given, for all practical purposes. In 1947, this constraint was informed by the perception that Soviet communism, presumably in the interest of creating a "new man," tore its society, root and branch, from those customs that sustained group solidarity. As in social democracy, the European counterpart of American progressivism, of which Schlesinger became a leading spokesperson, the two rules of economic and political transformation are gradualism within the liberal democratic state and cultural conservatism.

It is no wonder that, once again, a significant portion of the intellectuals associated with modern liberalism such as Irving Howe and Schlesinger find themselves, even if uncomfortably, allied with neoconservatives, most saliently, for our purposes, Irving Kristol and Hilton Kramer, editor of the militantly modernist *New Criterion,* in the crusade against the disunities sown by polyglot cultural innovators. As Talcott Parsons, that great theorist of modernity, never tired of reminding us, preserving the cultural system is the very presupposition of social stability, without which reason cannot flourish. As we will see in the discussion on political correctness, current debates are, in part, a replay, in different cadences, of this much older dispute.[9] In the second part of this introduction, I want to elaborate on some of these problems and indicate how this book intends to address them.

I have called this book an "interpretive genealogy" of cultural studies. By this term, I mean to distinguish my perspective from at least two alternate approaches: cultural or literary history and a straightforward account that might delineate the categories, styles, and institutional contexts that have marked the development of cultural studies. In each of these ways of seeing, the object is taken as given; it has a definite history, a cast of characters and well-defined mode of intellectual interventions *within* a fairly well established field of academic knowledge.

To be sure, there is no doubt that the development of cultural studies has been influenced by both the impetus to depart from traditional disciplinary demarcations and, especially recently, by the imperative of institutionalization that is perceived by proponents of cultural studies to oblige them to integrate themselves more securely within the disciplines, specifically the humanities. And, particularly in English and, to a lesser degree, comparative literature, cultural studies tends to become a weapon in internecine wars, especially of those who wish to practice studies of popular culture and what has been described as "theory." Of course, these confinements subvert the whole project of cultural studies, which, as I will argue, seeks to transgress the boundaries between humanities and the sciences, and even to transcend the boundaries of formal academic sites. At its best, cultural studies is not interdisciplinary; it is antidisciplinary.

If one adopts this perspective, the object of investigation has two quite distinct aspects: on one hand, there are the *actually existing* programs, centers, curricula, foci of cultural studies, each with a history, a mode of existence within the institutional contexts that spawned them, and a series of works that represent their specific intervention(s). In this book, actually existing cultural studies is an important, even if subordinate part of my considerations. On the other hand, I want to attend to the *tendency* of cultural studies toward intellectual transgression that, as we will discover, is already implicated in its roots. That tendency is rarely made apparent by the actors themselves, so throughout this book I try to tease out what is often unsaid.

For example, British cultural studies sought to overcome the occlusion of working-class culture from legitimate intellectual knowledge. In the process, it was obliged to examine the concept of culture itself as it had been defined by its Arnoldian legatees.[10] British cultural studies was known for this violation and then for the violation of the violation, when it shifted to the study of women, race, and youth and insisted, in opposition to a more classical Marxism, that the agency of these social categories involved legitimate objects of knowledge. Yet, it was only retrospectively that some of its major protagonists openly acknowledged the theoretical and ideological implications of this shift.

In a slightly different register, we often treat the social upheavals of the 1960s as an instance of immaculate conception that arose spontaneously from the loins of its main actors. In Chapters 5 and 6, I maintain that there were significant, largely ignored antecedents of the startling shift in aesthetic and political sensibility that marked this era and these were precursors in the sense that they influenced what followed. I do not want to deny that the cultural uprising of the 1960s was a sharp break with its past; surely, in comparison to the immediate postwar period, the intense focus on rock and roll and new explorations of sexuality and drugs that literally millions of youth experienced, made these original years. New Left politics rejected all forms of the old left, democratic as well as authoritarian; the counterculture proclaimed a "new morning" in communal ways of living. They rejected consumerism in favor of a different conception of desire, a conception that nurtured a mass ecology movement in the United States that has, in turn, inspired major critiques of what has been regarded as sacred and unassailable knowledge: the theories and results of modern natural science.

More to the point, I argue that the most profound stake in the crisis of cultural authority, briefly described in the previous section, is the authority of knowledge. Who has the right to determine criteria of validity? Who may speak truth to power? What is the responsibility of intellectuals with respect to their own knowledge?

So, in what follows, I "read" the tendency in the history of cultural studies as a lurching, often unexamined effort to reconstitute legitimate knowledge and its agency. From this perspective, I interpret the culture wars, not merely in the ideological terms in which they are framed, but in connection with the breakup of the old knowledge paradigms that have been ineluctably linked to economic and state institutions. Along the way, I find strange allies acting as gatekeepers for the established culture. From these alliances, I have concluded that the old definitions of "left" and "right" barely apply to cultural struggles. People who might find themselves opposed on issues of state economic intervention, market economics, party affiliations, and other proclivities might discover they can agree on the absolute necessity of defending civilization "as we know it" or, conversely, decide to join in an effort to attain a more libertarian educational system.

As I have already indicated, we are witnessing a basic shift in our acceptance of the validity of scientific claims, a shift barely twenty years old. For example, here is a judgment, written as late as 1964 by one of Europe's prominent intellectual journalists:"Sociology, one foot planted in metaphysics, the other tentatively poised on the elevator leading to the summit of political power, is the master discipline of our time. Other ages may have done more for philosophy, literature or art. Even the nineteenth century was better at the business of intellectual synthesis. But none can dispute our preeminence when it comes to the social sciences. There is nothing in the past to match the devoted labors of those trained researchers who have taught us how to quantify, tabulate and analyse our social environment."[11] So begins George Lichtheim's admiring but ambivalent review of David Riesman's collection of essays, *Abundance for What*. Lichtheim's judgment about the preeminence of sociology, grounded in the apparent triumph of the "ultimate authority [of] fact" for which the discipline, at least among the social sciences, takes responsibility, reflected the optimism of the first decades after the Second World War that Reason, embodied in the social applications of scientific method, would, after the long nightmare of fascist irrationalism, dominate human affairs. No longer would the social world be disrupted, even ruled, by mystical, racist, and openly ideological precepts, but instead, in terms of the prevailing "empiricist orthodoxy," would rely on the dispassionate exploration of the data and their integration with rational principles.

As a Central European intellectual, a veteran observer of cold war politics, and critic of ideologies of various sorts, Lichtheim is too jaded to accept the jaunty, optimistic American faith in enlightenment science as a new basis for human reconciliation. Yet, he can't help exhibiting a kind of jealous admiration of Riesman's naive self-assurance that the procedures of his discipline might significantly contribute to overcoming the world's economic and social ills. At the same time, with memories of death and destruction still fresh, Lichtheim has little sympathy for one of the major preoccupations of Riesman and other American sociologists: the problem of affluence and its implications for middle-class life. Next to the Nazi terror, chronic economic underdevelopment in the third world, and the contemporary threat of mutual nuclear annihilation, social problems in "advanced" capitalist societies such as alienation with its attendant symptoms of loneliness, the furtive search of many for "meaning," and displacements such as excessive consumption seem to Lichtheim parochial, if not trivial. Yet, until recently, modern liberalism, no less than Marxism, could not doubt the transformative power of critical social science with its combination of humanism with the rigor of the natural sciences.

Measured against the current widespread skepticism concerning science, Lichtheim's backhanded endorsement of scientificity as the way to salvation seems painfully outdated. Since the mid-1960s we have definitively entered an era where every precept of the scientific enlightenment is subject to scrutiny, particularly its application to human affairs. And there is reason to be wary of some of the products of the new science.

For example, molecular biology, which has all but overrun biology, has resolved itself into a virtual technoscience. In Richard Lewontin's words, it has become "an unchallenged orthodoxy,"[12] and for its practitioners "transcendent truth and unassailable power."[13] In the "dream of the human genome project," molecular biologists and their allies in government and private industry seek the "acquisition of all of the details of our genome" that "undoubtedly will affect the way much of biology is pursued in the twenty-first century."[14] These are the remarks of leading figures in this biological "revolution" which, even before the close of the century, has swept nearly all alternative views of the human organism from its path. Lewontin, as a dissenter *within* biology, raises all the pertinent objections to the relentless pursuit of the goals of the project: its grandiose claims cannot possibly be achieved, especially the expectation that when all information about the genetic makeup of humans has been collected, prescriptions for eliminating disease will follow, virtually automatically. Lewontin's argument is that this expectation is based on an erroneous model of the human organism. He invokes the metaphor of the fetish to describe the tendency to ascribe all power to the DNA molecule. Therefore although it is "correct in its detailed molecular description it is wrong in what it claims to explain."[15] Contrary to the three major elements of molecular biology's explanatory model that DNA is self reproducing, it "makes" duplicate cells and therefore "organisms are determined by it." Lewontin advances the alternative that human organisms are not only formed by their genetic composition but crucially shaped by their environment(s) as well: "A living organism at any moment of its life is the unique consequence of a developmental history that results from the interaction of and determination by internal and external forces. The external forces, what we usually think of as the 'environment,' are themselves partly the consequence of activities of the organism itself as it produces and consumes the conditions of its own existence. Organisms do not find the world that they develop. They make it. Reciprocally, the internal forces are not autonomous but act in response to the external."[16]

Of course, this is a minority view within contemporary biology, indeed within all natural science and philosophy, which have leaned heavily toward internalist explanations. Yet, in this public display of a scientific controversy, we see that the consensus that has marked natural science in one of its most dynamic branches is breaking down.

Other investigators of the consequences of bioengineering have contended that these practices are creating serious environmental hazards and, more problematically, have reintroduced eugenics into scientific discourse.[17] The debate about bioengineering has sharply posed the question of culture. For what is crucially at stake is who and for what purposes will the human body and its environments be controlled. On the one hand, recent alliances between universities and private corporations to plan zoological and botanical alterations raise the question of the private ownership and control over the patents governing the new organisms produced by cloning and other bioengineering techniques. The university-industrial complex that controls the products of molecular technology has revived the seventeenth-century vision of the domination of nature, including human nature, as a positive value to which the society must subscribe. Accordingly, they claim the risks associated with bioengineering are worth taking if, by cloning genes, we may eliminate the scourge of disease and even unwanted birth defects, among many other benefits. On the other hand, both professional critics and laypeople have begun to question the effects of bioengineering on democratic culture. They wonder whether eliminating human "defects" is the proper function of scientific discovery. Specifically, to the degree that molecular biology makes choices on the basis of predetermined categories such as superior and inferior traits, the biomedical industry is increasingly charged with harboring a profoundly elitist ethos.

Among the most significant interventions by citizen activists in scientific issues has been that of ACT UP, the major social movement involved in the struggle to overcome the AIDS crisis. While popular perception of ACT UP has been almost entirely framed by images of civil disobedience against the Catholic hierarchy and federal agencies such as the Food and Drug Administration and the National Institutes of Health, perhaps equally important have been the less-publicized but painstaking efforts of some of the organization's committees to contest the scientific knowledge produced by official AIDS research. To be sure, ACT UP does not speak in a single voice on questions of whether to seek a "magic bullet" to eliminate the dread disease. While pressing for speedy FDA approval of new drugs, some activists have suggested that the "solution" to the AIDs crisis is not exhausted by isolating molecules that are representing as "causing" AIDs or developing drugs that retard the progress of the disease. In contrast, some have offered an epidemiological approach to addressing the crisis, and have proposed an explanatory model that corresponds, in a rough way, to the views of Lewontin and other dissenting scientists.

Similarly, physics research has been redefined in terms of desired technological outcomes such as radar, nuclear weapons, and nuclear energy, and, more recently, the superconductor, each of which has recruited thousands of scientists, shifting their intellectual energies from "pure" discovery to overtly military and commercial uses. In 1990, there were literally thousands of jobs in solid state physics, the underlying science of the superconductor, but only a handful in cosmology and astronomy. The message is clear: join technoscience or teach undergraduates or high school.

The merger of science with the state, a phenomenon of both the welfare state and the permanent war mobilization of the past half century, has fatally eroded, if not obliterated, the veneer of value neutrality that conventionally legitimates scientific research. Since the 1960s a plethora of citizens groups have formed to raise, in one way or another, ethical questions about scientific investigation as well as the uses of scientific discovery. Public skepticism reached a peak with the successful campaigns of the 1970s and 1980s to halt the forward march of nuclear energy and the similarly powerful efforts to enact legal safeguards for the environment against industrial and other types of commercial pollution of air, water, and food.

Since the 1930s, American social science has not only been "poised" for service to those occupying the commanding heights of political power but has, with some exceptions, regularly taken the elevator to the summit. The entire profession of economics has become servants (and savants) of power, corresponding to the centrality of economic policy in contemporary statecraft. Of course, the most fervent wish of political science is to play a role as political adviser or polltaker (often the same thing) to a major candidate for public office. Criminal justice, education, social welfare, and military policy makers routinely rely heavily on sociological research, a turn that became even more pronounced during Great Society programs of the 1960s, and now in the current "war" on drugs and state programs to stem the AIDS epidemic.

In many areas, the status of "stubborn" fact as the arbiter of collective judgment has never been more in doubt. "Facts" once safely established by the procedures of scientific investigation, confirmed by the scientific "community," and supported by large sections of the middle class are hotly contested because the authority of those charged with establishing them—scientists—has eroded.

A summary judgment of these experiences leads to the conclusion that, far from the image of science and technology as sufficient indicators of human progress, we are in the midst of a profound reevaluation of the presumed beneficent effects of both and, more globally, the idea of progress itself. This event takes place in every corner of social, political, and especially cultural life. For what is at stake is nothing less than the legacy of modernity, especially the certainties that by the domination of nature (and a rebellious "human" nature whose treatment is left to psychologies of various sorts), the methods of science, and a similarly rational organization of social relations through market mechanisms, the state, and especially law, we may attain the good life. The assertion by science that its methods and ethos result in disinterested inquiry to support its claim that its propositions deserve the status of yielding certain, verifiable truth has defined what we mean by legitimate intellectual knowledge since the late nineteenth century. Beyond all doubt, the humanities and the social sciences have adopted these precepts as aspiration, if not fact. Social science never ceases to bemoan the absence of an experimental situation to test its claims, but does its best to simulate the laboratory through interviews, statistical correlations, models, algorithms, and other paraphernalia of physical and biological science. On the humanities side, Anglo-American philosophy has, for all intents and purposes, subordinated itself to the "hard" sciences, earnestly emulating Locke's declaration that the discipline can only be an "underlaborer," clearing up misunderstandings that may arise out of linguistic ambiguities and confusions of scientific statements. Literary criticism, since Matthew Arnold's *Culture and Anarchy* intimately intertwined with the belletrist tradition has, in embarrassment, periodically taken up "theory" to gain freedom from the charge of subjectivism and put the discipline on a more scientific footing. Consequently, the reception (as opposed to the motives of the producers) of such paradigmatic statements as Frye's Law that narratives are grasped through their mythological and symbolic signifiers, Saussurian semiotics as a method of analysis that reduces the text to its codes and signifiers, and Bakhtin's dialogic sociology of literature may be understood in the context of the will to scientificity.

I invoke these examples not to cast aspersions on the work itself, but merely to illustrate my argument that the separation of the hard sciences from the humanities made popular in C. P. Snow's celebrated Two Cultures thesis is an untenable gesture. For, despite the best efforts of some of its practitioners, modernity enframes all academic discourse in the image of science and those who refuse to adhere to these requirements risk marginalization. The critic who lacks a theoretical framework may be labeled a mere journalist, the social scientist who prefers to write in the genre of the learned essay rather than the systematic treatise may be refused tenure, the philosopher who engages in metaphysical speculation stands little or no chance of getting a job in a leading department or, in many instances, any academic department at all. After all, metaphysics is declared dead, thoroughly discredited by the achievements of empirically based science.

After centuries of assurances that modern science removes the need for speculative reason, we have once more become immersed in philosophy, if one takes that term to mean the critical interrogation of the categories by which knowledge is generated. This work, begun by Nietzsche's critique of science, especially the science of history, and taken up by Weimar intellectuals a half century later, has once again pushed to the surface due, crucially, to three contemporary influences: the rise of the ecology movement, which has challenged the scientific establishment's alliance with corporations and the state and argues that mainstream scientific knowledge cannot be separated from these relationships; the obvious failure of social science, after decades of effort, to provide the basis for a state policy in the most technologically developed societies that offers its citizenry a safe and secure life; and feminism's attack on science as a manifestation of patriarchal knowledge both with respect to issues of reproductive medicine and, equally, the paradigmatic reduction of all life forms to their physiochemical levels. On the more general plane, science is convicted of being the quintessential achievement of modernity, its worldview ensconced in the presuppositions of domination.

For the purposes of this book, it matters little whether one contends that modernity has not yet been exhausted (particularly with respect to universal human rights) or whether we pronounce the arrival of a postmodern condition with its renunciation of all universals. The various attempts by Habermas, Lyotard, Jameson, and others to periodize our culture in their respective terms are finally less interesting than the situation they are obliged to face. Both sides of the modernism debate acknowledge a massive legitimation crisis; at issue are the conditions by which consent for the economic and social system is secured, not only in late capitalist societies, but in most of the rest of the world as well. There have developed philosophical, sociological, and feminist critiques of science which even more fundamentally have engaged in an extensive reexamination of the received historical and cultural wisdom of the past century. Historical materialism, that monumental achievement of nineteenth-century thought, may not have collapsed, but has certainly been reduced to one among other possible modes of historical explanation; the very idea of history as vital determinant of the present has suffered pillory, if not total eclipse. From Benjamin's ironic narrative of historical law to Kuhn's account of scientific change we are persuaded that disruption, not continuity, marks history. Foucault has gone so far as to substitute the term "genealogy" as a means of distinguishing his own work from that of conventional historiography. Derrida shows the *historicity* of what is often understood as an intrinsic property of Mind, if not matter: formal and/or dialectical logic. And in social theory, students of politics have commented extensively on state legitimation problems, citing the decline of voter participation, a minimal sign of democratic vitality, in countries such as the United States and France, but also in the newly democratic countries of Eastern Europe; beyond voting, the increasing disenfranchisement of whole populations from making decisions that affect everyday life; the passivity of the world's advanced democracies in the wake of flagrant violations of democratic rights in developing countries, most recently Bosnia, Korea, South Africa, and Haiti. Nationalism, once believed to be in permanent decline, has demonstrated that reports of its death were, to say the least, premature. Various nationalisms challenge key modernist assumptions: secularism in education and morals, the institutions of political and economic integration put in place by leading countries after both world wars, the liberal democratic state as the pinnacle of political society and cultural cosmopolitanism. Perhaps most damaging to modernity's project has been the profound cultural shift underway, especially in what may be termed the metaparadigm of, in turn, ethical efficacy and human knowledge. Fundamental to this metaparadigm has been the idea that culture, like science, may have become closely integrated with the state—more specifically, that some self-evident "state" culture may be taken as a model for all culture, both with respect to forms of knowledge, including art, and with respect to everyday life.

I use the awkward term "metaparadigm" to signify the end, or at least the weakening, of social and cultural theory as it evolved out of eighteenth- and nineteenth-century philosophy, for which the development of the sciences of social relations, human affairs, culture, and psychology presupposed the natural sciences or, in the Hegelian mode, a fundamental dialectical logic that embraced both nature and history. In the various fields unified by the phrase "human sciences" (including arts), the past quarter century has witnessed an end to "theory"—if by that term we signify the historical burial of metaphysics and its replacement by a coherent account of a stable and apodictic knowledge object. After centuries on the margins, speculative, and especially metaphysical reflection has returned amid the ashes of the old positivist faith with a vengeance, and coherent accounts of various elements of the "external world" are widely taken by the cognoscenti as a sign of reductionism or, in current parlance, "essentialism."

Here coherence entails two stages: fixing the object (whether social or natural) in time and space; and establishing an algorithm of investigation whose normative validity for all objects of this type is unquestioned. These scientific rules have been placed under scrutiny because the knowledge object is no longer taken as prior to inquiry when writers do not accept certain representations. The status of "representation," not only of discrete objects but of universals such as "society" and "nature," is no longer taken for granted; even more fundamental, the concepts of evidence and rational calculation no longer enjoy unimpeachable status as the constituents of an ultimate court of appeal. And we have relearned from Nietzsche and his latter-day intellectual progeny that "facts" are adduced, not from pristine procedures, but from a complex of discursive elements that include the prevailing beliefs of scientists and other knowledge gatekeepers, their links with the state, corporations, and the normative codes of their own professions, and, more widely, the culture of their spatiotemporal contexts. The notion that knowledge—mathematical, scientific, or aesthetic—is ineluctably context-dependent is no longer intellectually shocking, even if most intellectuals are bonded to the old realist paradigm.

Characteristically, twentieth-century western art and philosophy have bifurcated along similar fault lines to those of the sciences. On the one hand, a widespread movement spanning social philosophy, the human sciences, and cultural criticism displaces the universals of eighteenth-century thought with a conception of the social world as a series of "fragments," the unification of which can only be conceived as a vanishing horizon. On the other hand, a substantial fraction of intellectuals, surely a majority, have responded to the defection of many traditional intellectuals by reasserting the universality of science as the pinnacle of rationality; affirming their faith in liberalism both economic and political; and, in the wake of what they perceive to be cultural malaise, have betrayed a certain passion for empiricism.

In our contemporary era of fallen idols, when ideas of canon have sunk to disrepute, or at least the traditional canon can scarcely be defended, we seem unable to avoid the temptation to construct our own "tradition of the new." Critics and historians have dredged up esoteric names, some of which were unjustly forgotten in the early postwar nationalist years, others not. While the "French" turn in Anglo-American cultural theory appears predominant, it is important to note that most of the work of the schools loosely known as structuralism and poststructuralism are elaborate metacritiques on works that emanate from German philosophy, particularly the Kantian and Hegelian traditions, with a more than liberal dose of Nietzsche, Husserl, and Heidegger. Kant and his epigones provide the referent for nearly all the major French philosophers and social theorists from Lacan, Lévi-Strauss, and Althusser to Derrida and Foucault. In fact, Deleuze's philosophy is unique since, in addition to Nietzsche, it privileges Bergson and especially Spinoza. Of course, Canguilhem and Bachelard provided Althusser and Foucault with more than the raw materials for their respective critical discourses on the human sciences.

Even Derrida's crucial demonstration that phenomenology of both the He-gelian and Husserlian varieties cannot escape the aporias of western logic works within this project; its ultimate aim is to realize it, not to abolish the quest for the things themselves.

Suffused with such discontents, some intellectuals, especially those deeply influenced by the new social movements that arose during the international generational revolts of the 1960s and early 1970s, have, following Wittgen-stein, concluded belatedly that knowledge, including art, was a mode of life. Thus, the academic division of labor into discrete domains and disciplines no more than mirrors the relentless analyticity of the industrial workplace. Frus-trated by Anglo-American philosophy's scientistic proclivities, literature's Ar-noldian program to teach only the "best that has been thought and said" on the one hand and social science's myopic search for facticity, on the other, a polyglot of humanists and social scientists have loosely affiliated under the sign of "cultural studies"—a heading derived from the famous Birmingham Centre for Contemporary Cultural Studies (which, for most of its almost thirty-year existence, was assiduously ignored by the traditional disciplines). However, as we will see, cultural studies in the United States and in other environments that use the term bear only an indirect resemblance to the orig-inal motives and activities of the Centre's founders.

In this book I treat cultural studies as a response to the profound shifts in the character of knowledge, its constituencies as well as its claims in contem-porary intellectual discourse. The Centre focused on recovering the collective memory of working-class culture and explored, at the beginning, the relation of this culture, in both the artistic and especially the anthropological senses, to the effects of British "mass" media on working-class consciousness. Inev-itably, it was obliged to enter the age-old debate about the aesthetic and social value of popular culture among environments that privileged high culture as the only worthwhile pursuit of the mind. However, since its heyday (about 1980), these debates have been extended. Feminist studies in Britain, the United States, and other English-speaking countries have produced one sig-nificant mutation in the character of cultural studies. At the Centre itself, women insisted on the exploration of women's communities, responses to mass culture, and creation of their own cultural forms, as autonomous objects of study.

The thirty-year-old explosion of linguistics, semiotics, deconstruction, and discourse analysis in U.S. universities occupies a liminal space between sci-entificity and the increasingly central place of cultural studies. For many investigators, culture presents itself as a hieroglyph that can scarcely be de-ciphered by the language of common sense. Cultural signifiers confound brute facticity. One the one hand, literary and other humanist intellectuals have grasped at these "tools" to decipher the otherwise hidden codes of art and everyday life. On the other hand, popular culture resists these surgical procedures. In recent years, nonanalytical ways of knowing, preeminently ethnography and autobiography, have been rediscovered by cultural theory. The new interest in the problem of the "subject" or "agency" is a symptom that analyticity has lost some of its luster. Critics have become fascinated by local knowledge; their self-conception as "local" (in Foucault's terms, "specific"), rather than universal intellectuals, has moved them to see themselves with the context of the university as a specific site of the knowledge production, especially their own.

In the wake of the eclipse of the universal values that animated modernity, everyday life privileges particularity; postmodernism in art, despite its renunciation of universalism, becomes the new universal. The 1970s and 1980s were marked by the rise of "new" cultural and political identities—gender, racial, sexual, national, and ethnic—that manifested themselves as challenges to established powers: over intellectual knowledge in media as well as universities and institutional hierarchies in workplaces as much as legislatures. Concomitantly, the old identities based on class have not disappeared but are in significant retreat. Or, more precisely, class issues are displaced to these new identities. At the same time, these identities are in constant motion, decomposing and recomposing, revealing their inherent instability.

Conceptions of unified knowledge through scientific method, the evolution of science into technoscience, and the political and social uses of knowledge in the service of domination and freedom have become new, perhaps the most vital development in cultural studies. This work goes on in science, technology, and society programs, feminist and women's studies, and cultural studies itself. Philosophers and former scientists, mathematicians and social scientists, historians and literary critics are joined in a sometimes brilliant, often halting effort to come to terms with this most hegemonic discourse in modern culture. Perhaps the singular notable achievement of this inquiry has been to demonstrate that science is inexorably intertwined with culture, that the sundered relation of head and hand, knowledge and everyday life is the outcome of human relations, especially language and power.

In the chapters that follow, I want to explore some dimensions of the current cultural transformations. Chapter 1 discusses the recent controversy over what is popularly termed "political correctness" in both its contemporary terms and historical roots. Through this investigation, we find that the culture wars are no passing skirmish in an otherwise consensual cultural system. Instead, they manifest the profound fissures among intellectuals concerning the proper function of the university, the character of legitimate intellectual knowledge and its political ramifications. One of the more significant fissures in our cultural situation is the challenge to artistic hierarchy in which what is conventionally designated "high" culture is taken as a signifier of "Western" civilization and the natural superiority of the established authorities. Chapter 2 addresses the emergence of the popular and the reaction of the guardians of conventional Art. In this inquiry we discover that the high/low debate, like education, makes "strange" bedfellows, that is, it realigns conventional ideological divisions. Chapter 3 is an extended essay on the "origins" of British cultural studies, the name affixed to the various counter-hegemonies that inhabit Anglo-American cultural sites, especially but not exclusively universities. I take the work of the Birmingham Centre for Contemporary Cultural Studies as one model of the cultural opposition and show the degree to which its project was transformed by events of the late 1960s, particularly the "French turn" in social and cultural theory. In this chapter, I focus on the contributions of three key writers: Richard Hoggart, the founder of the Centre; E. P. Thompson, whose *Making of the English Working Class* radically altered the character of labor studies; and especially Raymond Williams, whose theoretical reflection and revisionary writing on working-class and mainstream cultural traditions opened new avenues for research.

Chapter 4 carries the story to those who, building on the work of the three major earlier figures, shifted the focus of the project, first to the study of youth subcultures, then to feminism. In this chapter I argue that these shifts were propelled by the events of the 1970s, especially the rise of new social movements that experienced the exclusive preoccupation with class by the historical left as an oppressive constraint. Chapters 5 and 6 carry the genealogy to the United States. In Chapter 5 I discuss the specific contribution of the popular front phase in the history of American radicalism to cultural debates. I make the point that what is conventionally understood to be Gramsci's thesis of the "national popular" was actually the policy of the American (and the British) Communist parties during the period of the struggle against fascism. I also claim that whatever the considerations of this policy for political strategy, its cultural effects have become a permanent feature of American culture.

Chapter 6 is a snapshot of the rediscovery of popular culture by New Left intellectuals and others associated with the various movements in the 1960s. What unifies these chapters is not only their American location but also the degree to which they were cultural emanations and expressions of political and social movements outside academic environments. Chapter 7 carries the story to American universities, focusing especially on two signal developments of recent years: the debate about canon that is really an intellectual expression of the strength of the black freedom and feminist movements, and the critique of science arising from both disciplinary quarters and feminism. Chapter 8 is a brief examination of the implications of the cultural transformations of legitimate intellectual knowledge for the future of the disciplines as the chief form of the academic division of labor.

CHAPTER ONE

On the Politically Correct

I

ON SUNDAY, October 28, 1990, the *New York Times* cultural correspondent Richard Bernstein reported faculty approval of a new writing program at the University of Texas called *Writing on Difference*. Students "will base their compositions on a packet of essays on discrimination, affirmative action, and civil rights cases." According to Bernstein, the program earned the praise of many members of the faculty. But a few, like English professor Alan Gribben, dissented: "You cannot tell me that students will not be inevitably graded on politically correct thinking in these classes." Shortly after the article appeared, the university administration rejected the new curriculum, responding to pressure from some state legislators and internal opponents such as Professor Gribben.

It is odd that the idea of political correctness should reappear in the 1990s, for its genealogy can be traced to another era, a time when a substantial segment of 1960s radicals were engaged in reclaiming a Marxist-Leninist heritage they had previously refused.[1] To be politically correct meant that one had assimilated many of the crucial markers of left culture, particularly antiracism, a working-class ethos, and support for Third-World revolutions which, in the 1960s, were breaking out in many parts of the southern half of the globe. In many respects, the groups that sprang up in the wake of the demise of the New Left's democratic radicalism had a penchant for rigid applications of these values; in their struggle to become "truly" revolutionary, in an imagined emulation of earlier radical generations or contemporary revolutionary movements elsewhere, they were frequently given to excesses that resulted in some bizarre attacks on individuals who were labeled politically "incorrect."

Inspired by the example of the Chinese, Cuban, or even Bolshevik revolutions, a dozen or more groups were formed around 1970; by the end of the decade most had disappeared. Among the majority of leftists who had stayed away from these movements, the use of the phrase "politically correct" had a distinctly ironic, even abusive, connotation. It was a grim reminder of the losses, owing to the immaturity of the "revolutionary vanguards," they believed had been sustained, in the twentieth century, by the left as a whole.

Thus, its use by the critics of what appears to be an insurgent radicalism among intellectuals, especially a younger generation, may be regarded as suspect.

Although "politically correct" is, according to Bernstein, "spoken more with irony and disapproval than with reverence," he also wrote that "the term p.c. as it is commonly abbreviated is being heard more and more in debates over what should be taught at the universities." The "what" in question— race, ecology, feminism, culture, and foreign policy—has defined, in Bernstein's words, "a sort of unofficial ideology of the university." Needless to say, this did not apply to the University of Texas.

Of course, each of these categories has a content. Bernstein goes on to describe what, according to conservative and liberal critics of this unofficial ideology, are the crucial beliefs associated with p.c. Among them, none is more prominent than the view that there exists a "white male power structure" associated with European civilization. The phrase encompasses a constellation of oppressions, notably of race, gender, and sex, and the Third World. What is remarkable about the controversy over politics in the universities is not the ideas themselves. The judgment that European civilization itself, not merely a specific political party or government, or a series of regrettable but broadly held social attitudes, is responsible for such injustices as inequality, gender and race discrimination, and colonialism has a long history. The novelty, many conservatives and liberals believe, is that these judgments, either singly or in the form of ideology, are now widely supported among faculty and students, especially in some leading universities. For their purposes, they charge that a new polyglot "left" has entrenched itself within the university as in no other American institution. In this lexicon "left" encompasses a broad spectrum from ecologists—many of whom vehemently deny their association with the traditional left—to Marxists, deconstructionists, feminists, and African-American intellectuals, all of whom spend as much energy distinguishing themselves from each other as they are distinct from cultural conservatives.

In fact, in the wake of what, in 1989, Francis Fukuyama termed "the end of history," a reference to the apparently sudden and swift collapse of East European communism, the reappearance of the charge that some are imposing "ideology" when applied to intellectual knowledge seems, at first glance at least, anachronistic.[2] Fukuyama, deputy director of the State Department's policy planning staff and former analyst at the RAND Corporation, writes the communist demise is evidence of "the triumph of the west," or more specifically "the western *idea*" (emphasis his). There have been reform movements in the Soviet Union and China that, aside from major policy changes, were spurred by the "ineluctable spread of consumerist Western Culture" in diverse contexts.[3]

Fukuyama is acutely aware that "culture" and "ideology" were precisely at play in the West's prolonged effort to prevail over competing and alternative historical models. He points to a paradox in the defeat of the Hegelian notion that abstract ideas are worth risking life: on the one hand, neither the communist nor the capitalist states are able to avoid ideological categories such as the national interest or, indeed, the liberal or the revolutionary communist "idea." For the nearly three-quarters of a century since the Bolshevik Revolution these were the flags of economic and political struggle between the dominant competing social systems. On the other hand, liberalism seeks to naturalize as universal values its twin ideologies of the market as the best guarantee of freedom and representative democracy as the highest achievement of human communities, which is presented as a common sense whose violation constitutes nothing less than moral turpitude.

For Fukuyama the end of history that accompanies the supremacy of liberal ideas will also witness the triumph of the mundane—that is, the ascendancy of "economic calculation, the endless solving of technical problems . . . and the satisfaction of sophisticated consumer demands. In the post-historical period there will be neither art nor philosophy, just the perpetual caretaking of the museum of human history."[4] The age of the end of ideology, except that of technocracy, will be a "very sad time."

Among Fukuyama's respondents in the symposium by the conservative journal *National Interest* devoted to his article, Irving Kristol struck the one ominous note that may serve to comprehend the odd reappearance of ideological struggle in the early 1990s: "We may have won the Cold War," states Kristol, "which is nice—it's more than nice, it's wonderful. But this means that now the enemy is us, not them." American democracy is now at risk "with all its problematics—as distinct from mere problems—that fester within such a democracy." He lists some of these problematics as "the longing for community, spirituality, a growing distrust of technology, the confusion of liberty with license."[5]

In retrospect, Kristol, himself an old socialist ideologue who led a fraction of his generation into neoconservatism, may have proven a more accurate forecaster than Fukuyama, although neither denies the ideological force of liberalism. Fukuyama regards, with some foreboding, the prospect that the time has finally arrived for the confident predictions, widely held by liberal intellectuals of thirty years ago, that there are no historical problematics to face, that we are fated to a joyless technological/liberal utopia. But Kristol's adroit focus on the "enemy within" seems to foreshadow the 1990s, to have anticipated that the death of Stalinism would not prefigure the end of ideological struggle per se. For his generation, having become part of the constellation that forms established authority, must now face what Lionel Trilling once termed the *adversarial culture* and what they believe to be the new authoritarian threat of the marginals. As we will see below, the reemergence of the adversarial culture may prove more difficult to uproot than the political opposition.

Consequently, the demise of the "evil empire" was cause for only two cheers. The third had to be deferred pending the defeat of the nascent *internal* opposition that would abuse democratic privilege by cloaking itself in precisely liberal values: diversity, pluralism, difference—the other side of the quest for universalism in liberal political philosophy. For against the doctrine of centralism, the liberals argue vehemently for politics as a public sphere in which difference, guaranteed by the integrity of the private sphere, is the grist of democratic decision making. Yet the meaning of "difference" in liberal discourse is not identical with the postmodern use of the word. As Sidney Hook argued more than forty years ago, difference in the "democratic way of life" is always subsumed under the universal values of western culture: reason, the scientific spirit, individual freedom, representative democracy.[6] These values are not *necessarily* what contemporary advocates of difference have in mind.

A strong case has been made, most recently by Jurgen Habermas, that the social condition for democracy is the existence of a "public" of individuals who transcend group interest and are able, owing to free access to knowledge and information, but also their autonomy from the state, to participate in both the great and the small decisions of the commonweal.[7] In turn, difference is encouraged, not merely tolerated. Beyond divergent opinion within a commonly held series of assumptions, difference should accommodate systemic opposition. The possibility of an articulate, even if minority, opposition to consensual worldviews may be the basis not only for evaluating the status of "human rights" within a given community but also for determining whether a society can change.

In the universities, liberalism as an idea spans conservative and modern liberal camps and is, indeed, on trial. For the underlying assumption of this doctrine is that western civilization embodies universal values such as individual freedom. This formulation contains one of the crucial and explosive contradictions of liberalism: its claim that individuality is the telos of social evolution. Yet it also implies the ineluctability of difference, a characteristic that undermines the universalist claim. Individuality signifies more than the quest for human rights or the celebration of private interest. It has been intertwined with concepts such as democratic vitality, made the condition for the emergence of a "learning society," and is inherent in the very idea of modernity as the cornerstone of modern liberal thought.

Of the consequences of this philosophy, none stands higher than the idea that through the tolerance of diversity—in thought, culture, and politics—a democracy may thrive, individual aspirations be accommodated, and the "national" interest served not by pressure to conformity but by free discussion and debate. The trials of liberalism are concentrated in the characteristic claims of the so-called pcs. For, contrary to the earlier dominant alternative position to liberal democracy that there was a revolutionary truth handed down by the "scientific" discoveries of Marxism-Leninism, whether in Moscow or in Beijing, the new discourses of multiculturalism and postmodernism (two of the names under which this movement is known) want nothing more or less than, in the name of pluralism, to place eastern, African, Latin American, and other subaltern cultures next to European culture, thereby abolishing the claims of western culture to its privileged place on the evolutionary apex of civilizations. Similarly, heterosexuality is taken to be only one of several practices that constitute the range of legitimate sexual choices, the others enjoying equal status. And it refuses the claim of universal value except that inherent in the ideology of diversity: that individuals have the inherent right to free association and hold views that run against the current.

As with oppositional political ideologies, small and otherwise marginal publications and spiritualist, left-wing, nationalist, and feminist movements have, with some persistence, disseminated their orientations for decades. What is new is that they demand public representation in the curriculum of mainstream educational institutions at all levels, and seem to have the popular force to compel consideration by established authorities and, second, want to take their rejection of, and alternatives to, the privileged place traditionally accorded a literary/philosophical canon into the mainstream of U.S. academic and intellectual life.

Subaltern groups argue that the prevailing canon is conventional rather than a thing of human nature and has occupied a magisterial place only since the nineteenth century, when, most notably, Matthew Arnold, responding to the rise of contemporary working-class movements and a nascent working-class culture, defined the canon as "the best that has been thought and said" against the claims of this burgeoning social movement that carried with it popular class-based literature. According to the new educational reformers, these conventions are too narrow because they fail to make room for Third World, women, African-American, gay and lesbian writers and practitioners of other art forms and alternatives to western philosophy such as those of the East and Africa. But the challenge to the canon emanates from another direction as well. Since the early 1960s, a movement to valorize working-class, black, and Latino popular cultures as aesthetically valid works of art has contested the claim of "high" culture to aesthetic privilege.

In the pursuit of what is sometimes known as "cultural studies" there is a new challenge to the disciplinary basis within which legitimate intellectual knowledge is framed.

What is "cultural studies"? Historically (as we will explore in greater depth in Chapter 3), it was the name given to the movement to *aesthetically* and *politically* valorize popular culture. Cultural studies signified the refusal of a new generation of British and American intellectuals in the late 1950s and 1960s to observe the hierarchy between high culture and the culture, in both the aesthetic and anthropological sense, of the working class and, most saliently, addressed the ideological basis of such distinctions. In the subsequent decades as new, emergent discourses developed into social movements, particularly of feminism and race, but also ecology and sexuality, and found their way into universities, cultural studies became one of the names for what became a virtual revolution in literary and cultural-theoretical canon. These emergent discourses demanded the inclusion of women's, Third World, and African-American writing or, alternatively, claimed to contemporary, postmodern concerns the irrelevance of the established canon in literature, philosophy, and criticism.

Within the past decade, we have experienced an outpouring of critical studies of science and technology, the purport of which has been to demonstrate that what is taken as the pinnacle of legitimate intellectual knowledge, the "hard" sciences are, like other knowledges constituted by discursive practices, not exempt, any more than are the social sciences, literature, or philosophy, from the influences of the social and cultural contexts within which they are produced and disseminated.[8] These arguments have been made by historians, sociologists, and philosophers who have extended and revised Thomas Kuhn's celebrated thesis that scientific knowledge is not cumulative to mean that it is situated in its own milieu.[9] For example, feminists such as Donna Haraway, Sandra Harding, and Evelyn Fox Keller have argued that science, like any other knowledge, is "gendered";[10] historian Paul Forman found that Weimar culture, especially its disillusionment with ideas of determinism and causality, shaped the development of quantum mechanics;[11] and Latour and Woolgar and Ludvik Fleck disputed the idea that biological "facts" are the pristine outcome of experimental methods of discovery.[12] Latour and Woolgar showed how laboratory life, especially conversations among investigators, itself produces what is taken as knowledge. In some respects this more recent work follows Fleck's work who, in 1938, showed that the scientific community did not even recognize syphilis until it affected the middle class. His conclusion, that scientific "facts" are not discovered but are *constructed* from the interests and concerns of scientists acting within a broader social and cultural environment, has become one of the more powerful and recent concerns of cultural studies: to discern the conditions under which knowledge becomes legitimate and hegemonic.

The philosophical and ideological implications of these investigations constitute a new crucial dimension of cultural studies. As I will argue in the final chapter, they have revealed that cultural studies' real challenge to conventional

academic disciplines is *epistemic*. The demands of the popular and the subaltern to the status of legitimate intellectual knowledge remained tacit critiques of various conceptions of cultural sciences for privileging works whose
implied audiences were ruling and middle classes, mainly white and male. The
recent critical investigations of the social context of scientific knowledge have
demonstrated the stakes entailed by cultural studies. Perhaps most troubling
for the gatekeepers of tradition, cultural studies aims its fire at the disciplines.

Yet the term "interdisciplinary" scarcely describes the movement. For interdisciplinarity merely connotes the possibility that in certain instances new
knowledge may be obtained through the collaboration of two or more specialized discourses. Cultural studies interrogates the *adequacy* of the prevailing division of intellectual labor. Its proponents claim that there are unique
objects of knowledge and ways of knowing that cannot be articulated with
the disciplines. At its farthest outpost, the movement does not seek to create
a new discipline that can stand alongside others in the humanities and social
sciences, but instead to initiate new lines of inquiry that are unbound by algorithms, methods and models employed by schools of positivism, historicism, and empiricism that still prevail in both humanities and social sciences.
In the past two decades, philosophers and social and cultural theorists influenced by Marx and Wittgenstein, by the post-Nietzschean turn of French social thought, and by Durkheim's theory that what is called "truth" is socially
conditioned, as well as some trained in the natural sciences have made a fundamental critique of the social neutrality of science and technology.

During the past decade, these ideas have circulated with increasing force
in U.S. universities, but not without contestation and rancor. Cultural studies
has succeeded in establishing courses, centers, and advanced degree programs
within the humanities as either concentrations of English departments or, in
a few instances, as free standing institutions sponsoring research colloquia
and conferences. The names attached to these efforts are as diverse as the
emphases: the PhD program in Cultural Studies at the University of Pittsburgh is a program of the English department and its research program, which
spans faculty from several other disciplines, has not been able to reach beyond
the humanities; the History of Consciousness program at UC-Santa Cruz, a
free-standing PhD, predates the movement, but is widely perceived as one of
its premier outposts; programs connoting interdisciplinarity at the University
of Minnesota and SUNY-Binghamton remain, largely, within a humanities
context; CUNY's Cultural Studies Center is an interdisciplinary concentration and research program that spans the social sciences and the humanities
but has no faculty of its own and, despite course offerings, can offer no advanced degrees. Thus far, the disciplines have fought successfully to contain
cultural studies within established departments, especially English depart-

ments where, at least in the United States, it seems safely sequestered, at least temporarily.

Of course, African-American, Black, Latino, and women's studies programs have a much longer, even if troubled, history. With few exceptions, they are post-1960s developments. In almost no case are they permitted to award advanced degrees, although they have frequently won departmental status. This means a considerable number of these programs can hire and tenure their own faculty and award bachelor's degrees. Since the ebbing of the black freedom movements in the early 1970s, and the relative decline of organized feminism in the 1980s, they have been consistently under attack from the disciplines who claim they are methodologically flawed, their knowledge-objects ill defined, their faculty underprepared when measured by credentials and publications records, and their proclivity for unrigorous pedagogies a disservice to students. These charges are contested by the programs, but the sheer frequency of the attacks in an age of conservatism has made it difficult to shed the pall that surrounds some women's studies and African-American studies departments.

Needless to say, cultural studies suffers some of these charges, but the prominence of some of its advocates—especially in literary theory and criticism—and the strategic decision to seek a haven for cultural studies *within* the disciplines has spared the programs, until now, from some of the harshest judgments. Rather, cultural studies programs, while often overtly accepted intellectually, are restricted by bureaucratic entanglements that are adroitly employed by opponents unable to make intellectual arguments. Administrators and curriculum committees often grant the validity of the intellectual rationale and may even approve centers for Cultural Studies. However, there are still few cases of free-standing academic degree programs in cultural studies because disciplinary-based departments have jealously guarded their own prerogatives in this respect and have proven flexible enough to incorporate some elements of the movement into departmental curricula.

One of the difficulties in gaining institutional, as opposed to academic intellectual legitimacy, may consist in the relative distance of cultural studies from the historical successes of social movements outside the university. In the main, proponents have represented their educational ideas primarily in conceptual terms. This strategy has successfully opened up a major debate about the critical function of the university, the legitimacy of traditional knowledge, and its division of labor, but it has resulted in few *permanent* institutional bases for the movement. However, despite relatively little institutional power, the movements of multiculturalism, cultural studies as well as the older gender, race, and ethnic studies are perceived by their critics as the true "enemy within."

As long as these programs remained content to grasp a small piece of the institutional pie, restricting their purview and aspirations to that which characterized earlier *American Studies,* that is, asked to expand the knowledge object to include certain works and certain experiences, but were contained within the prevailing disciplinary framework of legitimate inquiry, the academic establishment could parsimoniously yield inches of space but, at the same time, manage to preserve its intellectual hegemony. There were no cries of "a new McCarthyism" of the left, only head wagging about "standards." A professor's choice to devote some energy to women's or African-American studies could be tolerated as long as it was perceived as a necessary but short-term effort by the individual to come to terms with her or his own "identity." However, at the end of the day, her academic standing would be judged strictly by the degree to which the work conformed to expectations conventionally made of those who were trained within the discipline. In other words, for example, be a nationalist or feminist if you want, but is the research and writing clearly identifiable in disciplinary terms? Is it recognizable as history, sociology, or literary criticism?

And, equally important, is the person a "congenial colleague"—a codeword for does s(he) make waves or behave herself? "Behaving" in the context of a typical academic department means playing the game in ways that do not challenge the structures of established authority. For example, the senior professoriate should not be called to account on feminist, race, or class grounds. Women charging sexual harassment by a male faculty member are, as in courts of law, frequently subject to persecution, although in recent years the situation has somewhat improved. In American colleges and universities, student admissions, faculty selection, tenure, and curriculum are decided by committees dominated, by consent, by the senior faculty. And, under no circumstances, except perhaps overt sexual harassment, can faculty teaching and office practices be challenged because these are subsumed under the rubric of academic freedom or free speech. The watchword of the liberal academy, live and let live, while under some pressure from women and minorities, remains in force. This phrase embodies the assumption that there are consensual views about key issues—the sanctity of the canon, of the literature of the discipline and of method, and the perquisites of the senior faculty to define the standards by which the department, and the discipline of which it is a part, lives.

The great divide of the last decade has occurred because there is no longer a consensus. Influenced by the *ethical precept* shared by feminists as well as its internal antagonists, the male-dominated New Left, that the "personal is the political"—a challenge to the conventional separation of intellectual, political and personal issues—a newer generation has emerged. As it has been disseminated in subsequent decades, the significance of the phrase is intensely overdetermined by the fact that neither feminism nor Marxism and other critical discourses *necessarily* imply a serious critique of academic conventions, particularly the century-old division of legitimate intellectual knowledge into a series of disciplines and subdisciplines.

Before addressing the specific charges that have been leveled against cultural studies and other challenges to conventional academic disciplines, practices, and values, I want to take a brief historical journey in order to ferret out the roots of the conflict. The controversy over political correctness resonates with similar, but not identical *generationally based* struggles that alighted the political landscapes of the 1930s and 1960s. In each of these periods, intellectuals debated the relationship between culture and politics, often with acrimony. Although the specific issues were different—modernism versus social realism in the 1930s, the dominant culture and the "adversarial" culture or the counterculture in the 1960s—in all cases, including the recent debate about pc, the disputants often talked past each other, but used similar arguments. The realists accused the modernists of "obscurantism" and were contrarily charged with making socially conscious art the only politically acceptable kind; in the 1960s, now in power, the modernists attacked the counterculture for mysticism, degeneracy, and anti-intellectualism and were asked to confront their own liberal authoritarianism by a defiant adversarial culture that refused the distinction between high and low, correct and incorrect, and, especially, the claim that western values were superior to others.

The generation that attained its majority after 1960 defined politics not only in relation to specific issues such as civil rights and the Vietnam War but perhaps more saliently as a struggle against the alienating effects of late capitalist culture—consumer society, suburbanization, fragmentation, and especially what they perceived to be liberal acquiescence to the policies of established authorities at home and abroad. Race and gender discrimination, the horrors of war, and class injustice are understood as manifestions, the latent content of which is their own *powerlessness,* especially to determine the conditions of daily existence and to chart a personal and social future that corresponds, in broad outlines, to the aspiration of freedom and, perhaps equally important, of community. The quest for community was engendered by the post-war dispersal of the American population: in the first place from the cities to the suburbs, from neighborhoods to shopping centers; from the old ethnic subcultures to assimilated Americanism.

This quest was, of course, shared by many who preceded the 1960s radical generation. In the main, in the early years of industrialization, protest against bourgeois culture was located in small groups—utopians, anarchists, communitarians who founded countercultural institutions—farm communities, alternative schools, art colonies, and consumer and residential cooperatives composed of people who were also political dissenters and sometimes sexual radicals.[13] What distinguishes this movement from those that settle for social reforms is crucially its will to make the future present, refusing the indefinite postponement of the ethical life. For this reason, the older counterculture consisted, typically, of philosophical anarchists and sexual libertarians (sometimes they were the same people, sometimes not) who were frequently hostile to communists and socialists for their authoritarianism and opportunism. For the basic program of the mainstream left had been, and remains, one of reform within the boundaries of the existing economic, social, and cultural system, postponing fundamental transformations, especially in the so-called private sphere of the family and friendships, to an indefinite future. On the other hand, intellectuals published journals and magazines, notably, before the First World War, *The Masses* and Emma Goldman's anarchist periodical *Mother Earth*. Writers such as Floyd Dell, Max Eastman, who also edited *The Masses,* Edward Carpenter, Havelock Ellis, and Virginia Woolf advocated culturally radical ideas, including sexual freedom.[14]

However, although these movements and individuals created their own small institutional bases, they could rarely intervene directly in the mainstream, largely because they disdained it. (Of course, when Eastman moved away from his early radicalism, he had a lucrative journalistic career as a conservative.) Cultural radical intellectuals were concentrated in urban bohemias, abetted by cheap rent and, consequently, could survive on low-wage jobs. Marginality was not only a badge of honor even if dictated by necessity; it had its own constituency. It was situated in large cities, particularly New York, Chicago, and San Francisco, outside what was widely perceived as the conservative university which, in any case, was much smaller than now.

Since, in the early twentieth century, many radical intellectuals perceived America as the modern Babylon—surfeited not only with crass business values but also cultural philistinism—political and artistic avant gardes were convinced, as often as not, that the mainstream was hopelessly corrupt. This view rendered strategies of intervention more than merely futile; they would inevitably corrupt the interveners. Consequently, some intellectuals and artists expatriated to France and England and Mexico in the 1920s and 1930s. Others huddled in European-like enclaves in large cities such as New York and Chicago, publishing "little magazines" such as the *Partisan Review (PR), Story,* and *The Little Review* that were typically politically cynical but dissident and/ or aesthetically high modernist at a time when the official left was bathed in the light of the popular front that extolled the virtues of Americanization and artistic social realism.

Like the First World War, which proved to be a watershed event that sealed the fate of the old socialist movement as well as the first generation of cultural radicals, the Second World War became another great divide: most radical intellectuals were torn between their hatred of fascism they shared with liberals and Communists and their profound disaffection from American politics and culture. They distrusted U.S. and Soviet war aims even if they agreed that the fascist threat went well beyond the bounds of ordinary imperialist aggrandizement. Not a few of them, exemplified by anarchist Paul Goodman, took the radical pacifist opposition to war as a too brutal and ultimately futile solution; others like *PR* editor Dwight Macdonald condemned American participation in the war as evidence that capital and the state wanted nothing less than U.S. world dominion.

However, Sidney Hook, writing in *PR*'s March–April 1943 issue, spoke for perhaps a majority of his intellectual community. Radicals who opposed the war and particularly the entrance, militarily, of the United States in the struggle against fascism exhibited shortsighted and potential dangerous tendencies. The failure of the left was its inability to see that this was no ordinary imperialist war, that the Nazis represented a threat to civilization *as such* which, on balance, required all who upheld the best traditions of democracy and enlightenment culture to defend liberal values by defeating Hitler on the battlefield. Radicals who persisted in sectarian views of the war betrayed their increasing distance from real politics. According to Hook, they had become "Platonists . . . they worship a system of Ideas originally projected as instruments of social action. Historical experience, having long since been impolite enough to reveal the inadequacy of these Ideas, is no longer capable of exercising a veto power over them."[15] These ideas, particularly the identity of fascism with capitalism, and the equal culpability of the capitalist democracies and fascists for perpetrating the world crisis, led rigid left fundamentalists such as Socialist leader Norman Thomas to insist that a tactical alliance with the Roosevelt administration would be morally and politically improper. For Hook, "historical experience" made evident that the doctrine according to which Roosevelt stood astride Hitler as an equal enemy of the people was completely preposterous. Hook argued, "If Hitler wins, democratic socialism has no future. If Hitler is defeated it is by no means assured that Democratic socialism has a future. But it has a chance!"[16] From this followed an exchange with, among others, Dwight Macdonald, Meyer Shapiro (writing under the pseudonym David Merriam), and Paul Goodman, all of whom stood by the traditional antipathy of the left of the socialist and communist movements to supporting imperialist wars.

At the time Hook was, together with Macdonald, an editor of *PR*. Although its editors did not openly support the allied position in the war, *PR*'s silence signified consent to U.S. war aims. At least, Macdonald, Shapiro, and Goodman shared this interpretation, which prompted Macdonald (whose differences with the other editors had been developing for some years) to resign from the editorial board and start his own magazine, *Politics*. Shapiro debated Hook's adherence to the allied war effort and Goodman wrote an impassioned letter to *PR*'s editors proclaiming, in the light of the magazine's pro-war neutrality, his own homelessness. But by the war's end only a small fraction of left cultural intellectuals remained outside the Roosevelt coalition. Although Hook recognized that *objectively* if not in spirit he had joined an alliance that included the Communists and their intellectual fellow-travelers, this pragmatic political choice, by its appeal to "historical experience," marked a fundamental turning point in the history of the interwar intellectual left.

Within a few short years, most left intellectuals outside the Communist party responded to the cold war environment of the late 1940s by "choosing the West."[17] Hook had already taken his stand by organizing, with Stephen Spender and others, the Committee for Cultural Freedom, formed to combat the considerable Communist party influence over U.S., British, and French intellectuals. Macdonald held his nose and, in a *Politics* editorial, virtually repeated Hook's appeal to historical experience and to the democratic socialist future and made the same choice. Having broken with Stalinism by the mid 1930s and reluctantly joined the war effort, it was a surprisingly short step for most (but not all) independent intellectuals to embrace not only their country's politics but to reevaluate their own contempt for its (high) culture.

"The American artist and intellectual no longer feels 'disinherited' as Henry James did, or 'astray' as Ezra Pound did in 1913."[18] So states the editorial statement initiating *PR*'s 1952 major symposium "Our Country and Our Culture," featuring many who had been firmly entrenched in the prevailing modernist view that most American writing, if not nonexistent, was little more than a pale imitation when not a series of degradations of European culture. This symposium marked a genuine reconciliation between the disaffected avant garde of the 1930s and the mainstream of American cultural life, just as Hook's wartime compromise signaled the definitive decline of intellectual radicalism, an event noted, during the same year as the symposium, by Daniel Bell in a book-length epitaph on the death of Marxian socialism in the U.S.[19]

The editorial statement speaks for its generation. "For better or for worse, most writers no longer accept alienation as an artist's fate in America: on the contrary, they want very much to be a part of American life. More and more writers cease to think of themselves as rebels and exiles."[20] This reconciliation was not without problems, particularly their collective perception of the unfortunate link between the democratization that marked the American century and the advent of a new mass culture that "involves an inevitable dislocation" between a higher culture and the schlock offered by most media.

Of the eleven individual contributions to the *PR* symposium, that of Lionel Trilling was the most tortured. As one of the key architects of the new accommodation, Trilling could hardly distance himself from this celebratory mood. "There is an unmistakable improvement of the American cultural situation over that of, say, thirty years ago," he declared, although he recognized "that no cultural situation is ever really good."[21] But after entering his own

ritual renunciation of the commercialization of culture and especially his belief that "the intellect of a society may be thought of as a function of money
in society (specifically of the money, not merely of the wealth in general),"
Trilling notes a truly remarkable new development in American society:

Intellect has associated itself with power as perhaps never before in history, and is now
conceded to be itself a kind of power. The American populist feeling against mind,
against the expert and the braintruster, is no doubt still strong. But it has not prevented
the entry into our political and social life of the ever-growing class which we have to
call intellectual, although it is not necessarily a class of "intellectuals."[22]

In a few highly concentrated paragraphs, Trilling sketches the contours of
the growth of this new class: increasing public administration to meet new
social needs; powerful labor unions who increasingly recruit college graduates
to fulfill their expanding functions; and "the increasing prestige of the universities." Yet, while the rise of the new class does not "necessarily make for
a good culture," he offered hope that its emergence might prefigure a new
group of "supporters and consumers of high culture" which, for Trilling, is
the only culture in question.

Still, Trilling's essay is not without dark ruminations. After noting that the
development of the intellect depends primarily on the state of universal education, he observes that education has fallen into the hands of "reactionaries
of the most vicious kind." At the same time, progressives and liberals "live
in a cave of self-commiseration and self-congratulation into which no ray of
true criticism ever penetrates." In sum, genuine intellectuals have very little
influence over education, the consequence of which is that the education editor
of the *New York Times* has more influence over culture "than any intellectual
has or is likely to ever have." So, the association of intellectuals with power
and the growth of the intellectual class allows only a ray of hope that American culture may emerge from its characteristic derivative and Philistine
existence.[23]

In the same year as this cautious marriage between intellectuals and power
was being made, Daniel Bell who, at first, had refused the post-war rapprochement and, in fact, entered a short period of political radicalization,
concluded that there was no longer—if there ever had been—a base for radical
politics in America.[24] Bell's critique of the left articulated what remained
somewhat inchoate in the *PR* symposium: the trouble with American socialism was that it was *in* but not *of* American society and culture. But, according
to Bell, this paraphrase of Marx's description of the radical chains of the proletariat was inappropriate for a social movement that sought popular roots
within a cultural context in which class discourse never enjoyed anything like
wide currency. Bell's point—that American Marxian socialism was tied too
powerfully to Marxist doctrine, developed within the European environment—was curiously parallel to the "Americanization" line adopted by the

Communist party during the 1920s and, again, during the popular front period after 1935. As Michael Harrington later quipped, the policy of democratic socialists should be "Browderism without Stalinism." (Browder was the leader of the American Communist party and led its Americanization phase.)[25] Needless to say, by the early 1950s, noncommunist left intellectuals were attracted to the same formula, but as they came to power *within* the mainstream, and, in some cultural spheres, were setting the mainstream taste, they shed their affiliation to the idea of an adversarial culture in proportion as that culture—modernism—became the standard of universal high culture.

However, the post-war era provided the chance for Kristol's generation to more fully identify with the ethical values and intellectual presuppositions of modern liberalism, many of which were inscribed for cultural criticism by Lionel Trilling in his fecund *Liberal Imagination,* for the noncommunist left-liberals by Arthur Schlesinger, Jr., in *The Vital Center,* and, somewhat more virulently, by Hook in his anti-communist tirade *Heresy Yes, Conspiracy No* where his earlier characterization of the Communist party as a "little more than the American section of the GPU"[26] (the predecessor to the KGB) became the basis of an argument against extending to Communists the privilege of academic freedom in the universities on the grounds they are opposed to the essential function of education to engage students in the free exchange of ideas.

Gone were the sentiments expressed most eloquently in *PR* editor Phillip Rahv's paean, six years earlier, to Arthur Koestler's "homeless radicalism," homeless because neither during the wartime alliance between the U.S. and the Soviet Union nor in its euphoric aftermath did Koestler succumb to blind, naive faith either in capitalism or Soviet-style state socialism.[27] For Rahv, the achievements of both were worth preserving: from the West comes the (partial) achievement of freedom and democracy; from the Soviets, despite their serious betrayals of socialism's legacy of "libertarianism," the valuable achievement of nationalized fundamental means of production. By the late 1940s most anti-Stalinist Marxian socialists were convinced that utopias are merely masks for totalitarianism and western democracy, although imperfect, was the best of all possible worlds. Some expressed reservations: Irving Howe, whose activist affiliation with an independent neo-Trotskyist movement that promulgated a "third camp" position between the West and the East, prevented his wholehearted approval of the generally middle-of-the-road sentiments of *PR*'s circle, and led him to found *Dissent* in 1954; and Norman Mailer who, in the 1952 *PR* symposium, reiterated the anti-capitalist faith that his elders were in the process of abandoning. But for most non-Stalinist left intellectuals on the road to accommodation and even outright alliance with the dominant class powers, the 1950s were a time for celebration of the legacy of western culture, now apparently irreversibly altered by the literature and painting of high modernism long advocated by the cultural avant garde, but also the triumphant politics of modern liberalism. What remained troubling for the literary radicals were the inequalities and exploitation of labor characteristic of the capitalist economic system. Their broadly pro-labor orientation was most directly expressed in Howe's works of social history, not only the best-selling later work, *World of Our Fathers,* extolling Jewish immigrant working-class culture and institutions, but also his collaborative work of the 1950s on Walter Reuther and the United Auto Workers.[28]

In fact, Howe, who worked on *Politics* with Macdonald in the late 1940s and belonged, with Bell and Kristol, to the next generation after Rahv, Hook, and Macdonald, never imbibed the literary taste of high modernism. His monograph on the realist writer Sherwood Anderson, his bold anti-modernist assertion of the close tie of politics and the novel, and his distance from literary avant gardes, preferring the life of a party intellectual, made him something of an outsider among intellectuals who all but abandoned the joys of ideological discourse after 1949.[29] Even as Bell and Kristol were trying on their brand new liberal clothes, and Macdonald went back to work as a literary journalist for mass circulation magazines, especially *Esquire* and the *New Yorker,* Howe retained hope that, for example, the breakup of the still formidable Communist party after 1956 would make possible the formation of a new, broadly inclusive democratic socialist movement, the organizational expressions of which had all but disappeared. Almost alone among leading left intellectuals who decisively broke with Stalinism in the mid 1930s, Howe retained a strong political identity into the 1960s, even as he shifted from the margins to the academic center.

By the mid 1950s many erstwhile homeless radicals were beginning to find a new home in the universities. In their circle Hook and Trilling remained, until this period, among the few left intellectuals with secure academic positions, although each had suffered a significant measure of anti-Semitism (not acknowledged except in their respective memoirs) along the way.[30] In 1954, Howe got a job in the English department at Brandeis and some radicals were catching on in sociology and history, notably sociologist Lewis Coser and art historian Meyer Shapiro. Equally significant, Clement Greenberg, along with Harold Rosenberg, the *PR* art critic, established himself as the gatekeeper for abstract expressionism and became chief publicist in its quest for aesthetic hegemony in the art world. His influence was so powerful that, by the 1950s, the so-called "social realist" artists found few outlets for their work; abstract expressionism and cubism had become the preferred styles of the successful high artist. Trilling was already on the way to becoming perhaps the leading academic literary critic in the belletrist mode of the postwar period; his essays helped establish an Arnoldian canon of English literature for two generations to come. He trained some of the leading critics of our own day, among them

Edward Said, who succeeded Trilling as the reigning literary presence at Columbia. Even the dissenter Dwight Macdonald, a journalist with few scholarly pretensions, played a leading role in affirming the high cultural tradition against the incursions of kitsch, best-selling novelists whose acolytes in the daily press regularly proclaimed their genius and, of course, mass culture.[31] His 1960 *PR* piece "Masscult and Midcult" was required reading for every budding literatum wishing to emulate the wit and wisdom of the older generation of New York intellectuals.[32]

So effective was their influence in literature that the once-towering figure of Theodore Dreiser was reduced, by *PR*'s canon-makers, to an unfortunate incident in American literary history. His influence, pervasive in the documentary novels of the 1930s, was now overshadowed by the "exile" fiction of Henry James and William Faulkner; of his vast output, by 1960 only *An American Tragedy* retained anything like canonical status. Similarly, Pound and Eliot displaced Whitman, who among other things was clearly the great American nationalist poet, precisely for that reason. As self-proclaimed cosmopolitans, their love of country had always been tempered by an acute sense of their European affiliations. Although both were American born, Pound and Eliot retained the exile image that, in art and literature, if not in politics, still resonated in the hearts and minds of the former literary radical generation. The marriage of modernism with political radicalism erased, at least provisionally, the fact that many of the leading modernist lights were political conservatives when not rightists whose anti-democratic virulence matched that of contemporary fascism. What mattered was the radicals' judgment that, in an era when culture had been reduced, in the mainstream, to a commodity, modernism provided the only possible resistance.

Along with Schlesinger's *The Vital Center,* Bell's *End of Ideology* (1960) theorized the transformation from modernist cultural radicalism to liberalism. The New York Intellectuals proved themselves in the decade after the war to be the most articulate guardians of the western tradition of high art, the great ideologues of a resurgent modern liberal democratic creed which, in the context of cold war struggles, played an invaluable role in defeating domestic radicalisms of all sorts. They were also the sharpest polemicists against the late 1940s remnants of the popular front. Whereas liberals like Max Lerner and Henry Wallace harbored a residual nostalgia for the wartime Big Three Alliance and advocated, for a time, a permanent rapprochement between the U.S. and the Soviet Union in the interest of world peace and against nuclear annihilation, Schlesinger led the cold war liberals in resolutely opposing this "soft" line. While conservative anti-communism could be dismissed as simply the ideological expression of bourgeois self-interest, the radical credentials of a Hook, the early Marxist-inspired historiography of a Schlesinger and the undeniable critical talents of Macdonald, Greenberg, and Rosenberg could hardly be ignored or relegated to mere anti-communist invective.

But Bell went far beyond polemic and policy formation. The essays published in *The End of Ideology* stated flatly that with the integration of working-class movements into the regulated welfare capitalist states there remained problems but not problematics, conflicts but not contradictions, programs but not utopias. Thus, in concert with his argument in *Marxian Socialism* a decade earlier, the "Americanization" of radicals meant that they had come to terms with the perspective that only reform was on the historical agenda. Bell's prognostications of the end of ideology foreshadowed Fukuyama's thesis of thirty years later. In effect, the traditional humanistic intellectuals had little to do, if their historical mission had always been to raise ideological flags behind which masses and classes marched. Their marching music—the discourse of alternative futures—was now relegated to the museum. For if advanced capitalism proved able to solve the historical problems associated with scarcity because, against Marx's dire prediction, it could develop the forces of production, there was room only for the agency of managers and other strata of the technical intelligentsia. The new marching songs were now made by the clicking of the computer's keys.

Bell was to make this last point more explicit in his *Coming of Post-Industrial Society* (1973) published thirteen years after *End of Ideology,* most of the contents of which had been written in the mid and late 1950s. Thus, as early as the 1950s, Kristol's generation (he and Bell later co-edited *The Public Interest,* a neoconservative magazine of social policy) turned from ideological struggle (except against the Soviet menace) to the task of fine-tuning late capitalism. Yet, as Bell was to later realize, whereas scientific and technological development and the provision of social welfare *within the framework of capitalist social relations* were able to contain most of the specifically economic problems of the system and thwarted the emergence of a mass-based political opposition founded on class inequality, there were few, if any, tools to overcome the *cultural contradictions.* In the aftermath of the rise of the youth movements of the 1960s and early 1970s, Bell, if not his fellow converts to the liberal state, presaged new, perhaps more intractable contradictions that could not be repaired by technical means.

It was evident that nearly all the intellectuals who followed the path to modern liberalism or neoconservatism after the war expected that the class struggle, socialist ideology, and historical contradictions would end with capitalist economic and political integration, leaving only the defeat of world communism as the remaining ideological task. What they did not see until much later was that having defeated the enemy without, the new historical question would be concentrated within, in "culture," an indefinite term that signifies everything from values and beliefs to rituals and customs to art and language forms. In no case did anyone, except orthodox Marxists and liberal economists, identify the great historical issues with western societies with their economic fate.

Yet here, too, liberal optimism proved shortsighted: by 1970 it was apparent to informed opinion that something was desperately wrong with western capitalism. Europe was experiencing the early signs of economic crisis as production stagnated and jobless rates began to climb to at least 10 percent in most countries. And, by the middle of the 1970s, the United States showed similar symptoms. At first, unions and some business groups insisted that imports made with cheap labor were the heart of the problem. But this explanation, while partially justified, failed to account for a host of other troubles. Technology in the U.S. steel industry lagged behind Asian and European competitors; cost savings could not be attributed to low wages, but to more efficient labor saving machinery in foreign plants. American products were not as well made as those of their competitors for foreign as well as domestic markets. Consequently, for these as well as other reasons, among them worldwide overproduction, the U.S. economy began its long slide in the last years of the 1970s and has not yet recovered, except ephemerally, during the middle Reagan years when, fueled by a ballooning defense budget and even more bloated consumer debt, some sectors experienced boom times that served to hide the underlying crisis. What remained to be explored, beyond strictly economic factors, was the degree to which "cultural" issues might have produced some of the features of the decline. Did the United States, during the cold war years, cultivate too much of a taste for military solutions—not only in foreign relations, but for economic problems as well? Did the political and economic directorate misperceive the character of the global restructuring of the 1970s and 1980s that has been marked by "disorganized" capitalism? Have the largest corporations, politicians, and state intellectuals become overly enamored with and stuck within "free market" solutions to economic problems that have proven inadequate to address deeper, more structural challenges, especially scientific and technological development? And, since this orientation, growing militarism, combined with the weakness of the labor movement, has led to a massive dismantling of the U.S. welfare state, has the corporate elite overplayed its power and permanently damaged the system's own infrastructure?

These questions imply a profound challenge to the thesis shared by this older generation of political intellectuals that there were no longer systemic contradictions and that ideological questions, except anti-totalitarianism, had lost not only their mobilizing force, but their social pertinence as well. They have cast a pall over many of the underlying assumptions of all varieties of modernism and modernity theory, some of which baldly state the thesis, while others presuppose it. For, as I argue below, many of the arguments of multi-culturalism, cultural studies, and feminism presuppose when they do not ex-plicitly posit: the persistence of exploitation, inequality, and oppression in which the economic, political, and cultural aspects are combined. That is, while many of the old modernists made a politics out of the ideological neu-trality of culture while acknowledging that some unmet social and economic needs remained, the new social movements insisted that cultural difference signifies economic and political difference, and that issues of knowledge are identical with questions of power. To put the matter succinctly: the New York Intellectuals were mistaken in their assumption that they were the last adver-sarial culture. Nor could they anticipate their own antipathy to the new cul-ture that displaced them. Their integration (and triumph) after the war did not signify the last appearance of what Trilling had called a new "class" of cultural intellectuals.[33] While, with the triumph of high modernism, there no longer remained a warrant for the assertion that such a class existed, if its formation was attributed to the numerical growth of those whose intellectual identity was bound up with opposition to an older mainstream, when mod-ernism became the Culture—in Trilling's use, a signification of the Establish-ment—it was certainly premature to declare the death of the vanguard.

2

Assimilation into American life was the preferred cultural practice of the first-generation, turn-of-the-century immigrants, especially the Jews. This de-cision was abetted by several features of contemporary economic development and political tradition that made a contrary perspective less attractive for most. First, U.S. law provided for a process of naturalized citizenship for those who could pass an examination in the English language and U.S. history. Ex-cept for radicals and other "undesirables" (sexual pariahs, for example), im-migrants suffered discrimination only if they clung to their language to the exclusion of English. Second, the first three decades of the twentieth century was an era of rapid growth for the U.S. economy which, despite its frequent panics and depressions that affected immigrants with particular force, pro-vided even the poorest with the material justification for hope for a better life. It was not chiefly a matter of getting rich; America promised deliverance, at least for a substantial fraction of the next generation(s), from backbreaking toil and the *opportunity* for a minority but substantial portion of the popu-lation for professional and small business occupations. Third, for many there was simply no alternative that was better. For Jews, the distinction currently made by U.S. immigration rules between economic and political migration did not exist. Every Jew was fleeing, to one degree or another, from anti-

Semitism and, in Eastern Europe, from economic privation closely related to discrimination. While American nativism harbored a powerful streak of anti-Semitism, it was never official state policy as in many countries of Europe where, for centuries, Jews were obliged to suffer for their cultural and religious heritage. Fourth, however uneven and violated, the prospect for freedom and eventual democratic rights, especially for dissenters and radicals, but also for oppressed national minority people, was far better in America, especially because it was prepared to accept large numbers of them, at least until 1920.

Assimilation took on a special meaning for Jewish immigrants. It was not simply a matter of shedding Yiddish, the more orthodox versions of their religious practices, or shtetl culture. Assimilation to an American identity promised *liberation* from the stigma of being a Jew in a Christian land. Many of the families of first-generation Jewish intellectuals, including Trilling's, practiced religious orthodoxy. For many reasons—the strict prohibition of Saturday work, kosher culinary practices, the routine observance of religious rituals whose origin could be traced to the medieval period, and the fierce patriarchal household—many young Jews were eager to find an alternative. On the Lower East Side of New York, in Williamsburg and the Brownsville sections of Brooklyn, the Tremont and Hunts Point areas of the Bronx, among others, the socialists fought the liberal-supported settlement houses for the souls of the sons and daughters of the new immigrants, while the socialists vied with the two old parties and sclerotic trade unions for their parents. The struggle carried over into the public schools, which, from 1910 to the Second World War, were crucial institutions of assimilation.

Public schools, socialist youth groups, and settlements were all sites of *secular humanism,* a phrase signifying faith in science and technology rather than God, a fervent passion for extending democratic and egalitarian practices to private as well as public life, and beliefs in the capacity of individuals to achieve their own goals regardless of class, ethnic, or religious backgrounds. The differences among them reduced to conflicting interpretations of the enlightenment. The dictum that knowledge is power and that "man" is the author of his own fate was commonly shared. The great debate was whether the problem of America was its imperfections within a broad ideology that it was the "best of all possible worlds," or whether as an advancing capitalist, even imperialist power, America shared the class dynamics of Europe. If the leaders of educational and reform movements were right, the task of schools and other modernizing community organizations was to assist in the process by which individuals became citizens, organized collective action to improve their lot, but realized their individual aspirations primarily through hard work and education and achieved their collective demands through trade unions, professional associations, and electoral action. If, as the socialists argued, the U.S.

was little more than a relatively privileged version of harsh, rapacious capitalism, whose political system remained closed to "others" than native-born middle-class Americans, the working class had no choice but to liberate itself through revolutionary action even as it struggled for a better life within the capitalist system.

To be sure, for both sides political action, that is, reforms by means of legislation and electoral politics, was necessary, even desirable. For example, there was a broad consensus within the community that workers should have some compensation, either by employers or by the state, when made involuntarily jobless; child labor should be prohibited by law; health and safety regulations should be imposed on landlords and employers among other ameliorative measures. Some liberals even recognized that workers needed unions. But, for them, the ultimate aim of collective action—reform—was subordinate to helping the immigrant to imbibe American and western culture, to shed his or her rural or ghetto heritage which, after all, was a heritage of oppression. The socialists insisted that all efforts to change the way in which the coercive power of the state and capital was exercised was always, at best, temporary and fragile. Without a fundamental transformation in economic relations, of property, liberation from exploitation and its social symptoms was out of the question. But, especially in America, the socialist vision was more pertinent as an inspiration for immediate struggles than a practical program.

Regarding culture, the secularists of the liberal, socialist, and anarchist movements agreed. Religion held back the possibility of realizing the enlightenment: it thwarted the full development of science, technology, and human labor because orthodoxy was, by definition, as much as its practices committed to tradition. And orthodox Jewish religion was, like Catholicism, quintessentially the product of the preenlightenment. Its antipathy, or at least skepticism, about modern technology was matched by its suspicion that modern education, whose fundamental premises were those of scientific enlightenment, corrupted the soul. In sum, liberals and radicals may have differed on the question of how Jews could achieve emancipation from discrimination and exploitation, but they were united in their fealty to modernity. Their intellectuals were committed to a cosmopolitan world view as opposed to nationalist and religious parochialisms. For radical intellectuals, the problem with liberal (or, in the vernacular of the day, progressive) solutions was that they relied, at the end of the day, on the nation-state to provide the context for democratic action. Consequently, as historical experience showed, there was a natural, if unintended, affinity between liberalism and nationalism, a conclusion borne out by the virtual unanimity among nonsocialist progressives, in 1917, in favor of U.S. entrance into the world war.[34] So, in addition to the distinction between revolution and reform, the second great divide between socialists and American progressives was between nationalism and cosmopolitanism.

Until the Communists defined their doctrine as "twentieth-century Americanism" in the late 1930s, radicals were generally marked by their class rather than national loyalties. As Marx argued, "the proletariat knows no national boundaries." It was in this environment that many New York Intellectuals were nurtured. Others, raised in middle-class families, could not help being influenced by radical ideas; in the first two decades of the century, they were in the New York air, especially among the Jews. Although it was never true that *all* New York Jews were somewhat on the left of American politics (indeed, the considerable religious community was indifferent when not openly hostile to the left, and the liberal wing of the Democratic party always had a considerable base in Jewish neighborhoods), the public representations of the spectrum of Jewish public opinion ranged from progressive to radical. From 1910 to the early 1920s, socialists were elected from districts on the Lower East Side to the state legislature, Congress, and lower court judgeships. Thus, in contrast to most areas of the country—except Milwaukee (dominated by German workers), Oklahoma, the Dakotas (where the socialists inherited the agrarian populist upsurge), and Reading, Pennsylvania—New York and, to a greater extent, lower Manhattan, were exceptions to the general rule that socialism failed to find a stable popular constituency in the United States.

In these early decades, the face of intellectual radicalism was itself cosmopolitan. Many secular Jewish intellectuals, most of them journalists and professionals, wrote in Yiddish, still the language of everyday life in the new world shtetl, even though Abraham Cahan, the editor of the Yiddish language socialist daily *The Forward*, tirelessly urged his readers to speak and read English to integrate themselves and their children into American culture.[35] With few exceptions, notably Morris Hillquit, a national leader of the Socialist party, and the anarchist tribune Emma Goldman, the great majority of the leading lights of the broad spectrum of literary radicalism until the Depression were native-born Americans of Christian parentage. Writers like Max Eastman, Floyd Dell, Jack London, Henry Demarest Lloyd, Lincoln Steffens, Reinhold Niebuhr, and a fairly large number of leading novelists, among them Dreiser, John Dos Passos, and James T. Farrell *were* the public face of intellectual as well as literary radicalism. They, and an assortment of French, German, and Soviet political intellectuals such as Lenin and Trotsky, not Cahan, Rudolph Rocker (the non-Jewish German-born editor of the anarchist *Arbeiter Stimme*), or the Yiddish-language novelists Scholem Asch, I. J. Singer, and Israel Zangwill provided the models for the generation of Jewish-American intellectuals who reached their adulthood in the 1920s and 1930s. The Yiddish writers, despite their secular, often modern values, represented the Old World; they used the language of the shtetl, their key references were those of the eastern European ghettos.

It would not be excessive to claim that, except for Lionel Trilling (born 1905) who, in the late 1920s and early 1930s, wrestled with the problem of how to reconcile his Jewishness with cosmopolitanism (and, finding this task beyond solution, abandoned it), the Jewish literary radicals of the 1930s and 1940s defined themselves in open-throated rebellion against *both* the secular and religious Jewish literary and political traditions except that of "rootless cosmopolitanism" that had always been a minority, if powerful strain in Jewish history. As first-generation Jews, they spoke and wrote in English; their intellectual and literary references were those of nineteenth- and early twentieth-century European, particularly continental, modernism: Marx, Lenin, Trotsky, Dostoevsky, Flaubert, French impressionism, and then cubism and surrealism. As we have already seen, their crucial English language canon was derived from the modernist sensibility they helped to define. In short, "the best that has been thought and said" was invariably European, but never identical with artifacts of a national or subaltern culture.

In 1949, in an issue of *PR* in which a symposium appeared on the controversy concerning the judges' decision to award the prestigious Bollingen prize for poetry to Ezra Pound (most Jewish respondents insisted on the connection between Pound's anti-Semitism and his poetry), Sidney Hook published an unrelated reflection "on the Jewish Question" occasioned by the publication in English of Jean-Paul Sartre's *Anti-Semite and Jew*.[36] The piece is remarkable for many things, among them the statement that Christianity, with its doctrine that Jews are responsible for the death of Christ, is the cause of enduring anti-Semitism. But perhaps the most interesting of Hook's contributions to the discussions underway at the time is his endorsement of Sartre's definition: "a Jew is one whom other men [sic] consider a Jew." This is, at once, a condemnation of attempts to find "essential traits" to define Jews such as physical, personality, and cultural characteristics that are said to be racially inherent, and opposition to concepts of Jewish identity that rely on historical or religious traditions.

Jewishness, thus conceived, has only a socially constituted, negative connotation. Negative because, on the one hand, it violates the modernist aspiration to achieve a community of people who share the universal values of western European culture such as freedom and the democratic way of life. On the other hand, the Jew is a product of anti-Semitism—the assumption being that if Jews had not, historically, suffered persecution they would have assimilated into national cultures. Despite this perspective, Hook arrives at some positive conception of Jews. After rejecting a definition based on essences, he concludes: "Far wiser, it seems to me, is to recognize the historic fact of Jewish existence, the plural sources of Jewish life and its plural possibilities. No philosophy of Jewish life is required except the democratic way of life—which enables Jews who for any reason at all accept their existence as Jews to lead a dignified and significant life, a life in which together with their fellow men they strive collectively to improve the quality of democratic secular cultures and thus encourage a maximum of cultural diversity both Jewish and non-Jewish."[37] From this he argues that "the ethics of democracy presupposes not an equality of sameness or identity but an equality of differences." Within the universalist view common by the post-war, cold-war era, in which liberal democracy now occupied the pinnacle of human endeavor, "diversity" and "difference as cultural choices are entirely acceptable."[38] However, Hook who, apart from his political interventions, was the leading legatee of the founders of American pragmatism, especially John Dewey, and a powerful advocate of that aspect of pragmatism that privileged the "scientific method" as virtually identical with reason, was also an implacable opponent of all forms of religious "unreason." While admitting that the historical scars of the Holocaust were imprinted on every Jew, making any effort to deny Jewish identity as absurd as it is improbable, he remained stridently critical of efforts to reconcile reason with superstition with which he identified religion. As long as Jews, or any other subculture, observed western values that he, along with his peers, regarded as warrants for social and political conduct, let them practice, privately, whatever beliefs they please. But they should not impose these parochial interests on schools (Hook was an important educational philosopher) or any other institution of public life.

For the two generations of Jewish liberal and left-wing intellectuals reared in the first half of the twentieth century, assimilation was more than a choice; it became intertwined with their modernist creed. While American culture may have betrayed many of the egregious features of industrial society, even if mass culture was the unintended consequence of democracy unmediated by high cultural tradition, any intellectual effort to forge a separate identity from that of "American" was a formula leading not only to isolation from the enlightenment mainstream, but would inevitably reduce the chance that America could become genuinely "Europeanized." Thus, Americanization was intended to achieve the opposite result—to facilitate the cosmopolitanization of American culture.

Until the rise of the New Left, the term "liberal" could, by 1960, be widely applied to nearly all of the former radical intellectuals. Ensconced in leading universities and key editorial and writing positions in book and magazine publishing, they gradually extended their reach beyond *PR* and the liberal weeklies to the *New York Times, Commentary,* and leading academic literary and philosophical journals. They became broadly affiliated with the postwar coalition of anti-communist trade unions and the main civil rights organizations and with the Democratic party and its New Deal, Fair Deal program.

Many young socialists, like Albert Shanker and Victor Gotbaum, became leaders of the new white-collar and professional unions, while others got jobs as organizers, business agents, and House staff of unions generally considered part of the anti-communist progressive wing of the AFL-CIO. Others were directors and important staff members of liberal political and social-welfare organizations such as the Americans for Democratic Action in which Schlesinger played a central role, the NAACP in which Roy Wilkins, a former anti-Stalinist radical, was the leader and of which Herbert Hill, a former Trotskyist, was labor secretary.

However, the early New Left, a combination of former communists who had repudiated Stalinism and a nascent student movement formed by a libertarian and populist democratic progressivism, was not only a more militant battalion of this coalition, proposing direct action rather than relying on legislative and bureaucratic processes to achieve consensual reform objectives. Even in the mid 1960s when its main organizations such as SDS still defined themselves as radical democrats, and followed C. Wright Mills's advice to carefully avoid becoming embroiled in the historic debates on the old left lest they isolate themselves from any incipient native radicalism, important segments tried to constitute an adversarial political culture. Concepts such as direct democracy implied a powerful critique of the perceived degeneration of representative government that had become one of the revered elements in the ideological arsenal of the old radical intellectuals.[39]

Moreover, the music of Bob Dylan, the Beatles, the Rolling Stones, and Janis Joplin became anthems of rebellion against such diverse features of American mainstream politics and culture as imperialism and war, racism, and most crucially given their own social backgrounds, middle-class respectability. Rather than celebrating the partial affluence that was a cardinal feature of postwar America, the New Left concentrated its critique of society on the persistence of widespread poverty and hunger, worker exploitation, and racial oppression. Most if not all of the young radicals explicitly renounced the consumer society that had become the proudest achievement of what Mills termed the "American Celebration."

However, equally important, especially in the late 1960s, was the penchant of many tendencies in this emergent movement to adopt communitarian practices. Although few tried to form production communes, living communes, food cooperatives, and income sharing were fairly common. Alongside this "new" left politics of radical democracy and egalitarian ethics arose a counterculture that both resembled and differed from antecedent bohemias, education experiments, and cooperatives of the earlier years. This counterculture was accused, by the organizers of the "old" new left, of being apolitical because it did not focus on making changes in the state, but sought to separate itself from the mainstream by practicing alternative "life-styles" which, variously, involved vegetarianism, drugs, communal agriculture, spiritualism, self-help and self-improvement, and interest in eastern religion. Taken together, these practices were interpreted by the counterculture(s) and their enemies as a separation, even a revolt against some of the main features of western rationalism. This perception was as irksome to many among the political new left as it was to old left intellectuals. Some elements of the counterculture discovered the pleasures of eastern religions, particularly Zen Buddhism, but more pervasively became persuaded that a new spirituality was required to save humanity from the various scourges that afflicted it, especially the alienating effects of urbanization and industrialization and rationalized science and technology.

A significant segment of the counterculture became enamored with mind-expanding drugs and marijuana, not only in its quest for some of the pleasures that it perceived had been denied them by the prevailing puritanical culture, but as a crucial aid in its search for the spiritual side of human existence that had been sacrificed by their elders on the altar of crass materialism. This was also a period of sexual experimentation for a whole generation of disaffected youth. Once confined to the lower rungs of working-class life, premarital sex became, if not a norm of the entire generation of the 1960s, at least a practice that was already at hand. In sum, the counterculture shared, with some parts of the New Left, a new morality that defined itself against the decision of old radicals to reinvent themselves as quasi-normal Americans, "quasi" because, as intellectuals, they remained outsiders, no matter how conservative they presented themselves.

As with other aspects of this revolt, none of the practices or ideologies was entirely new. What distinguished the 1960s from previous intellectual, artistic, and sexual avant gardes was that the adversarial politics and culture that once existed in small enclaves now spread over an entire generation. And the forms taken by this counterculture were richly various. In San Francisco, Emmett Grogan organized a group called the "Diggers" to distribute food and provide shelter to many dispossessed youth who had left middle-class and working-class homes, quit high school, and found themselves stranded in the neighborhood called Haight-Ashbury. The point of the activity was not social work: it was to show that needs had no price tag. In New York, young radical writers, musicians, artists, and political activists congregated in a part of the Lower East Side dubbed the "East Village," a reference to their aspiration to become a new avant garde as Greenwich Village had been before the First World War. They opened coffeehouses where they read poetry and sang their rock and roll compositions. Within this context new art movements developed: Among them, pop art, with its aestheticization of technology and advertising and a comic book sensibility; performance art and video art formed the basis for a new visual aesthetic that self-consciously abjured the older literary radical traditions. In Virginia, Vermont, Tennessee, and New Mexico young people bought farms and operated them collectively. Several still exist.

However, the main sites of youth radicalization occurred on college campuses. This was particularly significant because, by the 1960s, universities were experiencing tremendous expansion; they were becoming the main sources for the production of knowledge on which the scientifically based U.S. economy depended. More, they were training scientists, technicians, traditional intellectuals, and teachers for the burgeoning corporate and education institutions. In turn, once stereotyped as pleasant, isolated ivy towers of esoteric learning, the university was now modeled on the industrial corporations it faithfully served.

Of course, for millions of lower middle-class and working-class families the chance that their children would escape industrial labor and other kinds of relatively insecure work enabled them to comprehend the university expansion as a blessing. Even at the height of the anti-war, civil rights, and feminist movements in the late 1960s, perhaps a majority of college students dutifully attended classes, tried to achieve high grades, and eagerly sought decent technical and professional jobs. The student left was always a minority movement, except during specific moments of protest and demonstrations, but it had attracted some of the academically best students—especially writers and editors—and created other public outlets for the dissemination of ideas. The new political left was an elite movement, and for this reason triggered cries of anguish with the more sophisticated sections of the Establishment, among whom were not a few old radicals.

White and black student participation in the civil rights revival of the late 1950s and early 1960s did not upset the established leadership, except in the South. But the transformation of the student movement from a support group for black civil rights efforts to a *left* that defined itself in opposition to the corporate capitalist system and its major institutions was not only cause for consternation in these circles, but became a subject for considerable debate. For the truth of the early New Left was that it saw itself as a force for democratization *within* and not against the progressive coalition. Its radical cultural interventions were, at least at the beginning, somewhat independent of its left-liberal ideology.

In the pursuit of dialogue with a tradition it believed had been repressed, undemocratically, during the McCarthy era, the tiny Students for a Democratic Society (SDS) although distinctly anti-Stalinist, agreed that representatives of a Communist youth organization could observe its June 1962 Port Huron, Michigan, convention. At the time SDS was affiliated with the League for Industrial Democracy (LID) whose chairman was Michael Harrington. Harrington, who had been a neo-Trotskyist militant, in 1958 followed his mentor Max Schachtman, the leader of the small Independent Socialist League

(ISL) into the Socialist party. Harrington reacted to the events at Port Huron with indignation and considerable consternation. He summoned the SDS leaders to a meeting to discuss their political errancy. The meeting resulted in the eventual split between the parent and the child: the mild-mannered and somewhat innocent SDS people were, in a few short hours, brought face to face with a history they only dimly perceived. For Harrington, like his somewhat older friend Irving Howe, had been schooled in the collective experience of independent left intellectuals, for whom Stalinism represented the antithesis of democratic socialism and humanism and should, therefore, be barred from access to the democratic left.

Howe and Harrington, who both remained organized socialists, did not go as far as Hook in advocating the denial of academic freedom and some other civil liberties to Communists and kept their distance from the penchant of some anti-Stalinist intellectuals to collaborate with government repressive efforts. But they openly expressed alarm at many of the evolving proclivities of the New Left, especially its distrust of the labor-liberal coalition and the Democratic party as well as its apparent blindness to the still potent Communist threat. By the 1962 Port Huron SDS convention, Harrington was well on his way to working with the Kennedys, a move that was stimulated by the favorable reception liberals accorded his best-selling *The Other America,* a brief chronicle of the persistence of poverty amid abundance and a call for a massive, government-led effort to end it.

This focus on the poor, if not Harrington's phobic reaction to the Communists, appealed, at first, to SDS leaders like Tom Hayden. But they differed on the best way to make sure that the "war on poverty" that Harrington was helping the Kennedys to organize would not become another welfare program administered from the top by bureaucrats, social workers, and politicians. SDS wanted "an interracial movement of the poor" to insure that the clients of the government's efforts became, themselves, agents of the changes. Only such a movement could guarantee that the poor were truly represented in their own economic emancipation. Thus, although SDS split organizationally with LID, much of its next few years were profoundly influenced by Harrington and the Kennedys. Yet by far the larger *ideological* influence was a kind of radical democracy fused with a home-grown romantic existential philosophy in which middle-class students and the poor would, through mutual interaction and aid, both achieve authentic existence. For Harrington and his fellow socialists for whom participation in Kennedy's New Frontier represented a rare opportunity to come in from the cold, the populism of the student left was nothing short of an invitation to retreat, yet another time, into sectarian obscurity.

In 1964 the Free Speech movement in Berkeley condemned not only Chancellor Clark Kerr's idea of the university as a rationalized, corporate, and military-dominated institution, but offered the rudiments of a critique of curriculum, the academic division of labor, and authoritarian styles of pedagogy. Many white as well as black students who became active in the civil rights movement were not only committed to the objectives of equal rights, especially in schools, public facilities, and voting, but became acutely aware that black culture and history had been systematically occluded within the liberal curriculum—when it was not entirely excluded. Others became interested in working-class history, especially the dissident and radical movements that defined themselves not only for workers rights but against capital, and found in the universities a conventional history of the established labor organizations. Still others, because they began organizing in working-class communities and in workplaces, discovered the main body of knowledge about class outside the classroom.

Whatever their specific critiques, the new radicals agreed that they wanted, and expected, that universities would meet their needs for an education that prepared them to participate in the struggle for social change. They took seriously the critical function that had always been the key legitimating ideology for the university. Instead of being prepared as agents of change, they discovered that "Cal" expected them to take high-paying positions in the corporation and state establishments. Instead of education, they were offered training.

At the University of California-Berkeley, sociologist Seymour Martin Lipset, a political contemporary of Howe, and philosopher Lewis Feuer, once close to the Communists and now also a liberal professor, were, to say the least, horrified by the ideology and tactics of leaders of the Free Speech movement. They recognized that the student occupation of the university in opposition to its increasing rationalization and industrialization, as well as its cold-war-inspired ban on political activity, was an entirely new kind of movement. In the 1930s, the student movement, although led, in the main, by Communists and Socialists, was chiefly a peace movement. Many radicals were excellent students and, on the whole, identified with the mission of the university to transmit the best in western culture and to train a new generation of technical and traditional intellectuals. No incident of the period demonstrated more clearly the gulf that separated the old left from the new. Feuer became an antagonist of the most radical efforts of the students to democratize the curriculum and held fast to the idea that the university was privileged space that ought to be immune from direct political action. Lipset and Feuer were open adversaries of the students. True to their own traditions, they saw in the protest nothing less than a subversion of the enlightenment mission of the university, and charged its leadership with communist or at least authoritarian tendencies. Feuer added his own psychoanalytic interpretation in which the students were portrayed as classically caught in their Oedipal problems which did not, however, vitiate the dangers inherent in the protest.

The originality of the Free Speech movement was, in retrospect, its challenge to the role of the universities as repositories of legitimate intellectual knowledge. It began in early 1963 as a protest against the policy of the UC-Berkeley administration's prohibition of political activity of any kind on the campus. Within eighteen months, many students, some of whom had spent summers in the southern civil rights movement, extended the issues to the character of education at Berkeley. With this challenge came a severe critique of the role of the scholar and intellectual attached to academic institutions. Students began to ask whether the professoriate were agents or opponents of the bureaucratic state and, equally important, in whose interest was the curriculum formed. In consequence of this skepticism, students demanded a voice in shaping the curriculum, specifically the right to propose courses that were not part of the traditional curriculum and to recruit instructors, with or without legitimate academic credentials, able to teach them. This notion violated traditional faculty prerogatives. Moreover, it expressed the outrageous idea that students possessed sufficient intellectual competence to intervene in their own education, if not entirely determine its content. Another outrageous demand was for direct student representation, from top to bottom, in the committees and departments of the university. And, finally, but very tentatively, the movement questioned admissions criteria, especially with respect to minority applicants. Although the demand for open admissions did not take root until much later in the decade, the Free Speech movement presented, nascently, the initial arguments for the democratization of the student body, the curriculum, and the professoriate. By 1965–1966 the Berkeley campus was thrown in turmoil by a torrent of anti-Vietnam War activity, that, among other targets, focused on the university's massive defense contracts that had, by that time, virtually taken over major departments of science and engineering. This situation simultaneously described developments at Wisconsin, Michigan, Harvard, Columbia, MIT, and many others. The key issue—President Lyndon Johnson's relentless expansion of U.S. military involvement in the Southeast Asia wars and his concomitant reimposition of the draft—was certainly the efficient cause explaining the magnitude of the movement, one that surprised its organizers. But the movement showed that what passed for disinterested intellectual research was really subordinate to the war effort. The university had become complicit with the war aims of the government; its capacity for critical inquiry was substantially impaired. For many student activists, president Dwight Eisenhower's 1960 farewell address seemed surprisingly prescient. Whereas he warned against the domination of American life by an emerging "military-industrial complex," students were adding "university" to comprise an unholy trinity of death and destruction. That these institutions were tightening their grip over public life under a liberal Democratic administration was among the crucial sources of radicalization.

As the Free Speech struggle was creating turmoil among the liberal professoriate, the summer projects of SDS and the Student Non-Violent Coordinating Committee (SNCC), the militant wing of the southern civil rights movement, were central radicalizing experiences for the activists of this generation. Hundreds of white students participated in SNCC's voting rights campaign in Mississippi and other southern states while the SDS concentrated its efforts, initially, in large northern cities and the mining area of Hazard, Kentucky, in poor white working-class communities and poor black neighborhoods. The consummation of these activities came with the challenge by the SNCC-supported Mississippi Freedom Democratic party to seating the regular, segregationist delegation at the Democratic Party's Atlantic City convention.

While the convention's credentials committee pondered the issue, Lyndon Johnson marshaled some of the leading lights of the left wing of the party to thwart the challenge. What remained of New Left faith in Senator Hubert Humphrey, March on Washington organizer Bayard Rustin, Schlesinger, and Harrington was completely shattered by the debate. The interracial delegation should call off its challenge lest the Democrats' effort to reelect Johnson against the most conservative Republican candidate for president since the 1930s, Barry Goldwater, be fatally weakened as a result of the divisions within the party that would ensue. Needless to say, Goldwater was swamped in the November election, but a new conservative movement was born that has dominated the past twenty years of American politics.

However, the depth of the disaffection on the left led, together with Johnson's subsequent escalation of the Vietnam War, to this generation's mass radicalization in the subsequent four years. By 1968, tens of thousands of people who had voted or otherwise supported Johnson under the slogan "Part of the Way with LBJ" either joined the primary campaigns waged by Robert Kennedy and Eugene McCarthy against Johnson's renomination, and/or joined the efforts to force Johnson's resignation or impeachment. Johnson declined to run for a second full term and his appointed successor, Humphrey, was defeated in the general election in part because millions among the traditional Democratic constituency sat out the election, voted for Nixon as a protest, or supported third-party candidates, especially in New York and on the West Coast.

As an organized ideological force, the New Left virtually disappeared by the middle 1970s as a substantial segment of the leaderships of its institutions became fatally attracted to the ideologies of the old left—not the Communist and Socialist Parties—but to "new" communist groups that were inspired, in various ways, by the Chinese or Cuban revolutions and by other Third World revolutions. Most of the new parties petered out not only because of the crisis in the Chinese leadership that resulted in their alliance with the United States after the Vietnam War, but also because they had violated the rule of "Americanization" that had animated all kinds of reasonably successful radical movements since the turn of the century. Simply put, they were unable to find a constituency for their politics in any segment of the American population. They remained a series of isolated elites that, as the 1970s wore on, engaged in the politics of revolutionary illusion, sometimes violent, sometimes destructive of their own cadres.

Most who had been inspired by the radical 1960s got on with their lives. Although the dissolution of the movement produced a pronounced tendency among some toward depoliticization, a significant number of radicals became community and labor organizers, social workers and therapists, writers and artists, and remained radicals. They were among the founders of the new waves of feminism and ecology, active workers in the civil rights movement, peace activists. As experienced radical militants, they have made considerable contributions to the "popular" reform left.

Others who chose to pursue PhDs got university jobs in the late 1960s and early 1970s. They became leaders in some large and influential academic disciplines such as English and other languages, particularly French and German studies, sociology, economics, where Marxism is the semi-official alternative to neoclassical approaches, anthropology, and, in the natural sciences and psychology, constitute a definite, although minority voice. In American historiography, Marxist perspectives have achieved parity, if not hegemony over the field; surely, the radical-inspired "history from below" has become among the more respected innovations in the past two decades. And "theory," a euphemism for alternative approaches—deconstruction, feminist, Third World, Marxist, hermeneutic—today dominates the largest of all academic disciplines, literature and languages. Many radicals of the 1960s generation are currently academic stars, especially in the humanities and social sciences. The organizational expressions of the radicalized generation are all but dead, yet the cultural influence of this generation does not merely linger into the 1990s; it is more powerful within the university than it was in the 1960s. And, as new constituents have entered university life—African-Americans, Latinos, Asians—women and the gay and lesbian movements are more visible, their intellectual orientations have been incorporated, but not without Sturm und Drang, into the mainstream curriculum. In contrast, the criticism (but not the social history) of Irving Howe and Alfred Kazin widely read by students and junior faculty until the late 1960s are today largely ignored except by their contemporaries and liberal critics of the younger generation. Trilling, who died in 1975, has become a historic figure. His wide-ranging criticism is read by intellectual historians, not cultural critics. From his early *Matthew Arnold* to his last book *Sincerity and Authenticity,* a tacit reply to some of his own New Left students, his work subsumed under his membership in the generation of New York Intellectuals, a fate that has also befallen Sidney Hook, most of whose books have been out of print for years.

Trilling and Hook are unjustly neglected. Today, they are largely unread precisely because the current cohort of graduate students and younger professors has identified them as cold-war intellectuals but also because the genre of writing within which they worked has become unfashionable. For example, Trilling, although a sophisticated critic, was pointedly uninterested in theory, except psychoanalysis, his interpretation of which would now be considered old fashioned. He was a veritable master of the "learned" essay, that genre in which the erudition of the critic is combined with a distinctive voice, sensibility, and insights that persuade the reader by rhetoric more than by systematic argument. It is an old and honorable tradition which, however, seems to have faded or, more exactly, has been removed to the middle-brow periodicals.

Hook is victimized by his political views, which became extremely conservative after the 1950s. His open hostility toward the New Left matched his anti-Stalinism, and this inability to draw useful distinctions between the two movements earned him the enmity of all but the most professionally oriented students over the past three decades. Hook's objections to the New Left were more complicated than his anti-communism. He was equally exercised by what he perceived to be the irrationalism of the counterculture and its penchant for utopianism, in which he heard echoes of Stalinism, a trait that offended his naturalist sensibility.[40]

I do not want to claim that one may unambiguously ignore one's political career in order to save intellectual contributions that can somehow be separated from political commitments. It is entirely accurate to say that the quality of Hook's work in education, political philosophy, and epistemology deteriorated during the last quarter century of his life (he died in 1989), a period that corresponded to his sharp rightward turn. More specifically, he allowed his open-throated passion for the American intellectual culture he and his peers had created in the late 1940s and 1950s to overpower his critical eye. While he lost none of his vitriolic style in later years, he lacked the substance to make it palatable.

These caveats aside, Hook's contribution to a social theory and philosophy that tried to combine Marxism and pragmatism are incomparable in the literature. He was trained in Germany under the influence of Karl Korsch's historical Marxism and in the United States by John Dewey who wrote the introduction to his first book, a sympathetic critique of pragmatism. His second book, perhaps his major work, *Toward an Understanding of Karl Marx* (1933) is arguably the most original contribution by any American of his generation to Marxist theory, a tribute that is particularly significant since this work was done in the so-called "red decade" when Marxism was fashionable among intellectuals. And his sequel *From Hegel to Marx* (1936) became, for a whole generation of American radicals, their first and probably only knowledge of the development of Marx's thought. In these and his 1930s essays collected in *Reason, Social Myths and Democracy* (1940), a rich potpourri polemic against Marxist orthodoxy, including its founder Frederick Engels, Hook provided the contour of a nondogmatic, anti-Stalinist Marxist pragmatics that unfortunately was not emulated by succeeding generations. In contrast to Trilling, Hook is equipped with a formidable analytic apparatus; he generates categories of understanding, adopts an explicit methodology of criticism, and employs the style of explication de texte to drive home his points. Even when he is not right, one is aware of being in the presence of a powerful mind whose learning is always subordinate to his arguments.

The legacy of the discomfited intelligentsia reared in the interwar generation reduces to this: in their condition of homelessness they created cosmopolitan space within which succeeding radical generations could breathe. But more saliently they reinvented the image of America as a democratic market place where, despite the degradations they perceived in mass culture, the popular front, and middle-brow art, this country had for them become the repository of modernist hope. The "democratic way of life" might not be exciting but, in contrast to the closed societies of Eastern Europe, China, and Cuba, it provided space for dissent, creativity, and even new ideas.

However, when new countercultural movements arose in the aftermath of the turbulent 1960s precisely within the precincts of their greatest influence, the university, the liberal intellectuals recoiled and even warned that the university itself was in danger. The New Left made only hesitant critiques that focused on the ideological neutrality of the U.S. academy, on the authoritarianism of university decision making, and on the political bankruptcy of the liberal professoriate that it accused of collaborating with the war machine. However, even as, at the end of the 1980s, statues of Lenin were unceremoniously toppled in East Germany, Poland, and other East European countries, the iconic artists and intellectuals of high modernism, and the canon they had carefully constructed through thousands of pages of critical texts, were being torn down at home. As 1960s radicalism matured intellectually it has taken on the bewilderingly difficult task of recasting what we mean by legitimate knowledge. From the perspective of the modernists, it has turned on progress itself. As Kristol had quipped, "the enemy is us." The row over political correctness is produced by a strange alliance: right-wing ideologues like Alan Bloom, whose attacks on progressive education, Marx, Nietzsche, and Heidegger as veritable authors of the decline and fall of the West, and the 1960s as a period of the wanton quest for pleasure, are already legendary; older and young neoconservatives grouped around magazines such as *Policy Review,* a journal of the right-wing Heritage Foundation, and the neoconservative champion of high modernism, *New Criterion*; liberals connected to *Partisan Review* and the *New Republic,* each of which has run a special issue on the controversy, with a characteristic declaiming unanimity among the contributors; social-democratic periodicals such as *Dissent,* whose editorial board is barely distinguishable, in its majority cultural opinions, from the *New Republic* but quite distinct on issues of social justice; and a fragment of older Marxist-oriented professors like Eugene Genovese and Stephen Thernstrom who themselves feel victimized by the young politically correct.

3

In the burgeoning literature on the subject, the "Thernstrom" narrative reappears with deadening monotony. For some years, Thernstrom and Bernard Bailyn, both prominent Harvard historians, had conducted a course in race relations in American history. Thernstrom read from slave-master narratives in class and was promptly accused by students of racism for this indiscretion. In despair, the instructors eventually dropped the course, but the student charges still dog Thernstrom. This incident and that at Brown where, in 1990, the university's administration expelled a white student for publicly engaging in symbolic acts of racist aggression, have become emblematic of the frequently repeated charge that universities are in the grip of "a new McCarthyism of the left." Of course, there are some other cases where professors have been attacked for expressing the view that African-Americans are intellectually inferior to whites, among them philosopher Michael Levin whose utterances have provoked student and some faculty protests and led to an investigation by New York's City College administration.

Clearly, these instances illustrate that there is a strain of anti-civil libertarianism among some anti-racist and anti-sexist groups and individuals. There is, indeed, reason for disquiet, especially in the face of the long struggle to realize academic freedom and other facets of civil liberties that libertarians and radicals have waged since the birth of the Republic. The U.S. government, employers, and, more generally, institutional authorities have never passionately defended the right to dissent from established policies and consensual values. In fact, America has a long record of witch hunts, show trials, political prisoners and more recently, absence of public debate about vital political issues. Although this is not the place to rehearse specific features of this illiberalism, one may cite the virtual absence of congressional discussion of the U.S. invasion of Panama, the stifling of public protest after President Bush ordered the bombing of Iraq in January 1991, and earlier cases where official versions of the national interest were the only voices heard in print and visual media. In addition, academics outside the mainstream social sciences and humanities have experienced sharp tenure and promotion battles during this period.

For example, during the 1980s, sociologists Theda Skocpol and Paul Starr, literary theorist and critic Linda Brodkey, and education theorist Henry Giroux were merely the most publicized of outstanding scholars and intellectuals who suffered from the vindictiveness of the established academic generation that felt threatened by their innovative work. Although the victims were by no means uniform either in their politics or in their intellectual orientation, their work, in various ways, challenged the dominant paradigm of the discipline. Skocpol and Starr violated the unwritten rule in sociology that junior professors confine their research to modest, discrete studies; in each case they departed from dominant thinking in their respective fields. Brodkey and Giroux overtly challenged the penchant of educational studies to avoid, at all costs, contemporary social and cultural theory, especially theory that falls outside the dominant functionalism. That each of them landed on their feet is a tribute to their immense talents, not to the far-sightedness of the university faculties or administrations.

Nonetheless, it is extremely dangerous for those who have been traditionally victimized to occupy the space of prosecutor as if reverse censorship is justified by these illiberal practices. Given its history, it behooves the left to become the most vigorous proponents of First Amendment rights, and especially to defend, wherever possible, those on the right whose views, however repugnant, are still within the purview of constitutional guarantees of free speech.

Yet the dispute over academic freedom does not entirely encompass the debate. More far-reaching is that many professors currently at the height of their prestige and power are widely perceived by a new radical generation as hopelessly tied to older knowledge paradigms, to an outmoded conception of the university, namely, as a fount of neutral scholarship, and to a politics curiously insensitive to subaltern social movements and their value orientations. The fact is, the cliché applies: between the generations there is a failure to communicate. The senior liberal faculty, joined somewhat cynically by the popular press and the right, reproduces, sometimes unwittingly, sometimes not, the generational conflicts of two earlier periods: the 1930s when the young cosmopolitan left intellectuals broke from the nationalism that inhered in prevailing traditions, and the 1960s when these erstwhile radicals having become the university establishment were confronted by a new generation challenging their newly acquired nationalism.

In the 1990s, those who occupy the position of defending tradition have offered comparatively feeble arguments against what may be the most serious challenge yet. For as opposed to earlier struggles when arguments over *knowledge* were often inchoate within contemporary political "issues" such as the war and demands for student power, today's radicals are more theoretically prepared to argue about intellectual traditions. They have focused, in the first place, on curriculum issues within some of the core disciplines of western culture, especially literature but also some social sciences and philosophy. At stake is who speaks for the intellectuals. On this question may hinge the legitimacy of the old hegemonic paradigms.

At the same time, the concept of "political correctness" can be separated from its ironic usage in the late 1960s or its sometimes regrettable deployment as a battering ram. The term may possess validity when interpreted as an ethical precept not to engage in racist and sexist speech or to sexually harass women students and faculty members. Surely, any community has a right to set limits on what it considers acceptable speech, and even establish rules by which communicative intercourse is to be conducted, just as long as individuals are able to express their dissent, in democratic forums, from these norms. Even as we do not sanction verbal abuse in everyday interaction, so individuals and groups who have suffered, historically, from the effects of racial, sexual, and gender discrimination may not tolerate openly racist statements in spheres where public debate and discussion occurs.

Now, we can distinguish abusive behavior from the exercise of opinion. The student or professor who holds that blacks are unable to learn and should be excluded from certain educational sites should be able, freely, to give these views in print, university committees, and other public forums, including the classroom, just as the expression of radical political, social, or cultural views, including the right to organize around them, is reserved for all citizens in every sphere of public discourse. The difficulty arises when students from subaltern groups exercise *moral*, rather than physically or administratively coercive pressure to silence repugnant speech. Surely, efforts to call professors and students to account when their opinions and their actions are perceived as harmful to its objects cannot be stifled on civil libertarian grounds so long as the right to express views is preserved.

Granting the right of a professor or student to make such utterances, the question is whether members of the institution have an obligation to insist on the distinction between the exercise of these rights and utterances where subaltern groups and individuals are abused. At issue is whether speech may be abstracted from the conditions of its utterance. What in an appropriate body may be considered entirely justified, say where a member suggests that women should be excluded from higher mathematics courses, becomes on the street or other public places harassment when expressed in an angry, threatening register. We may defend the right of anyone to utter expletives, but we do not expect individuals to do so in contexts where these utterances may be interpreted as hurtful to their victims. For example, when a white student yells at blacks the word "nigger" or scrawls some threatening sentence on a dorm wall, it is not unreasonable for the university to declare such behavior to be outside the bounds of propriety and to subject the perpetrator, who must be availed of due process, to a public hearing.

What is at issue here is not speech per se but context. Surely, one must draw a fine line between remarks made under various conditions. Where racist, sexist, or any other expressions of contempt for a specific category of person are made in a relatively "safe" environment, the targets of such statements may still condemn this speech as beyond the bounds of ethical practices. But they would not have the right of exclusion. On the other hand, such acts that are hurtful to others, especially historically oppressed groups, may be dealt with more severely, and penalties constructed that protect the safety of aggrieved individuals and groups. For conservatives to defend "free speech" by identifying criticism with authoritarian behavior is an act of bad faith, for there is no community that will tolerate speech that may be interpreted by them as harmful.

The past decade has witnessed the full force of conservative efforts to impose censorship by supporting legislation that bans pornography even when, as in the case of photographer Robert Mapplethorpe's work, it is presented as art. Related but not identical to this, they have favored obscenity laws that forbid expletives on television, radio, and print media. Many congressional conservatives such as Senators Jesse Helms and Strom Thurmond who abjure pornography have also sought to restrict a woman's right to an abortion and have effectively denied poor women access to federal funds for that purpose; they have also sponsored and passed legislation banning flag burning.

Clearly, the recent conservative concern for academic freedom and civil liberties, and their use of the "McCarthyism" charge to characterize some of the recent incidents, must be taken with suspicion that they are opportunistic, rather than principled in their opposition to censorship. It is hard to make a case that the several incidents that have marked left repressive tolerance explain the continuing p.c. barrage. For what is at issue is not merely this scattering of overt acts. More to the point, we are witnessing the passing of a whole hegemonic era in academic life. Those whose intellectual and political lives were wrapped up in it and a newer cohort who have identified with this hegemony, even at the remove of several generations, are struggling to regain their positions. What is at stake is not chiefly what one writer has described as the advent of "illiberal education," but a major paradigm shift in intellectual knowledge, culture, and political values.

Partly in reaction to the assimilationist Americanization of the old left, in both its major varieties, and to the loss of its radical edge, the 1960s generation, and those for whom some aspects of its culture and intellectual proclivities are a kind of model, is in the process of forging a new critical practice that owes its inspiration to European sources, chiefly from Britain and France, but also Germany and Italy. In addition, it has become attracted to post-colonial Third World intellectuals, many of whom have selectively appropriated European theory and criticism to argue against Eurocentric perspectives on, primarily, cultural knowledge. Moreover, to the extent radical academics have recognized the pertinence of American tradition, it is largely that of the subaltern and the popular, particularly African American, and has reached back to earlier feminist and working-class writers, political theorists, and agitators.

In this struggle the insurgents can no longer simply identify themselves as victims, any more than could Galileo and Copernicus who, despite considerable persecution, were clearly ascendant over their tradition-bound critics or James Joyce whose revolution of the word was, in the last instance, irrepressible. The values of the new intellectual radicals have already begun to permeate mainstream institutions such as the Educational Testing Service that designs various standardized academic sorting devices such as the Scholastic Aptitude Test (SAT) and the Graduate Record Examination (GRE). Knowledge of black and women's literature as well as the traditional canon are now included on these tests. Many universities, under pressure by younger faculty and students to institute major curricular reforms, are scrambling to hire African-American and Latino faculty to strengthen their disciplinary as well as their cross-disciplinary programs. At the same time, there has been a certain proliferation of interdisciplinary graduate programs, combining, especially, philosophy, the arts, and literary criticism. And, equally galling to conservative critics, some trade and university publishers eagerly seek out the work of the radicals and a plethora of new journals and magazines now crowd the bookstores. *PR* and *Dissent,* once the leaders of the small liberal political/literary magazines, retain only a fraction of their readership; their viability depends, to a large extent, on decades of accumulated library subscriptions but they have failed to win the allegiance of a substantial group of new readers since the mid 1960s. Nor are Marxist journals exempt from the judgment that their pages are stale with yesterday's ideas.

At the same time as the radicals have made significant inroads in U.S. intellectual life, neoconservative thought has revealed new vitality, if only by being willing to actively engage the new movements in combat. Aided by substantial sections of the daily and weekly press, Kristol, Bloom, and Nathan Glazer have drawn a younger generation of writers, notably Roger Kimball and Dinesh D'Souza, whose attacks against intellectual radicalism have received wide publicity and resonate with a substantial segment of intellectuals who have been silently watching their once secure positions erode. The growth of academic conservatism can be measured by the formation, in 1980, of the

National Association of Scholars with some 30 chapters and 1700 members, but also by the degree to which its views are now widely shared among the liberal intelligentsia.

Today, intellectual conservatism may be distinguished by two ideological positions: the resolute defense of the traditional curriculum—whether classical or modernist—against the postmodern turn; and its insistence on "excellence" as a euphemism for protecting the prevailing system of educational inequality against the attacks of subalterns. Of course, in his immensely popular best-seller *The Closing of the American Mind,* Bloom makes no effort to hide his contempt for curriculum reform that distances itself from classical texts. He bitterly castigates the handful of "first-class" private universities for pandering to women, people of color, and radicals who want to study Marx, Nietzsche, and Heidegger rather than Plato and Hegel; Richard Wright and Zora Neale Hurston rather than Charles Dickens; and whose critical sensibility is formed by their own time rather than the Greek city-state.

Bloom's rant has resonated with middle-class readers—whether intellectuals or not—who, buffeted by rapidly shifting economic, social and cultural winds, seek a prophet to rearticulate the old values for which they stand, regardless of whether they have read the philosophical and literary canon that girds the claim of the West to be the pinnacle of civilized society. But *The Closing of the American Mind* is also a call to action, a manifesto of the defenders of the faith. It argues, incoherently, that there is, for all intents and purposes, little, if any, philosophy after Hegel that cannot be charged with inviting the barbarians through the gates. It goes so far as to claim that, however democratic the recent efforts to open the doors of the universities to many who were formerly excluded, affirmative action and open admissions are futile gestures because blacks and other people of color are so overwhelmed by economic and social problems they could not possibly master a rigorous curriculum. Therefore they should be relegated to state institutions for training while the elite, private universities should resist reforms that "dilute" classical education and permit only the best and the brightest to occupy their classroom seats.[41]

Despite the attention that conservative educators have received in the past decade, and their ability to mobilize the media to disseminate their ideas, they are engaged in a rear guard action. Bloom and his acolytes have made a point of saying nothing new: they are committed to the good old things, since, by definition, the new things are always bad. For the modernists inspired by the now defunct New York Intellectuals, the distinctions between their liberalism and conservatism are, in the face of the rise of intellectual radicalism, increasingly blurred. They might advocate a different canon from that proposed by Bloom. Surely, given their own dissident, if not left-wing, roots Marx cannot be so easily dismissed. And it is hard to believe that Howe, who knows the difference between zealous anti-racism and McCarthyism, can adopt the cynical views of those on the right who hold similar ideas on the canon. He must remember his own book that showed how the right waved the flag of intolerance in the 1940s and 1950s.

Yet there is no doubt that the targets of the new intellectual movements are as much liberals as the right, for in many respects they have aligned themselves on knowledge issues similarly. The university wars have radically realigned ideological positions from their usual moorings around questions of economic justice. For the stakes—what is legitimate intellectual knowledge, who are the knowledge producers, and who can speak for "us"—question and otherwise threaten conventional authorities. The weight of the challenge has been so heavy that sections of university administrations that at first seemed more open to innovation, sensing their own positions under attack, have slowly yielded ground to preserve their own authority.

In one sense, the current struggles within the university reproduce the crisis of the middle class that has marked the larger social canvas. For the entire American ethos is intertwined with the well-being of this social category. Just as the ranks of middle management have been thinned by mergers, consolidations, and acquisitions of smaller by larger international corporations, and independent small businesses in virtually all production and service sectors face the most difficult times since the Depression, so the professoriate that benefited directly and indirectly from the dramatic expansion of universities through the early 1970s now face *both* economic and ideological battering.

Salaries of all but the top stars in each discipline are virtually frozen since the late 1980s and working conditions are progressively deteriorating. But, most humiliating, the guardians of the two major paradigms of western culture have been cut off from the younger faculty and the best students whose minds and hearts have wandered elsewhere. In a sense, their situation is poignant. The older generation were unable to experience the 1930s and 1940s as years of upsurge, since their eyes were fixed on the dual defeat they suffered at the hands of Stalinism and the New Deal. Their moment arrived only when the social movements ebbed and when they emerged it was on the side of the established power. Within universities the Hooks, Bells, and Howes *became* the established powers.

Then came the pain of the political youth disaffection just as they arrived in the prestigious chairs. If the immortality of the intellectual resides in the hearts and minds of the succeeding generations who venerate their elders by criticism as much as emulation, these figures could point only to the middlebrow journals for remaining sources of their renown. They stayed in their chairs during the political revolt of the 1960s generation and staunchly defended their newly won academic respectability.

Once again the political movement ebbed. And the Berlin Wall crumbled, vindicating the political choices of anti-Stalinist intellectuals. But the revolt of the 1960s was not over; now the *cultural* confrontation undermined the intellectual perspicacity of the New York Intellectuals. Postmodernism, the "French turn" in social and cultural theory, multiculturalism, and the neo- and post-Marxist revival has cut the ground from under them. Now they face something called "cultural studies," as a vision around which knowledge should be organized. To the generations who devoted their lives to rediscovering and remaking America, these trends must be perceived as nothing less than manifestations of disloyalty, as the coming of a new barbarism.

The cultural politics of the conflict may be expressed in terms of conflicting conceptions of citizenship. Those who have assimilated themselves into American culture have also conflated the idea of freedom with American nationality. Loyalty to the U.S. nation-state is identical with what they mean by democratic citizenship. One may criticize various policies of national or local government or even dissent from major foreign policy objectives of a given administration. But the precepts of the identity of the United States with what democracy and freedom actually signify has become a precept guiding mainstream intellectuals: their reconciliation with "their" country has meant that they have merged, politically and culturally, with the values of the dominant groups, even with the myths that have infused American nationality.

In contrast, for the past twenty-five years a minority has tacitly redefined citizenship to mean *cultural citizenship*. Cultural citizenship displaces, for many immigrants and adherents to new social movements, the notion of class loyalty that in earlier periods countered patriotism and nationalism. By this is meant that loyalty to the nation-state, conventionally tied to the meaning of citizenship itself, is shifted to subculture or gender, often taken as subculture. In turn, this cultural identity is frequently international as in the case of pan-Africanism or international women's solidarity. In short, cultural citizenship signifies a community of the oppressed and a statement that the nation-state is symbolic of the oppressor.

As I have already indicated, this cultural politics is inextricably linked to an intellectual project that entails the struggle for a paradigm shift in knowledge. The combination of the two aspects has elicited an enormous backlash, a storm of protest and contestation that, in the heat of the battle, tends to forms of representation whose meaning can be understood only strategically and tactically. However, cultural studies deserves its own genealogical investigation. It to this investigation that I now turn.

CHAPTER TWO

Culture Between High and Low

THE HISTORICAL distinction between "high" and "low" culture refers to the gulf that separates aristocratic and church culture, on the one hand, and the peasant culture of the late middle ages and the early modern, that is, bourgeois period, on the other. Bakhtin has shown the gulf was not as wide as supposed—indeed, each influenced the other in quite fundamental ways and so the assumption that, from the point of view of artistic production, there are two quite distinct spaces may be excessive. And the relationship has persisted to this day.[1]

However, his demonstrations and those of other writers who, as we will see later in this chapter, claim aesthetic and social value for popular "art" and culture, failed, until fairly recently, to impress the guardians of this hierarchy. Even after the passing of the feudal aristocracy, a new "high" culture was constituted by the middle class and its intellectuals, many of whom were themselves cultural entrepreneurs. The key to the historical preservation of the aesthetic hierarchy by which some modes of artistic production are called "high" lay in its important function with respect to maintaining the hegemony of the new bourgeois class in the wake of demise of the aristocracy. For one of the conditions of economic and political rule is, in countries in which the state requires broad popular consent for its legitimacy, to claim, as its inheritance, high culture, especially works that were appropriated by previous social elites.

I do not claim that the significance of the works themselves, or of the artists who made them, may be reduced to their cultural function. Art that bears an individual signature is a relatively recent development in western societies and corresponds to the larger social process of individuation that struggles with ecclesiastical tradition in the thirteenth and fourteenth centuries. We can see this struggle most clearly in Dante's exile, which resulted from the publication of La Vita Nuova and sections of the Divina Commedia. Recall Dante's guarded plea, in La Vita, for the replacement of Latin by the vernacular in literary works, which may be understood as the artist's attempt to supersede the existing audience of Church officials and the mandarin strata two centuries before Galileo's celebrated recantation of cosmological theories that contradicted those of the official, ptolemaic physics. For Dante, expanding the audience corresponded to his own vision that literature would take everyday life as its direct object, without the ritualistic mediation of the epic form. When taken together with the emergence of a new audience for writing and painting—merchants and even artisans—one can see the intimate connection between the appearance of the individual and the popular.

In the late feudal era, as the individual artist (or scientist) insists on (his) own agency, he can no longer expect the patronage of the church. Henceforth, artists are increasingly obliged to go on the road to make a living. For example, in the plays written and performed by traveling troupes in sixteenth- and seventeenth-century England, the popular becomes embodied in text and performance and is only later recuperated as "high art" after the specific context in which this work developed has disappeared. Such is the fate of William Shakespeare, Christopher Marlowe, and other, unnamed author/players who roamed the English countryside in search of audiences typically composed of a mixture of the social categories of the "productive" classes—squires, tenant farmers, artisans, and laborers. Clearly, the shift in the conditions of reception affected the content of these plays. As some recent critical work has demonstrated, Shakespeare's comedies bear strong resemblance to traditional folk legend, carry on traditions inherited from earlier minstrels, and incorporate their musical as well as dramatic form into the texts and performances.[2]

Working in a Germany that had not yet formed a unified nation-state, composers of the baroque period of the late seventeenth and early eighteenth centuries were almost entirely dependent on church or aristocratic patrons. Although, like virtually all high music of this or any other period, peasant dances, hymn tunes, and popular ballads formed the basis for melodic lines, one can discern the *signature* of the composer in the development of this material; Bach, particularly, calls attention, in the Goldberg Variations and the Art of the Fugue among other works, to the formal aspects of composition—which, of course, marks the distinction between "high" and "popular" music. Bach had been a church organist and choirmaster; Handel and Haydn were somewhat peripatetic but always court musicians.

However, Mozart was increasingly thrown on his own devices in the 1770s. He became an entrepreneur, performing his own works in concert halls and private homes, including those of the aristocracy but did not enjoy, in his later years, a permanent appointment or the patronage of an aristocrat. Although he composed in excess of forty-one symphonies and many chamber works, the real indication of the *individual* market status of the composer was his twenty-seven piano concertos, his five violin concertos (the authorship of the sixth is in dispute), and concertos and concertantes for virtually every solo orchestral instrument, as well as his prodigious output of piano sonatas. Mozart was a frequent solo performer and conductor of these virtuoso genre pieces. The later concertos were performed, in the main, for middle-class audiences in concert halls.

With some exceptions, especially his celebrated Quartets Numbers Seven through Nine, composed for a Russian count, and various commissioned works, Beethoven is the first truly bourgeois composer; that is, his career is largely made, despite some commissions from the nobility, on his capacity to sell his talent—both in composition and performance—to a popular, middle-class audience. From the early 1790s, when barely twenty years old, he established himself in the leading cities and towns of Germany by contacting agents who rented halls, advertised his arrival, and sold tickets. Beethoven himself performed at these concerts, often with a small chamber orchestra whose musicians were recruited locally. His nine symphonies, the violin concerto, and the five piano concertos are, perhaps, most familiar to contemporary classical music audiences but his more than thirty piano sonatas and his other chamber pieces—especially his sixteen string quartets, the two sonatas for cello and piano, and his string trios—were the bread and butter of his performances. As an entrepreneur, like most court composers, he knew that the *newly composed* piece was generally the main attraction in his tour which, of course, included performances in the homes of aristocrats and members of the new high bourgeoisie as well as in concert halls.[3] The solo piano work or works for small ensembles such as the sonatas for violin and cello were economically more feasible to perform than larger-scale compositions that required hiring many paid musicians and more elaborate orchestrations.

The symphonies and concertos were necessary to satisfy the *theatrical* requirements of a popular audience and so, like many after him who depended on these new patrons, Beethoven complied with symphonies, both numbered and named (Wellington, for example), overtures to never-completed operas (he only published a single work in this genre, *Fidelio,* which has three different overtures that have been folded into the standard repertoire), and occasional works such as *The Creatures of Prometheus,* themes of which were later incorporated into the symphonies.

Yet, even if the *class* that provided the patronage to artists has, more or less, passed into history, and musicians, novelists, and dramatists increasingly wrote and performed for a new popular audience since the sixteenth century, the notion of "high" art persists. In the aftermath of the American and European revolutions that extended from the turn of the nineteenth century until the early decades of the twentieth century, aristocrats and intellectuals who adopted their critical and aesthetic ideology have argued that mass democratic institutions and practices and the universalization of the industrial system, the cornerstone of which is wage labor, have, simultaneously, produced the decline of taste. This degeneration has, allegedly, occurred because the masses (that here include the middle classes) have taken social power.

For this reason, the canon of high culture is formed, retrospectively, by abstracting the works, particularly of the early modern bourgeois era from their historical and social context, forgetting or otherwise discounting the influence on the artwork of the audiences for whom they were composed and performed. In this respect, the valorization of the typical artworks as high culture after the middle of the eighteenth century depends on the historical amnesia of the canon-makers as well as a theoretical formalism that denies (when it does not ignore) the idea that signification is produced in a three-way relation of artist, context, and audience. Even the notion of the "artist" as a distinct figure is mediated: the artist is immersed in the imperatives of compositional and performance rules, including the formal requirements dictated by genres.

In this respect, musical composition and literary production differ not at all. A concerto, in the classic mode, has three movements, a symphony, four. The contemporary performance is a kind of ritual and so is the formal appearance of the literary work: commercial concerts of chamber music as well as symphonic works are usually performed in a hall; the story is published first in a magazine and the novel appears, typically, in a book (where once it might have been serialized in a daily newspaper or a special fiction periodical); novels and plays must possess their inevitable denouement and so forth. The departures from these rules—the twentieth century's one, five, or six movement symphonies, the novellas in book form—manage by their deviations to call attention to the norm.

I am not arguing that elements of individuality are not to be discerned in the artwork, only that these occupy a relatively small part of it. The artist occupies the *standpoint* of the individual creator even as the work itself is highly mediated by various conventions, including that of performance in which the audience plays a significant role. Since, as Wittgenstein has argued, there can be no private language and James and Mead argue that the self takes, in the process of its formation, the point of view of the Other, all art is dialogic, but the participants are crucially tied to each other at every level.[4]

The concept of high culture itself arises as a repudiation of the conditions of production as well as conditions of reception that are bound up with the universalization of the commodity—form. In an era when culture itself has become industrialized, the whole concept of distinction depends on the capacity of critics to empty the artwork of its social referent or, as in the case of Marxist criticism, to link the social codes to the formal innovation. Thus, the idea of high art becomes intertwined with the aesthetics of *form* and, from the middle of the nineteenth century, is identified by the proponents of high culture with the work of various artistic avant gardes that emerge precisely at the moment when bourgeois civilization can no longer hold on to its progressive claims and appears to have entered a long path of decline. Paradoxically, as Adorno and Greenberg have forcefully argued, avant garde art movements are bourgeois society's salvation, its mechanism for reconciling dissident intellectuals with the system, even as it signifies a protest against crass commercialism to which art is subjected.[5]

For art historians of the older schools, canon is constituted by *style,* by a breakthrough in color, composition, or, indeed, a new use of materials. For example, Picasso and Braque are heralded for their incorporation of artifacts of everyday life into their pictures and, by this technique, make the artwork self-referential. Musicologists construct periodization by noting stylistic innovation, the composer's employment of new instruments, and, as in the cases of Beethoven, Debussy, and Schoenberg, the disruption of older forms, but also a break with the building blocks of conventional music—tonality. In this way, they effect a break with the taken-for-granted presupposition of conventional aesthetics: that music be "beautiful" because familiar and reassuring. With the dissonances of his late quartets, not only disruptions in the melodic line but also inversions of the conventional four-movement form and addition of new movements, Beethoven denaturalizes classical form.

From the middle of the nineteenth century, conventional high art is industrialized by a powerful Culture Industry that disseminates it more broadly into the (middle-class) population. More to the point, high culture is degraded in two ways: by the systematic production of *kitsch*—perhaps the best examples are the multitude of operettas of the late nineteenth century designed for a popular middle-class theater audience;[6] and the mechanical reproduction of pretty pictures that adorn every middle-class home. Second, high music becomes the raw material of commercially produced popular music; advertising appropriates artistic form to sell products; and the novel-form becomes the shell of schlock, particularly the romance, adventure, and later the detective genres.

From this moment, western capitalist societies witness the emergence of artistic avant gardes.[7] The chief characteristic of the avant garde is its refusal, not of representation, for all art is representative of something, but of the banality *it perceives* is required by the Culture Industry. Against the tendency of late capitalist culture to subordinate art to its market value, the avant garde demands art's autonomy by calling attention to itself—its materials, its formal requirements, its process of production. Whereas, for Bach, Mozart, and Beethoven this self-referentiality remained largely inchoate (even many of Bach's efforts were framed as exercise books), the avant garde makes its art a self-conscious subject of artistic production.

For De Tocqueville as much as Ortega y Gasset democracy is the real culprit in the decline and fall of high art in the nineteenth and twentieth centuries. Writing of early nineteenth-century America De Tocqueville observed: "The inhabitants of the United States have . . . at present, properly speaking, no literature. The only authors whom I acknowledge as American are the journalists. They indeed are not great writers, but they speak the language of their country and make themselves heard. Other authors are aliens; they are to the Americans what the imitators of the Greeks and Romans were to us at the revival of learning, an object of curiosity not of general sympathy. They amuse the mind, but they do not act upon the manners of the people." Of course, in today's American universities the label "journalism" usually disqualifies a writer from the prestige accorded genuine scholars. The scholar may cite journalism as illustration, but the charge that one has engaged in it is no less damning than it was to De Tocqueville. In his view, the capacity of democracies to produce artistic "wonders . . . may occasionally be the case," but only "if customers appear who are ready to pay for time and trouble."[8] Whereas "in aristocracies, readers are fastidious and few in number; in democracies, they are far more numerous and far less difficult to please. . . . The ever increasing crowd of readers, and their continual craving for something new, insures the sale of books which nobody much esteems."[9]

A hundred years later Ortega carried the argument a step further. For him, the "accession of the masses to complete social power" is reflected in the emergence of the mass consumption of all aspects of culture. Ortega's argument against mass culture reduces to this: the rise of the masses to social power means, among other things, that we are witnessing a concomitant decline of the power over culture of the "minorities" he calls the "upper class." These minorities are "specially qualified" to appreciate and to direct the production of cultural things, while the masses (not to be confused with the "working masses") are the "average man. In this way what was mere quantity—the multitude—is converted into a qualitative determination: it becomes a common social quality, man as undifferentiated from other men, but as repeating in himself a generic type."[10] This generic type has no particular interest in what really qualifies an individual to imbibe culture: "to be surprised, to wonder . . . this is the sport, the luxury, special to the intellectual man." In contrast, mass man lacks the characteristic of the "visionary without which genuine art is not possible."[11]

Ortega does not object to the fact that the masses are enjoying themselves or that they have both "the desire and the means to satisfy" their cultural consumption. "The evil lies in the fact that this decision taken by the masses to assume the activities proper to the minorities is not, and cannot be, manifested solely in the domain of pleasure, but that is a general feature of our time." As for his aristocratic predecessor, Ortega's ultimate concern is that mass "taste" is increasingly identical with taste as such, that the special qualities of the intellectual are no longer capable of *imposing* high culture as the aesthetic common sense of the time. "The mass crushes beneath it everything that is different, everything that is excellent, individual, qualified and select."[12]

These lines, written on the heels of the 1931 Spanish revolution—the last one in modern Europe—a mass democratic uprising against an entrenched and ancient class of landowners and traditional aristocrats and their military retainers—have their echo on the "left" during the same period.

The American social critic Thorstein Veblen had, in the first decades of the century, darkly ruminated on the advent of consumer society, particularly the replacement of the redemptive values associated with useful work with a regime of leisure marked by such practices as "conspicuous consumption" and the consequent loss of inner directedness and individuality in favor of "pecuniary emulation."[13] His critique of American society and culture rested on the deeply conservative foundation of puritanical values, as conservative as Ortega's and De Tocqueville's invocation of the virtues of productive leisure whose premise, however, was not the pleasure of cultural consumption. Veblen's was the quintessential bourgeois critique of mass society: it fatally weakened the instinct of workmanship and, consequently, discipline, without which humans degenerate into greed, invidious comparison, and other narcissistic practices.[14] I have already alluded to the connection between questions of political and social rule and those of culture. It is now necessary to delve a little deeper into the precise nature of the relation. The theory of mass culture implies the theory of the massification of society and the transformation of the conception of polis. From one that assumes, in its ideal form, a public sphere consisting of individuals who, because they are freed for large chunks of their time from the banalities of everyday life and can, in consequence, know the common interests and legislate in their behalf, we have entered an age of mass passivity where citizenship consists merely in giving consent through the ritual of voting. The ultimate referent of mass society is the historical moment when the "masses" make the (still) contested demand for the full privileges of citizenship, even though they are obliged to work at mundane tasks, are typically and systematically untrained for the specific functions of governance, and are ensconced in the routines of everyday life. For the high cultural intellectuals these banalities are certainly dignified activities but disqualify the "people" for making aesthetic and philosophical judgments. To the contrary, good taste must be protected from the masses, lest civilization itself degenerate.

According to these theorists, the "masses" are subject to a division of labor whose effects, from the perspective of democratic ideology, are to limit their vision to the particular interests of their family and community. Moreover, as Walter Lippmann cogently argues, their ability to transcend the conditions of their own upbringing and immediate environment is virtually non-existent. These features of the rise of the "masses" have been among the persistent themes of political philosophy and, in my opinion, are the basis of the critique of mass culture. What is at stake is whether a larger conception of democracy than that of representative, republican government—popular control over economic and political life—is at all desirable, much less possible in a world increasingly dominated by standardization, fragmentation, and escapist plea- sure, what Herbert Marcuse calls "repressive desublimation." In short, de- spite the pervasiveness of democratic ideology since the French revolution, intellectuals, left and right, have questioned its consequences in terms that are remarkably consistent since De Tocqueville's lament.

Perhaps the most subtle and influential American treatise against the con- cept of mass democracy was Walter Lippmann's *Public Opinion* (1922). Lippmann had been a socialist, but discarded this allegiance in the wake of the Great War during which he discovered his own nationalism, but also the dangers of placing primary, much less exclusive, reliance on the decision- making power of the democratic polis. Lippmann's crucial argument presup- poses a social and, more specifically, an epistemological premise: that there is a profound chasm between "the world inside our heads" and reality. The world inside our heads is shaped by various stereotypes promulgated by habit and tradition but also by newspapers, magazines, and the statements of pol- iticians. The vast public forms its opinions according to these stereotypes that shape what we see: "For the most part, we do not first see, and then define, we define first and then see. In the great blooming, buzzing confusion of the outer world we pick out what our culture has already defined for us, and we tend to perceive that which we have picked out in the form *stereotyped for us* (my emphasis) by our culture."[15] This process is made all but inevitable by the fact that, individually, we occupy only a small part of the world—our family, our work, our friends are the context and the substance of what we call "experience." We may belong to organizations such as civic groups and labor and business organizations or even be professionals, such as engineers, physicians, and attorneys. Yet, according to Lippmann, none of us is exempt from perceiving the world as a series of stereotypes given to us by the culture. Thus, unlike most other critics of mass culture who carefully distinguish between educated minorities and the masses, he is not concerned to reproduce a picture in which the mass public is fundamentally different from "trained observers." Unlike his master, Plato, whose allegory of the cave places the philosopher, at least putatively, in a qualitatively better position to see reality than the mass of people, Lippmann *universalizes* the problem of shadow knowledge to embrace all of humanity insofar as they act as private individuals.

Given the necessary distortions in perception, there are bound to be nec- essary distortions of judgment mediated, in the main, by particular interests, by the fragmentation of everyday existence, and by the distortions of media representations. The "buzzing confusion of the outer world" is the mode of existence of humans. Although Lippmann is most interested in the problems of political democracy, specifically how the public may function as the *legitimating* base of any non-authoritarian system of governance, his argument rests, at its most profound level, on what might be described as a *social epistemology* in which "culture" is the crucial determinant of the ways of seeing social reality. His sources—the art critic Bernard Berenson and anthropologist A. van Genep—are much clearer about the Kantian premises of this argument. If there is no chance that the public can "see" beyond its own "self-contained community," the distorted communications of the news media, or even "education and institutions" that can sharpen the differences between images and reality, "the common interests very largely elude public opinion entirely and can only be managed by a specialized class whose personal interests reach beyond the locality."[16] This is usually an irresponsible arrangement when the specialized class lacks the disinterest as well as the expert intelligence required to identify the public interest and act rationally to serve it. Yet, in the absence of a theory of social transformation that can account, if not for the immediate prospect, at least for the *possibility* of a democratic and competent public able to intervene, much less control, processes of governance, Lippmann is, in the interest of preserving the institutional practices of democratic society, obliged to fall back on the hope for the creation of a professionally competent public bureaucracy that is, at the same time, responsible to what he later was to term the "phantom" public.

The conclusion of Lippmann's discourse is both tortured and ironic. Clearly, he recognizes the danger of placing such extraordinary power in the hands of experts who, as his previous examples amply showed, were not, typically, more reliable than the broad public. But by providing stability without which no intelligent and effective government can exist, the trained, expert bureaucracy may help unite "reason and politics." In the end, he argues that we must retain democratic institutions such as elections if only because the alternative—a self-contained oligarchy—is worse. Thus, the public must be consulted and, periodically, must "intervene" to keep the technical bureaucracy honest and assert its own needs, but the creation of a genuine public sphere where, like in the political theory that derived its conception of democracy from the Athenian example, citizenship is identical with legislative sovereignty, is utterly out of the question. In the end, embarrassed by his own reference, Lippmann turns to Plato's words in book V of *The Republic* as his epigraph: "Until philosophers are kings, or the kings and princes of this world have the spirit and power of philosophy, and political greatness and wisdom meet in one . . . cities will never cease from ill—no, nor the human race."[17] For Lippmann, Socrates' decision to "retire in anger" in the face of the utopianism of his demand on a state whose governance was propelled by the destructive effects of "culture" was no longer an acceptable alternative. Whatever their pitfalls, only the humanistic and technical intellectuals could provide hope that reason would control political life, and the prospect that culture which, in this discourse, is the determining agent of social distortions, could be subordinated to intelligence. Only then could the "common interests" be revealed and become the basis of public life.

Lippmann appropriates John Dewey's concept of *intelligence* as the standard against which the current confusion of public life could be measured as well as the goal to which it must aspire. Yet Dewey himself, however much he admired the power of Lippmann's analysis of our contemporary malaise, was constrained to reject his conclusion that the time had come to abandon the ideology of popular democracy for a more realistic democratic elitism.

To be sure, in his book length reply to Lippmann's conception that the modern democratic state is in crisis, Dewey accepts Lippmann's judgment that the public has been severely weakened, if not destroyed, by the ascendancy of mass culture. The difference between the two positions consists of Dewey's stubborn faith that democracy can be reconstructed through an act of *will* that promotes the revival of community.

Dewey begins his crucial chapter "The Eclipse of the Public" with the somber statement "Optimism about democracy is today under a cloud." To Carlyle's celebrated comment "Invent the printing press and democracy is inevitable" Dewey adds: "Invent the railway, the telegraph, mass manufacture and concentration of population in urban centres, and some form of democratic government is, humanely speaking, inevitable."[18] Yet, for Dewey, the historical experience of industrial and urban democracies is no cause for celebration, surely no cause for the self-congratulation that he saw in the America of the 1920s.

Democracy may be the entailment of industrialism, urbanism, and technological change but, according to Dewey, its roots are agrarian: "American democratic polity was developed out of genuine community life, that is, association in the local and small centres where industry was mainly agricultural and where production was carried on mainly with hand tools." Here he lays stress on "pioneer conditions" to account for the stability of early American democracy. These conditions "put a high premium upon personal work, skills, ingenuity, initiative and adaptibility, and upon neighborly sociability." Therefore, public institutions, such as schools, developed under local conditions and the appropriate form of governance of these institutions, given the ecological and economic basis of association, was direct participation among citizens, through the town meeting, in the decisions affecting these public goods.

"We have inherited . . . local town-meeting practices and ideas. But we live and act and have our being in a continental national state." Yet our political structures do not hold the national state together. According to Dewey, in modern industrial society, "We are held together by non-political bonds, principally those of communications—railways, commerce, mails, telegraph and telephone, newspapers."[19] But these instrumentalities, while creating a fragile unity, are not sufficient to maintain a genuine democratic polity: "It seemed almost self-evident to Plato—and to Rousseau later—that a genuine state could hardly be larger than the number of persons capable of personal acquaintance with one another."[20]

Here Dewey sounds the theme that animates much of American philosophy and art since the United States embarked, in the 1850s, on its century-long journey to world power. American democracy was born of the necessity arising from the conditions of its settlement where the "pioneers" were obliged to share social and political power in order to negotiate their relationship with an obdurate nature that did not yield its fruits easily. The people who occupied this "virgin land" were fiercely individual, and cherished, above all other values, their freedom.[21] But, in the interest of survival and then prosperity, they were obliged to constitute a political system based on the principle that all who engage in the labor of making of this wilderness that created America as a civilized community, shared equally in its governance.

This system of direct as opposed to representative democracy flourished on a foundation of face-to-face interaction among people who, whatever their differences, understood and therefore trusted each other within the limitations of any political relation. The root sites of this remarkable public life were the small towns of New England in the first half century of the American republic. Dewey gives the example of the school district: "They get a schoolhouse built, perhaps with their own labor, and hire a teacher by means of a committee, and the teacher is paid from the taxes. Custom determines the limited course of study, and tradition the methods of the teacher modified by whatever personal insight and skill he may bring to bear."[22] What impresses is the informality of the process; the state is constituted through the face-to-face interactions of its members. One can extrapolate from this example the formation of committees to build and maintain a local road, another to oversee the work of the tax collector, a third to develop a water and sanitation system, and so forth, and a community where final disposition of the recommendations of these subbodies is made by the town meeting.[23]

This political idyll was short-lived. Dewey recounts that "the temper and flavor of the pioneer evaporated" when "The wilderness is gradually subdued; a network of highways, then of railways unite the previously scattered communities. . . . Our modern state-unity is due to the consequences of technology employed as to facilitate the rapid and easy circulation of opinions and information, and so as to generate constant and intricate interaction far beyond the limits of face to face communities."[24]

Of course, the United States was a pioneer in the democratization of the political system, even as it forged a breathtakingly vast communications system that facilitated not only the spread of information but also of goods. Universal white male suffrage was enacted without the struggle that the English and other European workers conducted to win similar rights. With this veritable technologically based communications revolution came a new *culture*. For thinkers of Dewey's generation, the ability of technology to maintain nation-unity was purchased at an enormous cost. "The public seems to be lost. . . . If a public exists, it is surely as uncertain about its own whereabouts as philosophers since Hume have been about the residence and make-up of the self."[25] If a free society *means* not only the right but the ability of its citizens to participate beyond voting in the decisions that affect their lives, to the extent mass communications and its culture has replaced the "face-to-face" community, American democracy is, indeed, in serious trouble. For democracy is the same as community life itself, where the idea of community entails participation among equals, at least for the purposes of public activity.

For Dewey, as much as for Lippmann and other postwar writers, political apathy and, even more, the absence of intelligent political discourse among those who participate in elections and other public forms on the basis of "habit and tradition" or self-interest, is a function of

The power of bread and circuses to divert attention from public matters. . . . The members of an inchoate public have too many ways of enjoyment, as well as of work, to give much thought to organization into an effective public. Man is a consuming and sportive animal as well as a political one. What is significant is that access to means of amusement has been rendered easy and cheap beyond anything known in the past. And these amusements—radio, cheap reading matter and motor car—with all they stand for have come to stay.[26]

Dewey is forced to admit that there are no certain paths to the formation of an articulate public because the conditions for community life have been disrupted, perhaps forever, with the advent of complexity and heterogeneity associated with industrialization and urbanism. Moreover, while his framework of analysis is democratic rather than aristocratic, the invocation of a rural culture on which to mount a critique of contemporary society leads to nostalgia rather than reconstruction. Dewey describes contemporary American society as a mass society, constituted by the vast information networks whose volume and complexity overwhelm the individual and all but drive (him or her) to retreat to the other "instinct"-induced activities such as consumption and amusement. In current language, privatization is the consequence of massification. But, if these implements of mass culture "have come to stay," and, since these judgments were rendered in the 1920s when consumer society was still in its infancy and before television and VCRs became the main sources of information, it is hard to see how the public may be reconstituted short of some unforeseen cataclysmic event that recreates the wilderness in which small groups of survivors may, finally, form democratic communities.

Dewey's thought contained a significant and characteristic tension. A strong advocate of scientific and technological progress as a method to "liberate individuality," in Paul Kurtz's words, he nevertheless saw clearly the unexpected consequence of putting science in the service of the state:

Bacon's action in using his own knowledge as a servant of the Crown in strengthening Great Britain in a military way against other nations now seems more prophetic of what has happened than what he put down in words. The power over Nature which he expected to follow the advance of science has come to pass. But in contradiction to his expectations, it has been largely used to increase, instead of reduce, the power of Man over Man.[27]

The question here is whether scientific and technological development is capable of shaping human ends or whether their uses are always subordinate to the will of human masters. Dewey's answer is that science increasingly holds sway over human culture but does not possess a capacity for moral judgment. Hence as with the demise of genuine democracy, the real cause of the current state of affairs can be traced to our collective refusal to take responsibility for controlling our own destiny. Hence, scientifically wrought technology tends to drive human affairs, rather than humans driving science and technology. As with the democracy, unless humans take control over their own achievements, unless we find the "method" to harness our knowledge in intelligent ways rather than taking the path of least resistance, the quest for the Good Society is doomed. Finally, Dewey rejects the inevitability of the coming of Mass Man with its implication that only the rich and powerful and their intellectual retainers or, in its liberal technocratic version, experts, can be effective in solving social problems. However, since "human nature" is itself complex (we are pleasure seekers as well as moral agents—the two for him are incompatible on the social level), we are compelled to recognize that democracy and freedom are not given by historical law. They are moral imperatives, the achievement of which depends on whether we have the will to employ our innate reason to suppress those features of human character that, especially since the nineteenth-century scientific and technological revolution, have proven to be both powerful and amoral.

Like Veblen, whose roots were in the Scandinavian immigration that transformed the plains and prairies of the American Midwest using their inherited artisanal skills as well as their communal ties, Dewey's native American heritage is deeply religious. More specifically, he has a faith that social problems can be solved only when the individual is both the end and the means of human activity. This aim can be attained through the development of what might be described as an *intentional* culture, the deepest source from which habit and tradition, according to Dewey as well as Veblen, the actual governors of public activity are formed. Instead of submitting to habit, this culture would stress the unity of head and hand. That is, it would promote the application of intelligence—whose instrument is the scientific method—rather than its technological applications, to regulate our relations with nature and among ourselves.

Dewey tried to define a radical democratic vision of the future in which individuals, constituted as an independent and articulate public, could stem the tide of both totalitarianism and authoritarian democracy. In the early 1930s he worked with Paul Douglas (later a U.S. senator from Illinois), Reinhold Niebuhr, Norman Thomas, and others to form a third party as a practical vehicle to promote a new public life against the corrupt, apathetic, and narrowly self-interested political parties, but failed when the progressive George Norris refused to run in 1932. Yet his commitment to social action never waned. He intervened throughout his life in practical political issues—trade unionism for teachers as well as industrial workers, schools (as well as education), and the defense of the rights of persecuted minorities, notably Leon Trotsky and his Soviet followers. Despite his fundamentally pessimistic intellectual cast of mind concerning modern culture, Dewey displayed an almost classic "optimism of the will"—one that could only be grounded in ethical rather than logico-scientific theory.[28] This ethical dimension was rooted in a faith for which there was mainly local precedent in the New England town meeting as a signifier of a beloved community of individuals who, through dialogue and debate, were able to negotiate their differences on the way to defining common interests.

At first glance, this ethical stance would appear as foreign to the experience and theoretical beliefs of the Frankfurt Institute for Social Research as their Marxism seemed to be to Dewey. Stemming from Georg Lukacs's powerful metaphor that under capitalism "the commodity form penetrates all corners of the social world" and their own theory of science and technology, in which Bacon is a key interlocutor, in which these practices, far from liberating, have become instruments of human domination precisely through the degree to which they magnify human domination of nature, their analysis of contemporary politics and culture is strikingly similar, if not in its methodological premises, at least in its description, to Dewey's. In Theodor Adorno's essays on mass culture, his canonical *Dialectic of the Enlightenment* (1944) written with the Institute director, Max Horkheimer, and Herbert Marcuse's "Some Social Implications of Modern Technology" (1941)[29] later expanded into *One Dimensional Man,* which together shaped a whole generation of cultural critics, the Frankfurt School (Critical Theory) elaborated the intrinsic link between science and culture.

In Critical Theory's perspective, contemporary mass culture was not so much a product of the emergence of the masses to social power as it was the inexorable result of the technologically wrought advent of consumer society that arose at the turn of the century when capitalism appeared to be in its deepest crisis. Far from a diversion, mass communications gave bread and circuses a global reach, and entertainment made seamless the path between mass production of material goods and mass production of culture. Consumerism brought into being a fundamental transformation in everyday life. At stake was more than the usual degradation of art of which others had already eloquently spoken. The "masses," the subject of historical materialism's hope for human emancipation, had, indeed, been emancipated by modern technology from the most onerous features of manual labor. Working hours were shortened, wages raised, credit extended to them, and the number and variety of consumer goods increased by mass production and technological innovation.

Yet, far from constituting the cornucopia announced by technology's celebrants (including twentieth-century Marxism), the prospects for *self*-emancipation receded with every new gadget, with every technological toy, with every minute withdrawn from the labor process and expended on frivolous leisure activities. Instead, the working class in the countries of advanced or late capitalism was blocked from forming itself into a new proletarian public sphere and was in thrall to the fruits of its own labor; it had become the victim, not only of technology, including mass communications, but also had entered into a Faustian contract with late capitalism. In Marcuse's terms, capitalism would now "deliver the goods" by developing the productive forces, in return for which the working class renounced its historical dream of liberation through the creation of new relations—both of production and of social life as a whole.[30]

In the analysis of the rise of fascism, Critical Theory together with Wilhelm Reich, with whom it shares many psychoanalytic premises, boldly asserted the thesis that Hitler's triumph owed as much if not more to the mass appeal of his racialist, nationalist, and productivist ideology as it did to terror, and would not have succeeded without broadly based mass support, including that of a significant portion of the workers.[31] To which Reich (and Horkheimer) added, the significance of the power of fascism's identification of the traditional family with its authoritarian father, its substitute—emotional, especially sexual—satisfactions were manifested in staged spectacles, and rituals of obedience, especially of women and youth, and erotic ecstasy.[32] In this account, fascist ritual—its flag, salutes, militarization of the entire population through invocations of discipline in every corner of everyday life, parades, quasi-religious mass celebrations—were only one variant of the political function of mass culture. The other, more appropriate to the capitalist democracies, was typified by the pioneering industrialization of culture, particularly the arts, in the United States.

In his influential essay on popular music, Adorno makes the direct link between the tin-pan-alley songs of the 1920s and 1930s and the chief characteristics of industrialization: repetition, standardization (interchangeable parts) and mass production: ". . . the harmonic cornerstone of each hit—the beginning and the end of each part—must beat out the standard scheme. . . . Complications have no consequences . . . regardless of what aberrations occur the hit will lead back to familiar experience, and nothing fundamentally novel will be introduced."[33] These comments are a fairly characteristic example of the crucial point in Critical Theory's view of the Culture Industry. Above all, it suppresses *difference,* disruption, and innovation, hallmarks of avant garde modernist art which, for Critical Theory, is the only art worth having. While Adorno understood that even the most subversive art was subject to incorporation and by its dissemination was a vehicle for the reconciliation of the dissatisfied individual with the prevailing order, the body of work that situated itself on the cutting edge—works that were dissonant with the power of mainstream art to integrate through harmonious representations in their formal features—retained hope that reason would stay alive, even if not triumph.

Although, along with other German-Jewish refugee intellectuals, the Institute's members valued highly the democratic freedoms that prevailed in the United States at a time when all of Europe seemed to be bowing to dictatorship, they held out almost no hope that what Hans Magnus Enzensberger later called "the industrialization of the mind" in democratic countries could be overcome and the masses gain their own political and cultural agency. The Enlightenment had signaled an irreversible turning point in the history of culture. We learned to live with domination but also to prefer it to the risks that would ineluctably attend the struggle for emancipation. Under the weight of relative affluence, the masses became conservative; in Erich Fromm's terms, they "fear" freedom. Marcuse's metaphor for the transformation was that technology had penetrated the soma and altered the human gene. This "mutation" expressed the degree to which massification had foreclosed the chance for a different future.

For example, contemporaries might have laughed at the "Eisenhowerisms" in words such as "finalize" where adjective and verb are instrumentally merged. Or railed against the increasing autonomy of private and public bureaucracies from public accountability, and the consequent shriveling of public life, manifested in the much criticized phenomenon of "voter apathy," which, as Dewey was to point out in the 1920s, was indicated by the persistent statistic that only half of the eligible voters turned out to the polls, a figure that has not substantially changed in this century. Or, as in the case of American critics, bemoaned the spread of pulp fiction and its elevation by the mass media into works of artistic merit, even "genius." What the Critical Theory of the Frankfurt School suggested is that these "problems" were symptoms of a *system* of domination that inhered in the emancipatory enlightenment project and signified, definitively, the end of the democratic and socialist prospect, if by these terms is meant a radical democratic vision in which economic, political, and social life come under popular power.

Yet there was more than a tension between this libertarian Marxist vision, which members of the Frankfurt School had inherited from Rosa Luxemburg and the anti-Bolshevik German communists who had broken, in the late 1920s, with Leninism and its leading tendency, Stalinism, and the aristocratic conception of art and culture that they shared with cultural intellectuals. Leo Lowenthal, a member of the Institute who later became a professor at the University of California, states the case succinctly:

The counterconcept of popular culture is art. Today artistic products are losing the character of spontaneity more and more and are being replaced by the phenomena of popular culture which are nothing but a manipulated reproduction of reality as it is; and, in doing so, popular culture sanctions and glorifies whatever it finds worth echoing. Schopenhauer remarked that music is "the world once more." This philosophical aphorism throws light on the unbridgeable difference between art and popular culture: it is the difference between an increase in insight through a medium possessing self-sustaining means and mere repetition of given facts with the use of borrowed tools.[34]

Here we can observe the influence of Nietzsche's idea of mass culture as "counterfeit practices" that "harangue the dark instincts of the dissatisfied, the ambitious, and the self-deceivers of a democratic age."[35] I want to note two features of this comment. The basis of the idea of popular "art" as a *simulacrum* of the real thing, a category that has resonated in virtually all leading theories of contemporary "mass" culture from Adorno and the Frankfurt School and the major American cultural critics who emulated aspects of its analysis—Clement Greenberg and especially Dwight Macdonald—to more recent writers such as Jean Baudrillard, Gilles Deleuze, and the science-fiction novelist Philip K. Dick.

In the terms "counterfeit" and "simulacrum" there is always the implication of an authentic referent. However, just as a dollar bill is a print of an engraving—itself a copy and "authenticated" only by bureaucratic fiat—so the notions of kitsch, degraded art, and other prerogatives signify the existence of an individual, auratic original whose source is the sensibility, craft, and imagination of the artist. But, in Dick's novels, most notably *Do Androids Dream of Electric Sheep* and *We Can Build You,* the question repeatedly posed is whether the "original" can be distinguished from the copy, whether the distinction makes sense any longer: can we separate ourselves from our technological doubles such as robots and other types of artificial intelligence when we are all totally integrated by the electronic circuits of information and communications technology?

Of course, even as Adorno was dismissing the aesthetic value of the popular music produced by the Culture Industry as just another commodity, Walter Benjamin was proclaiming the universality of the popular and the definitive demise of "high" art in the wake of reproduction technologies that extended back into history to the development of lithography, the printing press, and the photograph. Everything, as Deleuze was later to remark, is a copy of a copy.[36] The referent is the process of production itself, rather than the pristine object or the individual who stands behind it.

Benjamin's discovery more than troubled his friend Adorno; it alarmed him. For, Adorno feared, if the age of mechanical reproducibility foreshadowed a truly democratic culture, all art was destined to become a variety of popular culture and the last source of resistance within late capitalism—genuine art—would disappear.

My second observation is that the history of the mass culture debate reveals the pervasive *fear* among many intellectuals of the consequences of mass democracy, a fear that transcends and realigns traditional ideological divisions. For the right, such fear is fully consistent with the doctrine, developed during and after the French Revolution, that claims that the perversion of the Greek idea of the democratic polity consists, precisely, in the historical amnesia that forgets the fundamental condition for the creation of a public sphere: a leisure class freed from the burdens of everyday life and labor. That is, for the conservative the attack on mass culture is part of its traditional claim that genuine culture can only be produced and sustained by an elite. Culture's catastrophe, ascribed by many to the advent of the Culture Industry in the late nineteenth century, was coincident with the process of democratization itself. Yet modern liberalism and the left are inevitably caught in the contradiction between their acceptance of the privileged place of high art in a democratic culture and their defense of popular power. To be sure, the neo-Marxist theory according to which democracy itself is not equivalent to mass society relies on the twin categories of commodification and technological domination. Under these conditions, far from being responsible for their own choices, the "masses" are the object of forces beyond their control. At the same time, since Critical Theory expressly integrates psychoanalytic categories into this analysis, the condition for the advent of consumer society is the introjection, by the masses, of their own domination. Thus, the eclipse of the subject corresponds to the eclipse of reason in a regime of social life marked by the pseudo-satisfactions of consumerism.

Nevertheless, regardless of Critical Theory's ascription of mass society and its culture to objective, historical tendencies, the formula that with the arrival of consumer society "popular culture equals mass culture" leaves only the small and diminishing coterie of marginal intellectuals and dissonant artists to bear the burden of refusal. How can we recognize the "real" thing in a world of Total Administration within a regime that subordinates all reason, when means themselves become ends, when rationality has become identical with technology, that is, instrumentalities for the domination of nature and man? Since the middle of the nineteenth century the avant garde has cobbled together a modernist aesthetic; instead of employing narratives in which a fragmented, alienated social world is sutured in order to represent social life as seamless, modernism shows the disruptions, the breaks. Georg Simmel's critical sociological method, appropriated for social theory as much as literary criticism in the earlier writings of Georg Lukacs and later transformed by Benjamin for literary and historical studies, captures the fragments in "snapshots" of the social world—the photographic metaphor shows the seams in the very act of abstraction.

In contrast, according to Adorno, mass culture consists, precisely, in the reverse. There is a beginning, middle, and end to narratives; the popular, "classical music" remains dominated by a tonally harmonious methodic line, is repetitious, and pieces are "resolved" into the dominant key and so forth; visual arts are figural, the more "true to life" and banal, the more popular. As for film, there is virtually nothing truly redemptive in the mass-produced commercial genres. Their narratives correspond to Lowenthal's idea of "borrowed tools" since many derive from themes found in the classical Greek drama and modern novels. Whatever "formal" innovations film culture may introduce are, for Critical Theory, taken as little more than examples of technologically induced manipulations of the audience's emotions, undertaken to produce certain effects for their own sake, merely illustrative of the rule that within the regime of mass technological society, means become ends.

It is hard to see how an audience whose aesthetic sensibility is ineluctably shaped by incessant battering can retain the sense of distinction without which critical thought is all but impossible to cultivate. For the function of genuine art is, invariably, to remind its audience of the value of *difference*; it constitutes, by its presence in the field of vision, a disruption in the boredom and rote of everyday existence, including "leisure" time. For Critical Theory, it is already too late for the masses. The integration of mass entertainment by electronic means into national and international circuits of capital and communication, that is, the loss of its local character which, in the nineteenth century, limited the influence of "bread and circuses," signals the passing of the *possibility* of a popular alternative. Cities and towns are linked by the vast communications networks described by Dewey; advertising is the same in town and country, pointing to a nearly complete standardization of products—in clothes, food, reading matter (in national newspapers such as *USA Today,* the *New York Times,* and the *Wall Street Journal*), and surely in television where syndication has all but eliminated local programming, even in the so-called public television network.

On election night 1980, as I was following the returns with some friends, one of them, a professor of philosophy at a southern California university who was deeply molded by Critical Theory, complained bitterly, when Ronald

Reagan's election had been confirmed, that "The Democrats had failed" to protect "us" (the liberal intelligentsia) from the people. Marcuse had died the previous year and I am sure my friend's blunt remarks were owed to the fact that we were still mourning the absence of our friend and teacher. Yet there can be little doubt that in the wake of the commonly held judgment that the United States had long since witnessed the eclipse of the public in any meaningful sense of the term, critical intellectuals had to rely on the disposition and effectiveness of political elites—for whom civil liberties were, in their own terms, useful—rather than upon a people who had been rendered incapable of independent judgment and action. It was, therefore, not accidental that Marcuse's last work, *The Aesthetic Dimension,* reiterated the classic theme of art's marginality as the last best hope of humanity.

Of the three leading figures of Critical Theory, Marcuse was perhaps the only one who lived long enough to witness the emergence of the feminist movement and, as a resident of the United States, was impressed by the civil rights and the youth movements of the 1960s. These movements significantly modified but did not alter his judgments of the possibilities for social transformation. As one can see in his turn back to high art in the 1970s, neither he nor his students made an attempt to reverse or otherwise alter the theory of mass society or the culture it allegedly produced. Marcuse remained, even after retirement from the University of California-San Diego, generous with students and others who sought his counsel. In the year before his death, he participated in a student-generated study group on the work of Benjamin, especially the essays "The Work of Art. . . ," "Author as Producer," and others that disputed the special position of art in capitalist society. Like Adorno, years earlier, Marcuse found these essays troubling. For the core of Benjamin's argument is that technology breaks the domination of aristocratic culture. Equally disturbing, he implies that commodification, rather than constituting a yoke around the popular neck, may itself be subversive of the old social relations to the extent art was now made available to those to whom it had been previously not accessible. In contrast, Critical Theory holds to a conception according to which art's subversion consists not only in its *formal* difference from that of the integrative mass culture but its spatial difference as well. The artist, once the servant of the mighty, lives in late capitalist societies at the margins, his or her work imbibed by small audiences, most of whom are themselves consigned to various marginal cultural, if not economic positions. Thus, Beethoven's partial break with the consonant music of the eighteenth and early nineteenth century courts with his transformation of the minuet into a scherzo and, perhaps more to the point, the dark, dissonant, formally transgressive late quartets prefigure the great twentieth-century revolution in music initiated by Schoenberg in the second movement of the second quartet where tonality is abandoned and a new idiom is founded. As is well known, Beethoven's symphonic music was inevitably incorporated into the middle-brow "classical" canon. In turn, Schoenberg himself ultimately submits to the pedagogic requirement that tonal dissonance and transfiguration be transformed from a series of practices linked to concrete musical works into a system, a shift that subsequently routinized serial music and made it academically acceptable in proportion as it lost its vitality.

The passing of the avant garde in music after the 1920s was accompanied, as Adorno shows in his sociology of music,[37] by the incorporation by the Culture Industry of the canon of the baroque, classical, and romantic periods. The institutionalization of the symphony orchestra in the late nineteenth century corresponds to the formation of what Macdonald was later to call a "middle-brow" audience composed of ruling and middle-class patrons whose demands on the repertory condemned the concert hall to infinite variations on the "top forty" hits of classical music. In recent years, we can see this process repeated in the proliferation of commercial and "public" radio stations devoted, almost exclusively, to broadcasting classical music for such audiences.

The morning music program that originates at WGBH in Boston is, perhaps, the characteristic illustration of this genre. For five hours, seven days a week, the program offers a potpourri of music drawn, in the main, from the eighteenth and nineteenth centuries punctuated by a selection of late romantic symphonies such as those of Bruckner, Dvorak, and Mahler, a sprinkling of twentieth-century music, primarily that of Stravinsky and British composers such as Vaughn Williams, Bax, Bliss, and Britten. On the occasion of a birthday (in summer 1991 it was Dvorak's 150th) the listener is treated to a cycle of the (nearly) complete works of the composer but, as the host reminds us, only the very greats are accorded this honor and Dvorak's standing was, in his view, a bit ambiguous. Bach, Vivaldi, Handel, Mozart, Beethoven, Mendelssohn, Chopin, Schumann, and Brahms are, by far, the most played composers, even though the selections from among this pantheon may be wider than the top forty. Yet, even among this limited elite, we rarely hear Beethoven's late quartets or, indeed, chamber music of any kind. And, needless to say, the works of post-Schoenberg modernists such as Webern, Berg, Carter, Babbitt, Subotnik, Feldman, all of whom are Americans, or, indeed, the music of Stockhausen, Boulez, Berio, Henze, or contemporary Soviet and Polish composers are played so rarely that the commemoration of Karel Husa's seventieth birthday with a retrospective of some of his works was quite noticeable.

The dissemination of classical music by electronic means to new audiences and the development of a mass, middle-class public for the works of the "masters" of painting shown in highly publicized museum exhibits have, in the last two decades, indicated the degree to which "high" culture has itself become

mechanically reproduced and massified. This mechanical reproduction generated, of course, new techniques and a new "school" of visual arts, "pop"
art, which, as we will see, became in the 1960s one of the crucial sources for
a new popular art criticism that, inspired by it, attempted to valorize popular
culture as legitimate art. For pop art was simultaneously an ironic comment
on the degree to which the elite character of art had itself deteriorated into
the spectacle and a strong visual argument for the legitimacy of the aesthetic
value of commercially produced, mass audience art.

CHAPTER THREE

The Origins of Cultural Studies

I

IDEAS TRAVEL across cultures, continents, and time, but do not survive intact. They are, it seems, inevitably altered both in meaning and in form by the social/cultural context in which they are situated. While this proposition is widely accepted for translations of fiction or even cultural criticism controversially, it may be argued that neither natural nor social sciences are exempt from this rule. Neither the language of mathematics nor the falsifiability of experimental results has succeeded in removing the imperative of *interpretation* in physics and biology.

Certainly, philosophical, sociological, and cultural ideas have rarely escaped the transformations that accompany appropriation. For example, in Europe the term liberalism means the adherence to a market economy combined with individual rights and parliamentary democracy while for the past century in the United States it has signified a politics of more equality through state intervention as much as a strong adherence to protecting the historic middle class from being swallowed up by large monopolies. Similarly, twentieth-century socialist ideology has at least 57 varieties, and Marxisms are no less plural, depending on the national or regional situations within which they are deployed. On a different note, we know that when Europeans receive, often enthusiastically, American jazz their effort to reproduce the musical form(s) is as indigenous to their own traditions as it is to its African-American origins. Listening to Django Reinhardt's jazz renditions of American popular ballads, we are once again reminded that subalternity has no necessary universal referent.

Closer to the issues before us, the intellectual love affair between many American and British intellectuals and French social and cultural theory since the 1950s succeeds in extracting its political content (and its context) from representations. Today, an important fraction of the U.S. humanist academy is (still) enamored by the names Baudrillard, Lyotard, and especially Foucault and Derrida and not only avidly reads their works but writes and imbibes endless commentaries on them, while assiduously avoiding drawing out the philosophical, let alone political implications of this body of work. Perhaps feminism is the only theoretical discourse that may be exempted from the charge that the American reception of French cultural theory is relentlessly depoliticized. Otherwise, what is called poststructuralism has become a substantial cottage industry supporting publishers as well as scholars, generating many dissertations and monographs but also a substantial number of collections of commentaries by and about the leading figures of this movement.

But, just as Sartre's phenomenological philosophy and criticism were employed within the early postwar period as weapons of the cold war and only later were his American admirers on the anti-Stalinist left embarrassed to learn he had been almost continuously a fellow traveler of the Communist party, even in the period of his most vociferous criticism of Stalinism, so the specifically *national,* political, and theoretical environment that gave rise to the work of, say, a Foucault or Baudrillard, both of whom were part of the intellectual generation that inspired the activists of the French May 1968 uprising—perhaps the most important radical insurgency in any western country in this era—is largely ignored or bracketed by the American acolytes of these theorists. Instead, the "French turn" in North American social and cultural theory is largely inspired by issues of local *university* politics having to do with debates over legitimate intellectual knowledge and is directed toward certain intra-academic struggles, and engages in a resolute pursuit of political and historical amnesia.

Thus, the uses of theory can scarcely be separated from the theoretical accounts themselves. In the North American context, Derrida and Foucault are assimilated to the made-up word "poststructuralism" and stripped of their polemical edge, especially with reference to Marxism. Without an understanding of the political/intellectual environment within which this movement arose, it is hard to understand what is at stake, for example, in the radical return to Nietzsche.[1] Instead of exploring these issues, the linguistic cast of French cultural theory is deployed in North America against traditional criticism and literary history, analytic philosophy, and, more recently, against the anti-theoretic bent of historiography. In effect, French theory has become a weapon in the professional wars that have gripped the universities.

This is another way of reminding us that to grasp what the relatively "new" field of cultural studies is, we are obliged to situate it in its own historically specific context and not take the ideas as they were developed in Great Britain and France sui generis. At the same time, this is in contradistinction to most recent reflections on cultural studies that tend to define it chiefly in terms of either/or issues of canon and the struggle to legitimate popular culture. In this chapter I want to trace the development of cultural studies from its inception, both in relation to the founding of the *Centre for Contemporary Cultural Studies* (CCCS) at Birmingham University in 1964 and to the transformations of the postwar era to which the movement was, according to its own understanding, a response.[2] My aim is not to write a chronology for the sake of the record, but instead, by selectively rendering the development of this "movement" in Great Britain, to illuminate some of the issues that have been lost in transit. More to the point, we can see what has been lost by the specifically North American appropriation, particularly the political and theoretical content of the movement. As we will see, some of these foci are very specific to the British situation, but some are not.

One of the major differences is that British cultural studies was directed, from its inception to the present, to linking the concept of the "popular" to that of *class*. Although the *problematic* of the relation of "high" to "popular" culture crosses the ocean, in British cultural studies asserting the integrity of the popular as opposed to conceptions that regard it identically with "mass" culture is a statement about the possibility of retaining working-class politics in the era of alleged "classlessness" of advanced capitalism. We will discover that cultural studies itself has undergone significant shifts of emphasis and even major changes in its theoretical orientation since its formal inception. These internal changes are barely perceived in the United States for, among other reasons, "western Marxism" aside from the Frankfurt school, itself a relatively weak academic tendency, has barely taken root among North American intellectuals, much less students of contemporary culture. Nor did the work of Louis Althusser, a crucial influence on the later British cultural studies, receive broad dissemination and reception in this country. Consequently, the theoretical intervention of writers such as Stuart Hall, Paul Willis, and Richard Johnson, leading figures in the later development of the British movement, is barely perceived by their American followers.

United States cultural studies is obsessed, since the 1960s, with the "high," "low" distinction for reasons that parallel the early history of the British movement: popular culture signifies both the expressive forms and the everyday lives of notably blacks, Latinos, and other oppressed immigrant groups and, in a different register, women, gays, and lesbians. The social movements corresponding to alternative cultural practices, including those of literature and music, are both displacements of class and possess aspects of autonomy. However, the crucial distinction between cultural studies in the United States and that in Britain is that class is more or less silent as an explicit discourse in the United States; classlessness, whether connected to a large conception of contemporary capitalist social relations or not, is, since the emergence of cultural studies, a tacit assumption.

In Great Britain, the term "cultural studies" itself signified both continuity and a partial break from the perspectives of radical historians and literary critics of an earlier period who provided some of the inspiration for the field. In fact, far from having a single "origin," cultural studies is born of a hybrid between the rather conservative critique, albeit from the left, of the emerging "mass" culture of the post-Second World War period, especially the rise of television as a near-universal entertainment medium and the concomitant explosion of "consumer" society; and efforts of the same Marxist and non-Marxist intellectuals to counter this massification thesis by documenting, in the past as well as in the present, evidence of a vibrant working-class culture which, even if not fully immune from commercial incorporation, possessed, they argued, an autonomous character.

Clearly these strands are not really compatible, a tension that has never been fully resolved. A long line of critics from Matthew Arnold in the mid-nineteenth century through the 1930s and 1940s when F. R. Leavis and the *Scrutiny* group,[3] the right-wing anti-democratic philosopher Ortega y Gasset and the conservative T. S. Eliot excoriated popular and mass culture (the presumed distinction between the two came under increasing scrutiny by the earlier practice of cultural studies) in tones that were taken up, as we have seen, in the United States by the "left" defenders of high culture such as members of the group gathered around *Partisan Review,* especially the critics Clement Greenberg and Lionel Trilling, who was profoundly influenced by English cultural criticism, and, of course, the *Frankfurt School,* particularly Theodor Adorno, which, in its American stay, paid particular attention to the problem of cultural massification, identifying this world-historical event with what became known as "Americanization." Recall that Adorno inveighed against jazz and other popular, albeit commercially exploited, art forms that became dominant in the 1930s and 1940s, especially music. For Adorno, jazz is a perennially fashionable aspect of the Culture Industry that manufactures literature and film as well as music as part of a system of late capitalist domination of a mass audience that has all but lost its ability to make distinctions between art and schlock, much less produce its own indigenous cultural forms. Marcuse, deriving his aesthetic standards from Adorno, was more directly concerned that the degradation of artistic culture through its transformation by electronic media was a crucial component of the death of working-class social and political *agency.* In this sense the early efforts of British left-wing intellectuals to find working-class culture was consistent with the project of reasserting agency, a term that detonates E. P. Thompson's monumental *Making of the English Working Class,* one of the signposts of the cultural studies movement.

Indeed, both sides of these arguments are faithfully repeated in one of the fecund documents of cultural studies, Richard Hoggart's immensely influential *Uses of Literacy* (1957). Subtitled "Changing Patterns of English Mass Culture," Hoggart's aim is to substantiate his contention that despite a decline in "serious reading" among workers and the emergent consumerism that Guy Debord described quite independently during the same years as a "Society of the Spectacle,"[4] working-class people have sustained many of their traditional values—notably family and neighborhood loyalties—and have demonstrated a resilience in maintaining an "all-pervading culture":

> To live in the working classes is even now to belong to an all-pervading culture, one in some ways as formal and stylized as any that is attributed to, say, the upper-classes. A working class man would come to grief over the right way to move through a seven course dinner: an upper middle class man among working-class people would just as surely reveal his foreign background by the way he made conversation (the tempo of conversation not only the matter of idiom), used his hands and feet, ordered drinks or tried to stand drinks. Recall for the moment some of the routines of working-class life: as to clothes, the persistence of the Sunday suit . . . or the fifty year old formality of seaside postcards. . . .[5]

The early chapters of *Uses* are an account of English working-class culture punctuated by reproductions of speech, rituals, and beliefs. It is drawn as much from Hoggart's own experience as a child of a working-class family in the 1930s as it is from the formal categories he constructs: conceptions of mother, father, the neighborhood, working-class fatalism, the attitude of "live and let live" (tolerance) and the penchant of working-class people to dwell in the present: "they are substantially without a sense of the past. Their education is unlikely to have left them with any historical panorama or any idea of a continuing tradition."[6]

But, like the entire English cultural studies tradition that arose, in part, on the strength of the enormous influence of this book, Hoggart skillfully invokes these traditions as evidence against two contemporary claims: that consumer society heralds a bright new world of "classlessness," at least insofar as visible distinctions based on income differentials are embodied in affluence for some and deprivations for most. Like those who follow him, Hoggart acknowledges that postwar Britain has witnessed a dramatic rise in popular living standards brought about, in part, by higher wages and the credit system. But he disclaims a second thesis: that if workers can now buy cars and refrigerators, working-class culture, if not obliterated by mass culture, is marked, predominantly, by its negative features and is really a culture of deprivation. In which case, television and other media of mass communications may be a boon to literacy, to finally make possible the elevation of this deprived class. In a later essay, published more than a decade later, Hoggart writes that his book was directed toward refuting the latter view.[7] By narrating, in considerable detail, the language, customs, and rituals, of what he takes to be an autonomous culture, Hoggart sought to prove that it was not a lack but a set of affirmative attributes that marked the working class off from the middle class it was supposed to have become. What is remarkable about Hoggart's analysis is his ability to face up to the core conservatism that constitutes many aspects of his own ancestral culture. His description is, consequently, not without critique.

There are two important theoretical points here: first, in contrast to prevailing wisdom, Hoggart rejected the economistic argument that the relative affluence of the postwar era signifies the end of class society. That is, he rejects and attempts to refute the contemporaneous sociological theory according to which class identity may be defined in terms of income, or, alternatively, given the rise of the installment plan that enabled workers to multiply their consumption of "big ticket" items, the Weberian notion that class was a function of an individual's access to "goods" and job markets.[8] Second, although by no means a theorist, Hoggart forcefully demonstrates that culture, in the anthropological sense of customs and mores (in current terms, "practices") rather than as a sign of artistic formation or of "manners," is the crucial determinant of class identity. Hoggart resolutely mediated the more conventional aesthetically embodied idea of culture with a deft use of his own memory (later to become an important category of cultural studies) with social linguistics (although not in the formal methodological mode) to show that, despite the incursions of mass culture, workers, living in families and working-class neighborhoods as well as engaging in industrial labor, maintained their identities as an act of *resistance* (later, Hoggart's intellectual children memorialized this formulation in a phrase "resistance through ritual," but altered the theoretical terms of the concept considerably).[9]

At the same time, Hoggart's self-professed anti-romanticism obliges him to describe and analyze the influence of popular magazines and other purveyors of fashion—in clothes, leisure activities, anti-intellectualism, and, most especially, the "penetration of indifferentism," the tendency among workers to increasingly withdraw from public activity. This direct appropriation of Matthew Arnold's mid-nineteenth-century rant is, perhaps, the key to Hoggart's ambivalence. While pointing out that what appears as a parochial, almost inchoate indifference to the outside world marks working-class life, he seems to defend it as a necessary means to fend off the "monstrous" effects of a "valueless" mass society, "a world in which every kind of activity is finally made meaningless by being reduced to the counting heads." What appears from the outside as an instance of privatization, even fragmentation due to what C. Wright Mills called the battering of the media, is also the condition of cultural survival. As we will see, this dialectic is to bedevil cultural studies until the present.[10]

Yet Hoggart's brutally honest account of working-class culture cannot fail to see its conservative features even as he describes the erosion of what he believed to have been an autonomous, authentic mode of life. For him and many others, the changes wrought by the war and its aftermath fatally weakened the capacity of the working-class movement to protect its constituents from the overwhelming tendency of mass society to reduce its objects, the "people," to conforming numbers in the endless game of production and consumption. Perhaps the most painful change in the postwar era is that entertainment has replaced art. As a Cambridge "scholarship boy," Hoggart, like his contemporary Raymond Williams (also a scholarship winner) can hardly escape being imbued with the values of "high culture," even as both writers situate working-class culture in a unique oral tradition and in a dense amalgam of informal associations such as those provided by social clubs and the neighborhood pub, as well as the institutions of the working-class movement, particularly, at least for Williams, the trade unions.[11]

Hoggart's conception of "literature" is as far from pulp fiction as mass, technologically dominated society is from democracy. Thus, for him, what is most depressing is that the huge quantity of titles emanating from the pulp writing mills in romantic fiction cannot be "deliberately conceived from the outside. Writing like this, maintained so consistently, and so unerringly in its sense of what the reader wants, can hardly be constructed intellectually; and certainly not by minds of the calibre usually revealed in these works. They are, rather, produced by people who possess some qualities in greater measure than their readers, but are of the same ethos. 'Every culture lives inside its own dream'; they share the common dream of their culture."[12] In other words, we are experiencing a loss of critical sensibility even among the intellectuals whose historical task it was to be its guardians.

While carefully noting that traditional working-class culture retains some of its resilience in the wake of the invasion of popular commercial entertainments—for example, in the 1950s there are still local singing societies and there is a fairly strong workers' education movement after the war—Hoggart evaluates the situation as a "crisis." As with all who hinge democratic hopes not only on the achievement of a greater degree of redistributive economic justice, opportunities for technical and academic higher education, and the chance to select, through voting, among competing political elites, but also on the possibility of sustaining a public sphere in which popular participation in "meaningful" political decisions and cultural self-production is accepted as an integral part of the definition of democracy itself, Hoggart cannot avoid ending his rich and disturbing book on a note of ironically tinged despair:

> So much is profoundly encouraging. And it may be that a concentration of false lights is unavoidable at this stage of development of a democracy which from year to year becomes more technologically competent and centralized, and yet seeks to remain a free and "open" society. Yet the problem is acute and pressing—how that freedom may be kept as in any sense a meaningful thing whilst the processes of centralization and technological development continue.[13]

Taken as a whole, Hoggart's book lives the contradiction of his reluctant deep-seated respect for the Arnoldian privileging of Art against the leveling tendencies of society that led to the master's lament for the demise of critical thinking in the wake of urbanism and industrialism; and his valiant argument for the dignity of working-class culture as complex of thought and feeling that derives from specific, "all-pervading" experience. In the end, like his contemporaries E. P. Thompson and Raymond Williams, whose equally influential work on, respectively, working-class history and dissenting intellectual culture are credited by Hoggart himself as among the seminal books that gave rise to the cultural studies movement, the divide between mass or commercial culture and popular culture remains vivid and itself constitutes a political and intellectual program.

2

The slender preface to *The Making of the English Working Class* is Thompson's only sustained attempt in nearly 900 pages to stake out a theoretical position, although the extraordinary details of popular struggle in late eighteenth- and early nineteenth-century England in the subsequent text may be taken, simultaneously, as theory as much as history. The work, in Thompson's words, is intended to substantiate the "agency of working people, the degree to which they contributed, by conscious efforts, to the making of history."[14] Equally important is the position, shared by such critics as Hoggart and Williams and historians, notably Christopher Hill and Eric Hobsbawm, that "we cannot understand class unless we see it as a social and cultural formation, arising from processes which can only be studied as they work themselves out over a considerable historical period."[15] Class, in Thompson's conception, is a "relationship not a thing" that comes into being not as a concept imposed from the outside on events, as critics charge, but through struggles in which, eventually, "English working people came to feel an identity of interests as between themselves and as against their rulers and employers."[16] The "making" is a self-conscious activity that entails social and cultural formation as well as a common relationship to the ownership of productive property.

In fact, in Thompson's account, the "class" forms itself out of artisanal traditions that are threatened and gradually decomposed by the industrial revolution that extended from the seventeenth through the nineteenth centuries. Class formation occurs in Thompson's narrative because as "free-born Englishmen," that is, independent mechanics and craftsmen, they were precisely *not* subject to the many chains of industrial dependency that was the lot of the unskilled labor whose social position typically derived from the historical experience of having been born in bondage. For Thompson, among the crucial strands of cultural formation are the artisanal traditions that were not only work centered, but entailed some of the major elements of what Habermas identified as a "public sphere" of debate, discussion, and controversy through which identities could be congealed.

Making demonstrates, convincingly, that the tradition of what its author terms "popular radicalism" is constituted by artisans who are not yet subordinated by a fully developed capitalist regime of production, even though they are invariably engaged in commodity production. In fact, it is the space between what Marx called the "manufacturing" phase of capitalist production and its industrial phase that provides the basis for Thompson's claim for the emergence of a specifically *working-class* political culture in contrast to the popular radicalism that pervaded the period of transition. The popular radical movements between 1780 and 1832 with which Thompson is chiefly concerned struggle against the specifically capitalist forms of industrialism, not technological change itself. And their ideas are as much libertarian as they are of social justice. The sinews of class identity are brought together as much by free speech fights waged by single individuals functioning as popular tribunes as they are by industrial struggles such as those waged against labor-degrading machinery and the exercise of arbitrary authority by employers against the increasingly proletarianized skilled workers. "The radical culture which we have examined was the culture of skilled men, artisans and of some outworkers. Beneath this culture (or co-existing with it) there were more obscure levels of response, from which charismatic leaders . . . drew some of their support."[17] Among these Robert Owen, whom Thompson portrays as a great propagandist and a poor political strategist, is the key harbinger of a new socialist consciousness that, beyond class identity, defines the class in terms of "an alternative system" rather than a series of local or even national reforms. In the period traversed by *Making*, the "people" rather than a clearly defined working class is the referent of the radical movement(s). It includes small employers as well as skilled workers and independent artisans, but also desperately poor weavers and other textile operatives. At the end of the period Thompson reports that the sense of the "we" is beginning to emerge in specifically class terms:

The new class consciousness of working people may be viewed from two aspects. On the one hand, there was a consciousness of the identity of interests between working men of the most diverse occupations and levels of attainment, which was embodied in many institutional forms, and which was expressed on an unprecedented scale in the general unionism of 1830–34. On the other hand, there was a consciousness of the identity of the interests of the working class or "productive classes" as against those of other classes. . . .[18]

However, in his own narration, the "productive classes" were themselves quite diverse. They included wage laborers, but also small independent professionals and producers, indeed all "producers" as opposed to landlords, possessors of inherited wealth, professional politicians, and employers who never engage in production but are, instead, parasitical on the productive classes. As Thompson so brilliantly shows, the ideology of the "productive" classes contains not a small measure of puritanism and other variations of the same moral economy. Popular radicalism has its share of anti-clericalism, but it does not fail to embrace some of the hallowed beliefs of Christian, especially Methodist, religion such as temperance and the deep-seated faith that work may be redemptive of the individual as well as the collective spirit. In this culture there is little room for the playful, or, indeed, the "right" to be lazy. The popular radical theory of work is clearly "bourgeois," if by that phrase is here connoted salvation through productive work.[19] Moreover, as Thompson shows, the dominant radical theory was not utopian socialism but "advanced democratic populism," a movement of militant reform of the economic and political system to provide space for the powerless.

Thompson is eloquent in his explanation for why, in the face of his claim that radicalism was the most important political event in England during this period, revolution never materialized. Beyond the acuity of the ruling classes in extracting, through informers, detailed intelligence about the growing movement, was the presence of a powerful *middle-class* reform movement alongside that of the popular radicals. Later, Stuart Hall, referring to the state of working-class culture after 1880, commented that "There was no separate autonomous authentic layer of working-class culture to be found." Rather, recreation was "saturated by popular imperialism."[20] According to Hall, the emergent working-class culture was infused with an "oscillation between containment and resistance," an oscillation richly documented for this earlier period as well. The bare fact is that the English working class may have, in Thompson's terms, advanced from adolescence to young maturity until the 1830s but faltered in middle age, an injury from which it never recovered. By the time of Hoggart's reclamation in the late 1950s, the rich and varied public life of the era of popular radicalism, including its utopian-socialist wing, had dissolved into militant but also oppressively bureaucratic trade unionism and a desiccated version of parliamentary "socialism" more accurately described as welfare reformism.[21] What radical culture that remained was driven from the streets back into the factories and, according to Hoggart's successors at CCCS, to subcultural formations and remained there, largely isolated from the mainstream of public life.

The agony of the British intellectual left is bound up with its effort, against the evidence of the history of the last century, to discern a viable working-class tradition in the past as well as in the present from which to forge a theory of historical transformation along Marxist lines in which a mature working-class culture is posited as a vital component of militant trade union and socialist movements. In such movements the workers themselves are the key historical agents. Since the Hammonds pioneered during the years surrounding the First World War in researches that attempted to reclaim a history of the laboring classes, the existence of a "historical" as opposed to a "sociological," i.e., objective, statistical, working class has eluded investigation.[22] "The Workers" as a self-conscious cultural and political/historical force if not invariably, then overwhelmingly, resemble the "productive" classes rather than a self-conscious proletariat. Its "theory" remained that of democratic populism, even when the Labour Party, the chief political vehicle of this amalgam of classes and fractions after the turn of the twentieth century, proclaimed "socialism," albeit the statist, rather than popular variety as its aim. Moreover, as Hall is to later argue and Thompson demonstrate, the autonomy of workers' culture is never secure; as a subordinate social category its political program and, as we have seen, its culture, are always subject beyond "containment" to incorporation. Here Raymond Williams's three types of cultural processes—emergent, residual, and incorporated—come into play.

On the evidence of a rich panoply of historical cultural studies, it may be argued that there never has been an autonomous, authentic culture of the English working class nor could there ever be such a culture, precisely because the class itself never emerged in anything like a pristine form after the artisanal mode of production was replaced by industrial capitalism. The older working-class culture was indelibly stamped by the crafts, skilled workers who acquired their trades through traditional apprenticeships. When these crafts are partially rationalized after the 1850s and machine production decisively transforms the nature of skill and its indispensability and, above all, when scientific knowledge displaces or, more accurately, *incorporates* traditional knowledge as the main productive force, to the degree artisanal culture is identical to working-class culture itself it tends to exclude the great mass of unskilled and semiskilled workers, except perhaps in mining, which is historically tied to isolated rural areas. Although large sections of English wage workers shared what may be described as a common identity of interests that congealed in strong trade union institutions and struggles, and even forged a series of views that might be called, roughly, a "world-view" that persisted from Victorian times to the 1950s, the middle and ruling classes have always been active as well. What Thompson shows is not merely the emergence but also the incorporation.

The last chapter of *Making*—"Class Consciousness"—is not so much a narrative of the maturing of a distinctly class culture as it is a testament to the thesis that, even in the process of formation, the English working class itself was constantly mediated politically and culturally by the middle class, not only by adopting popular demands, but also because the middle class incorporated elements of popular culture as its own. And, of course, this process is not confined to England, but is in full display in the United States as well, particularly in the universalization of rock and roll, albeit in many varieties, as the popular music of all classes of youth, but also in the struggle for and maintenance of the social welfare state in the thirty years beginning with the mid 1930s.

After the war, Thompson was a member of the Communist Historians Group whose discussions and writings during the 1940s and 1950s anticipated many of the issues that were central to the legacy of cultural studies. Members of this group included Christopher Hill, whose social histories of the seventeenth century still dominate the English historiography of that period; Victor Kiernan, surely among Britain's leading labor historians; and Eric Hobsbawm, whose work on nineteenth-century social movements in Italy as well as England has paved the way for a reconsideration of the history of that century.

These were the veritable founders of a new social history—whose fundamental insistence is that history is made, if not exclusively, then substantially "from below." While standing on the shoulders of an older generation including the Hammonds and G. D. H. Cole, these historians broke with the earlier tradition of economism and institutional histories and asserted the central importance of cultural formation as an *explanatory* category. They restored, if not discovered, the crucial dimension of popular agency as a mode of historical explanation in opposition to the hitherto prevailing tendency to explain historical developments in terms of institutional conflicts, the decisions of great or dominant "men," or, alternatively, in teleological terms as the "blind" logic of inexorable forces. In this last perspective agents act to accelerate or retard the emergence of a future over which they have no effective control. Their conscious intentions notwithstanding, they are *objectively* agents of the cunning of reason. Thompson specifically repudiates these perspectives, even the teleology characteristic of some versions of Marxism for whom the "logic" of capital constitutes the motive force of history within the capitalist mode of production, or the "inherent" contradictions of capital accumulation, especially the struggle between capital and labor that leads, inevitably, to a new economic order.

For the new social historians, history is an indeterminate "process" rather than a script. The real choices of actors make a decisive difference in determining its course. Needless to say, as Marxists they are well aware of the limits of action, so the antinomy between structure and agency that still haunts social science is, to a large degree, avoided. At the same time, given the political and intellectual context of English history—writing that, since the turn of the century, had placed strong emphasis on economic conditions—their own historiographic interventions emphasized the importance of cultural formation in the historical process perhaps more strongly than they actually meant, in opposition to the determinism of the economic historians, even the Marxists among them. For Thompson and Hill, this process always remained indeterminate—that is, was subject to ways in which movements, individual leaders, and the cultural configuration of the class(es) themselves played out the game. There is, in *Making,* a tacit theory of what later was termed "multiple determinations," or, in Althusser's Freudian idea, "overdetermination." Of course, such shifts away from economism were extremely controversial in the first decades after the war.[23]

The 1940s were, perhaps, the zenith of Stalin's grip over the international communist movement. Most internal opponents had been wiped out by the Moscow trials (1936–1938) and their aftermath; he had Trotsky murdered in Mexico in 1940, and those who survived were condemned to internal exile or otherwise marginalized by the enormous prestige the Soviet Union and Stalin himself accumulated as a result of their central role in the defeat of Hitler and fascism. At first glance, the work of the Communist Historians Group appears anomalous in relation to these developments. Stalinist ideological orthodoxy was a peculiar combination of economic determinism and political voluntarism, within which "culture" was conceived as a tactical weapon in the strategic arsenal of revolution but, in the last instance, was dependent on the movement of the economic base and the ability of political vanguards to bring it to life. Nor were the immediate circumstances of the postwar years particularly favorable for the development of a new radical historiography. After a fairly auspicious beginning with the institution of National Health Scheme, the Labour government, elected in 1945, barely survived a single term and was turned out of office in 1951. Thus, the early postwar reform impulse was fairly short-lived in an otherwise right-wing hegemony. In fact, it was not until the late 1950s that the workers' movements and a fraction of intellectuals exhibited a fresh radicalization and that the breakup of the Stalinist left enabled the formation of a New Left.

Moreover, the 1940s and 1950s, the main period during which the Group flourished, were marked by a British version of McCarthyism. While somewhat less virulent than its American counterpart, anti-communism rode high within Labour as well as among Conservative circles; the Labour movement was rife with factionalism and the governments led by both parties were busily hunting Soviet spies. The British Communist party, never strong, was becoming more isolated, although it retained respect and achieved leadership in some trade unions, especially in Scotland and north England. And it had influence, owing largely to the prestige of the Soviet Union and communist-led national liberation movements such as in China among a fraction of elite intellectuals that far exceeded its strength in other elements of the population. As historians devoted to reconstructing popular history, the Group did not enjoy a particularly favorable environment within which to advance their work. Yet they did have the lingering perspectives of the Popular Front period of the 1930s, a theoretical and ideological orientation which, despite the "leftward" turn in Communist party policy in the cold war period, remains, to this day, the crucial guide to Communist practice.

The concept of the popular front has often been identified as the turn in Communist party policy, following George Dimitrov's famous speech at the 7th World Congress of the Communist International (CI), from international class struggle to class compromise, to defeat fascism. As General Secretary, Dimitrov announced, in 1935, the end of seven years of communist isolation from mainstream social-democratic and social-liberal political forces. The preceding period was one marked by global policies that committed the parties to "destroy" the reformist social-democratic and labor misleadership of the working class and build parallel "revolutionary" parties and unions in every country or, failing this, establish a series of militant factions organized to "capture" leading workers' movements.

The conciliatory program of the popular front was prompted by the disastrous defeats suffered by the left in Europe following the rise of the Nazis to power and the CI's changed perception, never uttered as a self-criticism, that the key task for the period was to defeat fascism and restore "bourgeois democracy" in Europe. Failing an alliance with democratic capitalist states, the Communists now recognized that the Soviet Union as well as these states were subject to Hitler's plan for conquest. The new turn involved two separate strategies: a united front of all working-class parties and organizations and a popular alliance with other classes, as long as they were prepared to defeat various domestic fascisms and to crush Hitler's Germany and Mussolini's Italy by military means, if necessary.[24]

This new policy signaled a concomitant turn from a focus on proletarian cultural formation, conceived as resolutely anti-bourgeois and revolutionary, to the development, through historical, folkloric, and anthropological reclamation of what Gramsci has called "national-popular" traditions from which the democratic claims for these capitalist societies could be sustained.[25] Beyond this, the communists sought to counter the dominance of patriotic/imperial accounts of national histories with a popular tradition that could offer to the working class its own basis for fighting fascism. In the United States, for example, along with its support of the New Deal policies of the Roosevelt administration, the Communists who had set up their own parallel unions to those of the AFL in the late 1920s and early 1930s rejoined the mainstream labor movement, in some cases even before the official change of line. On what became known as the "cultural front" they shifted from relentless excoriation of modernist art as examples of bourgeois decadence to a "live and let live" policy. The brief movement known as "proletarian" art, which always privileged realist literature, representational visual forms, and "program" music, was quietly dropped in favor of a policy of pluralism in which the development of art that was directed to the cultivation of the nationalist and popular elements in the arts occupied a special place.

Affirmatively, U.S. Communist intellectuals devoted themselves to reclaiming and reconstructing this national-popular tradition: they produced several "people's" histories of the American revolution; new histories of the American labor and farmers' movements stressing their democratic, populist character; and especially pioneered in the study of slave revolts, reconstruction, and the struggle for civil rights. The party promoted a new American theater movement in the 1930s that was closely linked to the new industrial unionism of the period and was prominent in a folk revival that not only reinvigorated the rather dry field of musicology but was especially important for the emergence of blues and other black musical forms into the mainstream of American high culture. Together with black musicians and critics, the party played an important part in the agitation for gaining respectability for black artists—both in jazz and traditional classical music. Moreover, in contrast to earlier years when Charles Ives and a few black composers were quite isolated in their use of popular and folk themes as the basis of American classical music, Aaron Copland, who was deeply influenced by national-popular themes, helped create the first specifically "American" school of composition that, rather than drawing from jazz idiom as he and especially Gershwin had done in the 1920s, produced a hybrid form thematically deriving from traditional cowboy and other Anglo-American folk and urban popular songs as well as folk dance tunes. Copland's program dominated American "serious" music after the mid 1930s and became for two decades a major source of inspiration for film scores—certainly for westerns, but also for dramatic movies. Needless to say, left populism has remained a powerful influence on American cultural studies.[26]

The Communist Historians Group was similarly influenced by the non-sectarianism of the popular front and especially its effort to appropriate national traditions, even nationalism for the struggle against the right which, for most of this century, has retained a near-monopoly over national traditions. In contrast to earlier efforts by socialist and communist historians to interpret English history predominantly in terms of economic forces, in which the problematics of capital accumulation or, in the case of Cole, capitalist greed, drove the class struggle, members of the Historians Group, in different degrees, shifted the emphasis to the conscious actions of popular agents, within which the *class* problematic played an important role, but was ultimately subordinate to the democratic-popular and was, moreover, national in character.

Since Lenin's sharp emendation, on the eve of the First World War, of the principle of proletarian internationalism by theorizing the progressive character of movements of national independence against imperialism, Marxists

have, in the main, recognized the validity of struggles led by incipient bourgeois classes for national independence against metropolitan imperialist
powers[27]—except when exhibited in the leading imperialist countries, in
which case it became known as "national-chauvinism." This dual perspective
carried within the international communist movement until the popular front.
By the late 1930s, the Communists were shifting from a narrow conception
of the proletariat as the most exploited sections of the working class to a broad
front in which not only the so-called "labor-aristocracy" of craftspersons
united with unskilled and semiskilled workers but the working class as a
whole was to join with sections of the petty-bourgeoisie and even the big
capitalists in the anti-fascist struggle. Consequently, the artisans and "progressive" middle-class democrats had to be written back into history.[28]

Hill almost singlehandedly restored the English revolutions of the seventeenth century to the radical canon; Thompson rehabilitated Jacobinism, especially its English variant, which, in his account, "resembled less the Jacobins
than the sans-culottes of the Paris 'sections' whose zealous egalitarianism
underpinned Robespierre's revolutionary war dictatorship of 1793–4."[29]
Their early base was among urban craftsmen; Hobsbawm's work on "primitive rebels" and sympathetic, almost adoring treatment of early "bandits"
moved against the strong tradition of respectable "civic virtue" that marked
even the more radical histories.[30] Similarly, as a counterpoint to the radical
democratic tradition formed around a concept of civil society as a public
sphere of intense but civilized debate, Thompson makes a spirited defense of
the Luddites. Rather than dismissing their machine-breaking as immature if
not entirely destructive, he portrays the movement as an appropriate response
by skilled craftsmen or sufferers of sharply reduced wages to their virtual expulsion from the workshops, "a violent eruption of feeling against unre-
strained industrial capitalism" rather than a "reactionary" movement directed
against technological progress:

Even if we make allowances for the cheapening of the product, it is impossible to designate as "progressive" in any meaningful sense, processes which brought about the
degradation, for twenty or thirty years ahead, of the workers employed in the industry.
And viewed from this aspect, we may see luddism as a moment of *transitional* conflict
. . . an attempt to look backward, to revive ancient rights in order to establish new
precedents.[31]

There is no doubt that these judgments belie Communist orthodoxy for
which industrial progress, although painful, especially for workers and peasants, is an absolutely necessary price to pay for eventual workers' liberation.
This progressivist position corresponded to the views of no less an ostensibly
anti-Stalinist Marxist authority on Soviet history than Isaac Deutscher, whose
notorious apologia, on these very grounds, for Stalin's brutal industrial and
agrarian policies first appeared in his *Stalin, A Biography* in 1949. The im-

perative of industrialization at (nearly) all costs for economically underdeveloped socialist states had become a fairly accepted position among Marxists concerning the history of capitalism as well: Marx's grim description of the so-called primitive accumulation of capital that was accompanied by corn laws and enclosures that drove millions of peasants from their lands and by an industrialization process that brutally degraded crafts by replacing them with machinery did not temper his general acceptance of this process as the price of progress. Marx does not minimize the brutality of the early years of capitalism. Yet, at the same time, he has no doubt that by revolutionizing the productive forces, capitalism was preparing its own demise.

But here are Thompson and Hobsbawm showing that the rebellions against capitalist "progress" by groups being destroyed or rendered marginal by the new labor process are vital components of an emerging working-class culture. Perhaps more than movements for parliamentary reform that sought such reforms as universal "manhood" suffrage, the Luddites were among the earliest of class-conscious working-class rebellions that, ironically, arose in protest against proletarianization. Hobsbawn's account of the "primitive" rebellions in England and Italy focuses not only on resistance but the fact that many of these movements developed millenarian theories of an egalitarian future. Whereas the dominant streams of Marxism after Marx ritualistically disdained utopianism, insisting that "scientific" socialism had permanently displaced it, Thompson's and Hobsbawm's treatments seemed to valorize the "spontaneity" of pre-industrial insurgencies as indispensable precursors of the modern working-class and socialist movements. Additionally, they "correct" the summary dismissal of what had been widely perceived as "immature" revolts, by showing the rational core of these movements, their sophisticated organization and communications networks and their advanced programs, at least in terms of what followed them.

Although populism had been dismissed when not openly opposed as a petty bourgeois movement seeking, vainly, to prevent the consolidation of big capital over land and small industry, social history now sought to valorize these sentiments as crucial aspects of the democratic tradition. And where Marx, Lenin, and Rosa Luxemburg had warned against a too complete reliance by working-class organizations on parliamentary and electoral processes, institutions that according to Marxist theory were perfectly suited to incorporation of working-class demands without yielding capitalist power, the communists became staunch democrats and libertarians in the 1930s, and encouraged their intellectuals to read these sentiments into working-class and popular history.

But the popular front required that the democratic traditions be identified not only in class, but also in national terms since now the communists were holding out their hands to sections of the old enemies, the middle classes and even parts of big corporate capital. The communist historians, particularly Thompson, proved more than willing chroniclers of the working class as a national-popular movement. As Bill Schwarz has pointed out, *Making* argues that the popular radical movement was composed, in the main, of "free-born Englishmen"; the intent here is to demonstrate that workers share in the national as well as their own class traditions.[32]

I do not intend my account to diminish the achievement of members of the Group by ascribing their histories to mere strategic considerations. On the contrary, on the evidence of their work they were part of a political culture that "lived inside its dream."[33] This is another way of saying that the popular front created a new left-wing ethos of democratic, national populism, a new social and historic imaginary, especially for those who, in its milieu, matured from adolescence to adulthood during this period. For just as the leader of the American Communist party, Earl Browder, had proclaimed communism "20th century Americanism" in the 1930s and probably believed it, so communists all over the world were seeking to reclaim national traditions as their own. In the course of these labors, they were changing the face of the left since, for all intents and purposes, the communists set the pace not only for the "revolutionaries" (even those in the opposition oriented toward the Soviet Union and the Communist party), but also for social democrats, many of whom agreed that the struggle against fascism superseded internecine conflicts, at least until the 1939 Nazi-Soviet pact. Perhaps unintentionally, their political unconscious, having intuited that the revolutionary phrases of Marxist orthodoxy performed an important ideological function for cadre formation but were increasingly anachronistic to the emerging politics and culture of postwar western capitalist countries, forced them to straddle the boundaries between class and "people," revolution and reform, the national/popular and socialist internationalism, and most especially between socialism and populism.

Nor is this ambivalence confined to the Anglo-American left. For example, writing from a fascist prison during the 1930s, Antonio Gramsci, one of the founders of the Italian Communist party, was insisting, without the direct benefit of popular front thinking, on the profound necessity for communists to come to terms with the specific features of Italian history. Three of his longer entries are *The Modern Prince* after Machiavelli's political philosophic masterpiece, *Notes on Italian History,* and *The Southern Question,* an urgent explication of the relation between the more industrially developed north and the agricultural, "backward" south of Italy as a crucial feature structuring Italian politics and culture.[34] A passionate internationalist, Gramsci was, nevertheless, acutely aware of the necessity of comprehending, beyond strategic considerations, the national context. Like Lenin and Mao whose accommodation to revolutionary nationalism was at the core of their respective

Marxisms, his own Marxism was deeply rooted in Italian intellectual and cultural traditions not only of those modern thinkers within the Marxist tradition such as Spaventa and Antonio Labriola, but also Machiavelli and the liberal idealist philosopher Benedetto Croce.

To be sure, Gramsci, Lenin, and Mao developed their theories within the context of societies where different modes of production and a multiplicity of cultural formations co-existed within the same national boundary. For them, there was simply no question of positing a long tradition of working-class culture as the basis for revolutionary activity; in each case, as late as the First World War, modern capitalism had not captured its own internal market, much less fully industrialized, even though Russia and northern Italy had considerable industrial development.

The 1930s were marked by a paradigm shift not only in communist strategy but in socialist and Marxist theory and culture. Despite works like *Making* and *Uses* which, for their authors, are, in part, intended to reassert the affirmative character of working-class culture by reconstructing it in the past and the present, by the late 1960s and early 1970s it was already evident that the older "workerist" ideologies, sometimes promulgated by left Social Democrats like Hoggart as well as Communists, were already being surpassed by the force of circumstances such as those evident in consumer culture, the development of mass higher education that made room for a considerable fraction of youth from working-class families, and the resolute reformism of even the most militant trade unions. With the help of the Historians Group and the publication of a selection from Gramsci's *Prison Notebooks,* a younger, largely non-communist generation that never experienced the 1930s directly learned that the term "working class" itself signified a polyglot social category whose historical pertinence was as much ideological as anything else.

One of Gramsci's major contributions to Marxist theory was the distinction, referring to revolutionary strategy, between the war of "maneuver" and the war of "position." Writing against the backdrop of the extraordinary interwar period, not only the Bolshevik revolution, the (failed) German and Hungarian uprisings, and especially the powerful, but short-lived factory occupations in the Italian north of 1919, but also the successful right-wing counterrevolutions of the 1920s and 1930s, he made the obvious but often forgotten point that revolutions are sporadic events that occur only after long and often imperceptible preparation, the elements of which are the many wars of position, particularly the necessity for classes seeking power to engage in a determined effort to capture the cultural and intellectual fields. In societies where rule by consent has replaced rule by coercion, class power entails achieving "moral and intellectual leadership" over society as much as direct political and economic control.

Thus, we are faced with the crucial importance of grasping the significance of hegemonic institutions of the old order such as religion and schools as well as the counterhegemonic institutions—both cultural and political—workers' schools, social organizations, newspapers, and journals as well as trade unions, which had traditionally been a focus of analysis and political intervention by the ideological left. These are class institutions whose function, in different ways, according to Gramsci, is to impose a new common sense on society as a whole. For Gramsci, without the intellectuals organically linked to the working class, its struggle for economic and political power was beyond achievement. For common sense defines the terms of public political discourse; it is embodied in social practices and, therefore, must be considered a material force.

In theoretical terms, the significance of *Making* may be its independent discovery that the mass demonstrations, petitions, and other "direct" manifestations of popular democratic struggle were both accompanied and prepared by its "army" of organic intellectuals—Cobbett and Carlyle among the most prominent—and the hundreds who have been forgotten because, in Thompson's words, they were "impudent, vulgar, overearnest or 'fanatical.'"[35] The radical popular upsurge of this era relied as much on these organic intellectuals (some came from artisan ranks, others did not) because, among other things, they provided the communications links for thousands of militants in local communities throughout England who read their articles in the independent radical press as expressions of their own views; the radical press helped create a new common sense in which the world looked different from that represented by the dominant middle-class press. We can see, as Thompson's narrative unfolds, the interlinking of the story of the uprisings and the various *representations* produced by intellectuals of the moral content of these events. Over and over, Thompson takes pains to show the pertinence of literary representations, in the wide meaning of the term, for the development of the social movements he describes and of counterrepresentations of these events by ruling-class cadre, such as police and military authorities.

However, the New Past generated by radical historiography could only inspire a new generation of intellectuals; on the whole, although most of them became prominent *public* intellectuals, appearing on television and radio and writing for the journals of opinion that penetrated a chunk of the middle classes and the activist wing of the labor movement, the past was distant from the present in more than chronological ways. Even though Thompson, Williams, and the others taught for years in the Workers Education Association, there was no question of their becoming organic intellectuals of a popular radical movement, much less of a conscious mass socialist workers movement.

Initiated by a request to revise A. L. Morton's *Peoples History of England,* a popular front document of the 1930s, the Group (which never accomplished its task) made elaborate plans to offer, through a new popular history, a work of cultural memory to the working-class movement, but did not (or could not) succeed, for immediate as well as historical reasons. If Hall is right, such hopes may have been already part of the past by the turn of the twentieth century. Popular radicalism as a mass movement of the productive classes had definitively disappeared, to be replaced by stable reform institutions such as the Labour party and powerful unions that dominated the public spaces of working-class life. The radical press, connected to various left-wing political formations, lingered and even attained some influence in local areas and, under specific conditions, could affect national politics.

However, in the era of high imperialism, the English workers maintained only a mediated class identity and culture. And, contrary to economistic expectations, neither the definitive passing of this era of British capitalism in the postwar era nor the steep descent of the economy accompanied by mass unemployment and trade union resistance to shutdowns such as the monumental 1979 and 1986 miners' strikes and other struggles could revive a kind of culture in which workers, in Thompson's narrative, as self-conscious agents, intervene in a sustained manner in the "making" of a new history. Rather, the stories of working-class struggle, if not invariably at least typically, are those of *resistance* in which Capital retains the initiative.

Yet, due to its global scope, and the intellectual power of its categories, English Marxism has, until recently, shown its own resilience in the face of the counterfactual example of a national culture that has remained dominated by the middle and ruling classes. In the end, the infinite postponement of the revolutionary phase of the popular movement, even in the wake of an enormous growth during the postwar years of British trade unionism, was to produce a series of theoretical and discursive shifts in the character of English Marxism as a whole and cultural studies in particular.

3

It was left to Raymond Williams to theorize the incipient movement that came to be known as *cultural studies*. His earlier work, particularly *Modern Drama from Ibsen to Eliot* (1952) and *Culture and Society* (1956), remained basically within the Leavisite and even Arnoldian mode of moral literary criticism, despite the strong political concerns of the latter book. But with *The Long Revolution* (1961) he began a twenty-year effort to provide a solid conceptual basis for a new approach that would embrace historical, anthropological, and social conceptions of culture. Perhaps the most important move in this work was to "define culture as a whole way of life,"[36] thereby obliterating the conjunction "and" between culture and society. This strategic intervention introduced into social as well as literary theory the significance of culture in the anthropological sense, that is, the ways in which everyday life rituals, institutions, and practices were, alongside art, constitutive of cultural formation. Williams, at the end of the day, was a somewhat murky thinker whose thought manifests itself in a characteristic British disdain for abstraction and complex theoretical formulations; it was his insistence on the persistence of practices that were ordinarily viewed outside culture that inspired the generation that elaborated cultural studies after 1965.

Of course, Hoggart's early work had been suffused with this dimension, but only implicitly. And, unlike Williams, Hoggart never considered the *institutions* of the labor movement, especially unions, as signifiers or even sites of working-class culture. Nor did Hoggart's understanding ever extend explicitly to the category of *practices* rather than representations as the core on which cultural formation is constructed, although the best parts of *Uses* concern what, in contemporary terms, would be "discursive" practices that might be considered distinctly working class. On the other hand, Williams significantly broadened the concept of culture to embrace its materializations.

Now, the notion of language as a series of material practices had already been introduced by linguists who wished to break from the Cartesian premises of the discipline. At one moment, Williams appropriates this shift in his definition of culture as "signifying practices,"[37] thus preserving, not unwittingly, the distinction between the production of meaning and the objects to which they refer. Similarly, in the wake of Althusser's frontal assault on the Marxist orthodoxy's separation of base and superstructure by acknowledging the determination of the economic, but only in the "last instance" (which, according to Althusser, never comes),[38] Williams struggled to retain a class perspective despite his fairly tangled effort to show that determination was not a one-way street. Of course, in his influential essay on the subject, he acknowledges complexity.[39] Yet, in the end, he remains reluctant to throw out the power of the Marxist formulation of the primacy of the economic lest the political significance of class relationships be diluted.

Nonetheless, Williams's later work marches steadily in the direction of sundering the older Marxist categories. Williams spent nearly a quarter of a century, until his death in late 1987, trying to resolve the dilemma of spanning representation and material practices, and to cobble a conception of culture that avoids the landmines of epistemological realism. That he did not succeed is not surprising. The problem of all efforts to overcome correspondence theories, which posit the distinction between the knowing subject and its object, resides in the political as well as philosophical question of *agency*. If there can be knowledge without a knowing subject and objects are always constituted discursively, how are human agents constituted? Together with his colleagues, especially at CCCS, for whom he was a constant referent and inspiration, by the late 1970s Williams determined that culture is not entirely encompassed by art, artifact, or those representations that have been hegemonically valorized as "civilization." At the same time, unsatisfied by the persistence of the base-superstructure gulf, he worked with a play of alternative formulations that could satisfactorily overcome, if not entirely overturn, the scientific worldview, such as categories of determination and causality. That his work remained relentlessly discursive and bore the telltale traces of his moral training remained an object of pity and even scorn for the next generation of Marxist theorists, notably his pupil Terry Eagleton and Perry Anderson, who wished to produce a sophisticated but ultimately orthodox Marxist theory of culture on the basis of analytic categories from which what Williams understood as *experience* could be properly interpreted.[40]

With *Marxism and Literature* (1977) and *The Sociology of Culture* (1980) Williams entered the murky waters of *theory* but failed to shed elements of empiricism and especially historicism that had marked his earlier writings. He was trying to figure out how to articulate the two meanings of culture: "it became a noun of 'inner' process specialized to its presumed agencies in 'intellectual life' and the 'arts.' It became also a noun of general process specialized to its presumed configurations in a 'whole way of life.' "[41] In the latter instance, culture is seen as "constitutive social process." Thus, it cannot be understood as a category of the superstructure within the framework of determination by the economic infrastructure. This conclusion permeates all of Williams's work in the last fifteen years of his life and, in consequence, it is not difficult to discern his skepticism about the effectivity of base/superstructure as well as its premises, the reflection theory of knowledge and the correspondence theory of truth, themselves grounded in epistemological realism. At the same time, and not unexpectedly, he was unable to generate a satisfactory alternative, in part because of his deep-seated ethical belief in the class basis of socialist politics and the suspicion, shared by many of his generation, that the many varieties of post-Marxism that began to surface in the late 1970s threatened the emancipatory project for which he had devoted his life.

Still, Williams, like Stuart Hall, Richard Johnson, and many others in cultural studies, was plainly influenced, as Thompson and Hoggart were not, by structural linguistics and the epistemological claims for language and discourse that informed it. Meanings were not embedded in history or in the Mind underlying the utterances of essential subjects, but were produced within specific contexts; language has no fixed referent but, instead, involves practices whose "meanings" are spatiotemporally contingent. Williams never went so far as, say, Laclau and Mouffe for whom the social itself is impossible precisely because, following Foucault, human relations are interpellated by discourse. Moreover, if the idea of a subject is problematic so is the notion of human or social relations, for "relations" imply subjects who interact, a posit that is logically inconsistent if, indeed, subjects are context-dependent. In place of the conscious subject Foucault, Laclau, and Mouffe substitute a "subject position" whose rules constitute the space within which discourse takes place.[42]

In contrast, Williams never adopted the position that language/discourse displaces human agency. He remained wedded to the notion that practice is an effective counterweight to both mechanistic materialism (associated with some versions of Marxist orthodoxy that emphasized the determination of cultural, ideological, and political practices by the already given economic infrastructure) and idealism which, while insisting on the active side of cultural practices, lost sight of all but the signifying subject.

In what is perhaps the most powerful statement of his position, Williams displays the most "dialectical" of all his cultural writings, showing the degree that he wants to separate himself from the passivity associated with structural linguistics while, at the same time, declaring that "language is material" and the sign active. Here, Williams makes plain his adherence to a concept in which relations between various aspects of the social totality are indeterminate *in advance*.

In the interviews with the *New Left Review* published as *Politics and Letters,* Williams seems to agree with the conventional distinction between economic and cultural relations, even if he inferentially refuses a one-way determination of culture by production relations. Nevertheless, in context, he was drawn ineluctably to a position that "cultural production was material," a perspective that leads to this: "Because once cultural production is itself social and material, then this indissolubility of the whole social process has different theoretical ground [than classical Marxism]. It is no longer based on experience, but on the common character of the respective processes of production."[43] So what we have here is a productivist conception of culture within a broad theory in which material production loses its exclusive connection to what might be described as "physical" need. Thus, production of various kinds *together* constitutes the whole social process whose relations of determination are contingent not on a priori metaphysical categories but on concrete circumstances.

As we will see in later chapters, the course of British cultural studies is fundamentally altered since the mid 1970s by these shifts. Following Williams, cultural studies refuses to abandon the emancipatory telos of Marxism even as the shift away from the "always already" to a more contextualized position is elaborated. Cultural studies, in the interest of maintaining a political as well as theoretical standpoint, is required to retain categories such as the totality, albeit altered from its Hegelian connotations, production, and agency without imputing finality to the ways in which they are employed. In fact, with Williams, cultural studies enters its greatest period of growth as it opens itself to the critique of scientificity, to feminism, and to other subaltern discourses that arise on the ruins of a withered ideology of class.

CHAPTER FOUR

British Cultural Studies

I

AS CONCEIVED by Hoggart and Stuart Hall, the first assistant director of the Centre for Contemporary Cultural Studies, cultural studies was defined by two key distinctions: between the dominant, ruling and middle-class culture(s) and popular culture; and between popular and mass culture. Each of these differentiations was politically loaded. The first project of reclaiming the popular was initiated by Hoggart, Williams, and the social historians quite independently of each other but was propelled by their common effort to assert the existence of a (relatively) autonomous affirmative working-class culture, in the anthropological meaning of the term, that survived the power of the dominant classes to incorporate it through middle-class ideals of education; consumption as a way of life; and, especially later, the dispersal of working-class social and cultural space through urban redevelopment and industrial deterritorialization.

The second program, to delineate the differences between popular culture and the products of the commercial media, was somewhat more complex. For mass culture could be seen either as a pure fabrication of a "culture industry" in which case it had few, if any, redeeming features; or, despite this fact, might be understood as a series of incorporations of a still vibrant popular culture, a judgment that would merit more serious study of commercial forms. Hall's 1964 *The Popular Arts* was an attempt, using literary methods, to discern aesthetic and social value in what were considered, especially by the mavens of high culture, degraded forms. Together with the second part of Hoggart's *Uses* and Williams's *Culture and Society*, it relied for its meaning of culture on "a set of texts and artifacts" and "even less the 'selective tradition' in which these texts and artifacts had been arranged, studied and appreciated."[1]

As I argued in the last chapter, Hoggart's work reproduced the tradition in which mass culture was seen as a *displacement* of the texts of both high culture and an authentic popular culture that, albeit expressed, for the most part, within the oral tradition, lent itself to textualization through the translations provided by a dramaturgically mediated social linguistics. Thus, although committed to working-class culture, Hoggart's Arnoldian proclivities resulted in a work in which practices were translated into "values and ideals," another approach that Hall was explicitly to repudiate: "the abstraction of texts from the social practices which produced them and the institutional sites where they were elaborated was a fetishization even if it had pertinent effects."[2] This reflection, written almost fifteen years after CCCS was founded and at the end of the decade that he, as Hoggart's successor (Hoggart left in 1969 to work at the UN) more than any individual, contributed to a radical transformation of its theoretical and political basis, may be taken as a final judgment of his own mentor.

Hall pays tribute to the three spiritual and intellectual parents of cultural studies (they tried to offer a coherent radical response to the "parameters" that "were set by the post-war 'settlement'—defined by the revival of capitalist production, the founding of a welfare state and the 'Cold War'—appeared to bring economic, political and cultural forces into a new kind of relation, into a new equilibrium.")[3] For this reason, according to Hall, they did not really initiate a genuinely radical departure in cultural studies; culture was still understood as logically distinct from "society" connected by the conjunction *and*. Hall implies that Hoggart, Williams, and Thompson had not yet offered a transformed conception of culture for they still relied on texts and artifacts for their studies and were caught in the practices of literary criticism.

For Hall, the publication of Williams's own *The Long Revolution* was a seminal event in English postwar intellectual life because it "shifted the whole ground of the debate from literary . . . to anthropological definition of culture."[4] In this work, the anthropological sense is defined as a "whole process" in which economic, political, and cultural practices were seen within a totality of social relations. According to Hall's account, *The Long Revolution* points the way toward what for Hall is the decisive break in cultural studies, the turn toward French structuralism, particularly the work of Roland Barthes and other semioticians and, above all, Althusser's categorical fusion of Marxist categories with those of structuralism and Lacanian psychoanalysis. It points the way, but does not itself go beyond its own Hegelian-Marxist invocations. That is, Williams's work still bears the marks of humanism in which the subject is unproblematically invoked.

From the mid-1970s to the late 1980s, British cultural studies, like most of British Marxism, including, even if reluctantly, Williams (but, at least on the conscious plane, not Thompson whose vitriolic polemic *Poverty of Theory* is directed against this move), is marked by the replacement of Hegelian categories such as "process" by structural relations. Henceforth the context for cultural studies is the English "social formation" of the capitalist mode of production. The assimilation of structuralism to cultural studies "was part of the project to develop a materialist definition of culture" as opposed, especially, to Williams's lingering Hegelianism signified by his invocation of such concepts as society as an "expressive" totality.⁵ Thus while *The Long Revolution* brought British cultural studies into Marxism, the literary idealist legacy of not only German Marxism but also of English literary traditions had not been entirely extirpated.

The first requirement of this "materialist" definition had to be an interrogation of the separation of culture and society. Althusser defined a social formation as a "structured" totality of economic, political, and ideological relations, each of which retained its "relative autonomy" and is, therefore, irreducible to each other. Like Emile Durkheim's insistence on the irreducibility of the "social," Hall argues for the same status of the cultural, but leaves the relationship between culture and ideology somewhat undefined. In the context of the efforts by many writers in the Cultural Studies Centre to grapple with a materialist definition, there appears to be no theoretical basis left for the category of culture itself after the influence of Althusser on the movement. On the contrary, Hall's effort to delineate the specificity of culture has all the characteristics of a variant of Althusser's crucial category of ideology. I want to return to the question of ideology a little later.

The second feature of this materialist definition is to remove it from its "authorial center," the subject who produces culture. At this point Hall makes his most original contribution, which amounts to a veritable paradigm shift in cultural studies. Recall Thompson's and Hoggart's strong emphasis on *agency*. Put another way, their discourse is directed toward showing culture as *conscious*ly radical or, even in its conservative manifestations, at least a class-autonomous practice. For them, culture is a "signifying practice" in which, in Hall's terms, "meaning" is its own "determinate product." This definition entails a "lived experience" that, if not wholly conscious, embodies worldviews that can be shown to be constitutive of class struggles, the content of history. Hall's deconstruction of this model of cultural practice begins with the strategic move to effect a "fundamental decentering of culture from their authorial centre in 'man's project.'" In the first place, "men are spoken by as well as speaking their culture . . . culture was as much constituted by its conditions of existence (economic, political, and ideological relations) as it constitutes them." Thus, the new structuralist thrust of cultural studies "established constraint and regulation alongside expression and agency in the analysis of structural practices."⁶

I want to unpack these apparently conciliatory sentences. At first appearance, what Hall seems to be saying is merely that he wants to correct some of the unfortunate, even if necessary overemphasis by the founding parents on "consciousness," "agency," and culture's autonomy from society. However, when he finally gets to his own "materialist" definition, we can see that the new theorization is to effect an *epistemological break* following Althusser from Marxist humanism whose essentialist categories are to be found in the corpus of the Frankfurt School, Lukacs, and, indeed, Williams and Thompson.[7] For Hall is signaling not only a shift to a middle ground in which both structure and agency find their appropriate space, but a theory of "culture" as a series of "structured practices": "Culture was better understood as the inventories, the folk taxonomies, through which social life is classified out in different societies. It is not so much the product of 'consciousness' as of the unconscious forms and categories through which historically definite forms of consciousness were produced."[8] This formulation is so closely derived from Althusser's crucial contribution to cultural studies, his "work on ideology," which for Hall had a "special relevance" that it is necessary to enter a brief discussion of this theory.

I have already mentioned Gramsci's pathbreaking theory of hegemony in which intellectuals, on behalf of classes contending for power, wage a fight to "moral and intellectual leadership" by, among other things, "imposing" a new common sense. Gramsci redefines "civil society" conventionally identified with market relations, as the sphere in which the struggle to define the categories of common sense takes place. Althusser takes Gramsci one step further to grasp common sense, the beliefs and values that are taken as self-evident descriptions of the social world to be *derivative,* not so much of the conscious interventions of intellectuals acting as subjects but, instead, of the work of a structured, unconscious relation that, following Lacan, Althusser calls "imaginary." Ideology is the "lived experience" of the world that is not "false" but whose truth is manifested in practices—political, cultural, institutional. Thus ideology is defined as material practices that constitute social relations. Among them are the interventions of intellectuals, but their effectivity cannot be measured except through the transformation of everyday imaginary relations and the practices to which they correspond.

In his celebrated article "Ideology and Ideological State Apparatuses," Althusser makes his most important, and controversial, contribution to the theory of ideology.[9] Ideology is not only embodied in discursive practices, in the stories we tell ourselves and those close to us, that is, represented as "experience" or common sense. The materialization of these practices is preeminently embodied in apparatuses of the capitalist state. For, if Gramsci is right that coercive institutions, although necessary for reproducing relations of production, are insufficient ways to secure the consent of the governed in modern social formations, then "apparatuses" of consent, material institutions with real functions that touch the lives of subordinate classes, must be formed.[10]

In this formulation, Althusser proposes a conception of the state that departs significantly from Gramsci's sphere of civil society. For the ideological state apparatuses—trade unions, religious institutions, and, especially, schools—are only relatively autonomous spaces, and this relative autonomy is determined by their function as producers of consent. In his last work, Nicos Poulantzas is to draw radical implications from this breach in the relation between the state and civil society retained from the Marxist legacy in Gramsci's work, and argues that the state, rather than being conceived as a complex of ideological apparatuses functionally linked to a definite class hegemony, may be considered a "terrain of contestation" in which the outcome is indeterminate.[11] That is, the state is, itself, relatively autonomous from a univocal conception of economic class power and subject to more than quantitative alteration by contending social forces. In effect, Poulantzas reinserts civil society within a *terrain*—the military metaphor refers to Gramsci's understanding of politics as so many variants of war—that Althusser has termed "the state." Hence, with Althusser the state embodies both coercive and ideological functions, but ideology's effectivity in behalf of a given hegemony is not determined in advance. Poulantzas succeeds, albeit tentatively, in breaking with the functionalism of his teacher; we are admonished to recognize the ubiquity of politics and the indeterminacy of the outcomes of political struggles *within* and not against the state. In the end, the concept of the specifically *capitalist* state, which signifies the always already hegemony of the economic in the last instance is called into question.

Althusser may not have agreed with his disciple, but his theory provided the opening to a radically new conception of the relation of ideology and the state. For if ideology is an imaginary relation to the "real" (a sphere that cannot be grasped except by means of scientific inquiry), linked to the formation and consolidation of common sense, and the ideological state apparatuses are the key institutions for securing consent, then ideological relations are always indeterminate from the perspective of their structural perimeters. These apparatuses are, themselves, subject to the conflict between the "lived experience" of this imaginary relation, and their own functional imperatives that are derived from the requirements of the symbolic order. In which case, Wittgenstein's motto "the limits of my language are the limits of my world" does not entirely apply.[12]

What is important here is how statements such as Hall's "men are spoken by as well as speaking their culture" may be understood beyond the Marxist commonplace that social being determines social consciousness. Hall is showing culture as an instance of ideology. For just as language constitutes subjects, so culture is, among other things, a linguistic practice that constitutes "men." To be sure, Hall's report on this profound transformation criticizes this Marxist structuralism for "bracketing out agency." However, despite his acknowledgment of some excesses, one that had to be informed by feminist critiques that argued that if agents are constructed by economic, political, and ideological relations, if in Althusser's terms people are "interpellated" by ideology, how to explain the emergence of social movements whose claim to their own agency *outside the determination by class relations* is precisely their point. That is, the Althusserian model is part of a larger strategic critique of humanism sometimes compressed in the slogan "the death of the subject."

With the rise of feminism in the mid-1970s, generally among British women intellectuals and within the Centre, it was no longer possible to maintain this slogan without acknowledging, in the context of the rise of feminism, its sexist implication. Among the new objects introduced by the feminist movement was a fresh examination of the family and school. In conventional Marxist theory these institutions are considered part of the ideological superstructure, in Althusser's terms transfigured as "ideological apparatuses of the state." As such they are grouped with other elements of "reproduction" of the relations of production. To be sure Marxist-feminism forced upon male Marxists a new appreciation of the significance of reproduction—especially the role of women as the central agent in the reproduction of labor power—as a fundamental condition for the existence of production relations. In turn, this was capable of altering some features of the economic infrastructure. Yet Marxism situated production in the system of wage labor, especially in factories and workshops.

Feminists demanded a "rethinking" of production that would refuse even the most accommodating efforts of enlightened Marxism. Rethinking meant that production now had two aspects: the production of social relations as co-equal with commodity production; and redrawing the map of cultural studies because it refused the primacy of a narrow conception of the economic, especially class relations, even in the last instance, if the economic signified, exclusively, relations within commodity production.

Marxism had always recognized that the family was an institution that participated, together with the school, to reproduce "labor power," but had never recognized its subversive side: the configuration of relations outside and even against the commodity sphere. Moreover, the family and school became in this revision—together with the neighborhood—sites within which the material processes of the production of class and gender took place through the processes of cultural production.

I will return to this formulation in a later chapter. For now, it is important to note that by the end of the 1970s, British cultural studies had already experienced a double shift: from a field whose crucial claim was the agency of the working class expressed, chiefly, through the coherence of an autonomous culture to a theory that refused the notion, not only of autonomy, but of the conventional concept of culture itself; and the struggle between Marxism (whether inscribed in the historical Engelsian orthodoxy of the two internationals that arose after the death of Marx or the structuralist variety of which Althusser and Poulantzas were the major figures) and the emerging discourses associated, however indirectly, with new social movements. The intellectuals within these movements were moving away from Marxism to the more radical, decentering practices of Deleuze, Derrida, and especially Foucault for whom not only conceptions of class, but the idea of the social itself were under interrogation. At the same time, the feminists associated, broadly, with cultural studies were challenging the "death of the subject" thesis posed as a leading proposition by post-Marxist social and cultural theory.

And, as a new discourse of racial freedom corresponding to the burgeoning black immigration to England from the Caribbean and Africa and a substantial Indian and Pakistani immigration as well, Hall, himself a native of Jamaica, recognized that the influence of these movements had the effect of "redrawing the map of Cultural Studies." Perhaps the most direct critique of cultural studies from a racial perspective was offered by Paul Gilroy.

Among the more insistent criticisms of the Centre's work was its failure to focus on questions of what has become known as "racial formation" in Britain and elsewhere. For even as women within the Centre succeeded in developing a strong program of feminist studies *within* the parameters of its major emphasis on popular and mass culture, it was not until the Brixton and Liverpool insurgencies that Hall, after he left the Centre, turned his writing to race issues. In the early 1980s, Hall was ineluctably drawn into the seething and sometimes violent race conflicts that erupted in the wake of the triumph of Thatcherism which, as he brilliantly theorized, was not merely a conservative government but a new right-wing ideology among whose central components was racism. Responding to the insurgency of young people of color in Liverpool, Hall's writing reflects the agency of these new political actors in terms that, while not entirely removed from his Althusserian moorings, are constrained to portray them as subjects. In his major contribution to a theory of British racial formation, Paul Gilroy expresses his frustration in no uncertain terms. His position is worth quoting at length:

The book has a second more parochial aim related to its origins in the field of cultural studies. It seeks to provide, more implicitly than explicitly, a corrective to the more ethnocentric dimensions of that discipline. I have grown gradually more and more weary of having to deal with the effects of striving to analyze culture within neat homogeneous national units reflecting the "lived relations" involved with the invisibility of "race" within the field and most importantly, with forms of nationalism endorsed by a discipline which, in spite of itself, tends to a morbid celebration of England and Englishness from which blacks are systematically excluded ... the marginalization of "race" and racism has persisted even where cultural studies have identified themselves with socialist and feminist political aspirations. This is perhaps a consequence of the imperatives of what are identified as "national-popular" struggles as well as a desire to construct national interests and roads to socialism using a political language which ... is saturated with racial connotations.[13]

This indictment was published in 1987 when after a quarter century of cultural studies, the "field"—in and out of the Centre—had dealt only cursorily with issues of race. To be sure, there are some Centre publications during the 1970s—Hall's stewardship—bearing on these issues. What was lacking, however, was a major effort, comparable to its turn toward feminism in the 1970s either to theorize or to explore the unique dimensions of race in Britain to which large numbers of blacks from the Caribbean and Africa have migrated after the Second World War. But Gilroy's critique strikes to another of the contradictions of cultural studies and especially Marxist cultural theory after the popular front. The specific interpretation rendered by Williams, Hoggart, and Thompson of the broad concept of the "national-popular" was plainly that working-class and popular culture had to be articulated with English nationalism. Thus, Thompson writes the history of the formation of the "English" working class, as if this rubric can adequately embrace the long Irish, Welsh, and Scottish influences *within* the British working class and its movements, as if internal migrations played little or no role even in the early decades of British industrial capitalist formation and of the modern British labor movement. And Williams never tired of expressing his pride of Englishness even as A. L. Morton had written a people's history of "England." Or the title of Hoggart's recent meditation on cultural studies, *An English Temper,* which carries on the enthnocentric focus of *Uses.*

Gilroy ascribes some blame to the left's postwar efforts to develop a national road to socialism, one that takes account of the peculiarities and the traditions of the English workers' movements, but also the specificity of British capitalism. One of them, the steadfast refusal of the mainstream of the labor movement to identify itself with Irish independence either at the turn of the twentieth century or today, not on traditional left-wing internationalist grounds but on the basis of its identification with the colonial policies of the state, has bedeviled the left. Racialism in England begins with the Irish question which, besides being an issue of colonialism, has never ceased to show profound tendencies toward ideologies of racial superiority that have remained virtually unresisted by English labor, except for the initiatives of the now defunct Labour-controlled Greater London Council in the 1980s to mount anti-racist education and cultural programs.

For Gilroy and others trying to understand the concrete process of racial formation in Great Britain, Gramsci's argument that the left must address itself to the nation as an affirmative instance of what Benedict Anderson has called "imagined communities" seems, from the point of view of colonial subjects, an invitation to disaster. The invocation of an affirmative national culture is ineluctably a category of *exclusion* and, in historical terms, has been used in what Gilroy terms the "overdeveloped" countries of the West, against immigrants, most recently from the south, notably the Caribbean, Latin America, and Africa.

The validity of this critique from a subaltern standpoint seems undeniable.

"Euro" or "national" communism signifies, ineluctably, the power of the nation and its culture as opposed to class, race, or gender identities, the other side of which is ethnocentrism. The history of the left, in all countries of the "overdeveloped world," especially the United States, Germany, France, and the United Kingdom, demonstrates the dangers of such identification. We can see it in stark relief during the recent Gulf and Falkland (Malvinas) Wars where U.S. and British workers were effectively rallied to imperial interventions, just as the mainstream of the French left, both communists and socialists remained, until the Algerian war, allied with "their" state in pursuing the goals of colonialism.

Yet, Gramsci's question remains. If one of the crucial tasks on the road to social transformation is to gain moral and intellectual leadership within the boundaries of the nation-state, how can the left, in the broadest connotation, avoid the claim that they are the genuine legatees of both the democratic intellectual traditions and the best of its cultural achievements? The failure, even refusal, of strong elements of the left to recognize the possibilities in these basically national traditions has often fueled the charge that the left is really not indigenous to national culture. To this day, for example, the left remains, among other antinomies, divided between its internationalist, often "Third World" wing and those for whom winning social and economic justice within the state are the crucial battlegrounds.

These debates demonstrate one of the genuine problems inherent in the project of social emancipation. Radicals cannot avoid showing the degree to which liberal society betrays authoritarian tendencies, and the nation-state as a site of exclusions, the manifestations of which have been all too apparent in the Anglo-American contexts during the past twenty years. At the same time, radicals are vulnerable to the charge of anti-Americanism, anti-Britishism, and so forth. This may be the price of a genuine anti-racist and anti-colonial perspective. Yet, if this defines the relation of radical movements to the nation, they risk political and cultural isolation. In consequence, the various European lefts and, to a lesser extent, the North American left as well, have felt constrained to stress a nation-class politics, even supporting high tariffs, patriotic wars, and restrictions on immigration.

This accounts for recent critiques, from subaltern perspectives, of the penchant of British cultural studies, indeed the whole British left, to privilege class movements over social movements, Marxism over postmodern efforts to comprehend the multiplicity of social agents and, consequently, the left's general failure, at least in Britain, to grapple with racial formation. As we will see in Chapter 5, the U.S. left, if not cultural studies, has made a more determined effort to theoretically grasp the significance, even the centrality, of race without, however, avoiding the agonies flowing from the imperatives of national identity.

2

The Centre was preoccupied for much of the decade of Hall's leadership with the important but elusive category of "sub" culture. In their theoretical essay "Subcultures, cultures and class" that introduces the Centre's collection *Resistance Through Rituals,*[14] Clark, Hall, Jefferson, and Roberts describe youth as an "emergent category of post-war Britain" that, rather than assuming an existence that is spatially distinct from the working class, may be understood as a "subculture" of the working class. It shares the formation of other working-class categories—especially with respect to its economic conditions—but "must exhibit a distinctive enough shape and structure to make them identifiably different from their 'parent' culture." According to the authors, subcultures occupy the boundary between these distinctive "shapes" and the cords that are "binding" to the parent class.

Before taking up, in detail, some of the major features of the theory of subculture which, in retrospect, was the most elaborated realization of the Centre's structuralist phase, I want to draw attention to two significant aspects of this work. The first refers to the discussion above on the difficulties that confronted the project of reclaiming an autonomous working-class culture in the pre-history of cultural studies, during its first five years under Hoggart and in the third phase of the Centre's embrace of structural Marxism which, notwithstanding its attempt to transform the field into a rigorous "scientific" discipline in its own right, retained a strong commitment to the long-term program as set out by Hoggart. The unresolved problem of linking culture to class led to two areas of investigation: media studies that rejected the older categorization of its products as "mass" culture and, instead, attempted to dredge up the popular, working-class roots of commercial representations. The key strategic move here was to suggest a different relationship between production and reception than that posited by those who understood the media in terms of mass society theory. For the Centre's media group the audience was, far from a passive receptacle of the media spectacle, an active participant, through reception, in constructing the meaning of television narratives.

In contrast to the older mass communication research, the audience was not constructed statistically, as in British and American sociology, but instead was studied, in the main, as most "empirical" studies of the Centre by means of the crucial anthropological method of ethnography.[15] Through in-depth interviews, sustained informal observations, and "hanging out" with television viewers, school-leavers, and neighborhood youth, Centre investigators produced a body of work on media that showed the connection between watching and the production of meaning. In this work, there is an epistemological assumption of the watcher as producer. In turn, the "consumer" (often a woman) is *situated* in the multiplicity of relations that constitutes her capacity for meaning-production—class, subcultural affiliation, gender, family, and other environments. The specificity and pertinence of the conditions of reception rule out the presupposition of the thesis, derived from the theory of mass society, that all relevant differences are wiped out by consumer society and especially mass communications.

Second, the discovery and development of subcultural theory became the Centre's first tacit recognition that the working class was not only a *problematic* in the Althusserian sense of inscribing a series of indeterminate relations, but was also a problematic category. Although the essay in question holds it, precariously, as the "parent" of subculture, its practical existence is hard to sustain except as a kind of structural ideological "unconscious," the last instance to which subculture refers, but like Althusser's invocation of the "economic" as the sine qua non of Marxist faith, it is one that never comes. In brief, for the authors subculture is an ideological apparatus whose "latent function is to express and resolve, albeit magically, the contradictions which remain hard to resolve in the parent culture."

Working-class youth form subcultures through music, rituals, a common relationship to authorities—parent, school, and police—and, most important, through struggles to "win space for the young" within their own neighborhoods and families. However, "there is no subcultural solution to working-class youth: unemployment, 'educational disadvantage,' dead end jobs, the routinization and specialization of labour, low pay and the loss of skills." Now comes the Althusserian/Lacanian discourse of this phase: subculture can only "'resolve' these issues in an imaginary way which at the concrete material level remain unresolved."[16] But here fealty to an ultimately economistic variant of Marxist theory creates a dead end from which there is no escape. The so-called "concrete material level"—economic relations—is still logically and ontologically separate from the ideological level which, despite the enormous advance represented by the discovery of subculture, retains the epiphenomenal status it was accorded in economistic Marxism.

In the context of the corpus of the Centre's appropriation of structuralism, such theoretical vulgarity is entirely unexpected. At its best, subcultural theory adopts, following psychoanalytic terms, the crucial category of *displacement* to show how working-class youth forge their own autonomous "culture" that presents itself as a political challenge, not only to the prevailing order, but to a largely indifferent working-class movement.

If as Gramsci argued the "magical" resolution of these issues through the reconfiguration of common sense is one of the conditions for any possible change, in other words, if discourse is a "material level," then perpetuating the distinction between the ideological and material (i.e., economic level), the distinction between the "material" and "ideological" levels made in this article, misses the point and unintentionally neutralizes the power of subcultural theory and practice.

The Centre's formulations of subculture are directed against those on the one side who made youth (sub)culture a truly independent category from class, race, or gender, and ascribed its postwar appearance to the way in which Karl Mannheim posed the problem of "generations," in which a cohort of people located in common spatial/temporal relations may, under certain circumstances, constitute itself as a separate social category; and on the other side, theorists of mass society for whom classlessness in the political sense was the logical outcome of permanent affluence and who, therefore, dispose of any culture except that which conforms to the requirement of mass consumption and ideological conformity. It seems that subculture was the imaginary resolution to the contradictions of class dispersal, but still reined in by class orthodoxy. In practice, for cultural studies, subculture was a way to hold on to class analysis while simultaneously displacing it.

Dick Hebdidge and Paul Willis produced superb ethnographies of various aspects of youth culture. Hebdidge's classic work on skinheads and bikers—young working-class men who were in full-throated revolt against conservative aspects of the parent—disrupted the images of affluence and consumerism promulgated by sociologists. Willis's study of bikers is a subtle addition to the claim that subculture is intimately linked to the parent working-class culture. But his most convincing book is the truly remarkable study of male working-class students of a comprehensive high school, *Learning to Labour*—perhaps the most powerful single theoretical contribution made by the Centre.[17]

Willis advances a theory of "how working class kids get working class jobs," a concrete example of the link between subculture and its parent; and a metatheory of how economic, political, and ideological relations interpellate social agents. For although the "lads" make their own histories, they cannot make them as they please. Willis's central argument is that working-class kids get working-class jobs through "failing" to master the middle-class curriculum. However, this is not a failure either of intellectual capacity or of will. Nor does Willis accept the sociolinguistics of Basil Bernstein that argues that working-class speech employs "restricted codes" because life and labor do not require them to use an "elaborated" code. Willis develops a perspective that is, in broad outlines, parallel to that of William Labov whose ethnographic work argues that American black speech contains conceptual strategies for complex discourse: logical, syntactical, and semantic.[18] The "lads" reject the authority of the school to deprive them of their class identity and since the terms of success are defined by making good grades, learning the boundless details of school knowledge, and, above all, following instructions, these kids almost invariably become early school-leavers, a decision that condemns them to unskilled and semi-skilled industrial labor. Needless to say, neither for the "lads" nor for Willis is this "condemnation" unwelcome; on the contrary, their rebellion against school authority is, at the same time, a definitive rejection of the middle-class promise of upward social mobility. In Willis's report they generate coherent arguments against the arbitrariness of school authority and the irrelevance of school knowledge, judgments that cannot be easily refuted in a world in which industrial jobs that required no specific educational credentials were available for most early school-leavers.

In this process, subculture functions as the mechanism of solidarity by which the "lads" resist losing their class identity. In contrast to the liberal concept of "educational disadvantage" that Clark et al. adapt to their litany of problems suffered by working-class youth, Willis turns the tables by arguing that failing the curriculum is a ritual of resistance, an anti-authoritarian rebellion which, however, entails unintended consequences. At the heart of his analysis is the persistence of class identities that are embodied in a series of practices, including linguistic practices, the surrender of which constitutes perforce an abandonment of class identities.

Willis's book appeared in 1976 and was based on studies done in the late 1960s and early 1970s when the English economy, especially in the midlands, was just beginning to experience its prolonged downward spiral. The school Willis studied was located in Coventry, a center of the British car industry that employed a considerable number of male early school-leavers. A decade later, most of the British-owned plants had completely disappeared except for Jaguar and Ford, an American-owned company. Like the somewhat earlier closures in the steel industry, the 1980s in Coventry were bleak reminders of the end of an era: the postwar settlement between labor and capital was irrevocably abrogated; the Thatcher government's program to dismantle the welfare state was only slowed by popular resistance, not reversed; the policy of privatizing and otherwise eliminating the Labour government's nationalized industries went smoothly, save for the ill-fated miners' strike in 1983. Britain was not only no longer the "workshop of the world" or even of Europe; it had settled down to a dual economy: high technology projects that were routinely exported, which did not benefit the sick goods production sector that remained "backward" by global standards; and a fairly buoyant financial services sector at the top; and a panoply of low-paid services or permanent unemployment for perhaps a quarter of the population, including several generations of youth. And, like the United States, many of these service jobs were offered only on a part-time basis to women, many of whom were single parents, a situation that made them the core of a growing population of working poor.

The bare fact is that neither the British nor the North American economies of the United States and Canada have created structurally valid spaces for literally millions of high school graduates, much less early school-leavers who, in the main, have for the past twenty years been bereft of hope for the future. Under these circumstances, the subcultural ritual of rebellion-school failure-working-class job collapses in its outcome. Rather, the young men and women who refuse to imbibe the curriculum are more unambiguously condemned because in the more secure niches there are few jobs for which reading and writing are not crucial skills. In this period of global economic restructuring, the concept of the job "market" itself is in doubt, if by "market" we mean a system of exchanges of labor for wages where, at times, labor as well as jobs are in short supply. Except for specific categories of highly skilled workers and during periods of economic expansion, low-wage service workers (mostly women) are not hard to find; those whose family and peer traditions have prepared them for semi-skilled production labor are, to an overwhelming degree, simply unwanted.

Yet there is little warrant for the view that economic developments have overcome cultural practices. To hold this position is itself an indication of economism. For the position that argues that working-class youth are better advised to conform to the expectations of school authorities because of changed economic opportunities has adopted the rationality against which the rebellion occurs in the first place. Save for a minority of high school students and undergraduates who choose technical curricula precisely because they want those jobs, schools are not about training; they are about obtaining credentials that tacitly imply, for working-class youth, shifting one's class identity. One does not simply ingest a series of "subjects" in order to qualify for possible administrative jobs or professional status. The "credential" includes changing the representations that mark class membership. Since working-class kids take their "imaginary solution," group solidarity against authorities, to be "real," that is, take their culture and peer communities as a material, and even rational choice, the distant shore of full-time employment at a decent pay is not enough to convince many kids to "clean up their acts."

But the persistence of the pattern of school failure goes beyond the assertion of cultural identity at the ideological level. Many working-class youth do not believe that the world of technical and professional work is a place of opportunity for them, nor are they convinced they want to do it. First, even these jobs have been disappearing in the new economic climate; yet more fundamental is the profound gulf between the middle-class, puritanical idea that work fulfills the obligation to God and Man or even the more liberal notion that work fulfills a personal need beyond its income-producing feature and the working-class practice of working to live, in which case the content of the job itself is clearly subordinate to its function to sustain neighborhood life or even shop-floor cultural practices that, for youth, is intertwined with peer relationships or, among older workers, family life.

It seems to me that the conceptual power of the Centre's theory of subculture consists chiefly in its emphasis on "'maps of meaning' which makes things intelligible for its members ... embodies the trajectories of group life ..., even if always under conditions and its raw materials which cannot wholly be of its own making."[19] Next to the capacity of this subculture to "cement and unify"[20] its members around a series of common practices (among them what Phillip Corrigan calls the "dialectic of doing nothing"), the power of the "dominant" ideology may be seen not so much in its ability to defeat these practices, but to stigmatize the kids, even in their own self-conceptions. A functionalist, Durkheimian analysis claims that school failure supplies a necessary validation for the education system's claim that it provides, if not strict equal access to professional and vocational opportunity, at least access to those formerly excluded from the chance to get schooling. Those who, for whatever reason, turn their backs on opportunity have only themselves to blame.

In this scenario schools are off the hook as long as they offer an "objective" basis for measurement of adequacy (rather than the more ambiguous concept of "success") such as standardized tests constructed around a universal, lock-step curriculum that is, as far as possible, indifferent to considerations of class, race, and gender. But, as Willis shows, whatever the outcome, kids who obey the rationality of the subculture as a "map of meaning" may interpret this whole process in a radically different way. Whatever its defects, especially its own rituals of economism, the Centre's subcultural theory reintroduced agency, at least of the young, as counterfactual to the "dominant ideology" thesis which, in some manifestations, sees only the imperative of economic power.

3

With the incorporation of the Centre, in 1988–1989, into the university's Department of Sociology for reasons, according to its last director, Richard Johnson, that if they could not expand and would perish from "exhaustion" without additional faculty and staff, the moment of the Birmingham Centre as an original intellectual site passed into cultural history. However, as I want to argue, this merger resulted from more than the relentless attacks to which the Centre was subjected by the university's administration: frequent evaluations; blocking their ability to make faculty appointments that were consonant with their large student enrollment; and requiring them, for the latter part of their history, to offer graduate and undergraduate programs with three full-time faculty. Added to these indignities was a series of theoretical and political challenges to the underlying project of discovering, delineating, and mapping working-class culture and its relation to media, subcultures, and the larger historical canvas. The serious and fundamental shifts of direction forced by emergent social movements and their discourses, chiefly of feminists and blacks, made problematic the underlying Marxist theoretical basis of the project.

Elsewhere, I have argued that what I called the "crisis" in historical materialism consisted in a conjuncture of the palpable failure of "really existing" socialism—notably in Eastern Europe, China, and Cuba—already evident in the 1970s, with the persistence of a reformist working class (at best) and the decomposition and recomposition of its most experienced and militant sectors.[21] To understand the depth of the restructuring of the working class in the 1980s, one need only review the grim record in all western countries, but especially Britain, France, and the United States of plant closings, bitterly lost strikes, and trade union compromises to provide management with more flexibility on the shop floor, especially the relaxing of hard-won rules that limited the employers' authority to direct and reassign the work forces. Needless to say, among the major components of this crisis was the growing chorus of radical intellectual work that questioned, deconstructed, and otherwise refuted the doctrine of the privileged working class historical agency in the struggle for economic, political, and cultural transformation. Feminists asserted, with particular force at the Centre, if not the priority of sex and gender relations to those of economic relations, its parallel significance; ecologists have shown Marxism, in its most broadly understood manifestations, to be a creature of the bourgeois enlightenment's insistence on the domination of nature as a condition of human emancipation. And, as I will try to demonstrate in the concluding chapter(s), feminists, ecologists, and other radical intellectuals have mounted a powerful, and for many, convincing critique of science, including Marxism's own claims to scientific privilege.

The Centre was in the middle of many of these debates (except for ecology, which seemed to have virtually no penetration in its work) but did not (or could not) provide a context within which the most radical critiques could be voiced. As a result, its affirmative contributions were largely if not exclusively undertaken within the Marxist paradigm—even in the wake of powerful challenges at both the political and intellectual planes—and, consequently, confined to working-class cultural studies—subcultures, media, and problems of working women. In addition Johnson, Schwarz, and others made fundamental contributions to a creative critique of the humanist ideology of Thompson and other precursors.[22] Yet because the Centre remained ensconced in the categories and problematics of Marxist structuralism, especially the concept of the primacy of the economic, it became indelibly identified with its most powerful intervention: to demonstrate the significance and power of popular culture to provide a map of meanings, and, beyond these, to show that "relatively autonomous" class-based cultural practices provided the glue that held class and class fractions together.

This primary focus so overshadowed the Centre's incipient work on science and technology, patriarchy and race that cultural studies as a field was, for more than two decades, virtually identified with the mass/high/popular culture question. To the extent that the Centre maintained, resolutely, a stance against forms of academic dilution, it became a model for all the others. This dilution consisted mainly in the tendency betrayed by, especially, some American academics to study popular culture outside its economic, political, and ideological contexts—in short, to treat such artifacts of popular culture as rock music, vernacular speech, and subcultural rituals as aesthetic objects or as neutralized objects of ethnographic investigation whose real subject was what is called in the social sciences *methodology*. Despite these limitations and criticisms, the Centre's achievements were nothing short of spectacular: there are at least twelve cultural studies units in English universities, many of them in the polytechnic colleges, largely populated by working-class and lower-middle-class students. In other parts of the English-speaking world including the United States and Canada, cultural studies is a rapidly growing movement and there are at least six prominent centers in the countries of Latin America that use the phrase cultural studies to describe themselves. There currently exist at least a dozen important journals in England, Australia, the United States, and Canada devoted to the study of popular and subcultures whose existence would be unthinkable without the Centre's influence. And, beyond these specific achievements, as we noted in the first chapter, cultural studies has become a rubric under which a multiplicity of intellectual transgressions are in progress.

How to evaluate the intellectual legacy of the Centre and its immediate circles? I have already discussed the strong anthropological conception of contemporary popular culture that the Centre played a major role in disseminating. However, this innovation was made at the price of carrying out, to extreme lengths, the virtual extirpation of recent literary theory and criticism; indeed, we can see the marginal place of textual criticism—apart from theory and history—in the Centre's collective writings after 1970. Of course, this absence reflects not a "neglected" area, but a sharp ideological and methodological break with the past. As we have already seen, the Centre, concerned as far as possible to remove the study of working-class culture from "representations" such as are embodied in literary texts, led to a primary, nearly exclusive emphasis on ethnography, methods of participant/observation, and informal sociological interviews of television audiences.

On one side, ethnographic research was necessary to retrieve those practices—especially rituals of resistance—that marked class and subculture off from the dominant "mass" consumer society. On the other hand, despite Hall's conciliatory sentiments in the direction of the literary founders noted above, after assuming the directorship, cultural studies disdained the strategy of textual analysis of art forms. Clearly, part of the explanation for this omission inheres in the character of the criticisms of Williams and Hoggart and through this Marxist-structuralist attack on the tradition of English criticism that owes its vitality, in different registers, to Matthew Arnold and especially F. R. Leavis, perhaps the leading critic of the generation between the wars.

In order to indicate the degree of difference between the Centre during and after the Hall era, and those who, together with their efforts to valorize working-class culture, simultaneously felt obliged to continue to pay tribute to the special nature of Art, a perennial theme of Arnoldian criticism, there is no better voice than that of Richard Hoggart. Here is Hoggart writing in 1976:

To be cultivated does not mean to be elegantly mannered. Nor . . . is it synonymous with being virtuous. Neither making of nor the responding to art can in themselves make us one whit better; if they could, the problem of the wilfullness of man would be a great deal easier to resolve. But art can widen the sense of possibilities, give hints of greater depths and other orders; it stands ready to assist us to make better choices if we so will; and in doing so it creates experiences—artistic experiences—which are so beautiful and moving. I think this is what Matthew Arnold meant when he said: "Good poetry does undoubtedly tend to form the soul and character; it tends to beget a love of beauty and of truth in alliance together; it suggests . . . high and noble principles of action, and it inspires the emotions so helpful in making principles operative. Hence its extreme importance to all of us."

To which Hoggart adds, "the life of the mind is a political activity."[23]

What is tacitly denied, in the past twenty years, by British cultural studies are precisely these sentiments. No doubt art is political—a form, in Pierre Macherey's terms, of ideology.[24] Yet, if we take all "high" art such as poetry to be an instance of the "dominant" ideology, then the function of criticism is to dismantle the claim that it can "widen the sense of possibilities" or, indeed, suggest "high and noble principles of action." The Centre spent considerable efforts with media texts, following Hall's program for a semiotic of popular culture aimed at decoding ideology in the representations of media productions such as advertising. Perhaps a larger portion of the Centre's media studies was devoted to a sociological examination of the function of television watching in the lives of its working-class audience(s), work that, however valuable, is fully consistent with an older, American tradition of communications research and scarcely consistent with, for example, Willis's and Hall's anti-empiricist polemics of the same period.

Stuart Hall's paper "Encoding and Decoding in the Television Discourse,"[25] delivered in 1973, remains a canonical exemplar of a semiology of television that comprehends media messages as a complex of distinct and relatively autonomous codes rather than a unified representation of the dominant ideology. Thus, television programs are taken as discourses rather than being viewed as a "behavioral event" of stimulus-response in which the intentions of the producers are mechanically and inexorably internalized by a mostly passive audience. To my knowledge, this is a very early attempt to introduce the term "discourse" to cultural studies. In context, it signifies not only Hall's concern to dispel a residual mass-society view, but to affirm that the dominant ruling groups must *persuade* an otherwise skeptical audience in order to achieve consent, that television representation is a rhetorical form whose outcome may be, from the perspective of its intentions, indeterminate. Thus, the article carries the ideas of resistance, contradiction, and discursive *difference* into the analysis of television. At the same time, it remains faithful to the idea of media as an ideological apparatus of the state that is relatively exempt from serious contestation despite the requirement that programs provide an imaginary relation to the real, that is, are an instance of Althusserian ideology.

In Hall's account, the *"dominant or hegemonic code* in any television representation competes with what Parkin calls the *professional* code(s) which the professional broadcasters employ when transmitting a message which has already been signified in a hegemonic manner. The professional code is 'relatively independent' of the dominant code" but Hall places more emphasis on the term "relatively" than "independent" since the hegemonic ideology has already specified the content of the message.[26] The discursive strategy appropriate to the medium may dictate formats, personnel, choice of images, the staging of debates, but the dominant or hegemonic code "defines within its terms the mental horizon, the universe of possible meanings of a whole society; and it carries with it the stamp of legitimacy—it appears coterminus with what is 'natural,' 'inevitable,' taken for granted about the social order." Oppositional elements may appear in the discourses of television, but Hall considers their incorporation to be ineluctable to the form as it is inevitable, given the pretext of the hegemony of the dominant ideology. What Hall calls *negotiated codes* between the dominant and oppositional ideologies *"operate through what we might call particular or situated logics"* that can only disrupt the "systematic distortions of a socio-communications system."[27]

This paradigmatic statement deftly weaves Gramscian, semiotic, and contemporary communications themes within the dominant ideology thesis that, despite the positing of the categories of discourse, negotiated and professional codes, and opposition, are fully consistent with a Marxist theory of the mass media as an instance of the *reproduction of the relations of production.* This perspective is elaborated in Janice Winship's work on advertising that draws heavily on Judith Williamson's canonical *Decoding Advertisements*,[28] which brilliantly weaves semiotic analysis with a political economy of advertising. Here advertising is situated in the process of commodity circulation, between production and consumption, and seen as a necessary element in the circuit of capital, the completion of which in the act of consumption is a necessary condition for reproduction on an expanded scale. Winship's article "Sex for Sale" is through the late 1970s among the most sophisticated fusions within the broad structuralist/Marxist perspective on media representations, of psychoanalytic and feminist categories.[29]

Winship shows that ideological representation of femininity "is completed through our collusion as we read and consume the ads. We are never just spectators who gaze at the 'images' of women as though they were set apart, differentiated from the 'real' us. Within the ads are inscribed the subject positions of the 'mother', housewife', 'sexually attractive woman' and so on."[30] Winship is concerned to show that "we" are part of the process of media production as much as reception because we always already possess the "knowledge" required to decode the ads. In this sense, the images of media production are always negotiated and do not constitute a "laying on of culture." Consistent with work such as that by film theorists Laura Mulvey and Teresa DiLauretis, the "penetration" of femininity by masculinity is asserted as a crucial component of the ads as well as a "construction" of femininity that is, however, contained within patriarchal relations.[31]

In the late development of the Centre, cultural studies was able to produce a small body of work in media studies that, together with the popular music criticism of Simon Frith and others (about which more in Chapter 6), attempted to obliterate the boundaries between production and consumption, especially refuting the prevailing thesis that the Culture Industry was a monolithic instrument of domination. By showing popular culture to be a series of discursive practices, including expressive forms such as music and (in an incorporated form) television as well as specific linguistic practices and rituals, it took a long step to dispute the historical *existence* of mass society itself. For, even if always oscillating between autonomy and incorporation, the integrity of popular culture as a mode of life refutes the implicit assumption of mass society theories that the audience brings nothing but its degraded, technologically mediated desires to watching or listening. Politically as well as intellectually this is a very significant achievement. It not only brings the "people" back into contemporary life as well as history, but it drives a wedge in the conventional claim for the superiority of Art.

Yet, with very few exceptions, notably the brief earlier work of the Centre's short-lived *Literature and Society Group* and a later contribution by *The English Studies Group*, also short-lived, work on literary theory is meager within the context of the Centre's program and the contacts with art history or even film and musicology, apart from rock critics, do not seem to exist, much less close readings of crucial novels and other "high culture" texts, except those done by feminists in search of a critical tradition. Although the characterization of cultural studies as (pop) cultural studies by its elite detractors has always been made in extremely bad faith, the grain of truth in this perception is reinforced by the indifference, even hostility, of cultural studies to the various "great" traditions. In this sense, the dominant ideology thesis has served cultural studies badly.

British cultural studies did not succeed in sundering the *distinction* between high and popular culture; it refused to acknowledge the political and aesthetic *value* of male, "bourgeois" expressive representations for a putative workers' movement. Thus, in practice, it *obliterated* high culture as a legitimate object of theoretical and critical inquiry. Of course, if the movement were consistent with its own theoretical perspective, it would recognize that the category of "high" art does not inhere in the object, but in its historical and social constitution. In which case, since high art is conventionally constituted, canonical novels, poems, paintings, and so on are appropriate subjects for both textual and ethnographic inquiry. Works of literature and other traditional arts that attract ruling-class and middle-class audiences are not necessarily consumed by the dominant ideology: Hall, Williamson, and Winship have argued precisely against this proposition in media representations, even though middle-class as well as working-class fractions watch television and see ads. If the point of media studies is to delineate the elements of ideological *struggle* rather than univocal domination in these representations, Art would still be a fitting subject for investigation. In this sense it would have paralleled David Bloor's program to treat rejected and accepted science as instances of the same social processes and, thereby, to refuse the privilege accorded by conventional histories and sociologies of knowledge to "true" science.[32] The Centre would have had to reverse the procedure. That is, to treat accepted Art with the same ethnographic and semiotic care as it did with any popular representations.

Why, generally, the omission of this dimension in cultural studies? At one level, a new generation of left-intellectuals was avoiding the sins of commission of their "parents," the virtually exclusive textual (literary) orientation of even some historians, much less critics. And it can be argued that just as Marx and Engels were aware that they were constrained by circumstances, not doctrine, to overemphasize the economic in contrast to politics and culture, cultural studies had a polemical motive for its focus on the working class and its culture. These are necessary but insufficient explanations.

More to the point was the powerful conjuncture of the *British reception* of structuralist-Marxism with its preoccupation with founding a *science* of politics and culture, as opposed to the "art" of criticism and the influence of a distinctly "workerist" version of the left tendency in Britain, most saliently identified with Trotskyism. It is not that the various groups *directly* influenced particular figures in cultural studies. Most left-wing academic intellectuals stay outside organizations of the ideological left, even in the 1930s, when a relatively strong Communist party succeeded in recruiting some of the more prominent members of the professoriate and independent intellectuals. What counts was the moral suasion exercised by these New Left Marxist-inspired movements. Since the overwhelming preponderance of academics are re-cruited from the middle classes, especially its professional layers, the strident anti-bourgeois sentiments of the groups, whose membership was often indis-tinguishable from academic ranks (although most had renounced their aca-demic aspirations upon entering those movements that required them to do so) had an enduring effect on cultural studies as much as other outposts of the left academy, especially in the 1960s and 1970s.

Although Hall, Johnson, Willis, Schwarz, and feminists such as William-son, Michelle Barrett, and Winship were clearly opposed to the empiricism and positivism of the English and American academies, the moment of cul-tural studies in England is suffused with a strong *will to scientificity,* an effort to purge social and cultural theory of its lingering humanistic, essentialist, and literary as opposed to theoretical turn of mind to which these intellectual sins correspond. In the 1970s, Hall, Tony Bennett, and others worked to constitute this new field as a rigorous scientific cross-disciplinary inquiry that leaned strongly on social science rather than the humanities, the founding sites of cultural studies.

Hence, these intellectuals turn on their own Oxbridge training, and, in-stead, opt to become useful to the broad Labour and radical movements by renouncing their own intellectual heritage. This, more than any other act, was their resistance to middle-class culture through the ritual of self-renunciation.

CHAPTER FIVE

Cultural Politics of the Popular Front

I

THE COLLAPSE of Communism in Eastern Europe and the decline of radicalism in western capitalist societies might tend to produce a new past in which only the calumnies and failures of the left receive detailed treatment and the genuine achievements of the historical socialist and communist movements are given short shrift. Certainly, even before the current disastrous fortunes of the ideological left, critics and historians were rewriting history in different ways. One example, in the immediate postwar period, was Robert Warshow, perhaps (next to Dwight Macdonald) the leading high cult critic of the movies and other popular forms. Warshow, an editor at the time of his untimely death (1955) of *Commentary* and a frequent contributor to *Partisan Review,* shared the ultimate disdain of most anti-Stalinist left intellectuals for the popular front and especially its cultural policies:

> [During the 1930s] if you were not somewhere within the (Communist) party's orbit, then you were likely to be in the opposition, which meant that much of your thought and energy had to be devoted to maintaining yourself in opposition.
> In either case, it was the Communist party that ultimately determined what you were to think about and in what terms.
> There resulted a disastrous vulgarization of intellectual life, in which the character of American liberalism and radicalism was decisively—and perhaps permanently—corrupted.[1]

But what distinguished Warshow's criticism from that of Macdonald was his meticulous effort to judge individuals by their works and not by their party affiliation or sympathies. Thus, the work of Clifford Odets, undoubtedly the representative playwright of the popular front era, is "By a considerable margin, the most important achievement in the literature of the American Jews,"[2] an evaluation that would have been as far from the criticism of a Greenberg, Macdonald, and Trilling who were, in every fiber of their being, gatekeepers of high culture.

That Odets was a "middle-brow" dramatist in the sense that he failed, for the most part, to maintain that cool disinterest of which "great art" is made goes without saying. His characters virtually bleed, with high melodramatic flourish, onto the orchestra seats. But, according to Warshow, Odets is capable of producing in one of his major plays a sharp and brutal picture of Jewish life that manages to capture the crisis of one significant fraction of the middle class in this era. Plainly, even if Odets in the mid-1930s was, like his fellow intellectuals, in the thrall of the party that "ultimately determined what you were to think about and in what terms," he managed a "brilliant" play. Whether *Awake and Sing,* the piece in question, was aberrant to party policy or consistent with it, Warshow does not say. Clearly, it did not share in the general "cultural failure" that was, for the anti-Stalinist intellectuals, the over-riding legacy of the 1930s.

In retrospect, the works of Warshow, Macdonald, Greenberg, and Trilling foreshadow the current reexamination of some of the major assumptions of the left intelligentsia about the revolutionary past. By far, the most notable development of the recent past has been a searching reexamination of left-wing traditions since the French Revolution. Francois Furet and his associates discovered the bloody, authoritarian record of that watershed event and, like many who discovered the American Civil War to have been an unnecessary adventure by a vengeful North, concluded the revolution was a colossal error. In the same vein, Theodore Draper's worthy successor, Harvey Klehr, continued the effort to eradicate whatever honor remained in American communist history. Klehr's position—that even in the heyday of American communism, the 1930s, the movement exercised very little influence over American politics—was conceived, undoubtedly, as an antidote to the plethora of social histories that cast a new, more sympathetic light on the otherwise despised Communist party and its periphery. Those radicals who reached their political majority in the 1960s and early 1970s searched for a living tradition and discovered, much to the consternation and condemnation of the older anti-Stalinist intellectuals, that the party, even when it generally followed the line laid down by the Communist International, can be credited with solid achievements in, among other arenas, the development of the mass industrial union movement, the struggle for civil rights, and the field of culture.[3]

Draper and Klehr make a compelling case for the claim that American Communists rarely, if ever, departed from the Moscow "line." And, in numerous memoirs and studies by former communists, notably that of George Charney,[4] we learn how utterly self-destructive the party and its once impressive ranks could be in the face of the obvious fact that their policies at various times were not working, nay were even counterproductive precisely because they were widely understood as having been imported from abroad. This was especially evident in the 1920s when every radical tendency to the "right" of the party was condemned as "social fascist"; the period of the Nazi-Soviet pact that the party loyally defended; and the post-Second World War era when the party once again took an abrupt left turn and succeeded in slowly decimating its ranks by a parodic effort to impose revolutionary discipline in a palpably nonrevolutionary political situation and eroding its popular influence by a combination of strident defense of Soviet foreign policy and a premature policy of "going underground" in the face of political repression. Buffeted by this repression and its own sectarianism, the Communist party had already lost much of the credibility it had gained during the New Deal and the war. In the decade prior to the stunning 1956 Khrushchev report outlining Stalin's crimes to the 20th Congress of the Soviet Communist party, the American Communist party managed to maintain a substantial chunk of its membership, especially the cadres, but witnessed a dramatic shrinkage of its periphery.

Of course, political repression took a large toll. But the communists also suffered from an undemocratic internal life where decisions were largely presented to the membership by the leadership. In turn, the members, whether they agreed or not, were obliged to carry the party "line" to non-communists. Although dissent was formally permitted before decisions were taken, it was actively discouraged, in most cases. Finally, the communists maintained their hostility to other radical movements even in the 1960s when, in the wake of the mass radicalization of large sections of America's youth, the party, still licking its wounds, all but turned its back on the New Left, even condemning the new radicalism as a petty-bourgeois movement.

All this is virtually incontrovertible evidence that a certain moral corruption has dogged the American communist movement since its inception. To which Harold Cruse, Chester Himes, and Ralph Ellison have added tales of the communist manipulation of black people, the party's racist practices even during the zenith of its influence in Harlem and other black ghettoes.[5] There are similar experiences in other sectors of American life that require further documentation.

However, there is surely another side of the story. For example, Gerald Meyer, Mark Naison, and Charney have made a good case that the party's role in Harlem and East Harlem, at least until 1950, was generally positive, even heroic. And it is hard to ignore Robin Kelley's and Nell Painter's painstaking work on the black-dominated Alabama Communist party during the 1930s.[6] According to their accounts, despite the party's lack of political influence among any significant sections of white workers and intellectuals (although it had some limited success among southern white farmers), it succeeded in mobilizing considerable resistance among black sharecroppers and workers to southern white supremacy, and played an important part in the early history of the modern civil rights movement.[6] Equally persuasive is James Prickett's critical study of the party's work in several CIO unions.[7] What distinguishes this work from others is its pitiless critique of the party's accommodation to the centrist CIO leadership when its influence was at its peak in the late 1930s. Prickett's argument is that the communists' self-effacement after 1935 and their serious and ultimately self-defeating compromises in the interest of anti-fascist labor unity accounted as much as political repression during the cold war era for their ultimate isolation and disappearance from those sectors of the labor movement within which they once enjoyed considerable strength. Further, he chronicles the party's increasing tendency to work from the top, another consequence of the popular front line, a strategy that contributed to the rapid erosion of its rank-and-file union base after the war. Yet, on his and the evidence of others,[8] communists played an indispensable role in building two of the three largest industrial unions in the CIO—the Auto Workers and the Electrical Workers—and were crucial for the growth of many of the smaller organizations as well; they insisted, in some unions such as the Packinghouse Workers (although not in others) on policies that pushed for promotion of blacks both within the ranks of their leaderships and within the industry. In other industries such as auto and electrical their record was much more suspect. Communists and left-wing unionists allied with them pioneered in building unions of white-collar workers, professionals, and the unemployed when most of the rest of the labor movement held fast to the idea that these categories were "unorganizable."

It is fairly well known that, after a period in the late 1920s and early 1930s when world communist parties maintained a rigid "bolshevik" hostility to social democrats and progressive liberals, the looming danger of the triumph of fascism forced an about-face in communist policy. From 1933–1934, even before Georg Dimitrov, the secretary-general of the Communist International, delivered his famous speech calling for an end to sectarianism and the formation of a united front against fascism with the socialists and their followers and, beyond this, unity with democratic capitalist nations as well, many communist parties, including the Americans, had made tentative moves toward working in the political mainstream of their respective countries.

In the context of this shift, the American party, among others, began to explore the question of what Antonio Gramsci terms the "National-Popular." The object of this investigation was to found an alternative to nativist patriotism by reconstructing the national culture as a popular culture that could be articulated with the economic and political struggles of subaltern groups. Now, the communists had, during the 1920s, already produced several works of history that highlighted American working class struggles, notably Anthony Bimba's *History of the American Working Class* (1927). However, Bimba's approach, despite a very valuable historical narrative of the development of labor militancy, was articulated by the general economic determinism and anti-colonial discourse that marked the generally sectarian communist versions of Marxism. Interestingly, Bimba's description of the economic background of the discovery of America could have been written today during the five-hundredth-anniversary controversy over Columbus's discovery of America. It reflects the general left-wing hostility to American nationalism which, in their account, rests on a long record of imperial conquest. Rather than extolling the marvels of Columbus's achievement, Bimba's sympathy is with the victims of the mercantilist explorations of which these voyages were a part: "The discovery of America at the end of the fifteenth century was mainly the result of commercial and business necessity. The thirst of the European ruling classes to acquire new wealth and the glory which goes with it inspired and made possible the famous voyage of Columbus across the Atlantic. . . . Once America was found, the sole aim of the first white explorers was to plunder the American Indians, resorting, when necessary, to the most murderous means."[9] Bimba finds little to praise in the national, political, or cultural traditions that, in any case, are contaminated by the fact of the United States as a commercial settler society.

Gramsci, writing in the 1930s, provides perhaps the most powerful alternative view of national history. In his *Prison Notebooks* he insists on the importance of the "southern" question for the Italian communists.[10] This region, the least industrially developed in the country, has traditionally been under the firm control of both the Catholic Church and segments of the underworld. It has been, overwhelmingly, an agricultural region marked by a system of land tenure based on small plots. In the century ending in the 1960s it provided the pool of unskilled and semiskilled labor for the developing northern regions of Italy and millions of immigrants to the United States, most of whom found employment in the mines, mills, and light industrial factories of the northeast and midwest. For Gramsci, the politics and economic relations of this area remained the Achilles heel of Italian socialism as long as it remained economically and culturally segregated from modernity, as long as Marxists insisted on characterizations such as "undeveloped" and "backward" to justify their failures with respect to the southern question.

Equally important, Gramsci argued that the struggle for hegemony required the party to appropriate the history of what he called the "national-popular collective will" in all its aspects: "the language question, the problem of intellectuals etc . . . the significance of Catholicism etc."[11] For Gramsci the failure in Italy to develop this national-popular will could be ascribed to the absence of a "Jacobin force" capable of mobilizing beyond the traditional opposition from within the aristocracy. But the problem for oppositional intellectuals was to locate those "urban social groups" who, having undergone industrial development, also possess sufficient cultural development to participate in the reform of "moral and intellectual relations." Thus, as Quintin Hoare points out, the concept of the national-popular should be understood as a part of Gramsci's theory of hegemony and not a bow to nationalism. Gramsci's whole theory of the possibility for social transformation depends on the success of the project of linking economic reform to moral and intellectual reform through the mediation of intellectuals. For without the latter, fascist and other authoritarian solutions to the capitalist crisis are more likely to the extent that the right successfully captures the moral high ground, while the left wallows in its economism.

Thus, cultural politics is much more than work at the level of "superstructure." Seen as part of a social totality, the national-popular will of which the investigation of a whole series of cultural questions is a necessary precondition, is conceived as perhaps crucial for the success of any possible struggle against the existing order. I want to suggest that where the communists grasped this fundamental point their political as well as their moral standing and influence among workers and intellectuals was profound. And the American example is perhaps one of the representative instances where a small, although militant and respected, Communist party grew to have substantial influence owing, primarily, to its ability to adapt, tacitly, the theory of the national-popular to its strategy. Of course, the Communist party did not have access to Gramsci's prison writings that became available only after the war. However, it is not difficult to show that Gramsci's perspective, far from opposing the main drift of international communist policy after the 1920s, was among its most articulated elaborations.

At the same time, the record is by no means entirely unambiguous. For, in line with Paul Gilroy's pointed critique of how the national-popular strategy can slip into nationalism, no better example can be adduced than that of the American popular front. During the 1930s the communists tirelessly pronounced their fealty to the principles of democracy as articulated by Jefferson, Lincoln, and Franklin D. Roosevelt. Earl Browder, the party's General Secretary, even went so far as to proclaim that "communism was 20th century Americanism," a blatant reference to patriotic ideology. While the Communist party participated in civil rights, labor, and other popular struggles during which it often collided with the national administration, it took pains to identify itself with *national* goals, especially those of the New Deal, and was widely perceived as a leading element of the left-wing of the Roosevelt coalition. After 1935 when the communists gave "critical support" to Roosevelt, criticism became increasingly scarce in its rhetoric and discourse (except for the period of the Nazi-Soviet pact when the party went, briefly, into opposition).

What follows is, in part, an autobiographical account, really a memoir, of the cultural politics of the popular front from the standpoint of a postwar teenager who was influenced by it, even after its heyday. I have employed this genre as a kind of ironic corroboration of Warshow's lament that in the immediate postwar years the decline of the party and the destruction of the popular front at the political level diminished its cultural influence to a lesser degree. Second, I want to argue that the fierce attack mounted by anti-Stalinist intellectuals gathered around *Partisan Review*—but also within larger university circles—was a sign that cultural politics retains a large degree of autonomy; in the United States the communist construction and valorization of popular democratic traditions—folklore, hidden aspects of American history, especially of blacks and workers, and on the widest plane their advocacy of the significance of America's "southern question" (both the land struggles and that against racism and white supremacy)—constitute a legacy that remains powerfully influential on contemporary debates, at least among intellectuals which, in my lexicon, includes political activists.

2

During the Depression, my family lived in the East Bronx (now the South Bronx) in what used to be called a "private house"—a building occupied by one to three families, including the owner. As for many Americans, these were hard years for us; my father did not have a steady job until the late 1930s when, thanks to the civil service and the Bronx County Democratic machine, he was appointed to a low-level clerical position in the Borough President's office. Actually, my mother was able to get more steady work as a salesperson in department stores even when she was fired after a failed sitdown strike at Alexander's Department Store in winter, 1938. I can remember that during the early years of the 1940s most of my friends' fathers were still out of work most of the time. One neighbor, whose daughter was in my elementary school class, made a living as a street singer; he played his banjo in neighborhood back yards hoping people would throw down money from their windows. Another kid's father was a frequently jobless truck driver, and several parents worked as cutters, pressers, or operators in the highly seasonal garment industry that was then, as now, the main factory employer in New York.

As for many other Americans, the war produced a reversal of fortune for my family—at least economically. Millions of men were drafted in the armed forces and millions more, including women, entered war production and the myriad of civilian jobs that had been vacated. In lieu of being drafted, my father was permitted to join the U.S. Army Engineers as a civilian employee, went to night school, paid for by the federal government, and became an engineering technician, an occupation he practiced until he suffered a heart ailment in 1960. Immediately after the war he worked for a private contractor but took the first opportunity to return to the public sector, when he was offered a job with the Port Authority and then moved to the Transit Authority where he remained until his forced retirement. My mother stayed in the retail trades until the mid-1950s when she became an office worker in union shops and rose to the job of bookkeeper by the time she retired at age 68, after almost fifty-five years as a wage earner.

Among a considerable group of first-generation American Jews from Eastern European shtetl background, both high and popular cultural formation was, as much as mastery of English, a vital part of the struggle for assimilation. English was not the household language in my grandparents' home, and my father's parents never really learned it. For him, as much as for the first-generation immigrant intellectuals discussed in Chapter 1, education—both schooling and other forms of cultural activities practiced in settlement houses, for example—was the key to making it out of the Lower East Side ghetto into which, as a three-year-old, he came from Lithuania with his parents and sister. My grandfather drove a seltzer wagon and, as a young boy, my father was obliged to help load, unload, and deliver the bottles. He graduated from high school which, in the 1920s, was no mean achievement and, owing to his talent for competitive sports, won a scholarship to New York University where, briefly, he studied journalism. His schooling was interrupted when he got the first of a series of short-lived reporting and writing jobs on newspapers. He worked for the old *New York World* and, when it folded, briefly for the Associated Press. My mother, whom he had married in 1932, insisted he get out of the newspaper game because it was killing him. After that, all of his writing was strictly for home consumption.

My father's father was a cantor in an orthodox Lower East Side synagogue; my grandmother, naturally, kept a kosher household. Although she was the leader of her home-town association and possessed a sharp wit, they were far from being intellectuals in the traditional meaning of the term. Nurtured by his leaders in the settlement houses where he spent his childhood and young adulthood getting a liberal education as well as playing basketball, my father lived the conflict between the popular and high cultures of his day. He surely knew the pop tunes, was a good dancer and a moviegoer, listened to the radio, and later watched television. While he was familiar with much of canonical American literature—Poe, Hawthorne, Melville, Dreiser—his tastes ran to nineteenth-century romantic poetry—Whitman, but especially Blake, Shelley, Byron, and Keats. Until he met my mother in 1931, he was almost completely ignorant of music and painting, except for popular music including the jazz to which young people danced in the 1920s.

The crucial event in my mother's life was the death of her own mother when she was twelve years old. From that moment until she married my father she lived alternately with relatives, especially her aunt Lil, her father's sister, a skilled dressmaker in the garment industry (she sewed the whole garment by hand as much as machine) and her father and his new wife, who had little use for a teenager in the house. Lil's husband was a Yiddish writer who became the labor editor of the *Jewish Daily Forward* for much of his career. Her mother's brother was a cloakmaker who boasted he was among the organizers of the union, but became a small landlord toward the end of his life.

My mother's family was inextricably linked to the socialist and labor movements, especially its "right" wing, that is, after the Bolshevik revolution, they were militant anti-communists. More important than their political sentiments and affiliations, they provided, together with my maternal grandfather who was a cutter, small businessman, and card player, an extraordinary high cultural environment in which my mother's considerable musical talent flourished. I recall, as a little kid, my grandfather playing the violin, holding it like a cello. My mother was a good, hard-practicing violinist with an impeccable musical ear, who nevertheless did not possess the confidence to attempt a professional career. She was also a talented painter—trained, at first, in the New York WPA Art School, then the Art Students League, and finally with a private instructor who greatly influenced her later work. Like many artists in the 1940s and 1950s she experimented with styles and landed on a very personal concern with spatial relations, although the surfaces of her paintings were varied, oscillating from figuration to abstract, geometric shapes.

Despite having left high school at fourteen, my mother was reasonably well read. But her talent for and knowledge of "classical" music and painting were, for my father, important attractions because he was well aware of the gaps in his own education and was eager to fill them. Even though he had a pleasant tenor voice, he never learned to play a musical instrument nor how to read music. But he became a voracious "classical" music fan, added to his love of poetry, and baseball and other sports. After the war, when audio technology exploded on consumer markets and there was some money, he became a prodigious record collector. Meanwhile, my mother made sure I attended the New York Philharmonic Young Peoples Concerts; she took me to the Museum of Modern Art and the Metropolitan Museum as well as the 57th Street art galleries; and, at the age of nine, enrolled me in the Bronx House Music School, a settlement for predominantly Jewish working-class kids and adults, where I studied the violin for five years with a teacher who was a violist in the Columbia Symphony Orchestra.

I never was much of a fiddler but, by the age of twelve, I "knew," if not to play, at least to recognize and sing the melodies of the standard repertoire of concertos—violin, piano, and cello; I could recognize and often sing many of the (late) Haydn, Mozart, Beethoven, and romantic symphonies, not only those of Schubert, Schumann, and Mendelssohn but also of the late romantics such as those of Dvorak and Brahms, and played a fairly large amount of baroque and chamber music in high school. By my teens, I had also read voraciously from the household and the public libraries the twentieth-century American novel canon from Dreiser and Frank Norris through Hemingway and other postwar writers—especially Farrell, dos Passos, Thomas Wolfe, and Fitzgerald—although it was not until later that I worked my way through Russian literature, especially Tolstoy, Dostoevsky, and those Soviet novelists who had been translated, especially Gorky and Sholokhov.

In the high school I attended, the High School of Music and Art, music students were required to take an art appreciation course and art students took music appreciation. The assumption, largely correct, is that few of us had even a superficial, much less an extensive acquaintance with the other discipline. I must admit that I learned something in class of ancient Greek, Roman, and renaissance art. But, if I had not been exposed to the galleries, I would have finished the course without having seen German expressionism, except Kandinsky, let alone American "abstract" expressionist painting and sculpture. For the art teachers had already absorbed the perspective promulgated by Clement Greenberg, who drew a direct historical line between cubism and Jackson Pollock, effectively marginalizing German expressionism, much less the mislabeled "social realist" painters of the 1930s and 1940s. Of course, we were shown Marsh, Hopper, and other members of the so-called "ashcan" school, but none was accorded much attention.

Similarly, for the performance curriculum Richard Strauss and Jan Sibelius were the composers at the furthest horizon of classical music. In orchestra and chamber music classes we played Bach, Haydn, Mozart, and Beethoven and the early romantics but rarely ventured beyond Brahms and Wagner. In the first postwar decade, the Copland school, including Leonard Bernstein and David Diamond, were the only contemporary composers we played; Schoenberg, Berg, Webern, Stravinsky, or even Ives were simply excluded from the repertoire. At the time, Music and Art was one of a select number of public schools which, like City College, had been designed to provide a leg up to children of the "deserving poor." The other special schools concentrated on science and technology and managed to become the recruiting ground for a significant portion of the scientific and engineering establishments—and still do. In contrast to the scholarship boys of my parents' generation and many of my contemporaries for whom the civilizing process—the passage from *both* the ghetto and the American popular culture of the streets was a prize devoutly to be attained—"classical" music and what was taken as high literature were on my plate from early childhood along with the Wheatena. What I had to fight for was to attain the same intimate knowledge of American popular culture. For my father, who was the guardian of the radio, the record collection, and the record player, had become an authentic classical music maven, except for most of twentieth-century music. At our house, my fight was to include jazz into the menu, a battle I won. However, when it came to the radio serials that gripped my imagination (especially the Lone Ranger), my father's power was quite absolute. The exception to the rule was the Shadow which, for a time, starred Orson Welles (for my father a kind of cultural hero); he tended to draw the line, although he gave me the money for the movies every Saturday afternoon.

While still in the southeast Bronx, my parents dragged me on their almost weekly pilgrimage to the Amalgamated, an hour's journey each way that involved taking two trolleys (later buses) through a large chunk of the borough to an isolated section near the Van Cortlandt Reservoir where the seven buildings of the cooperative stood as an urban oasis in what was still, in the mid-1940s, a semisuburban part of New York. Or so it seemed because the cluster of buildings we visited bordered Van Cortlandt Park which, although New York's largest, was almost totally lacking in civilized amenities such as amusements, a zoo, or extensive maintenance, although it boasted an eighteen-hole golf course that was the playground for my dentist-uncle and other professionals who gained entrance, during the Depression, into the development. Although hardly a "wilderness" area, there was extensive foliage, even woods in the middle of the park.

We didn't merely go there: every visit was a ritual. We usually ate one meal at my grandmother's house (she lived in an apartment building adjacent to the coop); then had a long visit with my father's eldest sister who had three boys, the middle one three months older than me. I was an only child, so I enjoyed playing ball with my contemporaries, although they were much better at almost any standard sport, except football. Then, we would end the day, sometimes for dinner, at my mother's aunt's house. There my two cousins, a boy and a girl, would take me in hand to listen to jazz on their small record player. Sure, I knew all the top forty ballads by Sinatra, Crosby, the Andrews Sisters, and the rest, but these were of little interest. The arrangements were slurpy, the interpretations kitschy—except Sinatra who had something different, but I was too arrogant to figure out what.

My mother's cousins, who were closer to my age than hers, introduced me to the New Orleans, Chicago, "Dixieland," and Swing schools of jazz, but it was not until later, when I was already in high school, that I listened to be-bop and "progressive" jazz, an encounter that was part of my first exposure, at the age of fifteen, to contemporary African-American culture, of which more below. In fact, most of my earlier acquaintance was with "white" appropriations of African-American blues and the New Orleans school of Jelly Roll Morton, Sidney Bechet, King Oliver, Kid Ory, the Dodds brothers— Johnny and "Baby"—and, of course, Louis Armstrong. But, apart from records, as a teenager I only heard white musicians in live concerts, mostly at the old Stuyvesant Casino on East 13th Street where Maxie Kaminsky, Muggsy Spanier, Wild Bill Davidson, and Pee Wee Russell among others offered rousing "Dixieland" versions of New Orleans jazz. I was tall for my age, pretended I was eighteen, and gained admission.

My great-uncle, who epitomized what is now a nearly extinct tradition of secular intellectual political and artistic culture within the Jewish working class, was nearly scandalized by the musical tastes of his children; after all, his daughter was an accomplished pianist and was attending Music and Art. Like many European-born socialists for whom western intellectual and aesthetic traditions constituted their *counterculture* to the dominant orthodox Jewish religion, he harbored nothing but contempt for popular entertainments, and regarded them as little more than the bread and circuses fed to the masses by capitalist masters. His fellow radicals in organizations such as the Jewish Socialist Bund, the main movement of East European secular Jews, the Workmens Circle, the organization of Jewish workers' welfare benefits, and the Jewish labor movement, chiefly but not exclusively centered in the needle trades, which had organized educational programs for immigrant Jewish workers: classes in English, but also labor history, Marxian economics, and politics taught at night in dimly lit union and fraternal organization halls. For them, as for the intellectual radicals of the same generation, "high" art was the only possible cultural legacy for a working class that sought to transcend the degraded conditions of its own subordinate existence. Thus, my great-uncle's living room was filled with the radio and record player's reproductions of the eighteenth- and nineteenth-century classical canon, while in my cousins' bedroom the contrapuntal sound of "classical" jazz was played on a much tinnier record player sotto voce. But my father, who was virtually a native-born American, caught on that something was happening that he did not quite understand so he bought records that he thought I would enjoy. I did and after a while he did too; he often reminded me that this music was similar to music he and my mother had danced to when they were younger. They would dance the two-step to the "progressive" as well as Dixieland jazz music in our living room, expertly, but, I observed (but never out loud), completely out of step with the most popular white dances of my time—the fox trot and especially the lindy.

Of course, by the 1940s, traditional jazz had already become an esoteric art form except, perhaps, in some parts of the south, and bebop and progressive jazz were well on their way to becoming what some critics like to call America's "classical" music. Those who listened to these genres rarely danced to them. The music was, instead, performed in concert halls and on college campuses; the older stuff to white, middle-class college students, and 'bop' in clubs as well as concert halls to both black and white middle-class people, especially intellectuals (probably because most of it was performed by small ensembles and reminded them of chamber music which, as is well known, became the mark of distinction between high and middle-brow classical music after the war). The process of incorporation of traditional jazz into high culture began with Milhaud's, Ravel's, and Gershwin's symphonic pieces in the 1920s; and its appropriation, in the 1930s, by classically trained white musicians such as Benny Goodman, Artie Shaw, and Glenn Miller, whose arrangers learned and then assimilated the work of the major figures of African-American jazz such as Count Basie and Duke Ellington into a hybrid swing genre that became the popular dance form of the big band era but also, especially in Goodman's small groups, a more or less conscious chamber form. And, after the decline of the big band, it found its way to concert halls where in both chamber and large ensembles, it found a new jazz-cult audience.

Even as a teenager I knew jazz was no longer a popular genre because we didn't dance to it, nobody really sang the standard riffs, and none of my neighborhood friends even listened to it. Like classical music, it was the choice of a select group of aficionados who formed a kind of consumer cult since almost none of us played it, or even wanted to learn to play appropriate musical instruments. But cult members read *Down Beat* and *Metronome* and other trade magazines, frequented the clubs, collected rare, out-of-print 78s with as much concentration as any classical collector, and flew out the door, taking the train to the Sixth Avenue record stores (now displaced by huge office buildings) to pick up the latest sides of Bird, Diz, Miles, and Monk. I remember how the "in" crowd in my high school loved to scandalize the teachers by walking the halls singing James Moody's recent release, "Moody's 'Mood for Love,'" rather than passages from Beethoven quartets.

By 1950, abetted by veteran's and FHA loans, many working-class and lower-middle-class people were buying one-family homes in the suburbs or in the less-developed areas of large cities. In 1951, my parents were able to move to the Amalgamated Cooperative Houses in the northwest Bronx (where most of their respective families had moved, including my father's mother and my mother's close relatives, including her father). The first building had been built with funds borrowed from the Clothing Workers' Union-owned Amalgamated Bank in 1927. My aunt and uncle got an apartment because they were part of the labor movement; my father's sister and her husband came in the 1930s, even though he was a dentist, for reasons that had to do, I suppose, with their ability to put up the down payment on the mortgage at a time when many clothing workers were walking the streets looking for jobs.

I had already left their house, dropped out of Brooklyn College in my freshman year after participating in a season of intense political combat against the repressive liberal college administration, and began my ten years of industrial labor by getting a temporary job as a helper on a truck that picked up and delivered fur coats to dry cleaning stores. I was laid off just before Christmas—a few weeks before my eighteenth birthday. By that time, I had already found another job, in a camera factory, and, a day after my birthday, I moved to New York's Hell's Kitchen, rooming with a friend.

On the night I was married, at age 19 in 1952, my new wife (a singer and recent Music and Art graduate) and I caught Ella Fitzgerald and Stan Getz at Birdland and completed the evening by digging Miles at the Half-Note down 52nd Street. We "appreciated" classical European music, but jazz captured our souls. New Orleans and Dixieland had real fans, just like any other music. But a large portion of the white (and black) followers of bop responded to its conceptual features, its intricate riffs, the brilliant improvisations on pop standards by the most famous jazz figures and, of course, were attracted, but not yet as participants, to the drug culture for which this genre seemed to be a crucial aspect. The musicians were as often as not classically trained, almost always could read music, and wove phrases from composers such as Debussy, Stravinsky, and other composers into their solos (later, with Ornette Coleman, among others, serial music found its way into the progressive jazz idiom). Many of the stars composed their own tunes, especially Ellington, Monk, Tad Dameron, Gillespie, and Bill Evans. The canonical tunes—Diz's "Salt Peanuts," particuarly the 1953 version with Max Roach's fantastic drum solo, Monk's "Round Midnight," Bird's "Ornithology," "Now's the Time," and "Billie's Bounce" and almost anything by Ellington—and the canonical performances were the common referents that identified members of the cult at concerts, in record stores, in school, even on Greenwich Village streets.

Our rebellion against the top forty "schlock" ballads performed by male crooners and their female counterparts, but also the "middle-brow" classical fare on the FM stations, was condensed in the work of the post-swing era that began with Coleman Hawkins, Basie, and Ellington in the late 1930s and reached its zenith with Bird, Diz, Miles, and Monk. For, by the late 1940s, it was plain that a new music based on African-American blues traditions had been born. Although rooted in tradition, progressive jazz was a wholly original form that in the mode of "classical" music was individually as well as collectively wrought. The key figures in the movement offered very different styles that, in time, competed with each other and spawned distinctive "schools" of progressive jazz.

Another group, drawn largely from the left, represented its revulsion against tin-pan-alley culture by leading and supporting what became known as the "folk" revival, some of whose products made their way, in the 1950s, onto the top forty charts; supported an off-broadway theater movement that, having been born as political theater in the 1930s, remained viable especially as a political theater throughout the 1960s and has been dying in the past twenty years. Parallel to these there developed a would-be literary "pop" avant garde, known as the Beats, that united "politicals" like Allen Ginsberg and Lawrence Ferlinghetti with populist, even conservative writers such as Jack Kerouac and Clellon Holmes in a full-throated rebellion against the pretensions to high art by the reigning literary modernists—Lionel Trilling, John Crowe Ransom, and the entire academic English establishment.

Only peripherally did I encounter the conventional literary avant garde or their antagonists, the Beats, but I was, in my teens and early twenties, intimately engaged in the off-broadway and later the off-off broadway theater. As a teenager, on the advice of my acting teacher, I frequented the New School's East Houston Street experimental Rooftop Theatre directed by the German leftist/expressionist Erwin Piscator, perhaps, together with G. W. Pabst, the leading figure in Weimar theater. There, for a contribution of one or two dollars, we received what amounted to an education in standard twentieth-century European drama—Strindberg's *Miss Julie,* Capek's *R.U.R.,* Andreev's *He Who Gets Slapped,* Gorky's *Lower Depths,* the Chekov repertory, and, needless to say, the Brecht canon, especially *Mother Courage, In the Jungle of the Cities, The Measures Taken,* and *The Caucasian Chalk Circle.* In the early 1950s, many of my friends saw plays directed by Gene Saks and Lloyd Richards that starred such actors as Sidney Poitier, Hesh Bernardi, Moses Gunn, Beulah Richardson (later Beah Richards), Alice Childress, Howard Da Silva, and Morris Carnovsky, many of whom had already been blacklisted by Hollywood. Richardson and Childress were also playwrights, as was Douglas Turner Ward, a young black writer who had been a key leader of the left-wing youth movement in the 1940s.

The cold war was already freezing the political environment, but the arts were, perhaps, the last holdouts to the curtain that was descending on left-wing politics. Although the blacklist had extended from Broadway to Hollywood, to art galleries where Clement Greenberg and other anti-Stalinist critics were doing their best to expunge remnants of what they considered to be kitschy communist-inspired social "realism," and to publishing houses, an alternative theater, music, and painting and publishing houses struggled for survival by creating their own audiences—many composed of young people who had not yet received the news that the left was dead.

The characterization of the artwork of Phillip Evergood, Ben Shahn, Anton Refreigier, Charles White, and William Gropper as "social realists" was merely a polemical device on the way to establishing what Greenberg called "abstract" expressionism as the true successor of French cubism and to declare, as did his master Leon Trotsky, that any possible political art in this era was inevitably tainted with mass culture, Stalinism, or both. Obviously, none of the leading left-wing artists of this period were exempt from modernist, especially expressionist and mannerist influences. For example, in Shahn's Sacco and Vanzetti series, as with other works that I saw in the huge Shahn retrospective at the Museum of Modern Art in 1948, the mark of Picasso's use of line leaps from the canvas; or the drawings of the African-American artists Charles White and Jacob Lawrence whose work also bears the cubist, as well as mannerist stamp. What Greenberg detested was the politics and that these artists were seen as occupying some of the same turf as his own favorites. Greenberg drew the line more sharply than would have been justified if the cold war (which definitively began in 1936–1937 for anti-Stalinist intellectuals) did not skew aesthetic judgment.

Of course, many expressionist painters, theater people, and writers were, despite Andre Zhdanov's notorious directive in behalf of socialist realism, drawn to the communist left, managing to survive the bitter era of ideological warfare on modernism waged by Stalinism until the 1960s. Clearly, astute critics such as Greenberg, Rosenberg, and Trilling could not have failed to notice the hybridity of left-wing art but, perhaps impelled by their political unconscious, chose to remain blind.

3

One day while playing stickball on the Bronx's Clinton Avenue, around the corner from where I lived, a slightly older kid on the block (he was fourteen and I was thirteen) invited me to attend a meeting of his "club" the following Friday evening. I knew he was involved in some "progressive" youth group and had often asked him about it. Finally, he extended the invitation and I went to a meeting. From that day and for the next decade or so, I was associated with American communist politics, ideology, and culture, an association that was only organizationally and politically severed by Khrushchev's secret report on the crimes of the Stalinist oligarchy.

Complementary to my love of baseball (as a kid I could recite the batting averages and other vital statistics of many major league players), and the discovery of jazz, my specifically American, as opposed to high (mostly European) cultural formation was also closely intertwined with the popular front, first as a teenager and then as a young parent who tried to imbue his children with anti-racist, anti-war, and pro-labor values. When you looked around in the late 1940s during my early teens to the late 1950s, when I was already the parent of two little kids, for the cultural forms that expressed these ideas in theater, children's concerts, records, and books, you were ineluctably drawn, even if unwittingly, to the legacy of the popular front. As teenagers, our dance music in the "movement" was culled from current hits, but also the Latino popular tradition and rhythm and blues, the dominant African-American popular form of the 1940s and early 1950s. Moreover, the teenage communist-inspired left was, like the Communist party in New York, Detroit, and Los Angeles, among other large cities, an "interracial" movement that, like my high school, attracted sons and daughters of the small black professional stratum as well as black political activists who had been part of the communist left since the 1930s.

Communist party policy in the years immediately following the war briefly took a distinctly sectarian turn in the wake of the Marshall plan and the Truman Doctrine that effectively isolated the Soviet Union and its affiliated parties in every western country, even France and Italy where they had attained mass proportions due to their leading role in the anti-fascist struggles. But left-sectarianism in politics did not translate into cultural leftism; the American party made only a feeble attempt to resuscitate one of its "third period" cultural policies—the creation of proletarian literature and art. The party and its cultural apparatus did encourage proletarian writing in the late 1940s and early 1950s. Writers such as Phillip Bonosky, Lloyd Brown, Robert Travers, Alexander Saxton, Thomas Bell, Margaret Graham, and Phillip Stevenson published novels about industrial workers' lives, all of which had distinctly political character. When they did not have communist protagonists, the leading characters were militant trade unionists—black and white.[12]

But, for the most part, communist cultural politics of the postwar period continued the program of trying to build a broad left on, among other platforms, the recovery and development of a native democratic "national-popular" tradition. At the same time the communist left tried to maintain, against the determined efforts of federal and state agencies to put them out of business, or at least separate them from the labor and other social movements, their own "counterculture" of children's and adult camps, theater groups, choral societies, and social benefits organizations which were tied to the still strong party-affiliated nationality organizations. Where private vigilante groups failed, in many cases the government succeeded, as in the case of the International Workers Order, the popular front's effort to create a social insurance program. Yet, on the whole, it was the virulent anti-communism of early 1950s American culture that did the job. In time, many people were simply too frightened to attend the cultural, much less the overtly political activities of the communist left.

One of the Communist party's most successful activities was its adult education programs. These were offered in non-credit schools that, especially in New York, Chicago, and Los Angeles where it had a fairly substantial membership and an even larger periphery, enrolled thousands of people in classes ranging from Marxist theory and political subjects to dance and theater. As a teenager I attended New York's Jefferson School of Social Science for about three years. I studied political economy in general outline and in a seminar on Marx's *Capital,* but also joined a theater group directed by an actor thoroughly versed in the "Stanislavsky" method (later shortened in its more mainstream incarnation to the "Method"). Between a close textual reading of the radical Torah *Capital,* an extraordinary year-long course in the history of philosophy that began with the pre-Socratics, passed through English empiricism, French rationalism, and German idealism, and ended with *The German Ideology* by Marx and Engels which, for my instructor Harry K. Wells, was the "outcome" and the last possible work in philosophy, and two years of sense memory, emotion memory, and the other techniques of the Method, I had received a pretty good education against which, in intellectual terms, my "special" high school and Brooklyn College paled in comparison.

In the early 1930s, these schools were typically named "Workers" School, but during the war they were renamed to conform to the party's efforts to claim and construct a national-popular democratic tradition. Jefferson, Lincoln, and Tom Paine were top choices, not only to adorn the signs and letterheads of the schools, but also for party-published collections of writings, edited by party historians such as Philip Foner, Francis Franklin, and Herbert Aptheker.

There is no doubt that the American Communist party "discovered" the concept of the "special oppression" of black Americans under the theoretical and political guidance of the Communist International. Yet interest in what was then known as the "national" question had been among the crucial Leninist innovations since the years prior to the First World War and was among the major concerns of Otto Bauer and the Austrian social-democracy.[13] Attention to issues of national liberation was not merely the result of directives from Moscow. In 1928, the American Communist party advanced the slogan that, owing to the special nature of their oppression and their demographic and geographic concentration, even majorities, in seven southern states, especially "black belt" rural counties, blacks constituted a "nation" within the American nation. In the subsequent decade, the "Negro question" claimed the political and ideological attention of many Leninists, including dissident communists, especially those who followed Trotsky out of the Communist party. However, since the party had fairly well-developed cultural and ideological apparatuses (at least in the comparison to the rest of the left), its efforts—first as the heart of the legal defense of the Scottsboro Boys and other cases of miscarriages of justice; in the struggle against Jim Crow practices in the south; and its more or less systematic work in folklore, black history, especially of slavery and reconstruction—earned it enormous prestige in sections of the black community. Moreover, its efforts for social as well as economic and political integration in the popular front period and after the war were unique for the period, in sharp contrast to the race "blindness" of the socialists and massive liberal ambivalence. Of course, as writers from Ralph Ellison and Chester Himes to Harold Cruse have shown, the Communist party was not free of racism—both in policy and in its internal practices—but was, after all, a predominantly white American movement.[14] However, on the evidence of recent social histories it can be shown that the one-sidedness of these judgments may be attributable to the situation of the early postwar period when the party, in its defensive posture, perpetrated some extremely brutal and destructive policies—alternately expelling and disciplining white members for "chauvinism" and black members for criticizing the party's frequent twists and turns from integration to proto-nationalism. To be caught in the wrong period with a position at variance with the current policy often invited anything from reprimand to expulsion. At the same time, communist-inspired and -supported cultural movements continued to contribute to the enrichment of American popular culture.

One of the crucial elements of the American construction of the national-popular front were the left-inspired folkloric studies of Charles Seeger and his son, the performer and songwriter Pete, John Lomax and his son Alan, and John Hammond—among the leading collectors and record producers of African-American blues. This work also uncovered a treasure of cowboy songs, Appalachian, religious and secular music, and labor songs, many of which consisted in putting new words to traditional religious tunes. And, of course, with the collaboration, even if not formally, of Roland Hayes, Marian Anderson, and Paul Robeson, who were themselves folklorists, these scholars plumbed some of the depths of African-American sacred music, especially the genres known as "spirituals"—most of eighteenth- and nineteenth-century origin—and Negro work songs, many of which were produced in prisons and especially on chain gangs (but not the gospel tradition that has only entered the commercial mainstream sporadically).

From the 1930s the popular front's work of cultural reclamation broke through its cult incarnations in two places: for almost a quarter of a century, ending about 1960, composers who themselves had adopted a perspective that attempted to recover and create a national-popular tradition, worked in symphonic and other classical musical forms that were imbued with themes borrowed from Anglo-American rural folk and popular themes. Of course, long before the popular front, Charles Ives and black composers such as William Grant Stills and Scott Joplin had been pioneers in this celebration of the national-popular at a time when most American "classical" composers such as Edward MacDowell and Charles Tomlinson Griffes were striving to emulate, in different ways, their European masters. When I was growing up, only Ives's Concord Sonata had entered the standard chamber repertoire but his symphonic works and his string quartets were barely known by even the most sophisticated music lovers. Stills's music was heard even more rarely and Joplin was virtually unknown until made popular by the film *The Sting* (1971).

Later, in the 1960s, spurred by the passionate advocacy of violinist Paul Zukofsky, pianist Gilbert Kalish, and conductors Harold Farberman and Leonard Bernstein, Ives's four symphonies, other works for orchestra, and his chamber works were recorded, although his place in the live performance canon is not especially secure to this day. It was not until the emergence of the second wave of American composers led by Aaron Copland and Virgil Thompson that the validity of materials drawn, essentially, from nineteenth-century folk, hymn, and patriotic tunes was gradually integrated by the leading symphony orchestras.

Of course, Copland was the most successful of the entire cohort of composers born around the turn of the twentieth century, in part because, at least until the 1950s, he carefully avoided the more radical modernisms of dissonant music or of serial techniques. Others—notably Ferde Grofe, Morton Gould, and Elie Siegmeister—were forced, by economic circumstances, to work for the movies, make their livings as arrangers and teachers, or, in the case of Gould, became conductors. Copland's itinerary from having been, in the early 1920s, a student of Nadia Boulanger in Paris, who informed all her American students of their obligation to their own national traditions, and his early "jazz" piano concerto (1926) which was in part a result of this teaching that Gershwin also took to heart, to the key figure in the rebirth of American classical music on (white) Anglo-American folk themes, is a story that can be told only in terms of the popular front influences.

Copland played a leading role in organizing the League of American Composers, an organization that in its early years closely paralleled the left-wing American Writers Congress and other politically inspired artists groups. But the degree to which he remained, at least until the end of the war, within the broad orbit of the popular front, is a large part of the explanation for what became his most influential body of work, despite his later move toward serial music. His compositions of this period—among them Appalachian Spring, Billy the Kid, El Salon Mexico, but also the cantata "A Lincoln Portrait" whose mythic populism is apparent—played an enormously important role in the development of a national-popular tradition in "serious" music.

Virgil Thompson, the *New York Herald Tribune*'s music critic, was also close to the left. His score for Pier Lorenz's Depression film *The Plow that Broke the Plains* was among the earliest applications of the new folk classical style to a popular form other than dance. Copland himself wrote several film scores and many scores for dance theater. The influence of his music on films and Broadway shows, especially in the work of Richard Rodgers whose artful combination of contemporary tin-pan-alley ballads with a folk style, exemplified in major hits such as *Carousel, Oklahoma, South Pacific,* and *The King and I*, dominated the American musical theater in the first decade after the war, and on Leonard Bernstein whose debt to Copland is both acknowledged and incalculable, did as much to establish a national-popular tradition in mainstream musical theater as anyone else. A host of Hollywood composers, notably Dimitri Tiomkin and Elmer Bernstein, adapted his style to the movies.

In Chapter 3, I discussed the importance of the work of British communist historians for dredging up the remains of a (past) popular working-class culture. This effort followed an earlier movement by socialist and liberal historians and found its way into the mainstream well before the 1960s. Owing to the relative isolation of American Marxist intellectuals from the academic mainstream until the 1970s, the Communist party was obliged to sponsor, more or less directly, the publication of a series of scholarly works on the American popular democratic traditions. The party's press published books by Francis Franklin, Herbert Morais, and Jack Hardy dealing with the American revolution; Herbert Aptheker, a professional party intellectual, produced a score of books on slavery, reconstruction, and other aspects of African-American history that, together with the work of Carter Woodson, a noncommunist black scholar working independently in the Negro colleges, began a process that fifteen years after the war when the direct influence of the party had already waned, revolutionized the writing of American history.[15] For even though Charles Beard, in his monumental *Rise of American Civilization,* had argued that the civil war was a second democratic revolution, it was the Marxists who drew most fully the implication of this thesis by linking slavery to processes of primitive capital accumulation as well as attempting to show that the slaves themselves were crucial agents of their own liberation.

Some of the most influential historians of slavery and reconstruction in the postwar period—Eugene Genovese, Herbert Gutman, Robert Fogel—cut their teeth on Aptheker's works as young communist historians. Fogel was national student director of the 1940s Communist party, but broke with the party (and Marxism) sometime in the late 1950s. Genovese remained a Marxist, sympathetic to leftist critiques of Soviet reformism until the fall of Soviet Communism, and Gutman, like many who had suffered the cold war hysteria in the universities, drifted away from the party orbit even as he became perhaps the most important historian that carried into the 1960s and 1970s the national-popular project. Gutman's work, of all social historians who emerged in the 1960s and 1970s, was closest to Thompson.[16] Their interest in the issues surrounding slavery and reconstruction was undoubtedly shaped by the party's focus on the "Negro Question."[17] Even when Genovese wrote his final "repudiation" of his mentor in the early 1960s it was, like many famous examples of intellectual patricide, suffused with the ambivalence of the prodigal. The major labor historian David Montgomery had been active in the United Electrical Workers, one of the major unions on the left wing of the labor movement, when *Labor's Untold Story,* Boyer and Morais' early 1950s history of the U.S. labor movement, was a canonical text. This book literally rewrote American labor history as the struggle between industrial and craft unionism; class struggle unionism versus class collaboration within labor's ranks and, characteristically, the struggle for "Negro" rights against white racism within the ranks of organized labor. As opposed to the conventional practice of portraying labor's "progress" as the activity of far-sighted leaders, of the sympathies of "progressive" mainstream politicians such as Woodrow Wilson and especially FDR, Boyer and Morais told the story, however crudely, as a rank-and-file labor struggle, following closely a version most prominently offered by William Z. Foster, the chief organizer of the 1919 Steel

Strike and later Chairman of the Communist party. Although Montgomery's work is by no means entirely in agreement with this account—he is much more sympathetic to craft workers of the late nineteenth century, for example—there can be no denying the influence of the "class struggle" approach in his latest and most comprehensive treatment of the period ending in the 1920s of labor's decline.[18]

These writers attempted to uncover the participation of groups George Rude was later to call the "crowd," in the American revolution, the civil war, and the period of rapid industrialization ending in 1910.[19] Their ideological perspective was "history from below" but also the idea of the two traditions of the revolution(s)—one of the national bourgeoisie and later the large corporate monopolies that sought to restrict democratic freedoms, especially for African-Americans and workers; the other, a radical democratic mass movement that was later to be given brilliant scholarly treatment by historians such as Bernard Bailyn whose *Ideological Foundations of the American Revolution* is perhaps the apogee of American popular-democratic historiography for the next generation after the popular front era; and, of course, Gutman, John Hope Franklin, and Eric Foner whose work on slavery and reconstruction continues this tendency in American historiography.[20]

The popular front was to be a broad alliance of communists and noncommunists, intended to defend and strengthen liberal-democratic institutions against the insurgent right. The communists extended their hands to non-Marxist historians such as Charles and Mary Beard, whose economic determinism the party intellectuals criticized, but ever so gently, especially during Charles Beard's militant anti-war stand in the years just prior to the U.S. entry into World War Two; the literary historian F. O. Matthiessen whose *American Renaissance* (1940) is perhaps the premier critical achievement of the sub-discipline of literature, American Studies; and especially Kenneth Burke, whose unorthodox, dramaturgical Marxist criticism was blended with Peirce's semiotics and neo-Aristotelian rhetoric to produce the most original works of cultural theory by any American;[21] in anthropology, Marxists such as Bernhard Stern and Gene Weltfish, but also non-Marxists such as Ruth Benedict and Franz Boas whose work supported the democratic and the anti-racist politics that were hallmarks of the party's line of the era.[22]

This alliance was particularly significant for it produced a rich tradition of both "scientific" and polemical works that systematically attacked the prevailing theories of physiologically based racial difference and substituted, with remarkable effect, a "culturalist" doctrine. In this position, physical differences did not account for economic, political, and social inequality. Rather, these inequalities were socially and historically constituted. While these views appear, until recently, unremarkable, in the context of the 1930s and even the 1940s Benedict's *Patterns of Culture* and Ashley Montague's *Man's Most*

Dangerous Myth: The Fallacy of Race were revelations, in their time, to even some varieties of mainstream liberal thought. By showing that racial difference was socially rather than biologically constituted they helped prepare the intellectual ground for not only the civil rights movement, but for broad assumptions of American jurisprudence that followed their approach.

As a teenager I frequently attended folk song concerts in a form peculiar to the pop front tradition, the Hootenanny. Sponsored by *Peoples' Artists,* an organization of left-wing folk musicians that included Pete Seeger and Woody Guthrie among others, these events brought thousands of radical kids of my generation to what had been forgotten or, in some cases, suppressed traditions of protest, labor, African-American, and rural American music. These events were showcases for the rich folkloric work of the party and its friends, but equally important they provided a stage for some artists who were later to find space in mainstream popular music. I heard Odetta, Peter Yarrow, Woody Guthrie before he was struck down by disease, The Weavers, Cisco Huston, and Ledbelly. Our songs around campfires under the George Washington Bridge, at youth group meetings, and in our homes were the same songs that spearheaded the "Folk Song Revival" that forced its way onto the charts ten years later. We sang "Tsena, Tsena," "Good Night Irene," "The Hammer Song," "Kisses Sweeter Than Wine," and dozens of tunes that never became big hits, but were later to influence the hybrid genre, folk rock, especially Bob Dylan, who in this tale is surely the link between the pop front, especially Guthrie's music, and the 1960s popular mainstream.

The youth and student left that constituted the audience for this music in the years just before the full blast of cold-war repression were of an intermediate generation, neither part of the Depression era nor fully integrated into postwar culture. Some of us were from professional and small business families, genuine sons and daughters of a radicalized middle class that had suffered its own Depression-made disappointments. But, unlike the student movement of the 1960s, many of us were children of working-class families that had been radicalized by the labor upsurge of the 1930s, by the immense prestige enjoyed by the Soviet Union during the Depression, especially among a fraction of Eastern Europeans and labor militants. Or, we came from families for whom the New Deal, which itself adopted some features of the popular front after 1936, provided the first opportunity in a lifetime for legitimate politicization.

For us, this music had resonances of political and cultural resistance, and functioned as one of the major elements of a counterculture that was much broader than the jazz cults to which I was loosely affiliated, broader for its embodiment of a worldview that tried to integrate a democratic-populist political ideology with aesthetic elements. One of its characteristic features was consonant with the popular-front fusion of anti-racist and anti-war politics and art, a theoretical and artistic tradition that had already been defeated by the late 1940s, largely by cultural intellectuals who, as we saw in Chapter 1, held as a cardinal principle of critical theory that art should be exempt from conscious political motives in an era when Stalinism ruled political art.

We had acquired an extensive repertoire of union songs, some of American origin, others from the English labor movement. And we knew folk songs from around the world—from Israel, the Soviet Union, Africa, and Latin America—a sign of our internationalism, even as we struggled to identify with some native American tradition, even if it was largely constructed. Of course, we sang Spanish civil war songs—the anthem of the Thaelmann Column, "Freiheit," and the songs of the Abraham Lincoln Brigade, but also the Spanish tunes such as "Viva la Quinte Brigada." Needless to say, we had no knowledge of the anarchist tradition or, indeed, the left-Marxist Poum that fought bravely against Franco. If they had songs, we were unaware of them and probably would not have sung them, a testament to our narrow education about what we knew had been perhaps the most significant anti-fascist struggle of the interwar period.

We dressed like "bohemians": the girls wore long dresses, peasant blouses, and long skirts and kerchiefs around their necks; and, of course, there was the obligatory long hair which, however, had not yet caught on for boys. We wore jeans, corduroy pants, work shirts, and leather jackets, all purchased at Army-Navy stores, which often provoked surprise and laughter among the clerks who took our money. My girlfriend from age fourteen to age sixteen wanted to dance with Martha Graham, Jean Erdman, and especially Pearl Primus. Her black schoolmate was studying at the Primus studio and working with Donald McKayle. Some of my schoolmates were trading their fiddles for guitars and banjos. My classmate, an artist, daughter of a communist house painter, went out with Dave Sear, at the time a budding banjo player who, some said, was already better on the instrument than Pete Seeger.

At school, our teenage organization (part of High School Young Progressives of America, an outfit founded in connection with the presidential campaign of Henry Wallace in 1948, but which outlived that campaign by a few years) had about 200 members in a high school whose enrollment was about 1800. We met in a room near the campus; needless to say, no student political organizations were recognized by the Board of Education. Around the city, there were clubs in about 20 high schools with a combined membership of maybe 2,000. In these years, Communist party university student clubs (the name, dropped during the war as part of the party's self-dissolution, was restored by the party as a sign of its resolve to break with past "opportunist" errors) on the four public college campuses, at Columbia, and NYU. In New York, the combined memberships of New Left groups was never larger at the height of their influence, 1968–1969, although they were more influential because they were a genuinely *generational* as much as an ideological movement. The Communist party's relatively strong presence in U.S. politics following the war was, to a large extent, still configured by its prominent role in the 1930s labor movement and the wartime unity against fascism. The left developed no new and imaginative political or cultural forms after the war. Of course, the New Left was nothing if not an *original* movement even if a considerable number of its early adherents were daughters and sons of communists, socialists, and left-liberal New Dealers.

Most of all, songs were powerfully effective in providing glue to our more or less isolated counterculture whose esoteric elements were all too obvious to us. Even when they were not ostensibly songs of resistance as were the labor, the Spanish Civil War, and African-American songs, they enabled us to identify with the oppressed and exploited and, in the terms appropriate to any subculture, they were markers of distinction. Largely influenced by the war and our collective perception that America was rapidly drifting to the right, our cultural practices were strongly democratic and anti-fascist rather than socialist. For the postwar Stalinist left, socialism had become, despite brave rhetoric, a millenarian utopia, more part of our culture than our practical political activity.

Thus, our teenage culture—the dances and other social events such as frequent picnics, the dress codes, the alternative education in working-class and revolutionary theory and history, and especially the music—became markers of social distinction that provided cohesion for this fragment of a generation. Distinction from what? In cultural terms, from the mainstream music, movies, and recreations that were offered to kids. For example, we were largely insulated from the white top forty during the 1940s and early 1950s, the era when rhythm and blues was still segregated black music. The kids in my crowd knew and danced to the R and B bands and, in other respects—literature and the theater but especially music—had more than a passing acquaintance with African-American culture.

More to the point, the lefts, including the non-communist groups, were among the few contexts of interracial social and political relationships in this country. "Our" crowd was not, in any sense, truly integrated, if by this term is signified a nearly equal proportion of blacks and whites. However, in high school we had social friendships and sexual relations between black and white kids, some of which culminated in marriage and long-term relationships. Our dances and parties were *typically* interracial and interethnic at a time when this kind of activity was extremely rare (although not as rare as today when racial and class housing and economic distinctions are much more pronounced than forty years ago, in part because of the mass suburbanization of the white working and lower-middle-class population).

When I moved to Newark, New Jersey, in 1953 to work in an industrial plant in a town a few miles away, we lived in the middle of the black community. A year later, I had become active in the NAACP Youth Council and, when I went to parties and dances, felt at home with black young people and their music because I was accustomed to interracial social groups and had been dancing to black music for years. Moreover, in those years, in addition to singing "Somewhere Over the Rainbow," which for a brief moment symbolized the NAACP's slogan "Free by '63," but also the aspiration of its predominantly black Essex County membership to end discrimination and racial oppression, we sang spirituals and, of course, R and B hits like "Great Pretender" and "Earth Angel" (in the vernacular, e.g., "will you be mi–ine . . ."). When Kay Starr, Elvis, and Peggy Lee "shamelessly" adopted the style and even some of the songs for their own, we bitterly criticized them. But, secretly, some of us realized that even incorporation was something of a political and social victory for the incorporated.

I never gave up my love for "high" art and, indeed, when I became smitten with the Frankfurt School in the 1960s, I "saw through" pop front culture and believed, for a time, it was to be understood merely as the inevitable communist accommodation to nationalism and patriotism that accompanied popular front strategy. Through my newly acquired intellectual lenses it appeared to be nothing more than a refurbished populism—shorn of any critical content. In my personal musical canon Copland and Bernstein were ditched in favor of high modernists such as Schoenberg, but especially Berg and Webern, Mahler and Shostakovich and, except for the rich historical and contemporary African-American musical heritage and the labor songs that, however, were almost never sung by workers on or off the picket line, I all but jettisoned the American folk song (except on long car trips when I regularly unfurled my repertoire for my kids in order to forestall boredom).

Needless to say, some of these judgments were made in the context of the 1960s when many of us who had lived through the demise of the *legitimacy* of American communism, even if not (yet) its organizations. The popular front produced a lot of execrable literature, but also some works of genuine worth in stories, novels, and plays. Its literature leaned heavily on allegories of working-class heroism and betrayal, of the crisis of a middle class jolted from its complacency by the Depression, and, especially in Trumbo's *Johnny Got His Gun* and Irwin Shaw's *Bury the Dead*, on themes of the injustice and the tragedy of war, from the perspective of its victims, "ordinary people."

4

Yet the ideological warfare between party critics and the "high" modernist tradition—of the Europeans Dostoevsky, Flaubert, Joyce, Kafka, Eliot (insofar as he was identified as a British poet), among the Americans Pound,

Faulkner, and Henry James—marked the party, in the eyes of modernist critics, as philistine. The popular-democratic canon, constructed by American
progressive literary intellectuals of the 1920s and 1930s, notably Van Wyck
Brooks and especially the towering figure of Vernon Louis Parrington[23] had,
by Trilling's admission, become the literary common sense of these decades.
In fact, Trilling delivered the main attack on this tradition in his essay "Reality
in America," first published in *PR*, February 1940. The essay appeared as the
lead piece in the collection that elevated him to national prominence, *The Liberal Imagination* (1950), and it might be safely claimed that it contributed
more to sinking the influence of popular front literary culture than any other
single work.

In an obvious effort to draw an essentially uninformed audience into his
argument because he assumes they have been shaped by Parrington's aesthetics, the essay begins by noting Parrington's "influence on our conception
of American culture . . . is not equaled by that of any other writer of the past
two decades."[24] It is precisely this influence that Trilling seeks to upend, especially his status as "standard and guide" for those who seek to "take account of the national literature."[25] Parrington may have been influential but,
according to Trilling, he "was not a great mind; he was not a precise thinker
or, except when measured by the low eminences that were about him, an
impressive one. Separate Parrington from his informing idea of the economic
and social determination of thought and what is left is a simple intelligence,
notable for its generosity and enthusiasm but certainly not for its accuracy or
originality."[26]

The rest of the essay is a brilliant explication of how Parrington came to
make such mistakes as comparing James Branch Cabell to Herman Melville.
Trilling traces this apparent lapse to his fundamental realist philosophy—the
idea that reality is "one and immutable, it is wholly external, it is irreducible."[27] On this foundation, according to Trilling, Parrington constructs judgments of particular authors by evaluating the degree to which the artist's work
reflects and is true to this solid, grim, and external reality. But Trilling detects
a contradiction in Parrington's thought that forever condemns his work to
mediocrity. For Parrington there is an unbridgeable gulf between mind and
reality that relieves the artist of responsibility for his own work. In brief, Parrington has no critical basis for a moral sense.

Later, Trilling gets to the real objects of his criticism: the then Communist
critic Granville Hicks, whose *The Great Tradition* (1935) was in some ways
for the 1930s Stalinist left what Parrington's *Main Currents* had been for
progressive nationalist critics a decade earlier; and F. O. Matthiessen's review
of Theodore Dreiser's last novel *The Bulwark,* which the reviewer, against the
preponderance of his own fine aesthetic sensibility, praises. Trilling is, after
all, trying to overcome the "vulgar materialism" that characterizes American

liberal and progressive thought, now abetted by the Stalinist left, a materialism that could exclude Poe and James from the national literary canon on the ground that their works were improbable from the perspective of the facts of American life. In his own terms, he wants to replace it with a sense of the "dialectic" that exists in some authors where "reality" and "mind" are understood in their mutual relation, where the social and economic determination of an artwork is no longer sufficient to remain the basis of judgment. Specifically, Trilling's modernist "guide" depends, in the last instance, on his own conception of the significance of form. This turns on the ideas of "style" and "sensibility," qualities possessed, amply, by Henry James and lacking to the extreme in the major figure of the Parringtonian canon, Theodore Dreiser.

In this and other writings, Trilling is concerned to recreate the nineteenth-century public for which literature was the presupposition of all thought. Clearly, Dreiser's novels do not qualify as literature any more than Parrington is a standard and guide to American literary criticism and history. Equally damning, the political literature and theater that emanated from the party's large cultural orbit were labeled by anti-Stalinist critics as kitsch—or worse—mass culture. In fact, although after 1935, communists became more "tolerant" as writers and critics were drawn closer, at least politically, to their anti-fascist goals, much of their ideological stance remained undisturbed. Its major elements were that art should be, among other things, a "weapon" in anti-fascist struggle (as it had earlier been in the "class" struggle), the leading elements of which had to be democratic and popular and, if possible, heroic. This position did not preclude the left's support of the grim, largely pessimistic dramas of an Odets or Arthur Miller or the ironic anti-fascist plays of Bertolt Brecht that were performed by left-wing theater groups throughout the popular front period and beyond. Nor did the left theater turn its back on the canon, either in literature or in drama. Chekov, Ibsen, and Shakespeare were part of the repertoire of many groups. But there was no theoretical or ideological basis for an aesthetics that could cast a wider net beyond political art, except that offered by Trotsky, whose writing was completely suppressed within the communist movement and its periphery, or Lukacs, whose writing was virtually unknown, except to some intellectuals, until long after this era. What the party and its critics called "realism" was never unalloyed, especially with modernist style; nor was the modernist tradition free of seamless narratives.

In fact, the realism/modernism debate of this period was *overdetermined* by turf fights, the political disputes between Trotskyists and Stalinists and by definitions constructed by critics on both sides. Clement Greenberg proposed a modernist canon in which anything approaching figuration was strictly excluded, even the works of contemporary artists whose work is plainly dissonant. Robert Warshow, whose film criticism appeared regularly in various intellectual magazines, especially *Commentary,* condemned such major films of the popular front as Billy Wilder's *Best Years of Our Lives* and *Pride of the Marines* for their crude, propagandistic content and their sentimental sensibilities. And, with enormous style, Trilling waged the literary war in behalf of a morally responsible, intellectually sophisticated literature.

Among the modernists themselves there was always a division between those like Ransom for whom poetry occupied a privileged, even exclusive place in the pantheon of great literature precisely because its materials, language, dominated whatever external content it might employ, and others such as Trilling whose main interest was in the modernist novel and who sought to generate a new literary canon based on it. Among the reasons for this difference was between Trilling's fundamental ethical approach to literature and the New Criticism's preoccupation with form, a focus shared by the radical critic Kenneth Burke. (Although Burke always understood the *ideology* of form.) Burke's major premise, that the referent of representations was signs, is, of course, widely acknowledged today. His three studies in the social semiotic of representation posited a dramaturgical viewpoint on language. Utterances derive their meaning from two contexts—the immediate environment and the social and historical frame; and from the rules of communication in which rhetoric is not regarded, as in its common usages, as subterfuge but as a strategy of persuasion that is intrinsic to communication. The "content" of form involves socially constituted "motives" of which actors may or may not be aware. Thus, whereas for Michael Fried "theatricality" is per se a kind of counterfeit formal device, Burke comprehends the dramatic mode as intrinsic to discourse itself. In this framework, his category "motive" may be translated as "interest," a necessary premise of communication as well as rhetoric.

Of course, most of Greenberg's writings in the late 1930s and throughout the 1940s are focused on the ideology of form and consistently link the formal elements of painting to its social and political significance. But, unlike Burke, whose analysis precludes evaluative judgments of any particular discursive mode, following his own Marxist as well as modernist predilections, Greenberg rigorously maintains the distinction between ideology (which, in the case of painting, may produce the untruth of mass audience art) and "truth"—the subversive practice of the artist whose refusal of figuration and of explicitly social content signifies (his or her) rejection of mass culture and its middle-class permutations—the counterfeit practices of kitsch. In this reprise, Greenberg and Trilling are, from somewhat different perspectives, the key figures in the struggle to construct a modernist ideology of art, even if they construct the formal requirements of critical judgment somewhat differently.

Although Trilling and Rahv were by no means indifferent to formal considerations, their writing was, especially after the Moscow trials, obsessed with moral aspects of politics. Of course, Trilling himself derived his ideological framework as much from Matthew Arnold's critique of the consequences of unbridled industrialism as he did from Marxism; indeed, in the end, the triumph of Stalinism drove him, as well as his erstwhile radical colleagues, "back" to liberalism, literally back to Matthew Arnold who, in the interest of pedagogic excellence and aesthetic humanism, explicitly exempted art from the democratic imperative, except insofar as liberal democracy provided the best environment within which art might flourish.

However, despite the accusations of their detractors, heroic themes do not dominate the left-wing drama, fiction, and poetry of either the era of proletarian art or of the popular front. To be sure, the intonations of socialist realism in which a worker or middle-class protagonist discovers the imperative of social consciousness and/or political struggle infused many Soviet novels during the Stalin era (we read those too: I particularly remember the Soviet novel *How the Steel Was Tempered*), whose proletarian moralism had its American imitators. In this respect the "proletarian" novels of the earlier, sectarian period—Jack Conroy's *The Disinherited*, Robert Cantwell's *Land of Plenty*, even John Steinbeck's *In Dubious Battle*, Mike Gold's *Jews Without Money*, and Henry Roth's *Call It Sleep*—are more interesting than the triumphalism of Ruth McKenney and Clara Weatherwax, who carried on the tradition of the proletarian novel or of Howard Fast, whose battery of historical novels in the 1940s, little more than popularizations of communist historiography, sold hundreds of thousands of copies.

The left-wing novels of the early 1930s are, in the main, unsentimental narratives of working-class, everyday life, except Steinbeck's which can be read as an American version of Brecht's allegorical "The Measures Taken." Steinbeck, like Brecht, poses the dilemma of humanism in the context of revolutionary class struggle and asks whether there is not a different morality that governs social relations in these situations. In Steinbeck's account of an agricultural workers' organizing effort, the strike leader pitilessly uses the occasion of the death of a striker as a weapon. Similarly, there is absolutely no "coming to consciousness" even in a mystical form in Conroy's account of a young man's wanderings during the early years of the Depression (as in the last scenes of Steinbeck's pop front novel, *Grapes of Wrath*, where in various ways the main characters, Tom Joad, his mother, and the preacher, Casey, each express sentiments ranging from populism—"we are the people"—to an abiding faith in mass stirrings). Roth's and Gold's fictional autobiographies, seen through the eyes of first-generation youth, straddle the borders between American culture and that of the Jewish working-class ghettos of the early third of the twentieth century. Roth's is veritably a modernist work of psychological introspection (understood in these terms only retrospectively) and the self-consciousness of Gold's fictional memoir is mostly in the coming-of-age genre of American fiction rather than anything resembling social realism.

The narratives of the middle-class crisis such as the plays by Clifford Odets, Josephine Herbst's novels, or Isadore Schneider's poetry tilt more to pathos than heroism. In Odets's plays of this period such as *Awake and Sing, Rocket to the Moon,* and *Golden Boy,* the political statement is embodied in the collective unconsciousness of the family whose disintegration takes place right before the viewer's eyes, but which its members cannot see as connected to the economic and social context. Except for *Waiting for Lefty,* a public agitational play, Odets is a chronicler of private troubles that, nevertheless, have social meaning. In this sense, he is, despite the specificity of his middle-class Jewish themes, a representative writer of the American Depression. Lukacs might have called Odets's immensely popular dramas instances of "naturalism" rather than realism for their documentary quality, especially the grim everydayness of the situations and the determinate outcomes. Yet Odets's work is suffused with the classical conflicts of the bourgeois family in the wake of both the sexual and social implications of modernity. The dentists, whose travail is the subject of *Rocket to the Moon,* live tawdry, even banal existences. When their energy is not absorbed by bills, one can find diversion only in extramarital affairs which, in Odets's portrayal, are exemplars of anti-romance. *Golden Boy*'s Faustian themes manifest themselves inside the supremely bourgeois aspirations of an immigrant Italian father (an echt petty bourgeois merchant whose best friend is a Jewish radical intellectual) for his talented violinist son. The son, Joe, smitten by the lure of fast money but also rebelling against the brutal discipline required of a professional musician, chooses to make his fortune as a boxer, breaking his father's heart in the process. This rupture is signified by the scene where Joe comes home from a fight with a broken hand, the proud stigmatum of the gladiator, but a catastrophe for any musician. Having rejected Art, the prodigal son is more deeply sucked into the vortex of success and its standard props: money, business, and exotic women.

For dissident left modernists these plays and novels were nothing more than ideologically constructed Stalinist efforts that pandered to degraded mid-cult taste.[28] Odets was perhaps the quintessential popular front artist to the extent that his plays were directed to the middle class able to afford the price of a Broadway show. In contrast to "mass cult," entertainments that were consumed by the workers and lower-middle-class people, Odets was an artist of what Macdonald called "mid cult," work that could more properly be labeled, in Clement Greenberg's terms, kitsch for it borrowed the themes of high tragedy but realized them badly. However, the categories of mid cult and mass cult miss in their dismissive sarcasm what is historically significant about this work. Odets was concerned with the boredom that suffuses the lives of middle-class Jews who have, to some degree, managed to "make it" in the modern world.

Like Orson Welles's dark ruminations on various moments of twentieth-century American life—especially *Citizen Kane* (the ultimate emptiness of ruling-class everyday life), *The Magnificent Ambersons* (the disintegration of what Wright Mills called the "old" middle class), and the postwar films *Lady from Shanghai,* a fable of working-class innocence in the dens of the duplicitous and decadent mighty, and especially the macabre deconstruction of small-town justice, *Touch of Evil* (*Kane* and *Magnificent Ambersons* were passionately supported by the popular-front left), the works of popular front artists were more complex than either their detractors or their acolytes imagined. For these works achieved with different degrees of success, in formal terms, a collective narrative of the underside of the American success story. In none of his work, or in the work of other directors who participated in the attempt to come to terms with the specificity of American social life, are heroic themes attributed to socialist realism in evidence, except as deconstructed objects.

For example, with the exception of the sentimental and immensely popular film *It's a Wonderful Life,* which is virtually a case study in popular front democratic and anti-monopoly rhetoric, and is characteristically read differently today, all of Capra's protagonists are anti-heroes or, in Preston Sturges's *Sullivan's Travels,* perhaps his best film, hopelessly guilt-ridden intellectuals whose misadventures in the quest for proletarian "authenticity" in the lower depths of Depression America contain the message that whereof one cannot speak, be silent. Yet, even in Capra's small-town epic, there is little attempt to glorify ordinary life. For Capra, it is clear that the mundane tasks of a small-town banker, however fulfilling a life of service may be in abstract terms, is mostly suffused with frustration, routine, and crises that can only be made romantic with the assistance of an angel, a kind of deus ex machina who must constantly prod the ever-fading, semisuicidal hero. Viewing it today, we can see that, despite its conciliatory, sentimental ending, *It's a Wonderful Life* remains, for the most part, a searing critique of middle-class existence in an era when small-town life was giving way to the corporate/urban sprawl.

Yet, there is the counterinstance of John Ford's *Grapes of Wrath* that fulfills virtually every heroic and populist intention of the left in this era. In Steinbeck's narrative, all of the elements of populist ideology are present: the expropriation of farmers from the land; the exploitation of agricultural workers and their struggle to resist; the dignity and truth of ordinary people as opposed to the banks, the corporations, and the government (except the New Dealers who are pointedly contrasted in their humanity with local police forces, as the only visible representations of the local state). These conflictual film styles reveal the degree to which the "progressive" filmmakers of the Depression (and the war) were representative figures of otherwise opposing camps. The party critics might approve or disapprove of this or that novel or film (e.g., Hammett's distinct epitaph to proletarian ascendancy, the various adventures of the Continental Op, later transfigured into the Sam Spade film, radio, and television series), but this did not prevent him from retaining his Communist party membership.

This is not the place to construct a canon of popular front art. Welles and his collaborator John Houseman; John Ford, whose film treatment of *Grapes of Wrath* would certainly qualify; John Huston, particularly his version of B. W. Traven's Marxist novel *Treasure of Sierra Madre*; Howard Hawks; and Frank Capra were the chief agents of national-popular dissemination inasmuch as film, together with radio, where Houseman and Welles began, had outstripped, in their influence, all other art forms. John Dos Passos' trilogy *USA* may have been the most important radical novel of this century, but it was only the most powerful of a genre of left *modernist* works that were entirely within the purview of popular front culture, modernist in the conventional meaning of the term: snapshots of a "fragmented" totality seen from the writer's standpoint that is situated in the text as the constituent from which all representation emanates.

It is plain that Dos Passos is deeply influenced by Joyce's fractured narratives that are framed by vernacular speech. If these novels lack Joyce's psychoanalytic perspicacity, much less his protean grasp of western literary culture, the Dos Passos of *USA* has, nonetheless, abandoned the seamless narrative and detailed character development for the subject/object borders. Here, history is told in allegorical terms, a history that ruptures the everyday as much as it mediates the self. Clearly this is as much a popular allegory as James Farrell's *Studs Lonigan* and the first novel of the Danny O'Neill series *A World I Never Made*. Yet the politics of these works had nothing to do with the heroic modes ascribed to social realism. (Even though Farrell, identified with the narrative and linguistic decodings of social realism, was to engage in bitter controversy with his fellow Trotskyists about the relation of literature and society.[29]

Of course, black communists like Richard Wright and Langston Hughes, whose writing coincides with these grand narratives of the American denouement, cannot be equated with the socialist realist genre. Wright's work, long before Ralph Ellison became the preferred black novelist of the critical avant garde, is plainly in the Dostoevsky tradition, not only in his novella *The Man Who Lived Underground,* but also his later novel *The Outsider.* Nor can the novels of Myra Page and Josephine Herbst, each of whom managed to maintain an individual voice within a collective political project, be easily subsumed under neat critical categories. It is fashionable to argue that both Hughes and Wright were always at odds with the party, which would explain why they were able to produce work that was of a higher quality than most of the hack writing of the popular front era. And it is true that the party line on the "Negro" question changed from militant defense of black nationality during the early 1930s—if not nationalism, in the "third" leftist period—to an integrationist, civil rights position when the party informally joined the Roosevelt coalition in 1936 (but briefly returned to the black nation thesis in the 1940s). Wright's bitter *Native Son* (1938) and *Black Boy* (1940) were written during this period, even if Hughes's political poetry of the late 1930s and early 1940s bears affiliation to sincere integrationism rather than nationalist anger. Two of his most famous poems, "Let America be America Again" and "I, too, Sing America," contrast the democratic claims of American ideology with racialist practices, proclaiming black loyalty to the dream of equality within the American context.

Yet, in the famous Scottsboro civil rights case, struggles for jobs and relief in black ghettos, and against Jim Crow hiring, promotion, and membership policies in basic industries and in the labor movement, the Communists, or at least a portion of their black cadre, remained genuinely radical. And the party line on the cultural front was much more flexible during the popular front. Wright's *Native Son* is by no means constrained by the softer Communist party policy on racism after 1936. Nor could most works of literature, poetry, or theater, other than overt propaganda pieces, be traced to some kind of direct intervention of the political apparatus. Rather, artists as much as other party members and party sympathizers followed the cultural debates in the party and left-liberal press, and interpreted these policies in their own way. Sadly, many of the errors are those of the artists themselves whose internalized political aesthetic, if not their loyalty, sometimes overwhelmed their artistic and political judgment.

Popular front culture was pro-American, even if of an "other" America than that portrayed in mainstream media, school textbooks, and artistic representations. The other America was the world of the grim, seemingly impermeable reality many writers and painters assiduously avoided. And it was one that had been systematically excluded from dominant representation— Woody Guthrie's Okies, and especially the African-American heritage and those of working people and farmers. Although the left-wing intellectuals cannot alone claim credit for this work of cultural scholarship and dissemination, their single-minded dedication to this work, propelled by socialist motives (or, more accurately, because they were so motivated) was *indispensable* for the effort to produce a national-popular countertradition to that proposed in the late 1930s by the American defenders of high culture. Such works as Richard Boyer and Herbert Morais's popular labor history, *Labor's Untold Story,* first published in the 1940s; Aptheker's many works of "Negro" history; Philip Foner's monumental multivolume history of the American labor movement and his edited collection of the writings of Frederick Douglass; the "labor" plays of Clifford Odets, Irwin Shaw, John Howard Lawson, Albert Maltz, and Paul Peters, and the deeply flawed but moving film *Salt of the Earth* have been read and seen by millions of Americans and have contributed to sustaining this culture.

But the greatest and perhaps most enduring achievement of the era was its attentiveness to the *oral* traditions of working people, black and white. For songs and stories are the expressive forms of nonliterate cultures. A similar effort was made by Irish, Welsh, and Scottish folklorists, but the process of recovering the national-popular has been (mostly) done by historians who, as we saw in the last chapter, privilege documents produced by and for craftsmen. In the United States the social history that arose from the impetus provided by civil rights and other popular left movements of the 1960s, inspired by E. P. Thompson, constructed a working-class past in republican images. As a result, we have an extremely meager record of the history of workers, who from the perspective of industrial hierarchy are called "unskilled" in part because they are unlettered. For republicanism is crucially associated with Jefferson's conception that the ideal citizen is "educated," that is, able to constitute a public sphere as a result of having been subjected to the civilizing process. However unwittingly, many of the new social historians, by adopting this perspective, omit or otherwise occlude the "masses" whose characteristic strategy for making history is the riot and whose main cultural/artistic form is the music handed down through performance rather than published texts.[30]

The folkloric legacy as opposed to the historiographic tradition gives us the snapshots we need to construct such a history. Its collectors, Lomax, Hammond, and also the great blues and folksinger Josh White, went south during the 1930s when slave narratives and songs were still on the lips of itinerant singers, sharecroppers, and tenant farmers. Others went to the mountains and to the plains and reclaimed the hymns and the Anglo-American folk traditions of white working people—mainly miners and farmers—who for generations live in isolated areas, among them Seeger, Jean Richie, and Guthrie, himself a native of Oklahoma, which, until the First World War was an old populist/socialist stronghold. Robeson and his accompanist/arranger Lawrence Brown were major collectors of spirituals. And, of course, Zora Neale Hurston, the black writer, although pointedly hostile to the left, was professionally trained as an ethnographer by Franz Boas. Her tales of southern black rural life are to be found in her own fiction as well as more formal, social scientific works.

No doubt, these leftists never saw themselves in the current that emphasizes the anthropological sense of culture: a mode of life in which representations are seen as part of everyday practices rather than placed chiefly in formal, artistic representations. Indeed the popular front encompassed ostensibly high cultural forms and even privileged them because they were means by which the communists gained legitimacy among many intellectuals. Yet, the art of

the popular front pales by comparison to its popular forms. (We cannot judge
its legacy by the often bowdlerized incorporation to which this work was
subjected during the [second] folksong revival when even the Weavers displayed an alarming tolerance for recording their songs against an orchestral
backdrop that could have been arranged by Lawrence Welk, Liberace, or
Montovani—not to mention the emanations of the Kingston Trio performing
"our music" in characteristic saccharine harmonies, or countless Muzak appropriations of the "Hammer Song" and "Tzena.")[31]

The popular front counterculture never wished to contest the space of high
art. Rather, its intervention in American culture was to insist on the *plurality*
of legitimate expressive forms to fight, so to speak, a war of position, on two
fronts. The first was to establish the status and legitimacy of political art—
especially art stimulated by the aims of the popular front—a battle that it
seemed to have won in the 1930s, even in universities, but provoked a fierce
counterattack that literally *wiped out* most of its gains by 1950; the second
was to constitute its most enduring intervention into American culture: to
have opened the way for a new American national-popular culture, particularly those genres that drew from oral traditions, black and rural narratives,
and music. Thus, the popular front fought what proved to be an opening battle
in two still-unfinished wars: the struggle for a democratic conception of national culture and the battle to obliterate high culture's designation of popular
culture as "low."

CHAPTER SIX

Cultural Study in Postmodern America

I

IN *1964*, the same year as the appearance of the gloomy prognostications of Herbert Marcuse and Jacques Ellul of a human future in the thrall of a technology gone wild, no longer subject to human control, a Canadian English professor, Marshall McLuhan, published *Understanding Media*. Although by no means pessimistic about the consequences of electronics, especially the communications revolution, he has offered no less than an apocalyptic evaluation of the consequences of the shift from the mechanical to the electric age:

After three thousand years of explosion, by means of fragmentary and mechanical technologies, the Western World is imploding. During the mechanical age we had extended our bodies in space. Today, after more than a century of electric technology, we have extended our central nervous system itself in a global embrace, abolishing both space and time as far as the planet is concerned. Rapidly, we approach the final phase of the extensions of man—the technological simulation of consciousness when the creative process of knowing will be collectively and corporately extended to the whole of human society.[1]

However, rather than regarding these effects of technology as an egregious disruption of traditional existence, McLuhan argues that we are on the threshold of a new human *community* that had been lost in the alienated modes of the mechanical age.

In his earlier and much less dramatic book, *The Gutenberg Galaxy,* all of the components of McLuhan's later analysis are present: he traces to the emergence of the printed word in the late sixteenth century the centralizing tendencies of modern literate societies and the increasing passivity of its subjects; the segmentation of human communities, "like little jarring atoms," and the split in cultural forms, for example, the separation of poetry and music; and the classification of human societies according to extent of their command over knowledge that can be transmitted by the printed page. Basing himself on the work of writers such as Siegfried Giedion and especially Georges Poulet, McLuhan's central argument, presupposed in *Understanding Media*, is that technology is not only an extension of human senses, but these senses are, in turn, differentially developed within specific technological regimes. Thus, printing and film are closely tied to the process by which the visual is privileged over, say, the oral and olfactory senses which, in western societies, are relatively undeveloped.

In *Understanding Media* we encounter phrases that have, indeed, been incorporated into our common vocabulary: taking his cue from Walt Whitman's celebration of "the body electric," McLuhan claims that by "abolishing space and time"[2] we have created a "global village." Whereas mechanical technologies fragmented humanity into nations, races, ethnicities in which the ideal of community seemed on the far shore of possibility, media, the principal product of the new electric technology, make the planet accessible to all through human extensions such as the telephone, television, and, after McLuhan's death, electronic mail and fax machines. We can reach across the globe, wiping out the old mechanical age cultures that, in this context, remain barriers to communication. As for his colleague Harold Innes, communication, according to McLuhan, as process is the only realistic content of which we can speak. The form speaks the content in McLuhan's bold aphorism "the medium is the message."

McLuhan distinguishes between "hot" and "cool" media—the distinction is based on the density of information provided by each—and argues that cool media are best for restoring communities constituted by face-to-face interaction. Cool media are defined as those that supply only skeleton information, allowing the receiver to participate by filling the gaps.[3] Radio and print media are densely "overheated," a term that signifies that they provide little or no room for the intervention of their receivers and are forms of knowledge that entail an oppressive power relation.

The famous phrase "the medium is the message" points to technology as material sign. There is no technological determinism here. The technological systems represented by the terms "mechanical" or "electric" signify modes of life, but there is no imputation of technological causation. On the contrary, for McLuhan the operative term is "community." He wants to find a way to close the gap between advanced industrial societies and the Third World, to overcome the deleterious effects of nationalism, itself a reflection of global inequality, an important dimension of which is distorted communication.

According to McLuhan the mechanical age was a continuation of the older regime of outward expansion. The electric age marks a reversal: time and space are "abolished" such that the extension of our bodies results in implosion. Moreover, the whole idea of a content that can be separated out as an object independent of its mode of production and dissemination has been rendered obsolete. The distinction between ends and means has finally been sundered. With McLuhan we have our first historically situated postmodernism located in the new means of production of what has become the crucial means-ends of human activity, communication:

Everybody notices how coal and steel and cars affect the arrangements of daily existence. In our time, study has finally turned to the medium of language itself as shaping daily life, so that society begins to look like a linguistic echo or repeat of language norms, a fact that has disturbed the Russian Communist party very deeply. Wedded as they are to 19th century industrial technology as the basis of class liberation, nothing could be more subversive of the Marxian dialectic than the idea that linguistic media shape social development as much as do the means of production.[4]

Needless to say, we have already experienced the realization of this insight as a prognosis.

McLuhan contrasts the oral-ear culture with the literate culture and argues that in the electric age the former is invading the West: what the enlightenment sought to occlude from the center of power is filtering back. Implicit in his analysis is the historicity of literate culture as the matrix of "high" linguistic forms. The imploding planet produces the conditions for a restructuring of the cultural scene. For example, the electric light "ended the regime of night and day . . . in a word the message of the electric light is total change. It is pure information without any content to restrict its transforming and informing power."[5] Whereas many of those reared in the literate culture remain, twenty-five years later, alarmed by the simulations of consciousness effected by the oral messages of, say, television, McLuhan sees the mass reproducibility not only of art but of communication as an epochal democratic communitarian innovation. The longed-for dream of equality may not have been realized in the Marxist program for the social ownership of the means of production but it is likely to be the perhaps unintended consequence of the body electric.

In this chapter I want to explore the consequences of the hybrid energy produced by the confrontation of literate and oral-ear culture made possible by the implosive effects of technological change for the emergence of the generational movement of the 1960s. McLuhan's influence on this movement was direct, since his vision was widely disseminated among young intellectuals in this period, some of whom rejected Marcuse's radical pessimism and saw in the communications revolution a way to overcome cultural estrangement associated with the old era of material and spiritual scarcity. His theme of achieving a human community through the relentless pursuit of futurity was far more appealing than the various evocations of an integrated past by, among others, the Frankfurt School and John Dewey.

Arthur Kroker has argued that, together with his less famous countrymen Harold Innes and George Grant, McLuhan was able to place technological change in the perspective of the emergence of a new global culture precisely because of the liminal position of Canada and its intellectuals.[6] Neither "Third World" despite its subordination to U.S. capital nor a full partner in the alliance of advanced capitalist societies, Canada became a likely site for the development of a future-oriented democratic theory of technology, linking it to a wide range of cultural transformations. For many intellectuals of the generation of Americans born around 1940 to 1950, it was McLuhan's ideas, especially his effort to fuse communitarianism with technology, spurning the dark vision of the European intellectuals who saw in the emergence of mass culture—greatly enhanced by the communications technology—a lethal weapon against reason, that inspired an enthusiasm for the products of what had, until the 1960s, been dismissed as degraded cultural forms. Ironically, as we will see, the critics who emerged from this generation, most of whom had been trained in English and American Studies departments, often in elite universities, could scarcely avoid reproducing some of the elements of the older criticism, particularly in their search for aesthetic grounds for the judgment that popular culture was valuable, and even their desire to develop a canon of, say, the popular music of the era: rock and roll.

Yet the 1960s pop critics who, influenced by McLuhan, refused a technophobia that was ineluctably linked to a parallel aversion to mass culture, sowed the seeds of a new journalistic criticism that has had a profound effect on contemporary cultural studies. Of course, writing in the 1960s and early 1970s, mostly for newspapers, mass circulation magazines for both youth culture and more general audiences, many of these writers, like the bands and singers they wrote about, shared the unique political experiences of their generation and especially that utopian moment that was the counterculture and, in a somewhat different register, the New Left. Even though some had been influenced by the academic criticism of Trilling, Leslie Fiedler, and others in the school of "moral" criticism and shared with their teachers a certain suspicion, if not contempt, for ideological orthodoxies such as Marxism-Leninism (which had, by the late 1960s, captured the hearts and minds of many antiwar and civil rights activists), they were equally unwilling to conclude that modern liberalism was the furthest reach of political imagination. And, although imbued with a powerful belief in the utopian possibilities of American freedom, and deeply committed to forging a new definition of a national popular culture, they were not imbued with the patriotic fervor that, in the end, overcame the previous generation, perhaps because they were not damaged by the earlier generation's firsthand experiences with Communists and arrived on the scene after Stalinism had passed its peak. Neither were they content to reproduce the world-weary skepticism of a Trilling who was never quite reconciled to American culture, despite a somewhat late appreciation of what he perceived to be its diminishing parochialism.

As a result, the split between the largely non-academic pop culture critics and the anti-Stalinist high culture intellectuals appeared much wider than it actually was. The young critics who emerged in the mid to late 1960s for the most part eschewed academic jobs, while their teachers had decided that universities provided the best possible space for disseminating ideas. Under the influence of what was commonly viewed as a "sexual" revolution, they were committed to a definition of politics in which *pleasure* would radically replace the old Victorianism; as opposed to Greenberg and Trilling, who labored mightily to argue that in a cold war environment the survival of art depended crucially on its separation from politics, the new journalist-critics were persuaded that politics and culture were ineluctably linked; and, although congenital nonjoiners, their political sympathies were clearly with the New Left which they understood as a generational movement of which rock and roll was an integral component.

Until the 1960s, we can discern three forms of reflection on mass-audience culture: popular journalistic film criticism in newspapers and magazines; commentary by belletrist critics such as Gilbert Seldes and Edmund Wilson, much of which was published in popular magazines, in "little magazines" such as *Partisan Review* and in journals of "opinion" such as *The New Republic* and *The Nation*; and the subfield of sociology and, to a lesser extent anthropology, that emerged prior to the Second World War that focused on what was called "mass communications research." These investigators, in the main, studied the response of audiences to such media as radio and film rather than providing a critical perspective on the products themselves. There were some exceptions—notably the work of Herta Hertzog and, in a somewhat different register, Rudolph Arnheim—but, as we will see, there were definite reasons for an emphasis on reception. By far the most visible were the short film reviews in newspapers and magazines, the great bulk of which were really advice to moviegoers, helping them, among other things, to decide whether to pay for a babysitter. In this genre there were, of course, attempts at a more serious evaluation of current offerings and, in the works of a small group of critics, notably Robert Warshow and Pauline Kael, critical work on the form itself as social commentary, its larger cultural influence, and its relation to other forms, particularly literature.

In contrast to the 1940s when cultural commentary was dominated by the standpoint of high culture, namely, the view that all of the products of the Culture Industry were variations on the theme of standardization whose differences were determined solely by the expectations of their audiences, a few American critics, following the example of the French, discovered "cinema" as a new art form. Even as Dwight Macdonald continued to rail at what he considered to be the illegitimate pretensions of certain novels and films to art, film historians working in a few American universities and critics inspired by, among others, Andre Bazin and François Truffaut who, aided by Soviet film director Sergei Eisenstein and others, elaborated a *language* of film art, argued that the figure of the director was a near analogy to the *author*.

The *auteur* theory provided the basis for constructing a canon of films and especially directors who most powerfully contributed to the development of this twentieth-century art form. Although Bazin, for example, demurred from the model that was rapidly achieving a consensus that privileged the innovations of the American D. W. Griffith, particularly his use of camera and editing to liberate film from its dependence on novelistic or theatrical devices and thereby explore its full visual potential, all agreed that the process of film production was infused with the individual imagination of the director. Bazin counterposed the still-camera work of the Japanese director Ozu to the "American" style that employed the camera and the editor's shears as a producer of a new, virtual reality. But, as for the others, the poetry of film was the outcome of the work of a single figure in this process. Even the later work of Christian Metz, who developed a structuralist film semiotic that assumed film as a more collective activity than that proposed by the postwar pioneers for whom existential philosophy constituted the foundation of their aesthetic, failed to overcome the power of the auteur theory.[7] For what was needed to establish film as a legitimate academic discipline was no different from what is required of any literary study: a history, and individual works and authors who could be identified with the form.

In 1967 Andrew Sarris produced his near-definitive *The American Film Directors*, a major application of auteurism and a veritable hierarchy of the great and the near-great, the "fallen" idols, and the talented but ultimately second-line figures. Whatever the merits of Sarris's canon or, indeed, its theoretical basis, its overarching virtue was to have valorized film art not in terms of the avant-garde margins, but with respect to the commercial center of the industry. Or, more precisely, he identified the avant garde within the industry, thereby shattering the assumption that came to prevail in cultural criticism throughout the postwar era, that the culture industry was a monolith of schlock and that only documentaries, the small number of art films intended for small, sophisticated audiences, and "experimental" films deserved the designation of "art."

The dissemination of auteur theory became immensely influential on high cultural institutions such as museums that, from the late 1950s, began to show retrospectives of leading directors, and to feature lectures by prominent critics. Inherently conservative, some major universities such as UCLA and UC-Berkeley and especially New York University initiated film studies programs a decade later. We can observe in the development of the new academic field of film studies a process that has marked the emergence of nearly all high art forms, if we take the position that disciplines are not constituted as epistemological transparencies. Products of a culture industry are appropriated by an emerging critical group, the members of which have "discovered" among the welter of film commodities a few nuggets that qualify as Art. A few directors and their films are anointed with the status of canonical works, about which issue a plethora of studies, commentaries, and theoretical writings which, together, elaborate the aesthetic criteria that mark status in an otherwise banal field that may be called mass-audience culture. Gradually, there are enough critical works about Great Films, their directors and their styles, to develop a canonical bibliography, enough to constitute reading lists from which to transmit a *tradition*. Gradually, the members of the academy, rather than the newspaper and magazine critics, are the official arbiters of taste. In the case of film as in journalism and, later, in rock music, some of the academics are recruited from among journalists. However, a fairly large cohort hold degrees in English or other language disciplines. Others hold degrees from the subdiscipline of American Studies, the errant and somewhat diminished offshoot of established English departments. Typically, they bring with them the methodological precepts of their "native" discipline and impose it on film.

Yet there was dissent from the effort to elevate film to a high art form, notably by Pauline Kael whose influential criticism appeared regularly in the *New Yorker* during these years. "Trash, Art and the Movies," originally written for *Harper's*, is perhaps emblematic of her characteristic attack on the notion of commercial film as Art and, simultaneously, her most wide-ranging exposition of her position. In this piece, Kael gets to the point, early and often. For example, in the middle of the second page, she summarizes the essential features of her position. It is worth quoting at length for these comments are, together with those of Tom Wolfe, among the most powerful—and influential—statements against the prevailing tendency to aestheticize popular culture on the basis of high-art production values, notions of authorial authority, and considerations of pure form:

Alienation is the most common state of the knowledgeable movie audience, and though it has the peculiar rewards of low connoisseurship, a miser's delight in small favors, we long to be surprised out of it—not to suspension of disbelief nor to a Brechtian kind of alienation, but to pleasure, something a man [*sic*] can call good without self-disgust.

A good movie can take you out of your dull funk and the hopelessness that so often goes with slipping into a theatre; a good movie can make you feel alive again, in contact, not just lost in another city. Good movies make you care, make you believe in possibilities again . . . the movie doesn't have to be great; it can be stupid and empty and you can still have the joy of a good performance, or the joy in just a good line. . . . Sitting there alone or painfully alone because those with you do not react as you do, you know there must be others, perhaps in this very theatre or in the city, surely in other theatres in other cities, now in the past or future, who react as you do. And because movies are the most total and all encompassing art form we have, these reactions can seem the most personal and maybe the most important, imaginable. The romance of movies is not just in those stories and those people on the screen but in the adolescent dream of meeting others who feel as you do about what you've seen. You do meet them, of course, and you know each other at once because you talk less about good movies than what you love in bad movies.[8]

One of the key sources of Kael's appeal is that she writes from the point of view of the "knowledgeable" moviegoer, sharing with her readers the experience of utter isolation in the movie theater. Certainly, at times she slips from this standpoint, providing a more technical discussion of a given movie, but never allows herself to stray too long in the persona of the expert. She will use words to describe a movie as "smart" (*Wild in the Streets*), reflecting her penchant for using the vernacular whenever she wants to say what she means. Here's another example: "There are much worse things aesthetically than the crude good-natured crumminess, the undisguised reach for a fast buck, of movies without art. From *I Was a Teenage Werewolf* through the beach parties to *Wild in the Streets* and the *Savage Seven* American International Pictures has sold a cheap commodity, which in the lack of artistry and its blatant and sometimes funny way of delivering action serves to remind us that one of the great appeals of movies is that we don't have to take them too seriously."[9]

Of course, Kael frequently alludes to Art, which "is still what teachers and ladies and foundations believe in, it's civilized and refined, cultivated and serious, cultural, beautiful, European, Oriental; it's what America isn't, and it's especially what American movies are not."[10] For Kael, movies are about *pleasure*; it's an audience's medium. And the movie audience is, for the most part, not "refined." The audience goes to the movies to laugh and to cry, for "excitement."

Pleasure, excitement, fun. These are the basic requirements of movie art: "Movie art is not the opposite of what we [the audience] have always enjoyed in movies, it is not to be found in a return to official high culture, it is what we have always found good in movies only more so. It's the subversive gesture carried further, the moments of excitement sustained longer and extended to new meanings."[11] The "subversive gesture" is "playfulness and the absence of solemnity" in, say, a Hitchcock movie while, according to Kael, the much heralded Joseph von Sternberg is really a "kitsch master, a master of studied artfulness and pretty excess," a description that might fit the contemporary filmmaker David Lynch, who enjoys an equally overinflated reputation among some critics.

What endears Kael to other contemporary critics is her utter contempt for respectability, and her forceful argument that what she calls "entertaining trash" bears a relationship to "art" insofar as "working on trash, feeling free to play, can loosen up the actors and craftsmen just as seeing trash can liberate the spectator. And we don't get this playful quality in art much in movies except in trash."[12] Where the norms of culture emphasize work, respectability, and self-denial, the movies let us relax, provide the space for subversion of these values. In the darkness of the theater, where the screen action (when successful) transports the spectator from the ruin of everyday life, we are given an escape from the prevailing puritanism of our culture.

Second, in contrast to many "serious" film critics and theorists, for whom the work of art may be explored by analyzing its technical apparatus, the conditions of signification, the ideological content of the film revealed by these formal considerations or, in another mode, the ethical, spiritual, or aesthetic elements of the product, Kael's reception-aesthetic focuses on what is precisely denied by high art and its publicists: pleasure. She constructs an audience that is inundated by everyday existence and "slips into the theatre" to experience something else and expects to be entertained. Entertainment, sustained excitement, are above all the fundamental presupposition of any possible movie art.

Inspired by this declaration, a whole generation of popular culture critics dove into the mainstream of tin-pan-alley, writing, where possible, for the biggest newspapers and magazines, trying to touch the alienated mass audience with which Kael had so militantly identified. Their project was in part inspired by Kael's truly pioneering emphasis on the conditions of the consumption of culture. As we saw in Chapter 1, in contrast to the dominant tendency of postwar English studies to focus on form, or on economic and political influences on writing, F. O. Matthiessen led a generation of critics and historians to a specifically cultural(ist) interpretation of literature. Literary historians and critics such as Henry Nash Smith and Leo Marx adopted a perspective associated with the work of Northrop Frye, but actually a much wider movement in American criticism that recuperates culture as *myth and symbol*. For example, Smith's major work *Virgin Land,* subtitled "The American West as Symbol and Myth," is an analysis of the *discourse* of the West, and draws widely from contemporary and historical accounts to advance his thesis that the West was constructed as a towering presence in historiography as much as fiction. Smith ends his book criticizing the agrarian tradition's "paired but contradictory ideas of nature and civilization as a general principle of historical and social investigation."[13] However, this binary, which for Smith remains a barrier to the American achievement of a cosmopolitan culture, is transformed into a *method* that can account for the peculiarities of the American "experience."

We can observe the immense popularity of the Western in both American literature and American film. The closing of the frontier so poignantly and powerfully depicted by Frederick Jackson Turner became the thematic constant of vast portions of American fictions along with the persistent demythologization of the West from the turn of the century when Theodore Dreiser homed in on the loss of American innocence, the key result of industrialization and urbanization.[14] John Dewey's recurrent invocation of the myth of the New England town meeting to mount a critique of the contemporary demise of political democracy;[15] and Frank Capra's unabashed advocacy, in a dozen films, of small-town values against the growing trustification of American life and especially the growing cynicism and manipulations that accompanied it, thematized the contraries of wilderness and the city, face-to-face interaction and mass society, and innocence and decadence into popular culture as well as political philosophy.

These themes were transported into the high journalism of Robert Warshow who, despite his considerable debt to the characteristic political and aesthetic critique of the Culture Industry, advances an iconoclastic conception of "mass culture" as a series of symbolic but public acts concentrated in mythic figures, especially the gangster and the westerner. Like later treatments of the Western by John Cawelti and Will Wright, Warshow situates his view between the high cultural critique of this genre as an instance of standardization and repetition and a perspective that calls attention to its wider cultural importance. Of course, for Warshow, the Western is a standardized story ("a fairy tale") whose mythological and symbolic elements dominate any particular exemplar. But, unlike Dwight Macdonald and other fellow *PR* critics, Warshow cannot avoid taking these genres seriously "when other, more consciously serious art forms are increasingly complex, uncertain and ill-defined" because, among other films, the canonical *Shane,* for example, "offers a serious orientation to the problem of violence such as can be found almost nowhere else in American culture."[16] Warshow shows that the Western is a genre that conforms, in its essentials, to the criteria of any art insofar as the standard pattern of narrative is marked by "minor variations" that give pleasure to the "connoisseur."

In fact, Warshow's ire is reserved for those "uncertain and ill-defined" film efforts to replicate high culture, especially political commentary, whether conservative, liberal, or Stalinoid. The hit movies *Best Years of Our Lives,* an early postwar chronicle of the veteran's adjustment to civilian life, and *Death of a Salesman,* which, for Warshow, was not a very good play and was badly adapted to the screen, both address social themes and are taken as good examples of kitsch and, in this respect, typical of the mediocrity of the social realist genre of American film (against which Kael was to rail as well). Yet, despite his reservations about the enduring value of *Death of a Salesman,* Warshow draws a comparison between the central figure of Willy Loman, the hapless salesman of Arthur Miller's drama, and the protagonist of David Riesman's sociological "classic" of this era, *The Lonely Crowd.*[17] For both, one of the elements of American ideology, that the "world lies open to them," that we can invent ourselves to reach the fantastic goals of wealth and power, turns out to be, in part, a cruel and perhaps tragic (at least pathetic) deception. Consistent with the myth/symbol school of criticism, Warshow finds even in "bad" movies representative themes and figures of American culture and, as he ruefully admits, perhaps all we can expect in cultural forms.

In the late 1960s, under the influence of the "second wave" of French film studies and its British acolytes grouped around the journal *Screen,* the field underwent its first serious intellectual shift. For in place of the once pervasive existentialism—Christian or otherwise—theorists such as Christian Metz, Stephen Heath, and Colin McCabe utterly rejected the Subject as the center of the cinema or, indeed, the whole apparatus of "representations" that accompanied the assumption that film signified anything beyond itself, in favor of a conception of film discourse that adapted the apparatus of Saussurian semiotics to film "theory." Now films were constituted by visual signs, codes, and narrative structure whose juxtapositions "constructed" the film as a self-referential art form with subjects, but no authors. In the vernacular, films refer to other films both with respect to their apparatus of production and their narratives.[18] In this work, aesthetic considerations were largely occluded although, since these writers were, by the 1970s, firmly anchored in universities rather than in the popular press, they could not avoid developing disciplinary trappings such as canon formation, organizing associations, institutes, and centers to perform funded research, and creating journals that provided public representation of their arrival on the academic scene as well as opportunities for publications for budding scholars and critics.

Although the new linguistically infused film studies has since achieved intellectual hegemony in the academic field, as in other disciplines of the Anglo-American academy, notably the languages, it has not succeeded in sweeping away historiography (which has recently staged something of a comeback); Marxism in terms of ideology-critique; or the older American Studies approach that leans heavily on historical research and a myth/symbol analysis of texts. Although interpreting texts in terms of their symbolic and mythic elements may, at first glance, appear significantly different from that of ideology-critique, Cornel West has rightly argued that some Marxist critics, such as Fredric Jameson, are influenced by Northrop Frye's work, perhaps the most fully elaborated body of writing in this critical mode. Nor has the most "advanced" manifestation of the linguistic turn, either in its semiotic incarnation or psychoanalytic theory in its Lacanian transformations, been universally adopted, although it is certainly true that what is called "theory" is ensconced in poststructuralism and its linguistic and rhetorical conventions. However, among feminists the work of Laura Mulvey, Teresa DiLauretis, Annette Kuhn, and others who employ these conventions is highly valued, in part because they have turned psychoanalysis into a weapon of feminist criticism of the exclusion of women by the form itself. DiLauretis demonstrated that the male "gaze" dominates cinema: the auteurs participate in the sexist objectification of women. Thus, like British cultural studies in the 1970s when feminists made a *paradigm-critique* of the field, or in the later criticism that it was ethnically biased since it virtually excluded the cultures of people of color, American film studies has found itself the scene of sometimes acrimonious political conflict played out in a field of theoretical dialogue and dispute.

2

Peruse any of the many collections of the critic who may be taken as the key figure in the older belletrist tradition, Edmund Wilson's writings—reviews, memoirs, epistles, rants—and one finds frequent commentary on issues in mass-audience culture usually, but not exclusively, framed as reviews of books, most of which are works of fiction. To be sure, Wilson shared the high art proclivities of most critics; for example, he evaluates a collection of stories by the "journalist" Ring Lardner, noting he also writes the text of a comic strip, but praises the collection, comparing Lardner favorably with two leading writers of the 1920s, Sinclair Lewis and Sherwood Anderson. In another vein, one encounters a review of Gilbert Seldes' pioneering *The 7 Lively Arts,* a review of a new vaudeville house and other occasional pieces about popular culture.[19] In some of these pieces, Wilson's playful, almost perverse sensibility shines through. His vaudeville review assures the reader that Minsky's Follies still has the best strip show in town. For his *New Republic* audience this information would scarcely be received as reassuring. However, in all of the writing, it is plain enough that Wilson is an ardent pilgrim, searching for the soul of a uniquely American art. Unlike the *Partisan Review*'s critics for whom this was a quixotic quest and whose cosmopolitanism is directed, among others, to the validity of this project, Wilson ignores no corner of American culture, even the work of a journalist like Lardner. Moreover, like Seldes, Wilson is able to praise Lardner's accurate grasp of the American vernacular, a talent that would entirely elude some later critics for whom Lardner's work did not qualify as a candidate for any possible American canon.

Equally significant, more than thirty years before Stuart Hall's similar effort for British popular arts, Seldes surveyed American movies, vaudeville, the circus, and other popular forms and, much to Wilson's consternation, began the long process, not completed to our day, of constructing a canon of film artists by designating Charlie Chaplin one of the greatest of the twentieth century. Even more "audacious" (the word is Wilson's), Seldes engages in theoretical discourse, attempting a level of abstraction that, on the whole, was strictly eschewed by the belletrist critics. For Wilson's immense popularity among the intelligentsia was due, in part, to his generosity but more to his *style.* In this mode, criticism is an encounter between a subject, himself, and a work of fiction, an event, or, indeed, any artifact of the social world. What made the essay interesting was neither the brilliance of its dissection nor the categories of analysis it generated that could be emulated by others.

To the contrary, Wilson's writing is distinguished by its individuality. His voice was ironic, but never bitter, generous but never fawning. Above all, we heard the *person* in the writing. The pleasure of the text was inseparable from the critical side of the writing. The "I," that is, the persona of the critic, is embedded, and not so deeply that it cannot be heard, in each thought. In contrast to the tendency of much criticism—then and now—to speak in subjectless prose, Wilson is unabashedly evocative of himself as a subject, and frames literary discourse as impressions that, on the whole, require no justification other than the authority of the critic as a transcendent ego.

Not that he writes as a literary subjective idealist. Throughout the short and long pieces of every collection one finds evidence of considerable historical erudition. We know that Wilson is a voracious reader, his references span the ancient and contemporary worlds, and he does not hesitate to use analogies to illustrate his points. Indeed, Wilson produced one of the better reflections written anywhere on the Russian Revolution, a chronicle of the hopes of a sympathizer turned critic.

But there is no pretense at scientificity here. Wilson's essays, most of them full of insight and delight, are crafted so that the reader is entirely captivated by the first sentence and a prisoner until the last word of the all-too-brief piece. That is why Wilson's collections must be more satisfying than the single review or essay, for we can take a measure of the writer in, say, the 800 pages of *The Shores of Light* better than in any particular instance among the essays between the covers. Yet nowhere are we instructed, nor does Wilson suggest, anything but the rule that each work must be judged on its own merits, that the chief criterion of judgment is whether the fiction is worth reading. In this sense, Wilson, like Kael, is a pioneer in the genre of criticism later perfected by Robert Christgau with respect to rock music—the consumer guide. Like Christgau's, his is a genre that transcends the limits of publicity, but recognizes the legitimacy of the concern of the typical harried reader: trying to figure out what to buy. In this respect, Wilson was both continuous with everyday criticism and keenly respectful of his popular responsibilities.

Seldes's project is different.[20] His overriding purpose is to establish the legitimacy of "entertainment" as art, with all of the aesthetic criteria that are attendant thereto, and to combat the relentless effort of the mavens of high culture to so narrow the scope of legitimate art that even middle-brow culture is excluded—for example, what he calls "lyric theatre," most of whose products were later to be labeled "kitsch." Here I want only to investigate a little more closely what was, perhaps, the most controversial essay in the book, *The Krazy Kat That Walks by Itself*.[21] The first sentence tells the whole tale: "*Krazy Kat*, the daily comic strip of George Herriman, is, to me, the most amusing and fantastic and satisfactory work of art produced in America today."[22] Plainly, his enthusiasm for the comic strip, expressed by the adjectives "amusing and fantastic," is entirely within the purview of the genre of belletrism. However, when he adds the "most satisfactory work of art produced in America today" he plainly exceeded the bounds of appropriate criticism, an excess that, in his extended review of the book, Wilson did not hesitate to note. "The qualities of Krazy Kat are irony and fantasy—exactly the same it would appear, as distinguished *The Revolt of the Angels . . .*" While acknowledging that he personally prefers France's work to that of Herriman, Seldes points out that "in America irony and fantasy are practiced in the major arts by only one or two men, producing high class trash; and Mr Herriman working in a despised medium, without an atom of pretentiousness, is day after day producing something essentially fine."[23] Seldes's conclusion is that a masterpiece of "second order" art is superior to bad examples of high art. Thus, by invoking the absence of pretentiousness in Herriman's work, does he rescue it from trivialization by "those who hold that a comic strip cannot be a work of art."

"Irony and fantasy" are fused with the artist's capacity for pity and compassion that Seldes added to the Keystone comedies to form a kind of critical set against which other art may be measured. For it is plain that he finds in the popular arts the best examples of comedy, humor, fantasy, and irony precisely because they are freed from literary pretension. Yet, no more than Wilson who compared Lardner to Sinclair Lewis and Sherwood Anderson in the years both were consistently best-selling writers, Seldes cannot avoid the high art referent, in this case to Cervantes, Wagner, and Dickens.

Now, one may make comparisons to show the degree to which high culture and mass-audience or popular culture influence each other or, in a more radical formulation, are simply variants of the same socially and historically situated discourses. Seldes's argument is that, however "second order" is the art of Chaplin, Herriman, and other producers of popular culture, they qualify by the same standards that make any work of art great, standards that were generated by critics of high art. But what distinguishes *The 7 Lively Arts* from other occasional explorations of popular forms by critics of high culture is that Seldes takes the popular seriously. For this reason, he takes the trouble to generate taxonomies of several popular forms as well as establish criteria for aesthetic judgment. For example, in the comic strip he distinguishes between "realism" and "fantasy" and finds two dozen worthy exemplars. Similarly, in his examination of the "One Man Show" Seldes's critical standard depends on the degree to which the performer manages to exploit every aspect of him or herself. At the same time he has no doubt that "there is something wrong with the idea" of a one-person show itself.[24]

Despite Seldes's intention to provide the categories by which judgment may become aesthetically and theoretically legitimate, his style betrays a strong affinity for the dominant belletrist tradition. He is opinionated—and passionate—about his preferences, which are not always argued from formal aesthetic criteria but rely instead on the ambiguous and highly personal idea of taste. The personal voice is never absent. In this sense, Seldes is a genuine precursor of what later became known as the "new journalism," especially its pop practitioners. In many respects he provides the first widely disseminated consumer guide to pop culture. Perhaps more than any single individual, Seldes introduced the "serious" consideration of mass-audience culture forty years before the high/low debate became a public critical issue.

As a part of the important intellectual migration from Europe in the 1930s, the psychologist Paul Lazarsfeld, an Austrian Jew and active socialist, distinguished himself from many of his humanist colleagues by a strong belief that the methods of natural science were suitable for the study of social relationships—especially experiment and gathering quantifiable data as the basis for concept formation and theory. In the late 1920s and early 1930s Lazarsfeld had directed an institute in Vienna that performed research using statistical methods as well as interviews on the problems of youth, especially unemployment, but also conducted studies of audience responses to radio and other types of media propaganda.

These were years of the rise of the political right in central Europe. Unlike earlier incarnations, the "new" right presented itself in populist intonations and revealed a remarkable grasp of the rhetoric and techniques of mass agitation, talents once reserved for the left. Radio and film became major battlegrounds in the propaganda war and, as an astute social observer, Lazarsfeld was quick to recognize the significance of questions about audience response to helping democratic forces to understand the right's ideological appeals.

There was another reason why his studies were to focus, in the main, on reception rather than on the texts of popular radio shows and the news. Textual analysis was, necessarily, interpretative and, from the point of view of scientific knowledge, speculative. Since under the influence of the legendary Vienna Circle that electrified some intellectual circles in the late 1920s and 1930s, Lazarsfeld became a convinced positivist (albeit, in his own words, "tinged" with Marxism), he adopted the axiom that being is being measured.[25] This perspective suggested that the object of reliable knowledge is subject to quantitative measurement and to tests of validity. Accordingly, investigators were obliged to tabulate the results of interviews and surveys and adduce generalizations from them; close textual readings and historical accounts, however persuasive, simply lacked the same scientific status.

From 1936 when, in the wake of a deteriorating political situation in Austria, he definitively settled in the United States, to his death in 1976, Lazarsfeld was not only a pioneer in mathematical social science, but the leading figure in what became known as mass communications research. A major subfield of sociology, especially in the 1940s and 1950s, the study of audience reception of radio, television, and film was pursued within universities, but also within the growing Culture Industry. In fact, by Lazarsfeld's own testimony, the academic-industrial complex, later notorious in the fields of defense, physics, chemistry, and biologically based medical technology, was Lazarsfeld's basic strategy for securing the survival and dissemination of this work. Lazarsfeld's remarkable exposition of this "latent strategy" is worth quoting at length:

Latent strategies and directional cues involve the interactions that always prevail between dispositions and situations. Latent strategies lead to elective perception of the environment and they also become crystallized, more precise, more self-conscious as they meet success in an extending sequence of episodes. But what makes for a relatively high proportion of successes? Here I must take recourse to a term like *structural fit*. Both the environment and the life style of the immigrant are patterned in a certain way. The elements of these two patterns may complement each other, and to some degree they did in my case . . . my quantitative interests, controlled by strong conceptual training, fitting well into some nascent trends in the American community.[26]

Lazarsfeld's structural fit showed strongly in two areas: the American penchant for scientificity of the positivist type and the eagerness of the media and other large corporations to employ social research to sell their products, including their ideological productions. In a remarkable autobiographical essay, Lazarsfeld provides, in candid detail, the elements of the alliance between mass communications research and the Culture Industry. His two associates at the Princeton Office of Radio Research were the psychologist Hadley Cantril and Frank Stanton, who was director of research and later to become the president and chief executive officer of CBS. In addition to relatively small administrative support from the university, Lazarsfeld solicited the support of two funding sources: the Rockefeller Foundation which, at the time, became a leading force in the effort to direct American social science to issues of social policy through the organization of the Social Science Research Council and, on a smaller scale, Lazarsfeld's Bureau of Applied Social Research (BASR), the institutional form that derived from the Princeton project; second, from the very beginning of his American period with Stanton's help, he developed a long-term relationship with CBS, performing contract research on consumer preferences for various radio shows. In addition, from his days at the University of Newark (which housed the Princeton Radio Research office) throughout the career of BASR, he and his colleagues performed contract research for other private corporations.

Needless to say, these commercial relationships raised some serious ethical questions to which Lazarsfeld was extremely sensitive. Lazarsfeld justifies his bold move toward building an academic institution that could perform all kinds of work including contract research for private interests on two distinct, but closely related arguments. First, he calls attention to the precarious financial position of mass communications research during a time of economic depression when he and his colleagues were unable to secure regular academic professorial positions. Accordingly, his "latent" strategy was to build a strong, if not invulnerable institutional base with private funds, if necessary. Stanton and Cantril provided invaluable contacts with which to pursue this strategy. "The money had to be begged from public institutions and private industry," otherwise the project would disappear. Second, the nature of the work required close cooperation with private corporations and public agencies who had to grant access to his research staff. Lazarsfeld argues for care in criticizing these corporations lest the doors be closed to them and the interest of gaining valuable knowledge needlessly frustrated.

Thus, Lazarsfeld provides a demonstration of the kind of critique that might jeopardize the entire project. He gives an account of Theodor Adorno's brief relationship with the Princeton Office, wherein he argues that Adorno's abrasive intellect was an obstacle to the maintenance of the close relationship with CBS on which the project depended: "Adorno came to symbolize a general problem. In a number of memos written in the Spring of 1938, to my associate directors I explained the importance of Adorno's ideas . . . I asked Adorno to summarize his ideas in a memorandum."[27] Adorno's memorandum, a 160-page, single-spaced paper, employed Marx's idea of the commodity fetish to analyze popular music. Lazarsfeld asked Adorno to translate his theoretical orientation into a typology that could suitably be adapted to listener response research techniques. After some time, it became evident to Lazarsfeld that "Adorno's type of critical research" could not be brought into the empirical framework of the communications field. The Rockefeller grant renewal "provided no budget for the continuation of the music project."[28]

Clearly, the passive voice of this passage reveals that Lazarsfeld was troubled by firing Adorno. While he recognized Adorno as a major cultural thinker, the difficulty of translating neo-Marxist theory into operational terms combined with the relationships he had cultivated with CBS and other corporations to make Adorno's presence in the project extremely risky. If the "phenomenon of fetishism could be described by a direct approach to a sample of listeners," in other words, could be incorporated into a positivist framework, it would be useful. But, the fetish was a critical category that, according to Adorno, "takes possession of practically every musical category in radio."[29] Clearly, such generalizations were beyond the scope of Lazarsfeld's research agenda. On the other hand, they could not "sell out" to their private clients lest the academic legitimacy of the project be impaired. From Lazarsfeld's memoir of his encounter with Adorno at this time, one may infer the complexity of his motives. While he admired Adorno's intellectual grasp of mass culture, it was precisely his stature as a critic of mass communications that potentially could deflect critics for whom the contracts with private or government interests constituted a barrier to disinterested research. Until the 1970s, when a new generation of radical critics entered the field, mass communications research did not hesitate to offer its considerable technical skills to the industry and to the government to the extent that its intellectual independence could be challenged.

For example, in contrast to Lazarsfeld's strategy of maintaining the corporate-university alliance within the framework of a single academic institution—the BASR—other mass communications researchers, such as the sociologists at the University of Chicago who had migrated from Denver, preferred to separate their academic work from their market contracts. This strategy led to the formation of private market research companies whose principals were professors and whose research workers were graduate students, many of whom used the data collected in the course of this work for dissertations. Of course, the key categories of social science, particularly class and stratification, needs and norms, infused even the most instrumental market research. From data collected in the course of fulfilling a very large study for a soap manufacturer, for example, Lee Rainwater and his associates published an important study, *Workingman's Wife*, only one of the more prominent among a fairly substantial literature in stratification analysis whose primary data was derived from the results of commercial contract work.

From the techniques developed by mass communications research and its kin, market research, a whole industry of voter preference surveys emerged that has, by some accounts, come to dominate the electoral and legislative process in the United States and many European countries. It may be argued that the distinction between politics and marketing soap is no longer fundamental in an age when the relationships between producer and consumer, bureaucrats and clients, elected official and voter are mediated by social science whose methods of collecting and correlating data are uniformly applied in these ostensibly different spheres. And, on the evidence of recent historical studies and autobiographical testimonials of social scientists themselves, the role of government, private corporations, and private foundations in redirecting social research from critical to positive, that is, policy perspectives is absolutely central. Although Lazarsfeld and his colleagues were ethically committed to disinterestedness in social investigation, the institutional imperatives combined with the character of the research itself tended to subvert these intentions.

Lazarsfeld reports that some of the early work of his organization was supported by the WPA and, during the war, by a plethora of federal government agencies. The size and complexity of these involvements led him to invent a new classification to describe his own function: "managerial scholar." For Lazarsfeld was among the early examples of a new academic type—part methodologist and theorist of contemporary social problems, part entrepreneur, and part manager of large-scale research directed at assisting the formulation of social and corporate policies. Today, the managerial scholar/entrepreneur is as commonplace in U.S. universities as are government and private contracts that support institutes and centers of applied research in the natural and social sciences. For, especially since the late 1930s when war mobilization partially revived the American economy and knowledge-producing institutions, the concept of unencumbered funding for research has slowly yielded to project-based financing in which the granting agency specifies goals as well as guidelines for research. Just as physics research is largely dependent on the Defense Department and on corporate funding and research—in the biological sciences increasingly a function of three-way arrangements with private bioengineering, pharmaceutical, and medical corporations, the National Institutes of Health, and the faculty of leading universities—so a significant portion of social research is crucially oriented to policy and market outcomes.

3

Nothing is more galling to someone who has spent half a lifetime shedding his parochial cultural formation in order to enter the space of an artistic and critical universalistic aristocracy than the *betrayal of classicism* by those who are born of the educated classes and, from childhood, were afforded the pleasures of cultivated taste especially in music, painting, and literature. I want to begin with an extended discussion of the work of the outrageous Tom Wolfe, whose 1960s journalism, first written for popular magazines such as *Esquire* and *New York*, was read avidly by hip intellectuals, many of whom were themselves budding cultural journalists.

If Wolfe had published his mid-1960s reports and remarks on popular and aristocratic culture in respected academic or literary journals he would have no doubt become the object of excoriation by the mavens of high culture who had by the late 1940s managed to nearly obliterate the status, if not the memory, of left popular culture and the artistic legitimacy of mass-audience culture. As we have seen, the dominance of Trilling, Greenberg, and other high modernists in and out of American universities cast a long shadow over cultural criticism that remained, and retains considerable power in many parts of the humanities mainstream even today. But Wolfe wrote for publications that, although visible to a general reader, did not even enjoy the status of, say, the *Times* magazine or the weeklies of opinion, much less the *New York Review of Books*. When not writing for mainstream newspapers that he calls "the totem papers," Wolfe's venue was that part of the popular press frequented by hip, somewhat unconventional readers. For he was surely the bard of an adversarial culture that, even more than popular front folkloric or social realism in an earlier moment, confronted the literary high modernists with their contradictory advocacy of liberal democracy and aristocratic culture, with their newly won intellectual as well as political nationalism and the harsh low-cult reality of what Wolfe took as the "authentic" national culture, the architecture of Las Vegas, Murray the K, a disc jockey and rock and roll entrepreneur of the 1960s, and in a somewhat ironic mode, pop art.

At first, his most salient cultural writings were ignored, when not dismissed, by university intellectuals because, despite possessing high academic credentials, he had chosen to become a mere journalist. And his adversaries, the intellectual guardians of Art, were still, in the mid-1960s, exuding confidence. They had beaten the Reds and the liberal pop cult symps like Seldes. All cultural debates were ensconced within high art and concerned form which, throughout the 1960s, was taken as the only content worthy of comment. Yet, as we will see, twenty-five years before the advent of the current high/low debate *within* the precincts of high cultural criticism Wolfe's voice, together with a small group of young university-trained journalists, was promulgating to a whole generation the obvious, but hotly contested thesis that there was a redeeming social and even aesthetic value in the products of commercially produced culture, and that they were "symbolic" of profound changes in American life. In contrast to the more circumspect cultural critics of the old left, they began the war to erase the distinction between high and low—a contention that remains as emotionally loaded today as it did a quarter of a century earlier.

Their supreme stratagem was to designate popular culture as the essential *American* culture, refusing the prevalent Europeanization of critical and artistic practice that marked the writings of the *PR* critics, and the so-called *Fugitives* group of southern critics led by John Crowe Ransom, Robert Penn Warren, and Alan Tate, whose newly forged nationalism and modernism derived from different sources. To peruse the pages of *PR* during the late 1940s and throughout the 1950s is to encounter this diversity. The *PR* editors, particularly Philip Rahv, William Phillips, Clement Greenberg, and Lionel Trilling, were not only congenitally enamored of European culture, but never tired of proclaiming its superiority over the art work of their own country. Trilling was a veritable Anglophile, and Rahv may have left Russia physically, but his emotional and intellectual commitments remained tied to its culture. Similarly, while Greenberg became a virtual publicist for a new style of American art—abstract expressionism—it was clear that he favored the movement precisely because of its continuity with the twentieth-century modernism of Picasso and Kandinsky.

Far from being emanations of a "degraded" high culture that Clement Greenberg had depicted in his major declaration "Avant Garde and Kitsch"[30] or simply variant products of a massive Culture Industry, the new journalists developed a theory whose key tenet is that whatever its commercial uses, rock and roll and other forms are a genuine popular culture linked to a definite social layer of U.S. society. This position implies that the traditional distinctions—between high and low, in which the former is privileged for various reasons and equally between mass and popular culture—are conjurings of elite intellectuals that bear no relation to the postwar situation and, especially, fail to comprehend the special position of youth during this period. This is the genesis of a postmodern sensibility that Wolfe contended, nearly twenty years before Jean-Francois Lyotard's celebrated report, was, in effect, a condition rather than a mental attitude, rooted in historical changes rather than mere opinion.[31] Here postmodern consists in the rejection of the high/low distinction, even if it does not abjure aesthetics.

As we will see, the new cultural journalism in America worked out both a generational theory of politics and culture *and* a conception of subculture or counterculture based on it. For some, among them Greil Marcus, rock and roll expressed in its myths, symbols, and social commentary a *national* culture. Rock and roll, plainly the popular music of the generations born after 1940, becomes, for these writers, a marker not only of difference but, more to the point, of rebellion. Specific songs—Chuck Berry's "School Days," Bob Dylan's "Like a Rolling Stone," the Beatles' "With a Little Help from My Friends" (an SDS favorite), the Rolling Stones' "Satisfaction," Janis Joplin's performance style—these and others formed a canon, but were also anthems through which this generation and, more generally, America in the 1960s and early 1970s experienced itself.

A Ph.D. in American Studies from Yale University, Wolfe pioneered at one of the totem newspapers, the *New York Herald Tribune*'s *New York* magazine, what is now known as "cultural reporting." Rejecting the objectivism and positivism of conventional reporting that rigorously excluded the voice of the reporter, the new journalists, following the example of an older generation of critics, combined their critical sense with their accounts. That is, in contrast to conventional reporting, which, epistemologically, tries to emulate some of the assumptions of modern science, most importantly that the object is a pre-existent, closed system that through observation and interviews is reflected in an "objective" report, the new journalism *constitutes the object* through its encounter with it. The object is taken as open and therefore its constitution as part of a universe of meaning is subject to the intervention of the act of reporting. While these assumptions are largely made in the practices of the reporter rather than in anything like a theoretical or methodological statement, one can discern, allusively, an incipient theory in Wolfe's blunt polemics, incorporated in his investigative pieces.

One of the major elements of Wolfe's style is that the reports are always framed in the first person. The piece is as much an account of a process of investigative *discovery* as it is of the results of the investigation. In fact, the distinction between the two is usually blurred, so that results are represented as the outcome of a discovery that is never articulated in neutral terms. Wolfe makes us aware of his own perspective, of what he is searching for. The model for this kind of writing is the hard-boiled fiction of Cain, Hammett, and Chandler rather than the muckrakers and other journalistic traditions that owed their inspiration to positivism.

The first collection of his articles for *New York* and other publications, especially *Esquire,* became for magazine and underground newspaper critics and other non-academic younger intellectuals a veritable manifesto. And it mattered little that most of those whom these pieces inspired were part of, or at least on the periphery of, the New Left, even as he never tired to remind his readers of his own skeptical, apolitical views, at least in terms of the issues of that day. The common cause of the new journalist-critics, regardless of their respective political affinities, was their rejection of the cosmopolitan, high cultural proclivities of *PR* and its wider circles. For, by 1960, critics such as Trilling, Irving Howe, and John Peale Bishop, an occasional but unlikely *PR* contributor, the philosophers Sidney Hook and William Barrett, art critics Harold Rosenberg and Clement Greenberg, had assimilated fully the cold war imperative to defend the West against communist barbarism.

Despite its quite different context, the introduction to this first collection, *The Kandy Kolored Tangerine-Flake Streamline Baby* (1965), reiterates themes of class and generation that are, absent any hint of scientificity, remarkably resonant with those of the work of Stuart Hall, Paul Willis, and Dick Hebdige rather than with the later manifestations of cultural studies in America. Wolfe places the new popular culture in the perspective of social practices as well as representations, where, as we have seen, the fact that cultural studies is situated largely in the humanities, especially literature and art history, meant, until recently, that the scope of the very idea of culture is inevitably narrowed.

The essays in this collection treat, in various ways, "what has happened in the United States since World War II." Rather than bemoan mass culture as an unmitigated disaster, a sign of the degeneration of aesthetic sensibility, Wolfe *explains* the sharp break from classicism as the result of a certain kind of democratization of culture:

What has happened . . . has broken that pattern [of the dominance of classical English high cultural style]. The war created money. It made massive infusions of money into every level of society. [Shades of Hoggart's lament.] Suddenly classes of people whose styles of life had been practically invisible had the money to build monuments to their own styles. Among teen-agers, this took the form of custom cars, the twist, the jerk, the monkey, the shake, rock and roll music generally, stretch pants, decal eyes—and all these things, these teen-age styles of life, like Indigo Jones' classicism, have started having an influence on the life of the whole country.[32]

Referring to the replacement of baseball by stock car racing as the South's most popular sport, Wolfe argues that "this wild car sport with standard looking cars that go 180 miles an hour or so, this symbolizes a radical change in the people as a whole." What is obviously infuriating to intellectual elites about these changes is that they are led by "proles, peasants, and petty burghers [who] suddenly got enough money to start up their incredible car world."[33] The new culture, greased by new money, is that of the uneducated and corresponds to Thompson's "productive" classes recently enshrined within political rhetoric as the "working, middle class."

Wolfe: "Stock car racing, custom cars—and for that matter the jerk, the monkey, rock music—still seem beneath serious consideration, still the preserve of ratty people with ratty hair and dermatitis and corroded thoracic boxes and so forth. Yet all these rancid people are creating new styles all the time and changing the whole country in ways nobody seems to record much less analyze."[34]

"Ratty people with ratty hair and dermatitis," descriptive metaphors that tell of a cultural *movement* composed largely of "proles and petty burghers" who have used their newly won affluence to assert their own *agency,* one that left a panoply of cultural critics simultaneously terrified and awed. Wolfe's allusions refer both to what Thompson had called the productive classes that included small businesspeople as well as industrial workers, and to the young generation. His antagonists are clearly the intellectuals who, by 1955, were firmly in control of both the high cultural apparatus as well as the mid-cult criticism that pervaded the totem newspapers. They were the guardians of distinction, telling us—even those who never would or could enter an art gallery, museum, or classical concert, or read the canon of high modernist poetry or fiction—what is real art and, with it, genuine cultivation. "High" art can always be defined in formal terms by its complexity, awareness of the traditions within which it is ensconced as well as those it has overturned, its capacity for abstraction from the particulars of objects, and, most of all, the centeredness of the subject—the artist. This centeredness is signified by a distinctive, personal voice constructed from the colors on the artist's palette, by the originality of (his) conception of space, by the ruptures with the banalities of conventional, by now middle-brow, styles, by the refusal of figural representations. Most of all, as we saw in Chapter 2, the "high" is defined by its reflexivity, that it calls attention to the material process of the production of art as well as its gestures.

After all, any cultivated music fan can hear Shostakovich's angular ironic voice in the first eight bars of any piece, at least until the last decade of his life when playfulness gave way to a somber, almost silent mood reminiscent of Webern's late style. His signature, especially in his early and middle works, can be recognized by the mannerism of the scherzo movements of any symphonic or chamber work. Webern's music is marked by its silences and refusal of narration; Stravinsky's style is immediately recognizable. And who can fail to spot a Picasso? His individuality is indelibly inscribed in every painting, no matter what style he has invented or temporarily adopted.

The journalist/critics of popular music, like Wolfe himself, were profoundly wrenched from their own high cultural bearings by pop art, which, together with minimalism (which, however, retained all the trappings of high art), challenged the hegemony of abstract expressionist painting and, indeed, the whole apparatus of legitimate culture. What Andy Warhol, the most visible figure in the pop art movement, did was this: he used the institutional apparatus of the art world—museums as much as collectors—to declare obsolete the fence separating museum and commercial art. The innovations are well known: the air-brushed hyper realism of the Campbell's soup can inserted in a picture frame and hung on gallery walls; the portraits of the rich and famous, most of them, like Marilyn Monroe, mass cult icons; and, finally, Warhol's work as sponsor of the rock group The Velvet Underground, themselves a "border" band that broke both with the circumspection of popular ballads and rock music by identifying not only with cultural radicalism but also with an anti-utopian sensibility exemplified by songs such as "Heroin" and "Walk on the Wild Side," the most famous song of the group's lead singer, Lou Reed, which appeared after the band broke up. But the Velvets also incorporated, through John Cale, Lamont Young's eerie minimalism, suggesting, in the combination with rock, a new polyglot genre in which the categories of high and low are simply exploded.

And, of course—and this is especially accented in Wolfe's and Marcus's work—the indelible traces of the dominant myth/symbol paradigm of American Studies are ever present. No artifact can be discussed apart from its status as social and cultural representation, especially the degree to which it symbolizes the sensibility and cultural preferences of class and generational groups.

The alternative newspapers and magazines—especially the *Village Voice, Rolling Stone, Crawdaddy, Creem,* and the collective underground press of the late 1960s—promulgated Wolfe's earlier claim that popular culture was emblematic, not of the end of Western culture, but of the emergence of a new generation/class that, whatever its antecedent formation, aggressively asserted its claim to have produced a valid, alternative aesthetic against the art of an older, anachronistic but powerful critical tradition. The upstart critics vehemently denounced the categories as well as the judgments of the critical establishment: for them, there is no "authentic" art that opposes itself to mass culture; there is only good and bad art. In fact, there is no mass culture, if Warhol, Rauschenberg, and Johns are right that what is taken as "schlock" by the Greenbergs and Rosenbergs—especially images borrowed from Madison Avenue and comic strips—are really authentic expressions of the world that emerged after the war. If we are surrounded by advertising and comic strips—and for Wolfe this signifies the triumph of the proles, burghers, indeed the ratty people—the effort to deny the aesthetic value of commercial artifacts could result only in the construction of reactionary attempts to make the past present and, for this reason, is doomed to failure.

In the debate between the 1960s journalist-critics and the high cult establishment we can observe a sharply divergent aesthetic. Greenberg, for example, exalts the value of a minority culture against a thoroughly abhorrent political and cultural reality. The best the prevailing political environment can provide, in this perspective, is the space of an oppositional aesthetic sensibility at a time relentlessly committed to conformism. Thus, the artist and critic play within the distinction between liberal democracy and the cultural leveling that inheres in the commodity form. Opposition consists principally in the *gesture* since it cannot find political space, nor contest economic power.

As we saw in the writing of Kael, what exercises the aesthetic elite is precisely what is most subversive about mass culture: its capacity to bring to the surface normatively unarticulated eros. The critical establishment takes the point of view of the artist against the audience which, for the most part, has been adversely affected by the flattening of culture, but more particularly the crowd's unquenchable thirst for immediate gratification. The new critics were themselves fans of pop culture, part of the audience for it. They grew up with it, sang the songs and savored the movies and made love to it. They saw in the moment of the 1960s the merger of pop culture as a national culture with the movements to overthrow the institutions of domination, especially the civil rights and the youth movements.

The most contentious and ultimately deconstructive of their claims was that there was no "high" culture with the aesthetic authority to define alternatives such as rock, movies, and television as "low" forms. Moreover, like the Birmingham school, the young American rock critics, but also the alternative press's movie critics, insisted that so-called popular culture produced symbolic forms that had a social and historical referent in a contemporary political critique of mainstream culture, including the official cultural apparatus. That is, it was not a question of "cultural deprivation" that constituted the *choice* of certain forms and genres. Nor could these be evaluated on criteria that had always informed high cultural criticism.

So, following Wolfe's invocation of "ratty people with ratty hair" if not the proles and peasants among whom gangsters had become their vehicle, the pop critics constructed an aesthetic canon the criteria for which were no less ambivalent with respect to *distinction* than was Warhol. For, in many respects, the work of Marcus, Christgau, Dave Marsh, Ellen Willis, and Simon Frith, to mention only some of the most prominent, was informed by modernist sensibilities while at the same time, especially in their break with the scientistic apparatus of traditional journalism, they followed Wolfe's postmodern turn.

Their residual modernism consisted in their attempt to construct a pantheon of works and artists who best gave voice to their generation, who were part of its leap into History, not only in consideration of its political but also its cultural radicalism. In this sense, although Wolfe may have invented, or at least made public, some of the categories of the pop critical school—class, generation, the importance of affluence (post-scarcity society) for historical change, the refusal of the high/low distinction, and so forth—he was not prepared to take the next step. At the end of the day, he was a populist, at a moment when populism was a radical gesture. But by the late 1960s, it became clear that there was a difference between populism and radicalism. In aligning himself with populism, Wolfe had become a tribune of anti-intellectualism as much as a progenitor of one tendency of the postmodern condition.

As premature postmodernism, his provocative and absolutely central essay on Las Vegas as a liberated zone of postwar affluence is also an entirely original judgment of the city's architecture and culture. But the other side of his invocation of southwestern working-class defiance of the eastern cultural establishment, for which taste and not money talked, was Richard Nixon's pronouncement of the interests of the "silent majority." This in the midst of the civil rights explosion, and the most visible leftward movement among students in American history.

Wolfe's main idea is style. There is a clear Las Vegas style that can be demarcated from any other: "the incredible electric sign gauntlet of Las Vegas' strip, U.S. Route 91, where the neon amid the par lamps—bubbling, spiraling, rocketing, and exploding in sunbursts ten stories high out in the middle of desert—celebrate one story casinos."[35] This theme of "electronic simulation,"[36] imposed on nature in the guise of a desert, is the referent for this popular aesthetic. The "free form" of the signmaker identifies the glory of Las Vegas architecture. The proles and the burghers have finally been freed from scarcity by taking an otherwise useless, arid, landlocked area and converting it into a site in which a gaggle of dreams can be simulated. Las Vegas counters the boredom of the urban landscape and the equally numbing routines of wage labor with nonstop stimulation as well as simulation. It is not only gambling that stimulates or the signs that promise timeless pleasure, but the Las Vegas "buttocks decolletage" that, for the middle-aged (male) visitor turn the clock back twenty-five years when the sexual intimations of the stripper were, at least putatively, possible.

The hero of the piece is none other than the fabled gangster "Bugsy" Siegel, who, in 1945, pulled into the town with a couple of million dollars and, with the enthusiastic approbation of the city fathers, invented the scene by setting up its first gambling casino. Wolfe manages to retain some distance from Las Vegas, but he can barely contain his own enthusiasm for what he calls the

"Siegel aesthetic" of unbounded desire, that can be realized by anybody with a few bucks and a little time to spare. Next to the puritanism that pervades most of American culture in its industrializing era—the anti-drug mania, the passion for sexual propriety, and especially the relentless monuments to the work ethic symbolized by the office buildings that fill the skyscape of the large cities—this desert Xanadu is an oasis. Like Rabelais's depiction of the carnival's function in medieval peasant culture, Las Vegas provides a way to escape time, a *violation* of conventional morality. It is the physical space of the excess denied in everyday life, the mythic territory where dreams achieve legitimacy long denied by mainstream upper-middle-class culture.

This is definitely not the vision of the cultural critics of the pop music generation. Theirs is not of a proletarian simulacrum of the paradise that escaped with the car and mortgage payments, themselves symbolic of the postwar era. What they extracted from Wolfe was a full-throated appreciation of America and some of its most controversial protrusions: sex, drugs, and rock and roll, as exemplars of the possibilities contained in the post-scarcity epoch that was at hand. Their radicalism stemmed not *primarily* from the deprivations associated with the class structure of capitalist society (although class issues were important for them), but with its social and cultural repressions that, for many of this generation, were understood as the condition that made economic oppression and political powerlessness possible.

Here the influence of Herbert Marcuse's mid-1950s epic testament to the coming of post-scarcity society, *Eros and Civilization* (1955), as well as Paul Goodman's equally utopian statement, *Growing Up Absurd* (1959), were most apparent. Unlike the early and conventionally political New Left for which the influences of the black freedom movement and modern left/liberalism were the most salient (both movements were concerned with ending economic inequality in a land of abundance), the cultural radical critics were tuned into a different deprivation—pleasure—and some argued that, in the wake of America's technological and military power to provide economic abundance, the new issue was *freedom* to claim happiness, not only the "right" to survive. In this, there are strong elements of a position that resumes, albeit unwittingly, Walter Benjamin's claim that we can achieve liberation in a technological society only by going through the machine, not by denying it.

Like his colleagues of the Frankfurt School, Marcuse could not shed his anxiety about the popular, namely, that it would bring the irrational forces from their subterranean existence to the political surface, such as occurred in the 1930s. Determined to make a solid break from both liberal ideology and the intellectual ghosts of the thirties, Wolfe exulted in the popular as a symbolic act of defiance by a long suppressed class of common people (which, for him as for Ortega, was not confined to the working class) whose quest for pleasure had no transcendent existence beyond its capacity to mobilize the excluded. In contrast, most cultural critics in the 1960s and 1970s grasped the emergence of the popular, particularly rock and roll music, as a sign of radical hope. In this sense, although inspired to some degree by British cultural studies and Wolfe, they took a different turn.

While it would be an overstatement to argue that considerations of *class* exclusion were either ignored or absent from the writing of cultural journalists, especially Dave Marsh, who became a virtual publicist for Bruce Springsteen's variety of working-class populism, it is important to stress the degree to which these critics combined a tacit theory of class with that of generation. The scientific Marxism of British cultural studies, as we have seen, militated against any version of a theory of generations since the core of this idea is that a generation is constituted not primarily along class lines but as a historically specific cohort that shares a series of common experiences of its own time that results in new cultural and even political practices.

For example, we read in the literature of the Weimar period tales of the young men who returned, defeated, to Germany from the Great War, who saw the world turned upside down. Their worldview, inscribed in philosophy, science, and art marks the era of Weimar culture: Brecht's plays, Grosz's drawings, the tremendous influence of Spengler's epic *Decline of the West* on the intellectuals of the 1920s, and the new physics represented by Heisenberg and Niels Bohr signified a deep suspicion of the certainties of the past, particularly the repressive orderliness of Bismarck's Germany. They shared a cultural and political skepticism that, despite the democratic constitution of the new Republic, the rise of social-democracy to state power, and the growth of the Communist party to mass proportions, permanently supplanted the optimism of the pre-war period. One can see this sense of the brutality of everyday existence in Alfred Döblin's *Berlin Alexanderplatz* as much as in Kafka's stories, in Brecht's cynical *Threepenny Opera,* and Klee's spare, almost silent and despairing paintings.

Similarly, we may see the emergence of the 1960s movements in generational terms. Buoyed by the unparalleled economic prosperity of the postwar era, the generation born in the United States around 1940–1950, reared in the shadow of the Depression but having no direct experience of its hardships, shared two quite distinct perceptions: first, that the still powerful puritanism of hegemonic American culture was entirely anachronistic in the wake of postwar prosperity; and that the struggle for popular culture was an integral aspect of a new politics of pleasure. The slogan "sex, drugs, and rock and roll" signified that repressive institutions of work, family, and church had lost their cultural grip on the young even if many were obliged to hold down a job to put bread on the table and maintained strained relations with their families.

It would not be excessive to claim that the popular music of the 1950s and 1960s that replaced the old Hit Parade ballads may be considered the hymns of a new secular religion in which the politics and practices of pleasure acquired ethical, even moral standing. Listening and dancing to music was not considered frivolous or some kind of obligatory "recreation," but an aspect of an intense search for the spiritual significance of sensuous experience. Having rejected the mind/body split, they neither trivialized sexuality nor viewed it as reproductive. Marcuse's utopian essay, *Eros and Civilization,* which reversed Freud's lament that, in the service of stability, the pleasure principle must be subordinated, was, perhaps, together with similar and parallel works of Norman O. Brown, Paul Goodman, and Theodor Roszak, the crucial document that alongside rock music inspired however indirectly the emerging youth culture. For the function of these writings was to articulate, at least for intellectuals, what had remained inchoate in the early postwar period—the yearning for freedom expressed in the slogan "free your body, free your mind."

But it would be a mistake to conflate the traditional intellectuals such as Marcuse and Goodman with the intellectuals of rock and roll culture. In fact, as we will shortly see, the intellectuals of this culture, the journalist-critics who were of the 1960s generation as much as their work was about it, distanced themselves, at least at first, from the older, academic and political intellectuals. This movement decisively changed the meaning of the term "radical," which in the late nineteenth and early twentieth centuries came to be identified primarily, if not exclusively, with the struggle for economic justice, the ideas of social equality, and, in doctrinal terms, with anarchism, socialism, and communism. In contrast to these earlier years during which the demands of workers movements dominated the radical and much of the liberal imagination and cultural radicalism was, in the main, confined to the margins of political life, the mid 1960s witnessed a time, however brief, in contemporary history when the politics of eros, in many forms, edged to the center of political discourse.

Of course, a powerful backlash against sexual freedom arrived, inevitably, almost coincident with its emergence as a public issue. Even as the Supreme Court issued its remarkable decision in favor of a woman's right to abortion in 1973, cultural conservatism recovered its voice in response to the dissemination of cultural radical ideas and practices well beyond the young. This anti-abortion, pro-"family" upsurge developed within the framework of a broader effort to repeal the 1960s, a counterattack that became the central strategy of conservative hegemony into the 1990s. Many expressed their rebellion against prevailing social mores by growing long hair, using drugs, and, even more egregiously from the perspective of conventional mores, including those of the traditional left, by refusing steady work at every opportunity.

Characteristically, the new rock criticism was, in the main, the work of twenty- to thirty-year-olds, many of whom were themselves engaged in the same drug and sex experiments as their subjects, the performers. They were, simultaneously, participants and observers of the rock revolution; their writings were indispensable elements of it. For example, consider the passionate statements of Greil Marcus, perhaps the boldest and the one who made the major theoretical claim for the movement. Writing in the late 1960s, Marcus chides two professors—presumably S. M. Lipset and Lewis Feuer—who, commenting on the Berkeley Free Speech movement, claimed that the famous passage from Marx's pamphlet on the counterrevolution of Louis Napoleon, the *18th Brumaire,* was most on the participants' lips. "Hegel remarks somewhere that all facts of great importance in world history occur twice. He forgot to add: the first time as tragedy the second as farce."

"Well," Marcus retorts, "the remark may have wide currency among some circles, but among students, it was another quote which provided the metaphors for our situation, from Bob Dylan's *Memphis Blues Again*: 'And here I sit so patiently / Waiting to find out what price / You have to pay to get out of / Going through all these things twice.'

"The differences in metaphors are important. One seeks an academic and intellectual conclusion, a truth that will last the ages, and the other tries to establish and confirm the present moment, and in doing so, to save one from it. One metaphor structures time; the other tries to escape it. More important to me, though, is the fact that one statement is drawn from the vast stores of academic knowledge, the other from rock n' roll." And, according to Marcus, the professors cannot really *know* rock and roll; they cannot "understand it instinctually, to know that any one piece of music is part of over ten years of experience, to be in tune with a medium, is not something one can pick up by a little attention or a casual listening . . . Rock n roll was is and will be a basic part of the experience, of the growing up years of present college or non-student generation. It will continue to be so for the generations that will follow."[37]

Later, in his major work *Mystery Train* (1975), Marcus was to announce that rock and roll had become *the* national-popular music of America. But in these earlier passages we observe some of the characteristic perspectives of the era: this generation sought to "escape time," to break the age-old pattern of repeating the past and even to defy the ideology according to which maturity signifies coming to terms with everyday life, with the world of work and family, those conservative practices on which the reproduction of the prevailing state of things rests.

In this connection, the philosophy of rock and roll resumes themes that, since Nietzsche and especially Bergson, have haunted contemporary thought. This philosophy tries to recover the "feeling" of duration, to value the present, when the idea of "progress" with its resonances for the value of forgetting as the necessary step for privileging the future becomes suspect. Thus, the presence of the past is either denied or ignored in favor of a notion of the "now" as future.

Marcus is not only the theoretician of rock music but perhaps among the few genuine theoretically minded of those writers who celebrated the 1960s youth subculture. In opposition to the romantics and conservatives, the rock and roll generation does not look backward for the integrated moment on which to base a critique of the present. It is a utopian movement, but not future oriented. Instead "Rock n' roll seeks to do something the earlier popular music had always denied—to establish and confirm, to brighten and deepen, to create and recreate the present moment." But, as if to anticipate the inevitable objection that repetition always reifies by obliterating memory, Marcus qualifies his formulation: "Rock, as a medium, knows that it is only up to a certain point that this can be done, To keep a moment of time alive it's necessary to make a song new every time it's performed, every time it's played." The point of the unique performance, of an original, entirely new hearing is to "*obliterate* time and allow you to move freely in the space that the music gives you." Bliss is achieved when "mind and body . . . merge with the music."[38] Marcus's formulation of the cultural significance of rock tacitly acknowledges that the American 1960s was a privileged "space" for discovering the dimensions of the body that in everyday life are systematically suppressed in the service of social and physical reproduction. The struggle against time was also waged, by some, with mind-expanding drugs that enlarged the space for this exploration by slowing time/expanding the experience of duration. Just as the dream-work is process that occurs in a few seconds during which complex narratives are experienced, so the merger of mind and body in LSD and in the rock song were opportunities to escape time by occluding the everyday in order to "know" the emotionally prelinguistic self.

This, precisely, is the reason that music became the crucial form through which the generational community of the 1960s was forged. Young people demonstrated against state policy—against the war—but also for drug legalization. Even more fierce was their refusal to work and generate nuclear families because these were the signs of the reassertion of the dominance of time. What children and adults perceive as boredom—having time on one's hands—became for Marcus's generation a possession to be sought and treasured. Perhaps the unarticulated slogan of this period was duration. For although novelty is produced by difference, it was not the difference between past and future that marked this quest, but its reconceptualization as a spatial metaphor. To the conventional evolutionary paradigm that envisions the inevitable passage, *through time* from the lower to the higher, in which everything comes into being and passes away, when death is simultaneously the beginning of new life, Marcus's meditation proposes the alternative of *merging* into new community as the weapon against death.

Just as the fury of the conservative counterrevolution was gearing up for its "decisive" assault at the end of the 1970s, Marcus acknowledged that the link between rock and roll and the "mass movements of the 1960s" had been severed, that the music no longer enjoyed a quasi underground existence because it had been disseminated among an audience that far exceeded the generation that once experienced it as their own uniquely subversive activity. Most of all the "political realities" had reinstated everyday life and reasserted the dominance of routine over life, a living death the escape from which appeared increasingly improbable. The Beatles split up, "Dylan eased up," and the music no longer had a firm identity in specific movements and groups.

In 1978, in the wake of the passing of the Age of Rock as a distinctive cultural movement, Marcus invited some of the best critics to contribute to creating a canon. Grouped under the title *Stranded,* they were charged to name one album they would like to hear if they were stranded on a desert island. The editor chose the biggest names of rock criticism: Bob Christgau, already a fixture at the *Voice*; John Rockwell of the *New York Times*; Ellen Willis, former rock critic for the *New Yorker,* at the time a *Voice* columnist; Simon Frith, in his own words the book's "token Englishman" and one of its two academic contributors, who writes extensively in the press and magazines, especially the *Times* of London; Lester Bangs, Dave Marsh; Janet Maslin, a *New York Times* film critic; and Langdon Winner, the other professor whose work on technology rather than his criticism got him a job at MIT.[39]

Of course, the writers chose different artists and groups. But what marked many of them was a fairly consistent aesthetic: they were looking for expressions of a rock avant garde and managed, collectively, to propose a fairly contemporary series of criteria. By the late 1970s (the book appeared in 1979), the artists that delved into the "demi-world" of the hard-edged urban environment (Christgau allowed that he had already "OD'd" on rural virtues) were clearly privileged over those that represented the older utopian sensibility. Now critics celebrated the "detachment" of the Rolling Stones, the "distance" of the short-lived late-60s group the Velvet Underground, the "sexual ambiguity" of the New York Dolls, their "sweet street-tough alienation" and especially their "crude, raucous, flashy" style and their punk, studied amateurishness.[40]

The times they changed, but not for the better. What these older and wiser writers found worthwhile was *irony,* without which critique invariably turns strident or, worse, sentimental. Even Lester Bangs's paean to Van Morrison's early *Astral Weeks,* which begins with a brief account of a period of personal depression, and shows how powerful is Morrison's encounter with life, cannot avoid describing the music in this way:

"What this is about is a whole set of verbal tics—although many are bodily as well—which are there for reason enough to go a long way toward defining his style. They're all over *Astral Weeks*: four rushed repeats of the phrases 'you breathe in, you breathe out' and 'you turn around' in 'beside you' in 'Cypress Avenue' twelve 'way up on's, 'baby' sung out thirteen times in a row sounding like someone running ecstatically downhill towards one's love."[41] Then "Van Morrison is interested, *obsessed* with how much musical or information he can compress into a small space, and almost conversely, how far he can spread one note, word, sound, or picture. To capture one moment, be it a caress or a twitch."

Bangs is plainly enthralled by Morrison's work, but the juxtaposition of "caress or twitch" is as jarring as the judgment—meant to highlight the very philosophical character of this music—that to escape time, Morrison becomes obsessively repetitive of words and phrases. The "tics" are Morrison's way of fighting death, but you can't help calling attention to the semi-comical obsession. But Ellen Willis's piece on the Velvet Underground brings to the surface what remains tacit in the writings of other contributors—the idea of avant garde rock. She identifies the Velvets as the "first important rock and roll artists who had no real chance of attracting a mass audience," since "the Velvets' music was too overtly intellectual, stylized and distanced to be commercial. Like pop art, which was very much a part of the Velvets' world, it was anti-art art made by anti-elite elitists."[42] Like the later development of "punk" rock that their work anticipated, this was music of "cultural opposition"—cranky, sometimes crude, "not only distinct from but antagonistic to its own cultural conglomerate, rock."

The possibility of the avant garde invariably presupposes the incorporation and dissemination of a once oppositional popular art where the term popular signifies the ability of the artist to attract a mass audience. The Velvets were avant garde precisely because their work exceeded the conventions of rock, reaching out to other musical genres such as minimalism, which had not yet found its ultimate audience; and because their ironic, often erotic comments on sexuality and other forms of pleasure are decoded in the songs, even as similar themes were still shrouded in metalanguages by the Beatles and the Rolling Stones, for example.

Perhaps the boldest move of Willis's assessment is her defense of irony, the sure sign of detachment. There is an unpredictable gentleness in a music that means to resist authority, even the authority of commercial success that in the late 1960s and early 1970s demanded that "cutting edge" rock music defy the conventions of art. And, in their intellectuality, the Velvets and, after their breakup, Lou Reed, went against the grain of the populism of, say, Bruce Springsteen, the predictable social commentary of Bob Dylan, or the flight from oppositional art that increasingly marked mainstream rock music. Willis argues for the Velvets as leaders of a paradoxical, spiritual, but distanced avant garde, an opposition that is aware of the ambiguity of its cultural position both in and outside the banality of America's representative cultural form. In this respect, she argues that the Velvets defended rock and roll from itself, and countered rock's tendency to surrender to Muzak by resolutely employing its conventions in a novel and disturbing way that restored to the music its inherent vitality.

Perhaps alone among the critics of her generation, Willis refused to surrender her sharp, ironic, distanced wit to the music that she so passionately loved. What she praised in the Velvets—irony, distance, the struggle against nihilism—she reserved for herself as well. Which helps to account for the dialectical prose in her criticism: she works within the oppositions of the Velvets' music: order and chaos, art and violence, commitment and distance, sincerity and irony. Her identification with these oppositions allows her to retain her own outsiderness since it calls for no religious conversion. For, as she observes, complete trust in a "hostile world" is the path to self-destruction and the utopian sensibility seems to have been permanently laid to rest in the 1970s, a "leaner, meaner time." What seems eminently utopian in Willis's criticism is her claim that an avant garde is still possible, a claim that retains the vehemence of the earlier judgment that popular forms are identical to "mass" culture. Yet, neither Willis nor the Velvets is prepared to "ease up" on their criticism, whose referent is the possibility of pleasure in a "lean, mean" time. This hope is masked in the ironic cadences of the fragment of a song about the encounter of "a woman (transvestite?) buying a night with a sexy young boy," from Lou Reed's late 1970s album "Street Hassle," that Willis says begins as "squalid; it turns out to be transcendent. Reed's account of the odd couple's lovemaking is as tender as it is erotic: 'And then sha la la la he entered her slowly and showed her where he was coming from / and then sha la la la la he made love to her gently, it was like she'd never ever come.' "[43] Here Reed takes the knife to the conformist binary of sex—work and eroticism—and explodes, simultaneously, the alleged certainties of sexual identity.

The 1970s and 1980s mark the end of the identification of the cultural politics of pleasure with populism and nationalism. For while during the 1960s, responding to what they perceived to be a brutal and immoral war in southeast Asia, hundreds of thousands of young people had occasion to renounce their national identity, many of the intellectuals of this generation clung to the hope that the energy of the youth revolt both against government policy and social mores and the music that both generated and was generated by it could help create a "new" America radically wrenched from its puritanical and expansionist tradition. This hope was particularly consolidated by the powerful civil rights movement whose successes provided for some reason to believe that racism was, at last, destined for oblivion. The resurgent conservatism of this period at the political and cultural levels drove hope to the margins. And Lou Reed, John Cale, and groups such as the Dolls, the Who, or British punk exemplified best by the Sex Pistols kept alive the possibility of a cultural opposition without the expectation that it could grip a generation, much less a national culture.

Avant garde rock, and the critics who dramatized and publicized it, lives a liminal existence: to the extent that rock actually displaced the sentimental ballads and became the national music of Britain and the United States and succeeded in challenging, along with other aspects of American culture, the folkloric and otherwise traditional cultures of Europe and the post-colonial countries of Latin America, the musicians of the cultural opposition elected to work, after a fashion, within the genre. At the same time, they developed hybrid sounds to signal their distance from the now almost entirely assimilated rock business. Some like the New York Dolls deliberately adopted a crude amateur style. Like proponents of avant garde progressive jazz, Reed, Cale, and Robert Frith, for example, work with or borrow from minimalist artists such as Terry Riley and Brian Eno; the result is, in addition to a novel sound, also a parody of the desire to escape time through repetition and variation.

The course of journalistic cultural reporting and criticism in the 1980s parallels that of rock music. Where once such a newspaper as the alternative (if not underground) *Village Voice,* the underground press, and youth-oriented, semi-trade magazines such as *Rolling Stone* were the chief sources of rock criticism, by the late 1970s the totem press had hired many erstwhile oppositional critics: the *New York Times* changed its format by introducing an entire cultural section in its daily coverage and, on Fridays, provides extensive reviews and reports on popular music along with its traditional high cultural criticism. John Rockwell and, a few years later, Jon Pareles, both part of the oppositional criticism, became staff writers for the paper. By the mid-1980s most major metropolitan dailies followed suit. Today, the mainstreaming of rock criticism is almost complete even as the *Voice* and *Rolling Stone* maintain their position as journals of record for the industry with a tinge of the older oppositional work. Their coverage is more extensive and their commentary tends to be more iconoclastic, but the days of the articulated cultural opposition in mass circulation newspapers and magazines are, for the present, over.

With few exceptions cultural opposition has passed, for better or worse, to some quarters of the universities—a small fraction of English and sociology departments, women's, Latino, and African-American studies, which, however, have undergone frequent crises owing to the ambiguities of identity politics (of which more in the next chapter), and among cultural critics ensconced in art history, communications, and cultural studies departments and programs. In these precincts, the overwhelming influences of European "theory" are in evidence whether these are of British, German, or especially French vintage.

The explicit theoretical cast of contemporary criticism reflects, in the first place, its academicization. While universities have, finally, made room for criticism and history of mass or popular culture—even rock music—they have placed severe constraints on these practices. Those who refuse to subordinate their criticism to traditional literary and sociological methods have been obliged, at least, to present themselves as scholars and, consequently, adopt "theory" as a legitimating discourse. At the same time, with few exceptions, they (and criticism) have paid the price of a restricted audience. Much of the newer work appears as journal articles, book collections oriented to academic audiences, and is, accordingly, read by undergraduates in connection with newly created courses on various aspects of popular culture.

Although the struggle to gain recognition for the study of popular culture as legitimate intellectual knowledge is by no means won, universities throughout the United States, Canada, and Latin America are steadily retreating from their hidebound positions that only traditional disciplinary knowledge is worthy of the term "scholarship." Certainly, the conventional humanistic disciplines have yielded ground to arguments according to which all objects that can be called "art" embody the social and cultural context within which they are produced. While this perspective acknowledges that there are variations of form, these are accorded no particular privilege, except the prestige that is endowed on "high" art by its sponsors and its elite audience.

CHAPTER SEVEN

The Authority of Knowledge

I

CONTRARY TO the common sense of universities as ivory towers within whose walls humanist scholars plumb the treasures of the past, scientists labor through the night to make illuminating discoveries about the nature of the universe, and students sit at the feet of teachers who transmit the intellectual knowledge and the cultural legacy of western civilization in the image of a stern, but dedicated, John Houseman-style professor, the American academy may be characterized as a *knowledge* factory. Of course, in a system of higher education consisting of some 1700 colleges and universities, half a million full- and part-time professors, more than 14 million students, a private sector, and a public sector and many schools that are privately administered but largely publicly funded, there are a few examples of each of the popular cliches. And it is safe to say that without such scenes of research, thought, and learning "for its own sake" universities would perhaps experience a much deeper legitimation crisis than that which they currently suffer. Yet, despite budget cuts imposed by recession-torn state governments and administrations and the pervasive anti-intellectualism of North American culture, universities remain the main sites of scientific, technical, and policy research without which the economy and the state, including the huge defense establishment, would rust and eventually collapse. Moreover, they are the places where what counts as legitimate intellectual knowledge is produced and, perhaps equally important, where ruling and resistant ideologies are refined and disseminated.[1]

The concept of legitimate intellectual knowledge can be grasped only in comparison to what it is not: practical knowledge such as cooking, plumbing, and other crafts; "trivial" or useless knowledge because it cannot, except under special circumstances, be converted into a commodity (but is subject to monetary exchange as in the case of baseball cards); gossip, which is, typically, bartered. Of these, practical knowledge is surely legitimate, but in the socially and historically constituted division of labor it is not designated as "intellectual." However, like the shifting significance of the binaries "normal" and "pathological," the distinction between "intellectual" and "practical," even "manual" is not fixed.[2] Legitimate intellectual knowledge is entirely conventional, that is, it is not a natural fact. Since the late nineteenth century, it consists in the "humanities" whose scope has broadened from natural philosophy and history, of which culture, ideas, and art are increasingly important, but has recently included the practices of the arts: criticism—as we saw in Chapter 6—was once considered a branch of journalism and incorporated within the realms of practical knowledge; and, of course, the "empirical" sciences. The separation of sciences from crafts and natural philosophy is a consequence of the development of a more specialized division of labor after the sixteenth century and, especially, the special role physics played in the development of modern industry. From a discourse that as late as the eighteenth century remained largely removed from practical affairs, with the important exception of astronomy and mechanics which were closely linked to navigation, mining, and weaponry, nineteenth-century science became an integral component of industrialization.

Of course, the histories of music conservatories and studio art schools are fairly long. They succeeded the apprenticeship system that had trained generations of artists in a manner similar to the way carpenters and shoemakers learned their trades. The schools were necessary to reproduce the form when the patronage system dried up with the decline of feudalism and the Italian city-states. Some were subsidized by the Crown and other state bodies; others were privately financed. And, in recent years, music and art schools have become commercial enterprises such as the Art Students League and Parsons School of Design in New York or, as in the case of the Juilliard, Curtis, and Eastman schools, have received corporate patronage to defray much of the costs of operation.

Since the 1940s the universities have increasingly provided a safe harbor for the arts—writing, visual, musical, and theater—where artists may elide some (but not all) of the insecurities of the market. This movement from bohemia, Broadway, and the public concert halls to academic precincts has had a profound effect on the conditions of production of arts as well as their products. In each of these forms, there has emerged a dual economy: one in which works are subject to the vicissitudes of buying and selling; and another in which the fashion process, aesthetic "standards," and the current tastes of academic critics and colleagues constitute an *academic marketplace*. One is no less competitive than the other nor, much to the consternation of the arts professoriate, are they exempted from the judgments of various audiences. Indeed, writers have had a difficult time in universities in part because, unlike visual arts such as painting and film where no academic discipline previously existed, they are obliged to seek tenure within English departments where, typically, the faculty has traditional academic credentials.

The drift of artists to universities is a compressed variant of a much longer term tendency of practical knowledges to reshape themselves as legitimate intellectual knowledge. We can adduce many examples: management and other aspects of private and public business has become an academic discipline; the progressive incorporation of professions that were once considered species of craft—law, medicine, journalism, social work, teaching, accountancy, engineering, and, of course, science, whose affiliation to academic institutions corresponds to the high cost of research that accompanied the maturation of industrial capitalism in the late nineteenth century. As always, the corporations followed the example of education and were perfectly happy to transfer most of the responsibility for "basic" scientific research to public universities which, after the civil war, had been founded as "land grant colleges" to provide labor and organized intelligence to agriculture and industry.

This chapter concerns what Michel Foucault has called the "insurgencies of subjugated knowledges" that, in the midst of a tidal wave of global conservatism in the most economically and politically powerful countries, including the former Soviet Union, burst upon the United States as well as British intellectual scene in various guises—poststructuralism, Marxism, postmodernism, and, most recently, cultural studies. As we will see, even as these insurgencies proclaimed the disrupted history of humanities and the sciences by deconstructing the underlying, unifying assumptions of the division of labor in legitimate intellectual knowledge, perhaps behind their own backs they resuscitated the "dead" project of their forebears who, with quite different philosophical underpinnings, labored to find a nonreductionist common ground for knowledge. This project intends, among other things, to interdict the hierarchy of knowledges by showing the conventionality of all legitimate knowledge even as, contradictorily, it attempts, within the disciplines, to insert itself into the process of canon formation. Similarly, it asserts the historicity of the disciplines while fighting to gain positions of power and influence within them. Finally, it shows that far from reflecting the external world in a series of statements the unity of which consists in falsifiable propositions subject to repetitive demonstration, science is a form of discourse like any other, even as these insurgencies labor mightily, by means of discourses huddled under the tent of "theory" to legitimate their own critical knowledge. Even as critical theory shows that the privileged position of natural science in the panoply of knowledges owes less to its superior methods than to its links with power, its insurgent character is frequently eroded as it edges toward the mainstream.

Before the turn of the twentieth century, American universities were neither the master sites for the production and dissemination of the humanistic knowledges such as literature, historiography, and philosophy nor the privileged spaces of various branches of the natural and social sciences.[3] These knowledges were shared between universities and journalists, men of wealth, and freelance essayists and artists such as Pope, Swift, Godwin; in the United States, Emerson, Thoreau, Hawthorne, Whitman, and Melville, to name the best known; and scientists such as Newton, Boyle, and Priestley. In fact, it was not until Michael Faraday was appointed by the Royal Institution in 1821 and achieved semiofficial status a decade later after he invented the electric motor, that physics became an ordinary profession. And, as late as the years just prior to World War II, most scientific research in the United States and Britain was performed in connection with industrial enterprises; the role of the university in science was confined, on the whole, to basic research and theory.

Philosophy, in its early forms the secular displacement of theology, has a much longer tenure in the academy and, as is well known, had already made room for economic, political, and educational theory by the latter decades of the eighteenth century. Sociology was, at first, a branch of philosophy or the rising discipline of economics; the emergence of social sciences as separate disciplinary domains awaited another century. For example, sociology departments were first established in the United States at the turn of the twentieth century; most early practitioners were ethnographers or economists, although it can be argued that the work of John Dewey and William James, leading philosophers in the early twentieth century, contained strong sociological strains. Yet Charles Sanders Peirce, perhaps its most important philosopher during the latter half of the nineteenth century, was not a professor. Ethnography divided between sociology and anthropology at about the same time; the difference was conventionally described in terms of their missions to study, respectively, contemporary and "primitive" societies. While anthropologists adopted the rule that their warrant was to account for their economic, political, and social practices within a totalizing framework, American sociology happily accepted the boundary between itself and economics and politics, situating itself in the middle range and, concomitantly, accepted the prevailing division of labor in society with respect to its own specializations. This accommodation resulted in making sociology, together with the new discipline of political science, the ideal policy sciences, especially during the ascent of welfare capitalism from the turn of the twentieth century through the 1960s.

The discipline of political science was founded even later in the century and did not gain widespread recognition until the 1930s when Harold Lasswell, Arthur F. Bentley, and Robert Merriam argued for a program to transform politics from and art and philosophy into an empirical science. Among them, Lasswell made significant contributions to directing research toward the analysis of political power as a social fact sui generis, but also to comprehend the psychological dimensions of political behavior. Others employed survey research methods that were being developed by sociologists in connection with market research for corporations selling consumer goods to the analysis of voting behavior. In this respect, apart from the traditional affiliation of political theory to philosophy, political science is the first true *policy* science; its methods and presuppositions are almost entirely directed to analyzing state policy and providing the necessary data to elected officials and bureaucrats in public agencies in their quest for politically viable public policies.

Charles Sanders Peirce, who worked outside universities as a government scientist, developed perhaps the first sociology of scientific knowledge. His doctrine in the "Fixation of Belief" that the truth of any scientific proposition consisted not in its correspondence between ideas and "reality" but the agreement among professional scientists as to its validity.[4] This view, on which Thomas Kuhn based his theory of scientific progress, emphasizes that beliefs become accepted truths after processes by which scientists, their journals, associations, and academic disciplines, especially the leaders, have decided the issue is thoroughly sociological and political. It has come to mean that the link between what counts as scientific knowledge and power is inextricable.

The study of literature has always privileged its national contexts. Although in the United States, French and German departments have a relatively long history, the study of English language literature traditionally meant *British* literature. American literature, as De Tocqueville reminded us, was simply derivative of the master canon of Great literature and did not deserve the compliment of critique.[5] We have seen how, in the wake of the occlusion of American poetry and fiction from the English canon, this prompted, in the 1920s and 1930s, a nationalist movement to found American Studies. At the other end of the spectrum, critics and scholars developed comparative literature to provide a basis for breaking out of the straightjacket of the national literatures.

Similarly, the entrance of the United States into global economic and political relations, especially after the First World War and the new liberal and radical internationalism that questioned, when not opposed to, the more imperialist adventures, combined to broaden the scope of academic historiography from its almost exclusive preoccupation with American history, much of it in the patriotic, heroic mode to the study of world economic, political, and cultural life in a comparative perspective. In the study of the development of the United States new work has recently been done in social and cultural history, the pioneering area of which was immigration, but also labor history. I invoke these examples to illustrate the degree to which the division of academic knowledge into disciplines is entirely conventional. From the early twentieth century to the 1960s the tendency within the humanistic disciplines was to subdivide into ever narrower specializations, even as the objects of study proliferated into new areas.

Even as the social sciences and the humanities were fragmenting, the natural sciences displayed a synthetic trend. Biology attempted to transform itself into a "hard" science; it merged with physics and chemistry and its methods became more mathematical than historical, more structural than functional in orientation. The development in the 1950s of molecular biology brought this prolonged process that began nearly a century earlier with genetics to fruition.[6] At the same time, biology as well as physics demonstrated the fusion of science and technology. By the 1960s, parallel to the social sciences, theoretical concerns in the natural sciences were yielding to technoscience; today physics and biology are ineluctably linked to the *machinery of knowledge,* not only in the metaphoric sense, but literally. Doing high energy particle physics entails the perfection of accelerators that can more precisely record the effects of "objects" that can only be inferred from their presumed effects.[7] Similarly, the practice of molecular biology—bioengineering—relies entirely on its main procedure, gene-splicing.

The significance of university-generated knowledges extends throughout the society. Intellectual labor is the engine of modern "material" production and key *research*-oriented universities are symbiotically entwined with both government and leading economic institutions—not only manufacturing and financial services but also agriculture. With the expansion of state intervention into the economy, including the establishment of a "social" wage (more commonly known as social services or the welfare state), the social sciences were brought closer to government policy by means of research contracts "in the name of science."

What Talcott Parsons calls the cultural system—norms and values by which people measure their conduct—Habermas calls the moral order, Gramsci "common sense," and Foucault the "regime of truth," both everyday as well as scientific, have become central intellectual issues that span the humanities and the social sciences. There is now a widespread perception that the "consensus" by which our economic, political, and social relations have been successfully managed even as other societies are suffering what may be termed a "legitimation" or "cultural" crisis has broken down. Despite the overarching identification of Americans with their own country's imperial aims, as during the Gulf War and other recent U.S. interventions, the presumption of a shared worldview or even the more restricted notion of a *morality* may no longer be made regardless of the performance of the economy or the strong continuity of the political system. The centrality of what has been termed "social issues" or simply "culture" stems from a pervasive uneasiness in our growing collective incapacity to maintain the line between private troubles and public issues. The conventional sociological distinction between "macro" and "micro" spheres no longer applies. Neither public figures nor "ordinary people" defined customarily as those whose work and personal lives are lived, on the whole, in anonymity, can expect to avoid the unexpected consequences of a once personal catastrophe; today, not only mass media, but also the tangled lattices of the legal system and the public bureaucracies routinely monitor private lives.

The December 24, 1991, issue of the *Wall Street Journal* provided a statistical comparison between the 1981–1982 and the 1990–1991 recessions to show that, by nearly all measures, the earlier downturn was more severe, except in consumer spending. Yet people were far more anxious about the economic situation in the early 1990s. Whatever the objective *facts,* their perceptions were that the economy was in deep trouble and that the national administration was doing little, if anything, to reverse the slide. Without entering into a discussion of the specific economic issues in this recession, it was evident that press reports focused on the weakness of what economists term "consumer confidence." In a related story, President George Bush's campaign advisors were urging him to send a signal of decisive and quick action, rather than heeding the warnings from his own economists that such ill-considered haste might backfire. Clearly, this is an instance of how collective perceptions or, if you like, the discourse of economic catastrophe becomes both a burning electoral issue and also affects the economy itself.

Neoclassical economics has long been concerned with economic perception. Consumer and investor confidence has been made a significant factor in forecasting. But even though theory tries to account for consumer and investor choices in their calculations, on the whole they adopt a behaviorist approach to determining how these choices are made. The investor or consumer is said to respond to market conditions on the basis of a rational assessment of alternative courses of action. For example, if interest rates are lowered, investors will tend to put their money in productive activities such as manufacturing or services. If the rates are high, they will purchase Treasury bills, municipal bonds, and other forms of spurious capital and engage in usury. Similarly, government investment in defense, highways, or directly into jobs may increase the deficit and drive interest rates up as the government seeks new loans to pay off those who previously lent it money, thereby discouraging productive investment.

That pessimism and uneasiness may dominate investment and consumption decisions even when other favorable conditions exist from a rational choice perspective and may deter some kinds of activity prompts certain types of public discourse such as that engaged in by politicians who rush to action not merely to gain partisan advantage, but also to build confidence. The whole of economic policy is dominated by a reading of neoclassical theory. In rough terms, politicians as well as academics accept that the goal of economic policy is to achieve growth whose constituents are consumption maximalization and the condition to insure profit maximalization. Ancillary considerations such as the quality of goods, their effects on the physical environment, collective health, or on cultural things are considered only in terms of disincentives to production, investment, and consumption. In effect, in the contemporary social world, economic calculations of all sorts have displaced nearly all values and norms, and have themselves become a cultural system that pervades nearly all human activity.

This consensus, with the major exception of groups such as blacks, women, and workers whose consent for these goals was contingent on the provision of a measure of social and economic justice, has been eroded further by those who have proposed counterhegemonic cultural norms. The quantitative-economic basis for human association will remain politically and culturally powerful so long as the ideology of material scarcity is reproduced by various social systems. Nevertheless, dissident voices have asserted that scarcity is artificially produced by unequal economic relations, but also by the social and cultural regime that undergirds them.[8] Of course, these knowledges have been unevenly disseminated throughout the underlying population; for intellectual strata these counterclaims have nearly the status of a new common sense. Similarly, although the sexual and cultural counterrevolution has reached into universities and other cultural institutions, its lights have not been fully extinguished.

In the universities, everyday culture(s) as objects of legitimate intellectual knowledge have over the past twenty years spanned the traditional gulf between the humanities and the social sciences. Within the humanities—the various literatures, ethical philosophy—and the branches of the social sciences that address political, social, and cultural studies—mainly theoretical and ethnographic—intellectuals have attempted to ferret out the hidden dimensions of culture. Since people with opposed orientations agree that culture has become a sharply contested sphere, this work frequently takes the form of *ideology production,* a phrase that may not be counterposed to some transcendent truth but signifies, instead, efforts to produce and reproduce common sense. Counterwise, transformative or critical intellectuals attempt to forge a counterhegemony by means, alternatively, of a moral or "scientific" discourse on culture.[9]

Historically, the production and transmission of a discourse on culture is properly the function of traditional intellectuals who in ancient, medieval, and early bourgeois societies had a recognized position, respectively, in the polity, in the church, and in the courts. With the breakdown of the feudal order, intellectuals not fortunate enough to be manor born or to receive patronage from rich merchants or "modern" aristocrats were obliged to sell their wares in the marketplace and became journalists and novelists whose work, with the growth of the bourgeois public, was serialized in newspapers and magazines and also became, in the nineteenth century, the main purveyors of common sense, both mainstream and oppositional. Until the middle of the nineteenth century, the distinctions between art, philosophy, and criticism were ambiguous—witness the broad scope of the work, say, of a Goethe, a Blake, or a Coleridge.

Industrialism transforms the life world in its image of instrumental rationality—the sharp division of intellectual and manual labor, the distinction between nature and culture and with it the division of labor in the knowledge domain, especially between the sciences and the humanities. The division of labor, construed earlier as distinctions between whole branches of economic activity, say, between shoes, banking, and iron production, now extends to occupations. What Marx termed the "collective worker" arises with the development of modern industry and we now speak within industrial production of the distinction between skilled and unskilled labor. And at the same time, it is extremely rare to find a novelist of the industrializing era who, like Goethe, also offered a (rejected) scientific theory of color or a philosopher who composes poetry. The Leonardos are long gone. Science, art, and philosophy once welded together in a single discourse are sundered, perhaps forever. The agents of this diremption offer, characteristically, a quantitative theory to apologize for this new situation. They say the division of intellectual labor is made necessary by the proliferation and growth of knowledges. The individual is simply incapable of knowing more than a fairly narrow range of things. We coin the term "renaissance" man (*sic*), even today, to designate the anomalous figures in our midst whose talents and interests span wide areas of intellectual endeavor.

By the late nineteenth century the humanities and the sciences are, to all appearances, separated and when social studies emerge, they must choose between the epistemological stance of the natural sciences that hold their objects at a distance and mediate between observer and observed by means of quantitative and experimental methods designed to foster control, even domination of nature, and the historical, interpretative ways of knowing characteristic of philosophy and literary studies. To be sure, toward the end of the nineteenth century Wilhelm Dilthey attempts to stitch together the disrupted threads by insisting that there is one science of "man," what he calls the human sciences (Geisteswissenschaften) that must be radically separated from the natural sciences because, among other reasons, its object has feelings and consciousness.

But the powerful intellectual influence of positivism, the theoretical expression of the will to scientificity in the past century, overcomes this effort to reconfigure the social sciences in the discourse and image of the humanistic disciplines. By the 1930s, the older generation of social scientists trained in the curriculum of the traditional intellect has all but passed from the scene and is replaced by people for whom the term "geist" or spirit is identical with mysticism or at least "soft" literary ruminations. Philosophy is completely divided into different camps: many central and southern Europeans who simply reject the positivist bent, whether of German, Austrian, or French origin in which, in John Locke's famous phrase, philosophy can only be an "underlaborer" to the sciences, and those who, broadly speaking, follow Fichte and Hegel in adhering to the point of view of the totality in which matter and spirit, subject and object can be, once more, united. There are, of course, those who attempt to situate themselves in an intermediate position—the Hegelian-trained George Herbert Mead, and John Dewey, for example. Even though Dewey calls himself a naturalist and was enamored with the experimental method and Mead felt the influence of Darwin and Spencer in asserting the effectivity of biological influences on social life, their philosophies were profoundly anti-reductionist. However, by the 1950s, even these once influential figures in American philosophy are dismissed as essentialist and speculative by now dominant positivism.

2

The 1980s, the economics and politics of which spelled utter disaster for millions of people whom Gramsci has called "subaltern" groups—those historically excluded or occluded from substantial shares in U.S. expansion—also witnessed the blossoming of cultural politics. This disparity illustrates the nonsynchrony of these respective spheres. Even as workers' movements, the black freedom movement, and organized feminism entered prolonged decline, at the political level, and were obliged to concentrate their political interventions on defensive measures to preserve past gains, intellectuals, including artists, putatively associated with these movements made significant inroads in cultural institutions—universities, the "art world," and, to a lesser extent, into the institutions of mass culture, particularly television and radio. As we saw in the first chapter, these incursions evinced, at the decade's end, a counterattack from cultural conservatives who otherwise opposed each other within the traditional politics of social justice but saw the peril to their mutually reinforcing game in the postmodern turn.

The emergence of culture at the center of public debate has its roots in both the scientific and technological revolutions that, for the first time in human history, made possible the construction of an image of a *concrete utopia* of post-scarcity as a possible world and a reasonable alternative to the given situation, especially among sections of intellectuals and other elements of the middle strata; the rise of new social movements which, in one way or another, embraced elements of this vision; and the legitimation crisis of technological rationality that claimed, successfully, in the 1950s and 1960s to have subjected contradictions to "problems," struggle to conflicts and, as Bell and Lipset argued, ideologies into disagreements as to practical solutions. Just as the new right arose on the ruins of the society of more or less "total administration" and captured the imagination of millions of people with its doctrine that conflated freedom with the free market, so a nascent movement of intellectuals putatively linked to feminism, sexual, race, and ecology movements has challenged the hegemony of modernism over culture and particularly over intellectual knowledge. As we saw in Chapter 2, one tendency associating itself with modernism addressed its dark side, particularly the "bureaucratic society of controlled consumption" arising from the triumph of technological rationality.

However, in the past two decades postmodern critics have grasped the democratic possibilities connected to the coming of consumer society while, at the same time, rejected the description of late capitalism in the apocalypse of one dimensionality or total administration. On the contrary; they have asserted the imperative of diversity, of a new pluralism that may be possible only under conditions of post-scarcity. Thus, while critical of the uses of technology, particularly with respect to its implications for ecosystems and for the ability of women to control their bodies, technoculture has its radical defenders. According to some, cybernetics may be considered an open system that has already extended our collective capacities for communication, for play, and even for community. Certainly, the quest for technologically-driven things animates much of the world's economic quest. I have argued elsewhere that the breakup of the Soviet Union and Eastern Europe as well as recent movements for political democratization in Latin America may, in a large measure, be attributed to the failure of these respective economic and political systems to meet the cultural challenge posed by American and western European consumer society. Whereas the prevailing left cultural critique of the 1960s and 1970s labeled consumer society as a form of "imperialism" whose most deleterious effect was to destroy popular cultures and replace them with electronically mediated entertainments, the postmodern critics see, in the achievements of late capitalism, the possibility for exposing the irrationality of authoritarian systems. In any case, whether one views the scientific-technological revolution as a threat or promise, its cultural significance is indisputable. Contemporary consumer society signifies more than big-ticket items such as cars and houses; the application of microchips to electronic equipment has resulted in the availability of a vast array of new communications apparatuses for home consumption.

Of course, culture as a burning political issue was also connected to the resumption, after the relatively stagnant 1970s decade, of the expansion of post-secondary education that accompanied the artificially generated economic boom. Like the 1960s when universities and colleges experienced perhaps their most robust period since the immediate postwar years, the debt-driven 1980s was similarly a time for ferment in part owing to the coming of age of that 1960s student generation. As conservative critics have tirelessly argued, higher education became the last outpost of the "left," long after the rest of the country seemed to have definitively turned rightward.

However, there is more to it than the combination of a prosperity that produced thousands of new jobs in universities and colleges, especially in the humanities and social sciences, with the demographic maturity of African-Americans, women, and the erstwhile New Left. Equally significant were the intellectual transformations that produced a veritable paradigm shift in the human sciences. In philosophy which, in various displacements resonated in literary and social studies, positivism yielded, albeit kicking and screaming, to what might be termed critical epistemologies that, among other innovations, refused the common sense that asserted the immutability of the givens of the social and literary worlds. This conjuncture has created an explosion of interest in what is called "theory" among literary critics, historians, anthropologists, graduate students, and younger faculty members in many other disciplines. Since the late 1970s, French and German social and cultural theorists, especially Derrida, Foucault, Habermas, and Lyotard, have become crucial referents for much of the Anglo-American human sciences.

European thought—not only French, but also Italian and in other countries as well—is marked by a perspective that might be called postessentialist as well as postmodern. Its leading characteristics are, by now, fairly well known: the rejection of foundationalism, that is, the refusal of "first principles" on which a theoretical system bearing transhistorical truth might be constituted; the parallel statement that all knowledge is historically contingent, not only because it is generated at a particular time/space according to its social and political presuppositions but, instead, as Foucault has argued, according to the "regime of truth" within which particular knowledges function; the proclamation, echoing Nietzsche's famous dictum, of the death of the "subject." Accordingly subjects are constituted and interpellated by discourses. They occupy "subject-positions" rather than being conscious agents of history and have no a priori privilege with respect to the course of history.

Here "discourse" is understood as the narratives that claim to be descriptively valid accounts of social and intellectual spaces of all sorts that are inhabited by a moral economy, logical conundra, and other glitches that confound their status as scientific statements. Perhaps the most controversial statement in this new knowledge paradigm is that science, rather than being viewed as transcendental truth subject only to the rigor, both ethical and algorithmic, by which its own procedures are applied, is no more than a series of discursive practices, the eminence of which must be explained with reference to the conditions for the formation of specific, historically situated hegemonies rather than to the immanent meaning of its discoveries.

Whereas Anglo-American philosophy that adopted the positivist view of the supremacy of natural science defined the task of philosophy to remove the linguistic ambiguities of scientific statements or, at least, to secure agreement as to the meaning of words, concepts, and propositions, cultural critique adopts the position, inherited from Nietzsche of *genetic skepticism,* which asserts that scientific law is conventional, that the subject of history or otherwise is interpellated by the fundamentally contingent conditions of its production. That is, even when the notion of "totality" is not entirely denied, the term has come to mean a provisional unity of a subject that is, itself, produced discursively. Recent cultural theory follows the prescriptive statements of both Saussure and Wittgenstein that comprehend language as a series of semantic, if not syntactical rules of utterance whose validity in the last instance depends wholly on its uses within a specified mode of life. Language is neither an expressive communications vehicle for pre-existing subjects nor a transcendent signifier. Far from the master discourses of Marxism and humanism, contemporary culture critique is a series of probes of narratives, metaphors, and other significations the object of which is to discover how they function to produce the life-world rather than "representing" it. The body of work constitutes a collective deconstruction of representations. Knowledge that purports to signify the "other," for instance, ethnography, is shown to be self-signifying. Otherness is produced, it does not "exist" apart from its relation to the system of significations that constitutes a regime of truth rather than some kind of neutral knowledge.

Here permit me a digression on the problems of the invocation of the term "production." The concept is criticized as entailing a subject that in turn implies intentionality or the authority of a transcendent ego. One of the major moves of post-Nietzschean criticism has been to demonstrate the historicity of the doctrine of the subject, locating it within the contours of the discourse of humanism and in recent work identifies this humanism with masculinist and racist presuppositions. At the same time, while acknowledging the perils of essentialism, there has arisen a new "strategic" essentialism in the light of the perils of abandoning the agency of the subaltern by means of a thoroughgoing deconstruction of the subject. As we will see below, this strategic essentialism undergirds every proposal for an alternative literary, philosophical, or critical theory canon because canonicity is, itself, an essentialist category.

The dilemma reappears in the frequently used anti-essentialist term "social construction" to designate the multiple realities of everyday life often employed in the social sciences. One of the problems with this concept is the implication that on the other side resides the realm of truth; presumably there is, at least putatively, a discourse that is not socially constructed, but, when the alternative is not biological constitution, the binary to social construction corresponds to some transcendent reality, that we can, in Husserl's terms, return to the "things themselves." Here Derrida's critique is to the point. To Husserl's claim that, by means of the method of epoche (bracketing) we may transcend the thick layer of socially permeated meanings that mediate our relation to things, Derrida replies that all of the terms of Husserl's statement can be subjected to a Heideggerian destruction, the most crucial of which is to show that the "I" that experiences, feels, knows is itself contingent on a system of significations in which the I is a priori, stated as the author of perception, knowledge, actions.

Similarly, terms such as "history," "objects," "meaning" are not to be taken as transcendental signifiers—first principles of which the subject is the parallel term for the "actor" or the "knower." In consequence, Derrida calls attention to the series of double binds confronting the fervent deconstructor. All of the binaries—inside-outside, subject-object—for example, must be taken as provisional. Having acknowledged that language, the means by which knowledge is possible, is, nevertheless, ensnared in the vagaries of western logic, it is difficult to see how we may say anything that escapes the charge of essentialism. Needless to say, for African-American, feminist, and gay and lesbian intellectuals, anti-essentialism threatens to deprive them of agency, precisely at the moment of their ascendancy. For these emergent discourses, identity can scarcely be disposed of, lest the voice of male tragedy retain its hegemony, really occupy the space of the subject, albeit in the name of its impossibility.

In sum, the virus of skepticism has infected academic disciplines. For example, Anglo-American philosophy that, as late as the 1980s was and remains, to a certain extent, in the thrall of analytic studies of language within its self-appointed role of underlaborer of the sciences, has begun to experience "new" influences—new only in the sense of the return of the repressed. In fact, younger American and British philosophers are resuscitating not only the work of French philosophy that stemmed from phenomenology and Nietzsche, but also, to a much lesser extent, Nietzsche and Husserl and their successors. At the same time, the hybrid philosophy and social theory of the Frankfurt School steadily wins new adherents even as Marxism has suffered a partial eclipse in recent years. There is a veritable explosion of interest in "surpassed" American traditions, notably pragmatism and Whitehead. The discoveries, spearheaded by younger scholars, of the work of Peirce, James, and especially Dewey as precursors of a postmodern philosophy of anti-metaphysics without scientism articulates with the postmodern turn in cultural studies, specifically the simple but still controversial idea that all knowledge is context bound, just as contexts are knowledge permeated and cannot escape their historicity.

There is, of course, considerable discussion about the claims of science.

Richard Rorty's attack against the very notion of a "theory of knowledge" that establishes a fixed framework, most notably that knowledge "mirrors" anything and that truth is an attainable goal, seems to legitimate the argument that his pragmatic cultural critique is merely a relativism.[10] But the argument that science is socially produced does not, for Dewey, nullify the warrant of its assertions. Dewey remains skeptical of any truth claims that fail to call attention to their tentative character. However, he allows that its discoveries may be "true" within the generally accepted methods by which knowledge is obtained and within an always already given framework. Dewey's naturalism admits of a world independent of human understanding, but rejects its transparency. Later, I want to discuss these issues in the context of two discourses—the feminist critique of science as gendered and the results of the social and cultural studies of scientific practices. For now it is sufficient to note that the idea of universal knowledge, if not dead, is at least severely battered.

In a somewhat different register, anthropology has undergone similar changes. Traditionally, ethnography shares with other social sciences an almost tropistic aversion to metatheory and counterposes description grounded in the interaction between the field worker and the "subject" of investigation as a norm that distinguishes its practices from the more abstract sociological methods of aggregated statistical analysis based on surveys of individual attitudes.[11] Clearly, ethnographic traditions have, for the most part, refused both the presupposition of methodological individualism that guides most contemporary sociological research and the prevailing ideology that social relations may be studied by means borrowed from the natural sciences, especially quantitative methods. Yet, in recent years, particularly since the scandal prompted by revelations that some ethnographers accepted funds to conduct research that became the basis of the strategic hamlet and pacification programs of the U.S. military forces in Vietnam and were implicated in parallel elements of U.S.-Latin American policy, anthropology has been engaged in searching self-examination, not only with respect to the ethics of ethnography in the context of war and revolution, but also the intellectual presuppositions of the discipline.

One result of this reflection has been to oblige the discipline to confront the traditional scientific ethos of value neutrality. Social scientists inevitably adopt a definite standpoint, whether they want to or not; even the stance of refusing to take sides is a stance. Perhaps more unsettling, a substantial literature has emerged that challenges the epistemological assumptions of ethnography.[12] Using methods borrowed from contemporary critical (mostly literary) theory, this work has performed textual deconstructions on key ethnographies to show the degree to which, embedded in the language as well as the accounts, ethnographers themselves are profoundly tied, mostly unre-flexively, to their own culture, the elements of which are frequently imposed on the scene and the subjects of their field work.

Needless to say, the proclivity of social scientists for metatheory and self-criticism presupposes their recognition of the problematic nature of the col-laboration between social science and the state. This relationship has not detained many who gladly tailor their research to government-sponsored re-form or to assisting the development of more "rational" social policy. For example, much of professional economics is inextricably bound to the fact that both the professoriate and other practitioners routinely work for federal, state, and local agencies and for private corporations and provide the necessary in-telligence on which executives may make decisions. In short, economics is a policy science; its neoclassical theoretical corpus can scarcely be distinguished from the technologies of market manipulation, government intervention, and corporate strategies for profit maximization.

In fact, it may be argued that deconstructive strategies are inimical to the role of social sciences in contemporary cultures, one of whose main charac-teristics is the subordination of intellectual knowledge to productive and ad-ministrative practices. This perception may not deter the natural or social scientist eager to make a practical contribution to the overarching objective of achieving a more instrumentally rational world. Yet there is little or no chance for theories to be heard that question the efficacy of administration as the overarching strategy of social engineering.

However, many dedicated to the scientific ideology according to which the sciences must remain outside the mainstream of economic, political, and social affairs at least insofar as the choice of objects of knowledge, methods of know-ing, and the uses to which the results are put, have been obliged to take a close look at the ethical questions entailed by the link between contemporary scientific research and economic and political institutions. No discipline has placed these questions closer to its central concerns than anthropology.

Indeed in their examination of the current state of the discipline, Marcus and Fischer explicitly note the intimate relation between the "radically chang-ing world order" and the "crisis of representation in the human sciences . . . shaped by particular political, technological, and economic events." "At the broadest level," they argue, "the contemporary debate is about how an emer-gent postmodern world is to be represented as an object for social thought in its various contemporary disciplinary manifestations."[13] In their review of the paradigm shift in anthropology, Marcus and Fischer note that rather than examining social structure, interpretative anthropology began, in the 1960s, to discover "symbols, meanings and mentality."[14] Anthropologists concerned with culture critique employed two techniques of defamiliarization, that is, ways of knowing that challenge the prevailing common-sense view of objects of knowledge: crosscultural juxtaposition and epistemological critique. Each tries to "disrupt" our stereotyped understandings of the periphery of the world system (what used to be called "primitive" societies) and, perhaps equally important, to call attention to the "non-natural" reality within which we live. The work of Sahlins and Mary Douglas parallels Lévi-Strauss's linguistic effort to show that the traditional distinction between "advanced" and the "primitive," which always imply a hierarchical relation, cannot be sustained without bringing to the surface the progressivist assumptions of the ethnographer.

In contrast, through showing the crosscultural comparability of the uses of symbols and, especially in Lévi-Strauss's work, that binaries such as the raw and the cooked span societies of different regimes of economic and technological production, the myth of otherness yields to regional or ethnic specificity with no necessary values attached to their respective mentalities. While these efforts are suspect on the ground of their Kantianism, they have virtually revolutionized the discipline's conventional ideology of social science as an instrument of enlightenment, as a civilizing activity.

James Clifford's close reading of ethnographic texts, Vincent Crapanzano's sophisticated psychoanalytically informed North African ethnographies, and the earlier critique of "cultural reason" of Marshall Sahlins begin to form a corpus of a new philosophically oriented social "science" that departs radically from the mainstream by insisting, among other things, that ethnographies are texts whose meanings are subject to dispute, and whose objects are constituted rather than being in a state of nature. The ethnographic text therefore must be "read" like any other representation.[15] In turn, these texts refer not only to their overt subjects—people living in the periphery of a world order that often seeks to "civilize" them—but also to that world order and to the ethnographic activity itself replete with conventions, histories, and predilections. Since ethnographies are taken as instances of the social text, the epistemological turn in anthropology openly borrows from contemporary literary methods, themselves a specification of Derrida's argument that representations are self-referential. Far from constituting a "mirror" of the outside world, even if interpreted, discourses cannot reveal the things themselves since the space between the social text and the reader's interpretative apparatus is always undecidable. In this space of undecidability significations are produced that reach beyond the specific activity of the individual reader to the social text.

Critical anthropologists are still trying to come to terms with their own disciplinary traditions in order to discover what is living and what is dead in them. Not yet decided is whether field work is possible in the postmodern moment when the assumptions of enlightenment science have been shorn of their value-neutral veneer; whether it can, with ethical good faith, generate the categories, the positivities by which any social investigation comes to know its object, notwithstanding the complexities of its constitution. At stake here is the possibility of writing the social text in a way that simultaneously calls attention to the discourses it seeks to "represent" and its own apparatus of reading; that names the episteme by which forms of sociation are produced; and, at the same time, acknowledges the limits of description as a way out of the ideological imaginary.

Of course, similar concerns have been voiced concerning the uses of scientific knowledge by, for example, some biologists in the wake of the transformation of their field into a virtual arm of the medical and pharmaceutical industries or physicists who, since the development of nuclear weapons have, without ceasing research activities, called attention to the ways in which their discoveries are appropriated for questionable ends.[16] But what distinguishes the social from the natural sciences is the widespread, if not consensual understanding among the former that the world to which their investigations refer is a built environment, constituted not only by physical artifices but also by constellations of temporally bound meanings. In contrast, with few exceptions, the natural sciences may, from time to time, question aspects of the history of science such as the problem of paradigm shifts represented, say, in the transformation of physics and cosmology by the Copernican revolution or the displacement of the once dominant evolutionary and functionalist perspectives by the structural reductions of molecular biology. In each case, most ascribe the changed paradigm to "progress" owing to the rigorous application of scientific methods. While philosophy and social studies of science have responded to the crisis in representation by denaturalizing scientific knowledge, demonstrating, for example, that claims to value neutrality are violated by scientific practices and that there is a politics of scientific knowledge rather than positing a completely open scientific community, the natural and much of the social scientific community remains a bastion of modernity, persuaded on the whole by the fundamental insights of the Enlightenment that empirically wrought evidence and tests of their reliability are the path to truth.

The acquisition of legitimate intellectual knowledge of which science occupies a privileged place has become intertwined with economic, political, and cultural power. This power is not merely the consequence of the high status scientists enjoy in societies aspiring to technological development, or that scientific research is influenced by its government and corporate patrons. Or even that knowledge has become the crucial productive force of late capitalist societies of the West, a historical development in which science is routinely subordinated to capital. The heart of the power of science is that it remains, since the demise of universal religion, the only universal discourse in western societies. Science signifies what we mean by the concepts of "truth" and "progress" and physics stands at the pinnacle, for it purports, above all, to penetrate the secrets of nature, an achievement that has become virtually identical to what we take to be the fundamental condition for well-being.[17]

Thus, despite the long-term controversies concerning the degree to which social scientific statements bear the privileged space of truth, or the widespread perception that scientific work is context-driven, science's criterion of "proof" constitutes the measure of all statements, the basis for the classification of the plurality of human knowledges. While universities are now privileged sites of legitimate intellectual knowledge, the scientific community, consisting of researchers in private and public institutions as well as the professoriate, establish what counts as the most certain of legitimate knowledges. Other knowledges such as the human sciences—literature, narrative history, the visual and plastic arts and philosophy; practical knowledges such as that of the crafts or administration; and everyday knowledge arising from social intercourse are relegated, if not to the margins in the hierarchy, at least to secondary status.

3

Since the hegemony of the scientific enlightenment was established in western countries—in some cases even before capitalism had matured—the disciplines associated with the human sciences have, with some degree of insecurity, experienced an accumulation of knowledges that constitute their claims to legitimacy. In their attempt to establish a more solid footing the humanities have constructed a canon of indispensable works and have linked these with the imagined master discourse of "western civilization." For the traditional humanities, these works exemplify the values by which this civilization mirrors itself, but also the extent to which the West represents the human condition as such.

Given the current decentering of master discourses, this claim may, initially at least, appear nothing less than arrogant. On closer examination it is merely a logical inference from the more sweeping western claim to have achieved the highest level of maturity of all societies. This maturity is measured by the three fundamental characteristics of modernity: the permanent revolution of scientific and technological development, unimpeded by religious and other mythological precepts; the formation and reproduction of the liberal-democratic state that insures a broad base of citizenship in its affairs without which a society based on consent rather than coercion is not possible; and, despite much slippage, securing individual rights which, among other things, guarantee the free exercise of speech, assembly, and the press—rights that are the analogue of the free market, which may be considered the overarching but largely tacit principle of modernity. The ethical root of modernity is the Individual, conceived by philosophers since the sixteenth century to be the origin and the outcome of human activity. Thus, one of the characteristics of a modernist literature is its explorations of the depths of the ego as much as the social self—how individuals live in communities (narrative histories including the historical novel) and the individual self, exemplified by imaginative explorations of the depths of what since Freud, Bergson, and the phenomenologists has been termed inner experience both in its emotional and intellectual aspects. The motive force of literary criticism since Matthew Arnold first attempted to codify it as legitimate intellectual knowledge is to elevate literature, especially poetry, alongside philosophy as the most general expression of what is meant by the specifically human.

The modernist project spans philosophy, sociology, and literature. Indeed, the birth of economic science, as opposed to its somewhat orphan status within philosophy until the middle of the eighteenth century, is ineluctably tied to the new status accorded the individual by the bourgeois market. Adam Smith's celebrated doctrine according to which, notwithstanding the fact that humans were tied together by sympathy and the division of labor, self-interest-driven human interactions became the basis for the neoclassical view that economic activity consisted largely in the rational choices made by individual possessors of commodities, including labor. With the exception of Marx, nineteenth-century economics follows this prescription to ground itself in these choices, to examine the various motivations that may sway individuals, and to construct economic laws in terms of the influences that bear on individual propensities to invest and consume.

In turn, mainstream Anglo-American sociology and political science are based, largely, on Adam Smith's doctrine of "self-love" (self-interest) as the structural foundation of social relations: "It is not from the benevolence of the butcher, the brewer, or the baker that we expect our dinner, but from their regard to their own self-interest. We address ourselves, not to their humanity but to their self-love, and never talk to them of our own necessities but to their advantages."[18] To be sure, in this paradigm of human sociation the cultural system—the internalized norms and values to which people adhere—as well as the laws provide a measure of coherence to human conduct, mediating the excesses of self-interest. Yet the individual, taken not in her or his class, gender, or racial identity but as identical with a self, has become the object and the subject of social knowledge. Of course, there are competing traditions in the social sciences for which individuality is the vanishing horizon of social possibility that must be *achieved* in opposition to, for example, group, class, and national interests that constitute the boundary conditions for individual activity.

These counterlogics have recruited strong spokespersons. Just as Durkheim refers to "collective" representations and the division of labor as the constitutive categories of social life, so Marx insists that relations of production determine social identity. And the concept of ideology addresses the degree to which what is understood as individual "rational choice" is socially and historically produced in accordance with structural determinants such as class relations. Weber developed a historically mediated theory of rationality, showing through his taxonomic investigations that rationality is never "given" but has different forms and mutations. Yet these challenges have failed to supplant the doctrine of individualism that remains, in its Smithian form, to this day the basis of modernity. Where Marx placed individuality as the determinate end of a revolutionary social process, this process is descriptively reduced to the "given" individual who associates with other individuals and subordinates her or himself as a conscious political agent to the state in the interest of pursuing private ends.

After having attained positions of hegemony in the human sciences in the postwar era precisely because of their aspiration to scientificity, philosophy and the social sciences have fallen into relative eclipse in recent years because neither has acknowledged the postmodern situation as the context of their respective practices. In all of these disciplines dissident voices are becoming louder but, with the partial exception of anthropology, the will to scientificity prevails. Having affirmatively responded to the "crisis of theory," literary theory and criticism, which today occupies the spaces in varying degrees of the critical traditions of philosophy, sociology, and linguistics, has become the privileged discourse of postmodernism.

For this reason, more than its intrinsic merits as a discipline, many who covet the discursive positions of the subaltern have flocked to the various literary disciplines since the 1960s—to American Studies, English and Comparative Literature. For literary studies have positioned themselves at the crossroad of individual and collective identities; have sought the meeting ground between narrative, language, and social and historical context; and have become the site where the universal claims of modernity as well as the discourses of literary and artistic modernism are subjected to frequently withering examination.

Nota bene, literary studies have not always been in the forefront of critical theory. In the early postwar period when the social sciences seemed to be more receptive to the dire implications of the crisis of modernity revealed by the rise of fascism and the world war, the emergent academic literary criticism distanced itself from its own historical roots and offered the alternatives of a poetics that, in effect, proposed to repudiate the prevailing sociological and historical interpretations that dominated criticism in the 1920s and 1930s. In John Ciardi's felicitous phrase, the reader should be concerned with the "poem itself"—particularly the elements of its construction and its aesthetic dimension. The work of art referred not to social reality, but to itself; a poem "means" not its discursive practices, which always occur within a definite cultural or social context that includes its immediate reception by readers, but its relation to purely formal, poetic traditions. If there is a possibility of a history of poetry it must, like the conventional history of science, be purely internal. In John Crowe Ransom's words, "And as to the speech that the critic may use. We must say that ordinarily the critic's language, though less immediate than the poet's, should be less reductive than the philosopher's; in order that he may remember, and permit his gentle readers to remember, that the language of poetry is the language of feeling not the language of epistemology."[19] Ransom, together with Robert Penn Warren, Cleanth Brooks, and Allen Tate, founded the movement known as the New Criticism; he allows that critics can and should read philosophers but not to emulate their analytic sensibility and especially not their turgid style of writing that, more often than not, invents new names for ordinary objects and thereby defamiliarizes them and thereby reduces their intelligibility. Nor, he insists, can science, even the science of signs, contribute to helping us to better appreciate the poetic text. Ransom waged, tirelessly, a polemic against efforts such as those of Kenneth Burke and Charles Morris to combine aesthetic theory with anthropology and psychoanalysis, philosophy, and science. At the same time, his evocative use of the Hegelian concept of the "concrete universal" to characterize poetry's ontology showed the extent to which he was willing to borrow from philosophy but only to integrate into his own aesthetic system. The poem is the concrete universal of human experience torn from the mundane secular influences that disturb its formal integrity. Hence, the critic is the gatekeeper of form.

In the hands of lesser critics, aestheticism became a narrow, almost technicist discourse perfectly suited to the early postwar period when cultural politics consisted, precisely, in its avoidance. From the war to the 1970s critical theory in literature referred to the close reading of a pristine object, the poem, and strictly eschewed its social function, historical context, or political significance. Clearly, Ransom's arguments, for example, against Marxist literary criticism as a crude reductionism, bore, at least at the height of Stalinism, more than a grain of validity. And it must be noted that no less a dialectical critic than Adorno himself argued for the relative autonomy of aesthetics and for the subversive possibilities of *formal properties* of the work of art as a protection against the degradation by political and social forces of poetry and other literary forms. Yet, by the rigorous exclusion of philosophy or the social sciences, especially the remarkable social poetics of Kenneth Burke, and even its disdain of the ethical discourse of Lionel Trilling, for example, the universalist poetics of the prevailing literary studies was experienced by its victims as a warrant for undertaking literary warfare. This perception was exacerbated by the influence of one of the leading figures in the movement, Rene Wellek, whose grasp of European literary theory was quite broad but, until the 1970s, a decade that corresponded to the death of the New Criticism, held his piece, and only at the end of his career revealed his connection with Czech semiotics.

The space was opened in the 1970s by the crosscurrents of Marxism, given renewed life by the New Left, what became known as structuralism and then poststructuralism, and the revival of historical studies in literature. Although it can be easily shown that the conservatives' conflation of these tendencies in their attack on cultural studies contravenes the fact that these approaches to textual analysis, in their mutual relations, are fraught with tension, even conflict, what they have in common is a shared critique of the modernist hegemony in literary studies, New Criticism. The perception of a common enemy helped to effect a marriage of convenience that, in many literature departments, became identical with academic subalternity. In time, this unity proved too fragile to withstand the emergent discourses of feminism, ethnicity, race, and sexuality which, unevenly, took up the fight to break the hegemony of disciplinary traditions, but changed the keywords of the conflict to multiculturalism, phallocentrism, essentialism, and other terms that signified a new cultural logic that was used to characterize the prevailing powers. As with other emerging intellectual movements, the polyglot of Marxism, deconstruction, the new historicism, and structuralism set before themselves the task of displacing the prevailing critical modes by a relentless paradigm critique and, simultaneously, launched an indirect attack on the mainstream literary canon, especially the widely held proposition of New Criticism that poetry was the privileged literary form, relegating stories and novels to inferiority.

Frank Lentricchia's attack on the New Criticism, coming from a protégé of one of its leading lights, had the force of a sledgehammer.[20] His critique, which slipped in and out of Marxism, relied on arguments that showed the elitist social function of both the New Criticism and its privileged canon of high modernist poetry. Fredric Jameson's *Marxism and Form,* almost singlehandedly, revived an almost forgotten subtle western and dissident Marxist criticism, the major contributors to which were largely unknown, even if they had been translated, to many of the most sophisticated scholars and critics. Among the reasons for this state of affairs was the still potent cold war academic discourse according to which Marxism was little more than a vulgar materialism. Jameson's incontrovertible, and uncontroverted, demonstration of the absurdity of this characterization in the light of his review of Lukacs, Adorno, Benjamin, and Bloch, among others, cleared the space for a new generation of critics—Kristin Ross, Susan Buck-Morss, Jack Zipes, Andreas Huyssens, and Miriam Hansen among many others—to work within a neo-Marxism whose suppleness is apparent in their historical and contemporary studies. Guyatri Spivak's translation and monograph-length introduction to Derrida's *Of Grammatology* and the translations of a selection of the psychoanalytic essays of Jacques Lacan capped the decade.

More than any other work, Derrida's book supplemented by Spivak's commentary provided a sustained explanation of that mystifying term "deconstruction," but also supplied a *method,* a theory machine through which avid students could perform their own criticism. In critical practice, whatever its connotations in the works of Heidegger and Nietzsche, it came to mean the critical practice of exposing the essentialist presuppositions of literary and critical texts, what De Man termed the "blindness" that constituted the significations of the text.[21] But, while for De Man the blind spot was simultaneously a strength, a road to insight, less subtle interpreters often confused the deconstructive work with ideology-critique. And the implicit nihilism in this procedure relieved many critics of the obligation to adopt a standpoint. Derrida's infinite deferral of subject-position on the ground of undecidability was torn out of its French intellectual and political context and became, for some, a pretext for producing a New Criticism under the sign of poststructuralism. Taken together these works and the translations of works by Roland Barthes and Michel Foucault created new intellectual space for an entire generation of critics, but also forced many in the profession to hasten their own re-education lest they be swept aside by graduate students and young faculty who were greedily learning the new vocabularies.

Paul De Man became the leading U.S. figure in Derridean deconstruction. In the 1970s reading De Man became de rigeur for anyone who wished to enter the obscure thickets of philosophically imbued criticism. Around him, at Yale, formed the first "school" of criticism which, for a decade, succeeded in effecting a virtual turnabout in academic literary work. This group included not only Hillis-Miller, Hartman, and Bloom (although Bloom was included as a result of a misunderstanding), but also Shoshanna Felman, Barbara Johnson, and Margaret Ferguson who, in different ways, increasingly deployed the work of Derrida and also Lacan against some of the more masculinist implications of their teachers. This was the moment when the presuppositions of the discipline itself came under stern scrutiny, including the canon that the New Critics had carefully constructed to constitute the knowledge from which their critical enterprise gained legitimacy. The canon was a fairly restricted list, chosen according to criteria that focused, in the first instance, on the felicitation of imagery through language whose primary tools were tropes and metaphors. Even the early structuralists were in concert with this criterion, adding only an expanded taxonomy of mechanisms through which images were produced, particularly those derived from semiotics.

The second "event" in this movement was the plethora of critical writing that reread the established literary canon with new eyes. At the dawn of the

1980s, the debate turned on perhaps the most intense and ultimately crucial challenge spanning the multiplicity of cultural issues that fill the intellectual landscape: challenges to the authority of knowledge or, to be more precise, to the authority of *legitimate* intellectual and aesthetic knowledge as it is conventionally defined and disseminated. For, despite the relative decline of the organized resistance in this decade, feminist, gay and lesbian, and Latino and African-American discourses emerged that have succeeded in placing the question of "what counts as knowledge" squarely in the middle of the cultural politics of universities, at least in the humanities.

In the first moment this was plainly *destructive* of the prevailing claim that the established canon was the best that had been thought and said and, more sweepingly, "represented" the civilized self. In the 1980s English departments were engaged in a canon war that pitted especially feminist and African-American faculty and students and their supporters against the traditional literary canon and, more profoundly, against the idea of canonicity itself. That is, the new wave of critics questioned the notion of a privileged list, especially one that, in the main, excluded works by and about subaltern peoples. Canonicity was a kind of transmission of established western civilization; its works are chosen to exemplify the values and norms of the West—its views of sex and gender, its class and racial prejudices, and, equally important, its dominion over other civilizations, not the least of which are those of Africa, Latin America, and Asia. Most of all, the canon exemplifies the West's self-appraisal as a superior culture that is destined to civilize others. From this standpoint it was not difficult to show that the revered works within the English canon were inextricably bound up with the representation of the generalized subaltern as the Other—in turns silent and passive and violent and mendacious.

This canon-critique was part of the long wave of skepticism concerning the notion of a *master discourse,* that consolidates, even in the wake of a plethora of contrary evidence, ideological homogeneity and, equally, a *master historical narrative* that defined the major contours of a single culture. Abjuring these narratives signifies the breakup of unified conceptions of the Subject of History, whether the working class or the autonomous individual, the core trope of Anglo-American culture. The generation of critics who, having been trained to read reverently the Great Books of World Literature (or a fraction thereof), shifted their knowledge-object from literature to the heteroglossia of oral expression, folk tales, daily newspapers, movies and TV, and especially theory. For some, literature *as such* became suspect, with the possible exception of slave narratives, folk tales, songs, and other genres of the popular transcribed by anthropologists, folklorists, musicologists, and journalists. Older scholars and critics began to complain that their younger colleagues in English and Comparative Literature departments were uninterested in literature of any kind. Indeed, I have been told by more than one superbly trained literary critic that they rarely, if ever, read novels or poetry. Writing may not have suffered the fate of the canon, since the bread and butter of criticism is usually inscribed in written texts, but for those who agreed that canonicity was a signifier of culture as aesthetic self-formation, their rejection of the canon signaled their cultural disaffection. When not veritable ethnographers or sociologists, they are interested in metatheories, poetry and mainstream fiction genres having become, for them, a suspicious form that partakes in processes of social and ideological reproduction.

Some of the politically and theoretically oriented faculty have even become interested in the lowest status of the academic fields: teaching (called, in their vernacular, pedagogy). The recent interest in education issues among even the most elite-trained academic professionals may be ascribed, negatively, to their collective disdain of the New Criticism and other canon formers. But, perhaps more pervasively, many consider teaching more than an honest vocation, an opportunity to help bring out the voices of hitherto stifled women, minority, and working-class students. For these critics, pedagogy has become a *subject-position,* a politics that poses itself as an alternative to criticism. Needless to say, teaching may be understood as a series of speech acts that may be counterposed to writing. In theoretical terms, for the intellectual it provides, at least in democratic regimes, considerable freedom. At the same time, good teaching is the least rewarded of all academic activities, a reflection of the priorities of universities to reward "useful" scientific research, administration, and publication as privileged sites.

The political economy and sociology of universities and other cultural institutions is rapidly becoming an important area of research and debate among those in humanities departments as academics try to situate themselves in the larger society. Bruce Robbins, Paul Bové, and Stanley Fish, all literary critics, write about the social and political function of intellectuals and intellectual labor.[22] Samuel Weber, Wlad Godzich, and Jeffrey Kittay have produced critical, deconstructive histories of their discipline showing, among other things, the function of literature in the broader culture.[23] In short, one recent movement of cultural studies is to write collective autobiographies of the knowledge class. Here we have the beginnings, within the humanities, of a discourse that calls into question the division of intellectual labor into disciplines, especially humanities and the social sciences with their unique incommensurable knowledges.

Others, equally critical of the established canon, have moved toward the construction of, alternatively, a countercanon to signify the emergence of various subaltern groups within the university. Recall, in the 1960s and 1970s, under considerable pressure from students, especially blacks, Latinos, and women but also many others, academic institutions accommodated the de-

mand for the creation of departments and programs that, implicitly, acknowledged the once rejected claim that these voices had been excluded. A decade
later, these programs were under attack—not only from administrative bodies, but also from within. From the outside, they were accused of intellectual
sloppiness and of lacking academically high standards of admission and in-
struction. More to the point, some of the more discerning faculty within these
programs engaged in self-criticism, acknowledging that, among other things,
the most important weakness was that they had failed to develop the knowledge base necessary to validate their claim to disciplinary integrity. While a
new generation of social historians had begun to provide a rich literature of
historiography of the excluded, the theoretical basis for the development of
the field had not been laid. Among the central strategies toward this objective
was to propose alternative literary canons armed with a theory that justified
the selection of authors and works. At issue was the status in the curriculum
of literatures that were identified as subaltern and had been excluded from
consideration, except in courses offered in women's and African-American
studies programs.[24]

The emergence of a new literary theory derived from philosophy and linguistics had already been present in the literatures and even English, a relatively recalcitrant discipline, for more than a decade. The influence of "post"
structuralism associated with the names Barthes, Derrida, and Foucault
spread from Johns Hopkins and Yale to other universities so that by the late
1970s the conjunction of the new intellectual conceptions in literary studies
with the entrance of a critical mass of new social currents into the professoriate took shape as a series of skirmishes to revise the literary canon, and, at
the same time, to introduce what became known as the oral and written documents of "non-European" cultures.

In the first phase of this effort—roughly until the early 1980s—feminist
literary theorists and historians armed with new critical weapons attempted
to demonstrate that much of the literary canon as well as its champions were
deeply enmeshed in the signifiers of male supremacist patriarchy. Some of the
major critical works corresponding to this claim—Kate Millet's *Sexual Politics,* Gilbert and Gubar's *The Mad Woman in the Attic,* in film theory and
criticism Teresa De Lauretis's *Alice Doesn't* and the writings of journalists
such as Molly Haskell and Marjorie Rosen—led to a searching reevaluation
of the English and American canon. At the immediate level, they called attention to the absence of women writers in the canon. The exceptions—the
Brontës, George Eliot, and Jane Austen (there were virtually no American
women writers on the list) and Virginia Woolf (who was not considered in a
feminist context, but was linked to the male-dominated Bloomsbury group)—
merely underscored the calumny.

The construction of a canon of women's literature, however, was not the first task of feminist critics. In concert with the generally destructive mood (in the Heideggerian, not the literal sense, for many of them were hostile to poststructuralist and even psychoanalytic criticism), they concentrated their efforts on showing *how* women were represented in male literature, including film. DiLauretis's category of the "male gaze" that relied heavily on Lacanian psychoanalytic theory perhaps epitomizes a central theme of the critique. In poetry, novels, and film the agency of women is denied. Instead, she is subjected to the male gaze, becomes an object incorporated into his dominion. The position of woman as object emphasizes the physicality of her being, instrumentalized to male desire, but yields little or no insight into her *agency* or her effectivity as a social actor. From the eighteenth-century novel of Richardson's *Pamela* to the recent past, feminist critics showed that even when women are represented, the perspective remains, epistemologically, male. As Rachel Brownstein argued, she is depicted as passive and "waiting" for the male.[25] In effect, there is no public female self, except the obscure object summarized in Freud's famous lament "What do these women want?," a confession, according to feminists, signifying that even the great psychoanalytic theorist is imprisoned in his own masculinist assumptions. As Gilbert and Gubar show, when she exhibits the hubris of self-directed activity, the woman is represented as the *other* of male normality and this becomes merely another form of objectification. To be female is to be a (deranged) object.

However, if the strategy shifted to constructing a canon of women's literature, focusing on the problem of representation was plainly not sufficient. The argument shifted to discovering hitherto neglected women writers and rediscovering some like Eliot and Virginia Woolf whose feminism had been expurgated by prior criticism. Feminism became a constructive standpoint that not only identified *which* women writers were to be included but also interpreted *how* they should be understood. Thus, for example, Mary Shelley, whose classic novel *Frankenstein* had been appropriated by the horror genre, especially in film, was now seen as a legatee of the late eighteenth-century feminist pioneer, her mother Mary Wollstonecraft. Similarly, for Eliot, whose *Silas Marner* was incorporated into the mainstream literary canon, a required high school text all over the English-speaking world, critics resuscitated lesser known works such as *Middlemarch* and *Adam Bede* as feminist classics. (Some critics claimed that *Middlemarch* is, perhaps, the best English novel of the century.)

Having taken the decision to construct an alternative subaltern canon and, finally, a struggle to make the existing canon more inclusive, many critics were obliged to drop or otherwise temper the strategies that challenged the idea of canonicity as a form of the reproduction of class, race, and gender hierarchies. In the process, they made an institutional and less radical compromise in their quest for institutionalization; as a result of the logic of the strategy of the "curriculum of inclusion" many were, as antagonists, nevertheless reincorporated into their respective disciplines.

The cultural politics of inclusion entailed the marginalization of the popular expressive forms in order to "win." Feminist and African-American critics were obliged to meet their adversaries on established disciplinary ground, not only to beat them at their own game but to recruit allies from conventional critical paradigms many of which, as we will see in my discussion of the science below, are undergirded by dubious ideological presuppositions. This tendency is especially marked among women social historians—notably Mary Jo Buhle, Susan Strasser, Elizabeth Ewen, Alice Kessler Harris, and Ellen Dubois as well as many others who were engaged in the work of cultural reclamation of the legacy of women's struggles for equality in the workplace, against slavery, and for their political and social enfranchisement in the home as much as the public sphere. In line with the generally positivist tendency of historiography, these histories stressed the agency of women but did not, except tacitly, undertake a theoretical examination of the problems of representation in their field. The critique of mainstream treatments was similar to that offered in the 1960s and 1970s by proponents of "history from below" which, at the time, focused on the absence of working-class movements from the writing of American and British history. In form, women and African-Americans were substituted for workers, but the complaint against working-class history was confined largely to the point that the object of knowledge was "incomplete." Absent was a critique of the positivism intrinsic to prevailing historiographic methods since many within the new practices of social history shared these presuppositions. To be sure, the discursive and ideological critique of historiographic epistemologies was undertaken by Hayden White, Joan Scott, and a few others who, perhaps to their consternation, found receptive audiences among some philosophers and many literary critics and theorists, but were received coolly when not with hostility and indifference among fellow historians.

4

In the 1960s and 1970s, literary and especially media criticism focused on the racial stereotypes—in both historical and contemporary contexts—in the representation of African-Americans. Critics had little difficulty proving that the history of the film since its silent days was replete with representation of blacks as lazy, subservient, and lacking intelligence. Major radio shows (*Amos and Andy*), leading films (*Gone With the Wind,* Disney's *Song of the South,* which featured the Uncle Remus stories), radio and television characters (Rochester of the *Jack Benny Show* or the film characters played by Hattie

McDaniel and Blossom Seeley), were merely the most obvious. More egregious was the degree to which the corpus of the films of America's great cinematic masters, D. W. Griffith, especially his *Birth of a Nation* and *Intolerance,* Howard Hawks, and other directors, was intertwined with a racialist reading of American history. Even where the representation of African-Americans does not reproduce the prevailing characterological stereotypes, few Hollywood films before the Second World War or radio and television shows before the 1960s avoided the representation of blacks in the slave mode, even if in modern dress.

The rapid spread of the civil rights movement was followed by the emergence of a new African-American cultural movement that, however, began as a black arts movement rather than in academic criticism. Houston Baker has argued that this movement was basically connative, that is, sought by acts of will and desire to bring into existence a new culture that refused the language and forms of the master and sought, instead, to find its models in Africa and the Caribbean, the putative originary sites of African-American culture.[26] As Henry Louis Gates has remarked, Baker's "position as the leading and most prolific theorist of Afro-American literature is . . . beyond debate." (His was the most compelling of recent attempts to discover the intellectual ground for the claim that an African-American canon be established.)

Indeed, Baker's *Blues, Ideology and Afro-American Literature* (1984) is a *tour de force* employing an extraordinary range of theoretical tools to address central issues in African-American culture. Baker's key descriptive and analytic categories "blues" and "vernacular" belie the book's title, for in these invocations Baker transgresses the boundaries of what his immediate predecessors the "reconstructionists" so forcefully argued. According to Gates, one of the more articulate spokespersons for this view, there is no "determining formal relation between literature and social institutions." Instead, according to Baker, Gates erects a closed "semiotic circle" around literature, but fails to recognize that, if as is argued literature may be comprehended as a system of signs, then language, the vehicle of articulated expression, is itself a social institution.[27]

Baker is sympathetic to Gates's effort to reverse the 150-year-old tradition that, since Jefferson, talked past black poetry to reveal the "humanity" of blacks behind the work but assiduously ignored its literary attributes, the degree to which black art may be grasped according to the same aesthetic criteria as any other art. Later in his influential book *The Signifying Monkey,* Gates provides ample evidence for a black aesthetic without, however, forging specific links between black power politics that arose in the mid 1960s and the black arts movement that was, consciously, a cultural analogue to it. Consistent with his earlier argument that sign systems are arbitrary with respect to the social and historical context within which they are produced, Gates pinpoints the specificity of African-American literature in terms of "signi-fyin(g)," the indirect, parodic, pedagogic, situational cultural practice that constitutes the heart of the black vernacular tradition. But this tradition in Gates's discourse bears only an indirect relation to the specificity of the his-toric circumstances—slavery, rural and urban post-reconstruction subordi-nation within which black expressive forms are produced.

Accordingly, Gates constructs an African-American canon, a "theory of tradition" based on the incorporation of this cultural practice into a literary practice: writers such as Zora Neale Hurston who, in Gates's pantheon, oc-cupies a unique, and central, place in the African-American tradition, Jean Toomer, Sterling Brown, Toni Morrison, Amiri Baraka, Alice Walker, and, in a somewhat different relation, Richard Wright and Ralph Ellison. In this work Gates mediates somewhat the semiotic circle by invoking the anomalous no-tion of "tradition," itself a historical term, but retains an internalist frame-work in which to justify the canon.

Baker's review of Gates's modified reconstructionist perspective notes this contradiction: "Rather than a referential semantics (in which) . . . words of a literary text stand in a one-to-one relationship to 'things' . . . what was im-plicit in the higher-order arguments of the Black Aesthetic . . . was an anthro-pological approach to Afro-American art. I think, in fact, that Gates recognizes this and is, finally unwilling to accept the critical responsibilities signalled by such an enterprise."[28] To accept responsibility would acknowledge the inti-mate links between Afro-American expressive texts and various "cultural in-stitutions or cultural systems (including language). Baker concludes: "The emphasis on close reading in Gates's formulations, therefore, might justifiably be designated a call for a *closed* reading of selected Afro-American written texts. In fact, Gates implies that the very defining criteria of a culture may be extrapolated from selected, written literary texts rather than vice versa."[29] Baker's ultimate judgment is that, by their insistence on a black aesthetic, Gates and Stepto have made an important contribution to the development of a new theory of Afro-American culture, but are curiously "apolitical."

Gates has become the leading gatekeeper of a new African-American lit-erary canon whose validity resides in the degree to which the various works, while retaining their cultural specificity, articulate with conventional literary values (e.g., the perspicacity of its metaphors, tropes, and so forth) by invoking a unique literary practice that qualifies its aesthetic, in this case, signifyin(g). His work claims aesthetic legitimacy for African-American literature *within* the boundaries prescribed by a fairly conventional critical theory. In effect, through the aestheticization of popular African-American cultural tradition, he found the strategic lever to achieve institutional legitimacy by transmuting a cultural tradition into "literature," an entirely mainstream form. For Gates has succeeded, through his polemically charged invocation of a "Marxist" black critical strawperson in which "race" replaces the "base" in the famous formulation of determination by the economic over the ideological superstructure, in providing a sophisticated intellectual basis for the (re)integration of the black tradition within the academic mainstream without adopting an integrationist point of view. According to two of its leading advocates, Richard Wright and Sterling Brown, the historical events in the quest for black freedom such as the Supreme Court decision outlawing school segregation, civil rights legislation, and other advances would erase the underlying logic of a separate Afro-American art that presupposed economic, social, political, and therefore cultural segregation. Blackness for this tendency only had negative connotations; its linguistic specificity and unique sensibility were historical developments and had no inherent value. Liberation consisted in abolishing the color bar which, at the same time, would bring a welcome disappearance of blackness as a cultural phenomenon.

It is interesting to note the exclusions as much as the inclusions in Gates's canon. Two of the more striking exclusions are Langston Hughes and Chester Himes. Gates praises Hughes' long poem "Ask your Mama" as a superb example of a subgenre of signifyin(g) the dozens. And one of the novels in Himes's series about two Harlem police detectives, *Hot Day, Hot Night,* "exemplifies all eight of (the) markers of Signification."[30] Yet neither writer enjoys canonical status in Gates's pantheon. After an initial period of almost complete indifference among the critical and the reading public in the United States (if not in Europe where, like Richard Wright who had emigrated there in the 1950s to, among other indignities, escape the marginalization of his work by modernist critics, he was celebrated), Himes's detectives became among the most admired figures in this genre, and enjoy a cross-over readership. A master of the black urban vernacular, his work included a major autobiographical novel, *The Third Generation,* and a deeply affecting autobiography of the black middle class, *The Quality of Hurt.*

Himes's bitter fictional account of a black union organizer during the Second World War who is also within the Communist party's orbit remains nearly a half century later a powerful indictment not only of the American Stalinist left, but of American culture. *Lonely Crusade* does not neatly fit into conventional literary genres; even as it presents itself as a "political" novel, it probes the psychological costs of race relations in the ideologically charged wartime environment. Himes's diction oscillates between the vernacular expression of which he is an acknowledged master and the conventions of political narratives. For those seeking a pristine aesthetic, this novel is transgressive and jolting, as is much of Himes's later writing that is channeled, almost exclusively, into commercial genres.

As Baker points out, for Robert Stepto, a reconstructionist, Hughes's work lends itself to "pedagogical contextualization" that might lead the student to seek the meaning of his poetry by referring to social and cultural conditions of blacks. In other words, Stepto objects that Hughes lends himself to the project of a specifically political art. It is true that despite the high praise he earns from Gates for his poetic virtues, Hughes never hesitated to connect himself and his writing to both the black liberation and civil rights movements and, more broadly, to black urban culture. His vernacular poetry as well as prose was intended for a popular, not a specifically intellectual, avant garde audience such as responded to the work say of Ellison, Ishmael Reed, and Amira Baraka. In fact, he may be described as a specifically "urban" and not academic poet; his imagery, especially in his "Simple" series, the major character Jesse Semple ("Simple" in the vernacular) is articulated with life in Harlem streets, its barbershops, gambling sites, and dance halls. Simple's speech is replete with statements of moral and ethical philosophy, social and political commentary, and personal reflection that have historicity, that is, can be situated at a particular time and particular place but are, at the same time, components of black culture and literary tradition. Moreover, Hughes identifies with the black working class.

Recently I discussed Himes's status in the emerging canon with a black critic working on a book on African-American literature. He told me that while he was an admirer of Himes, his work was still "too controversial" to warrant treatment as a central figure, chiefly because so much of his best known work is in genre fiction and, beyond the vernacular, is embedded in the lives of the urban subproletarian strata of the working class, a move that, by the 1970s, was the opening of an era of the ascendancy of the black middle class. For this ascendant class, looking down as opposed to looking back contravened their idea of "progress." And, like Wright, Himes can be convicted of having been much too much a "realist" writer, impervious to the modernist trends that swept postwar high fiction. Unlike many writers in Gates's canon, there is virtually no elegiac or pastoral sense; to the contrary, Himes is immersed in the black ghetto experience.

Baker's work breaks new theoretical ground, not only by his careful delineation of the major trends in African-American criticism or even his vernacular theory, which can be employed to identify a canon on the basis of the articulation of literary tradition with African-American everyday speech traditions. I want to call attention to two other significant elements of his work: while repudiating the integrationist approach to black literature, at the level of *standpoint* he tacitly retains its historical metatheory—the ineluctable and mutually determining relation between representation and its economic, social, and cultural context to which it (indirectly) refers. And he restores, in an undogmatic way, what he calls the "economic voice" in Frederick Douglass's autobiographical narrative: the undeniable connection between the history of African-Americans and the legacy of slavery which, as Dubois argued in his *Black Reconstruction,* is inextricably bound with their position as *workers.* For Baker, this is the void left by the black aesthetic, the nationalist rejection of the integrationist standpoint which, however valuable as a corrective to the proposal for the liquidation of a specifically black culture, ignores the class dimensions of African-American life. It may be said that Baker restores, however tentatively, class discourse to African-American cultural studies.

Baker represents his own critical shift as the difference between a symbolic approach to literature to one that stresses the significance of "ideology." While not repudiating the symbolic in literature, Baker now relegates it to one "moment in my experiencing of Afro-American culture—a moment superseded now by a prospect that constitutes its determinate negation."[31] At the same time, following Jameson, he seeks "an analysis that escapes all hints of 'vulgar marxism' through a studious attention to modern critiques of political economy, and also through a shrewd incorporation of post-structuralist thought."[32] Note the shift signified by the asymmetry of the terms "experiencing" and "analysis"—one a category of feeling, the other of science. The combination of attentiveness to critiques of political economy and, simultaneously, to poststructuralist thought may, at first glance, appear oddly inconsistent. Even the term "ideology" is firmly planted in the Marxist lexicon that, pointedly, Foucault sought to overcome. In one, the binary, "truth" is posited as a determinate negation; the other asserts the undecidability of comparison between one discourse and another. Each can connote a "regime of truth." Thus, for Foucault the notion of "false consciousness," the tacit content of the orthodox Marxist conception of ideology, is canceled.

The poststructuralist turn, then, may be seen as a repudiation of the critical Marxist categories of political economy, including class. Nevertheless, this perspective, as his explorations of the links between literary and cultural traditions, places Baker beyond typical literary criticism toward a broader, transdisciplinary critical practice. For him, as for many others who refuse the "new" New Criticism introduced by the decontextualized critical theory of the reconstructionists, this paradigmatic ambiguity is necessary. No other paradigm of cultural knowledge has displaced the Marxist conception of labor while, at the same time, retaining attentiveness to the "ideology of form" (Baker's phrase) necessary to grasp the specificity of culture.

In Baker's work, the high walls that separate humanities from the social sciences are lowered considerably. None of his moves in this regard is more dramatic than his appropriation for cultural analysis of Thomas Kuhn's theory of scientific revolutions. While noting the critical literature's argument that there are limitations for the universality of Kuhn's explanation for the process by which paradigm shifts occur, Baker finds important uses for

Kuhn's achievement. For him, the concept of paradigm may be understood as "tropological vehicle," not only for the understanding of science but for showing the change introduced by Stephen Henderson and other proponents of the black aesthetic in the "perceptual field of Afro-American literary study."[33] Baker is excited by the disruptive effects of a theory of knowledge shift that refuses the cumulative, progressive assumptions of chronological histories that form a closed circle in which past and future are seamlessly linked in the present. None of the contributions of the black aesthetic is more transgressive than its insistence that the black cultural expression not be confined to literary texts, but that music, the oral traditions, were constitutive of the aesthetic.

Thus, Baker makes a powerful argument for comprehending Afro-American expressive forms within a cultural rather than exclusively literary framework. By describing this critical view as a "paradigm" that first appears as a trope of the history of science, Baker makes another tacit shift: the distinctions between theoretical categories in the sciences and humanities become, thereby, moot. For example, in the course of discussing the role of the "blues matrix" as "a cultural invention" that "generates its own referents," Baker is constrained to compare the procedure by which his analysis will proceed; he undertakes a methodological excursus in which he introduces the concept of "normative relativity" to acknowledge that he has engaged in model building similar to that done by physics.[34] The components of every model are selected from a vast array of elements in the cognitive field, but the theorist cannot include them all. Therefore, "no object, process or single element possesses *intrinsic* value. The 'art' objects," like the object of scientific knowledge, "are selective constructions" whose epistemological status, having been axiologically extrapolated, is radically uncertain since it refers to the critic's (the scientist's) "tropes and models," not a pristine a priori reality.[35]

The analogy between physics and critical theory may be taken in a number of ways: as a felicitous metaphoric "borrowing" in order to illustrate the character of the purely cultural phenomenon; as an attempt to *legitimate* a literary theory in terms of the master discourse of the West, science, much as Ransom uses Hegel to "signify" the ontological weight of poetry without entering into a truly philosophically informed theory of literature; or to make a larger claim consistent with the "perspectival relativism" of recent philosophy and social studies of science that "natural" and "cultural" objects—especially those that are not subject to the evidence of the senses—in the "post-Heisenbergian" world are selective construction and are, for this reason, subject to normative considerations. While Baker calls the physical analogy a "metaphor" and follows it to invoke categories such as "energy and spacetime" to describe the influence of the "blues matrix" on the blackness of Afro-American culture, he cannot escape the deeper implications of blurring the boundaries between science and culture.

The implication of this standpoint for cultural theory is immediately obvious: if the object is bereft of intrinsic value, but only acquires its value in relation to others within a model and, more widely within a paradigm with "perceptual and semantic ramifications," one might take the next step to develop a theoretical critique of the authority of existing knowledges—not only the literary canon but also of science itself—that proclaims their independence from the perceptual and semantic ramifications associated with cultural paradigms and contexts. While Baker limits his discourse on science to analogy and metaphor, the past decade is marked by significant strides in developing a discourse critique of the gender neutrality of science.

5

Some of the most powerful—and controversial—challenges to the authority of legitimate knowledge have occurred in the once staid fields of philosophy, history, and sociology of science. As previously noted, the received wisdom of contemporary positivist, analytic philosophy was, in the words of one of the major figures of the Vienna Circle, that "epistemology can never issue decrees that lay down what is, or is not to count as scientific knowledge; on the contrary, its task is only to clarify and interpret that knowledge."[36] For Schlick and several generations of scientists and their philosophic underlaborers, "we can carry out our work quite well in the sciences without providing them with epistemological foundations but unless we do so we shall never understand them in all their depth."[37]

Thus, the difference between philosophy and the particular inquiry called the philosophy of science is often indistinct since nearly all philosophers have accepted that their work is "only to clarify and interpret." In this mode of thought, science is equivalent to what counts as reliable knowledge because its methods are so constructed as to insure, by rigorous application, the "neutrality" of its results with respect to the historical, social, and cultural context. Thus, while philosophy intervenes to elucidate the nature of scientific inquiry—especially its methods—on which the apodictic character of its discoveries depends, the history of science tells the stories of the resolute progressive march of science on the basis of an internal history that shows that each generation sits "on the shoulders of giants." Until recently, the story of modern science (modern in the sense of postfeudal, enlightenment inquiry) has been told as all traditional history is recounted: in the conjunction of apparently insoluble problems facing scientists in their laboratories and in their imaginations, some of which are left by the previous generations and take on the significance of redemptive issues for the current community of scientists, and, what is in the last instance the determining moment, the individual genius, the true agent of scientific discovery.

Copernicus, Galileo, Kepler, Newton, Faraday, and Einstein have acquired so much iconic value that their names and their "discoveries" possess as much—or more—canonic value than parallel literary works. Like folktales that bear infinite repetition and are told in many variations, the biographies, studies, and semifictional narratives of the great moments of scientific discovery when their theories changed the world are part of our collective imagination. And, of course, there is a similar pantheon in biology—Aristotle, Lucretius, Darwin, Pasteur, Mendel, Watson, and Crick.

When "social problems" intrude to spur research as in the case of an epidemic of anthrax in Pasteur's France, they influence only the space/time within which knowledge is generated.[38] But the science itself is rigorously independent of these conditions. When such intrusions occur, the covenants of the scientific community must, and invariably do, relegate such work to the realm of *rejected* knowledge.

The development of the sociology of science by Robert Merton and others only mildly challenged the standpoint of history and philosophy.[39] Influenced by the work of the Soviet scientist and historian Boris Hessen, Merton's early work demonstrated that the paradigm of classical, that is, Newtonian physics was influenced by navigation, mining, and military materiel, not unlike Hessen's claim, and that of some other historians, that the economic and cultural conditions of early capitalism bore on the character of the mechanical world picture, including determining the *problematic* or the object of knowledge. In other words, the early modern focus on cosmology and mechanics had roots in practical economic affairs, in this case mercantile capitalism. Similarly, as Ludvik Fleck demonstrated, Ehrlich's "magic bullet" for the syphilis treatment, the results of experiment 606, could not be explained entirely with reference to the purely experimental history, but was closely linked to the "social hygiene" movement in the turn-of-the-century Germany that was prompted by the disease's spread from the lower classes to the middle class.[40] However, under Merton's later tutelage, the sociology of science steered clear of problems of the social determinants of scientific knowledge and focused, instead, on the reward systems within the scientific community, producing a number of valuable studies that demonstrated the importance of institutional context of scientific discovery for explaining how scientific careers were advanced or thwarted.

Since the late 1960s, the emphasis has shifted in the social studies of science. Under the influence of both the emerging intellectual skepticism of the era and the concomitant revival of a nondogmatic Marxism and more theoretically oriented reading of the work of Emile Durkheim, sociologists and historians began to explore the concrete links between knowledge and the social context within which it was produced. The process of scientific discovery, especially the laboratory, became the crucial site for this inquiry. In their study of the Scripps laboratories at La Jolla, ethnographers Latour and Woolgar identified three determinants of the knowledges produced there: inscriptions, the tools and other materials of inquiry, and conversations among researchers, and tried to weigh the degree to which these became constitutive of the results.[41] Others—notably Andrew Pickering, Karin Knorr-Cetina, Sharon Traweek, and ethnomethodologists Michael Lynch and Eric Livingston—following suggestions of Harold Garfinkel—performed similar investigations, emphasizing one or another of the categories.

Philosophy and the history of science were moving in parallel directions. Of course, as we have seen, the work of Thomas Kuhn has had more influence outside professional disciplinary circles than the writing of philosophers Norwood Hanson and Paul Feyerabend, or the historiography of Shapin and Schaffer. Yet each in his own way subverted the hegemony of prevailing discourses about science by, among other things, showing the incommensurability of past and present knowledges, the degree to which not only the problematic but the claims of science to universal validity were rooted in cultural and, in Feyerabend's account, authoritarian presuppositions.[42] Perhaps Shapin and Schaffer sum up best the most general conclusion of these studies: "the history of science occupies the same terrain as the history of politics."[43] And this involves not only the selection of problematics or objects of knowledge but the specification of how we know and what we know is, in the final instance, a political, that is, a philosophical question insofar as they understand philosophy as a form of life. Their study makes problematic the efficacy of the notion of an empirical way to knowledge ("seeing is believing") in the debate between Thomas Hobbes and Robert Boyle concerning how scientific knowledge may be attained. They are undeterred by the historical fact that Hobbes's anti-empirical position may now be classified as rejected knowledge and can safely be consigned to obscurity. By reviving the debate, the authors mean to show that, far from representing self-evident rationality, the outcome of the controversy in favor of experiment was part of the history of politics, that Boyle's status as a canonical figure in the history of physical science may be considered as symptomatic of specific historical, especially discursive/ideological circumstances rather than the triumph of reason.

Among the more important aspects of this superb study is that the investigators asked the question of the politics of scientific discovery. That their answer is essentially *historical* rather than normative raises a profound methodological issue: under other circumstances, could Hobbes's view that valid scientific knowledge need not depend for its legitimacy on experimentally induced observation be considered the more reasonable? By showing the historicity of the experimental method, more particularly the politics of epistemology, Shapin and Schaffer succeed in defamiliarizing what has become absolutely axiomatic in western culture—that reliable knowledge, in the last instance, must rely on the evidence of the senses.

Feminist critiques of science are inseparable from the general challenges mounted by feminist intellectuals to the authority of other forms of (male) knowledge and are also linked to the new sociology, philosophy, and history of science. The work of Donna Haraway, Ruth Hubbard, Evelyn Fox Keller, and Sandra Harding has had enormous impact not only on feminist studies of science, but also on the relationship between feminism and legitimate intellectual knowledge, in its institutional settings as well as on the discursive level.[44]

Studies of the relation of women to "hard" sciences are primarily of three types: biographical and sociological studies of women in science that emphasize the extent of their participation and their achievements; in works such as Evelyn Fox Keller's study of Barbara McClintock's career in biology feminists have shifted the earlier emphasis to study their occlusion within the scientific community and even their effective exclusion from basic research in some fields;[45] and, as the feminist movement has placed renewed emphasis on a woman's right to control her own body, especially her reproductive organs. Barbara Katz Rothman has studied the uses by medical science of new reproductive technologies such as in vitro fertilization that thwart the women's agency.[46]

Cynthia Eagle Russett has explored the Victorian construction of womanhood through contemporary "scientific" concepts—notably phrenology that measured girls' brain size, natural selection, studies of the physiological division of labor, and other dubious ideas whose purport was to demonstrate either the "natural" inferiority of women or their biological fit to be mothers and wives. According to Russett, as late as the turn of the twentieth century the cumulative effect of these studies was one of "diminished expectations" of women's capacity for public life. Russett's conclusion is that "science is not a disembodied inquiry; it is the product of particular human beings living in specific times and places, and these individuals . . . are affected by the circumstances of their lives."[47] This study draws heavily on the work of the social studies of science with its characteristic combination of sociological, historical, and philosophical categories.

Sandra Harding and Hilary Rose are among a small group of writers who integrate the core of these studies into a wider feminist problematic. On the one hand, they recognize that the gendering of science articulates with the marginalization of women in science and the choice of the objects of scientific inquiry illustrated by Russett's exploration of the way in which Victorian science became an instrument of male supremacy and Katz Rothman's demonstration of the ways reproductive technologies deprive women of moral and political agency. On the other hand, they are on the cutting edge of an attempt to fashion a new feminist scientific paradigm. Building on Rose's distinction between a male-dominated industrialized science and a craft-oriented "women's" science, Harding has made a strong critique of prevailing positivist models in which science is understood as value-neutral inquiry, to propose a postmodern approach. What are the components of this approach? First, and perhaps foremost, Harding tells the history and the ideology of science, including the work of historians, sociologists, and philosophers as a series of "stories," the cumulative effect of which is to produce discourse with powerful political consequences. This demythologizing work is the necessary condition for the development of a new science.

Among the crucial features of this work has been to show that, far from an idealized purely intellectual endeavor, normal science is a labor process, with a sexual division of labor as well as other hierarchical modes of social organization. The industrialization and institutionalization of science that accompany the maturation of industrialization in the nineteenth century provide the ground for an anti-romantic study of the social relations of science. One of the crucial features of this process, according to Harding, is the separation of scientists and their work from politics. The reigning myth is that science is a purely cognitive activity. Harding: "By locating the historical compromise that resulted in this division of labor, we can see the ideological components of a key concept in modernism's science: the commitment to value neutrality. The claim that science is value neutral was not arrived at through experimental observation . . . it was instead a statement of intent, designed to ensure to the practice of science a niche in society rather than the emancipatory reform of that society."[48]

In contrast to the earlier artisanal character of science, performed by amateurs as well as craftspersons, modern "big" science is a heavily financed industrial enterprise complete with the same characteristics of abstract labor that mark the labor process in general. The value-neutral ideology of science privileges a method of inquiry that rigorously excludes the experiences that might challenge not only the uses of scientific knowledge but its process and results. For Harding, as much as Rose, the precondition for a feminist science is fulfilled when science abandons its aspiration for unitary methods and its privilege of those branches that have most successfully excluded disruptive experiences that might contest the prevailing paradigm of value neutrality which, among other things, excludes women. Feminism insists that the modernist scientific paradigm be subject to the test of values.

The proposal for scientific pluralism in which feminist values can inform the intentions and procedures of scientific investigation joins with Feyerabend's call for an "anarchist" science. But to construct this new regime requires attention to the social organization of science with respect to its functions within the prevailing social order and, in particular, its technological cast, especially in contemporary particle physics, the "king" of the sciences, and molecular biology, one of its rising corporate stars. Harding's historical analysis is stronger than her contemporary assessment of the institutional position of science. However, by raising the question of what might be called the secular constitution of scientific knowledge and particularly the role of gender, race, and class discourses within the structure of science itself, Harding, Rose, and Harraway have made immense contributions to a science in the interest of emancipation.

CHAPTER EIGHT

The End of the Beginning?

IN DECEMBER 1991 the Board of Regents of the University of Minnesota voted virtually unanimously to abolish its Department of the Humanities as part of its attempt to "downsize" (it said), in response to a budget crisis that could not be viewed as temporary. Among the measures to achieve this goal, the university's administration proposed to reduce the number of departments. Toward this end, the university's president fashioned a triage policy to determine which of the university's departments could safely be eliminated without sacrificing academic standards. Instead of an arbitrary—or overtly political—process that would have invited protest and confrontation, the university administration proposed a series of criteria with which to measure the performance of the departments within the College of Liberal Arts. They were: quality, centrality, comparative advantage, demand, and efficiency.

In his testimony at a regents forum to hear arguments for and against the proposal, Gary Thomas, the department's chair, addressed the five criteria. As to quality he provided the members with evidence that, among other things, showed that with only eight members, the department's faculty had won the highest number of Guggenheim and National Endowment for the Humanities Fellowships per capita in the entire university; "half of the faculty has been nominated for the Morse-Amoco distinguished teaching award and one received it and its members had received other intra college awards." Perhaps equally revealing, "within roughly the last decade seven members of the faculty have published 17 books and these bear the imprint of the most prestigious university presses: Harvard, Oxford, Cambridge, California, Chicago, Duke, Princeton, and MIT. Four more books are currently in press, a good dozen in progress." Thomas went on to argue that, despite its uniqueness, its interdisciplinary curriculum "fields a set of courses available nowhere else in the college and very few institutions in the country."

Thomas then listed some of these: "Knowledge, Persuasion, and Power," "The Body and the Politics of Representation," "Gay Men and Homophobia in the Modern West," "The Ideology of the Master Narrative," and "Poetry as Cultural Critique." The department had a fairly respectable number of undergraduate majors, and, as to efficiency, its small faculty and its courses "have been the most popular in the university." At a time of declining enrollments in the college "the number of majors continues to rise. With one of the smallest faculties and lowest budgets in the CLA (College of Liberal Arts) we taught last year over 2600 students." Plainly, the Humanities department passed the president's tests with flying colors. Yet it was eliminated despite its success in fulfilling some of the stated objectives of the university to innovate in the direction of a multicultural curriculum that would bridge the various disciplines. One may speculate on some of the reasons for this astounding decision.

The bad luck of the Humanities department was to have arrived, in its own words, "on the verge of national distinction" precisely at the moment when the conservative, traditionalist backlash was in full flower, and conjoined with the nationwide budget crisis of public (and many private) universities that has included Columbia, Yale, and some other elite institutions. The corporate imperative to downsize provides traditional departments, sensing the new zero-sum game prompted by financial problems, where they are unable or unwilling to incorporate the innovations into their own program, an occasion to launch, in the name of "objective" criteria, an indirect assault on cultural studies. The growing prominence of a program within the university that can attract undergraduates in large numbers may diminish the standing of, say, English departments that, in many places, survive on the base of their required courses such as composition programs. And a department that can offer courses in "The Ideology of Master Narrative" or "Poetry as Cultural Critique" challenges the very foundations of modernism. Equally subversive is the tacit assertion in the course titles of the intimate relationship between knowledge, power, and persuasion, a standpoint that flagrantly confronts the value-neutral assumptions of the sciences with the specter of a discourse for which rhetoric is not regarded as "merely" a strategy of persuasion, but as constitutive of what counts as knowledge itself.

Of course, positing the knowledge/power matrix is not entirely recent; it appears in Nietzsche's *Will to Power* as well as Marx's analysis of the movement of physics, chemistry, and biology from independent disciplines to techo-sciences of industrialization and warfare. More contemporary is Foucault's argument, derived from Canguilhem, for the ways in which legitimate scientific knowledge about illness and health, the normal and the pathological, generates a normative regime that regulates and polices social behavior. Teaching that knowledge, including science, is context-dependent is an affront that can be tolerated only if this pedagogy is relatively isolated in a few obscure corners within the university. However, the institutionalization, in departments and programs, of the postmodern critique of the mission of the university to transmit the master narratives by which the structured inequalities of our culture reproduce themselves is another matter. It is possible that the limits of liberal tolerance are reached when the new paradigm accumulates some institutional power, but not enough to survive attacks from three directions: ideological, financial, and bureaucratic/political.

More to the point, as we saw in Chapter 7, the bearers of the new paradigm, in their quest for legitimacy, are obliged to seek institutional integration. In the Minnesota case, the formation of the Humanities department predated the paradigm shift. It began in the early 1970s as a response to both student demands for curriculum reform and the university's newly acquired tolerance in the wake of student protest. The mild "interdisciplinary" name for the department, "humanities," is a sign of the compromise that made the innovation possible.

As the department expanded in the mid 1980s, it recruited and obtained some of the best of the younger intellectuals in fields such as English, history, and musicology, most of whom were part of the shift. While as high achievers, in traditional terms, these rising stars received tenure, this was sufficient only to insure their individual places within the academic system. The breakup of Humanities at Minnesota will, if ultimately successful, result in the dispersion of its faculty, reproducing the anterior condition of toleration of individual dissent from prevailing modernist knowledge but will "protect" the institution from the erosion of its central reproductive mission.

The past two decades in American academic life have been periods of searching and sometimes painful reevaluations for the humanities and the social sciences. A new generation has entered university teaching and research informed by what can be described as a veritable *paradigm shift* in the theoretical assumptions by which knowledge is acquired, validated, and disseminated. But, as the Minnesota Humanities case demonstrates, these gains are subject to reversal.

The shift continues despite the institutionalization, even neutralization of cultural studies, women's, African-American, and Latino studies. We can observe this process in the contemporary and stifling confining of cultural studies in English and other humanities departments. In the wake of recent developments in this direction, we are obliged to take seriously Megan Morris's lament about the "banality" of cultural studies. In her view, this banality is exemplified by the endless rehearsals of "representations" of subaltern groups in media, the invocation of the idea that mass cultural reception is not a one-way street where messages flow from top to bottom but are reversed. This process is encapsulated by the category of "resistance" through interpretation, rituals, and other autonomous cultural gestures.

At the same time, American cultural studies has barely digested the radical intent of the Birmingham school. For in the United States and Canada, cultural studies still presents itself as an *amendment* to the conventional study of literature by expanding the canon to include new literatures; and enlarging the cultural object to include the study of representations of popular and genre novels, film, television, and sports, among other elements of popular culture. Boundary crossing between, say, the humanities and social sciences has barely begun.[1] In short, cultural studies has been colonized and reinterpreted from its European roots by the disciplines.

Still, as I have shown in this book, what has been described as the postmodern "condition" and the power of emergent discourses within colleges and universities may have irreversibly penetrated the core of knowledges. This shift may be signified by challenges to prevailing academic value systems: rather than seeking to achieve value neutrality in the production of knowledge, many of the new generation insist that every intellectual enterprise is informed by a *standpoint*, at least at the epistemological level, whether it wants to or not. The prevailing scientific and humanistic assumptions—positivism and empiricism—contain rules for research, particularly the privileging of the evidence of the senses over speculative knowledge. These are norms of conduct that have significant consequences for those who wish to perform legitimate academic research and teaching. As we have seen, feminists, African-American, Latino, and gay and lesbian intellectuals have insisted on the validity of their own standpoint, a claim that the academic system of American society has been willing to accommodate only with great difficulty; there is a growing acknowledgment among intellectuals that all knowledge is historically situated and is discursive. Far from being adduced from observation, facts are taken as theory laden. This perspective, a significant tendency in the contemporary philosophy of science, is associated in the United States with the work of Kuhn, Harding, and Feyerabend. French theorists such as Foucault, influenced by Nietzsche's insistence that knowledge and power form a matrix, acknowledge that each era/period has a "regime of truth" that guides what counts as legitimate intellectual knowledge. In turn Foucault, following Canguilhem, questions whether this truth may be considered apart from its normativity, that is, apart from the power relations of which it is a part. Knowledge paradigms are considered incommensurable with respect to their predecessors and successors. In recent years, the traditional idea of progress in the development of knowledge has been severely questioned. Since progressive reason is a presupposition of the self-conception of American ideology, this "europeanization" of historicality stretches the limits of liberal tolerance.

Consequently, the notion that the history of expressive forms may be written as a progression from the "lower" to the "higher" is repudiated. On the contrary, many, influenced by Bakhtin's discourse analysis of canonical literature, hold that popular culture and high culture mutually condition each other and that the novel canon is formed by those works in which the popular voices are present, despite the views of the writer. While there are tendencies among some critics to *reverse* the relation of privilege in favor of folk and other popular traditions, the program of reversal only mirrors progressive reason. The discovery that art forms, like science, are rooted in craft and other sites of the popular does not imply their superiority. The point is to reject hierarchies that are part of systems of social privilege. Yet the extent to which university education remains since the war—despite its dramatic expansion across classes, gender, and race—a privileged site, makes the postmodern project of insisting on the legitimacy of hitherto rejected knowledges still corrosive. While the high/low debate within intellectual circles seems to have resulted in a massive accommodation both in separate departments of communications, popular culture, and film and incorporation of these topics within literatures and sociology, the thesis according to which the liberal university has succeeded in the routinization of innovation is an illusion whose force seems to diminish with each passing year.

High art is constituted by this system of social privilege and forms, within the reception of all art forms, a specialized part of the cultural market. The sites of high culture are galleries and museums, the concert halls, the musical organizations that inhabit them and their audiences and patrons; and, in literature, the small number of readers of poetry, modernist novels, and short stories, except those published in mass circulation magazines that, for this reason, are designated as something other than high art. The specific conditions of the production and reception of artistic culture, not its contents, designate its position with respect to its location within the hierarchy of the Culture Industry. In this connection, even the most transgressive works, such as Picasso's early twentieth-century collages that incorporated newspapers and objects from daily life into the painting, are by no means exempt from their neutralization by the high cultural context within which they are produced. Similarly, Gershwin's "Rhapsody in Blue," which inspired Ravel, Milhaud, and Copland to incorporate jazz motifs within the concerto form, does not, thereby, qualify as a work of popular culture. These compositions have taken their place within the "classical" music repertoire and themselves spurred what was once a cottage industry of imitations that would currently be described as pastiche or kitsch. Conversely, jazz, whose roots are within the blues, a popular expressive music of black rural and urban workers, has, to some extent, become a high cultural form as its audience, sponsorship, and venue have shifted in both class and industrial terms.

As Clement Greenberg argued more than fifty years ago, the distinction between kitsch and mass culture is that the former is a degraded kind of "high" art, but the latter is intended for a different purpose and audience. Thus, high culture is not to be confused with questions of aesthetic value; within the high culture market, there is good and bad art and, if one can imagine an aesthetics of entertainment, the same standard would apply within the limits of the genres that constitute it. For Greenberg there is no point to a critique of mass culture since it is intended to be merely entertaining and has nothing to do with art.

However, at its most radical place, the new paradigm denies the category of aesthetics itself since, at least historically, it is inevitably affiliated with metaphysics. "Value" is understood as a historically situated discourse linked ineluctably to issues of hegemony; that is, aesthetic questions are taken as political questions. At the same time, even these more militant postmodern critics are required to justify the selection of their critical objects in terms of problematics that exemplify a cultural situation. These may not be described as aesthetic choices, but they seem to entail some kind of priority, at least with respect to the decision whether to engage in critique and exposition. In short, even if politicized, it is difficult to avoid elements that constitute any aesthetic: value. Insofar as value remains crucial for the selection, it may be held to be an equivalent of an aesthetic, although not necessarily one that is implicated in the swamp of "beauty."

Academic disciplines are conventional and not properties of nature. This implies that their development may be traced in terms of economic, social, and cultural contexts. This does not imply that they do not generate a legitimating intellectual basis, a canon of theoretical or literary works that "represent" the mainstream ideas and methods of the discipline or that the research projects generated within them are not warranted in their own terms and by the contexts within which they emerge. However, to regard them as constellations of produced knowledges means that their standing emerges primarily by processes of institutionalization, not only in terms of their role in the curriculum of socialization, but also with respect to their relation to state policy, what may be described as the production of norms and values for an entire culture, and most recently for the relationship of the social and the natural sciences to the military, major corporations, and private foundations that together provide most of the research funds. The historical context within which they generate knowledge is closely linked to institutional power struggles that result in their growth or decline.

Methodologically, historians, literary critics, and social and cultural critics have adopted discourse analysis, that is, close reading of the texts of the disciplines to discern both what is said and what is unsaid in them, their "blind spots" that often yield insight and innovation but frequently belie their claims. Although we have now a considerable body of critical work in the disciplines and on the disciplines, and there are conventional chronological histories of scientific and technological knowledge—MIT Press published a series in science and technology that presented itself as the story of progress—we have no critical history or genealogy of the disciplines that traces their internal and external relations, the issues that motivated and animated their development, their links with other institutions both within and outside universities in society. There are certainly some efforts in this direction: Fischer's study of the rise of the Social Science Research Council that has played a powerful role in turning American social science from a critical discourse on social relations to a policy science; work in the history and discourse of ethnography discussed in Chapter 7; Kittay and Godzich's wonderful prolegomena to a genealogy of prosaics, *The Emergence of Prose,* in which politics, history, and epistemology are articulated within the same narrative space to show the ineluctability of the articulation of knowledge and the state; and the much older work of Wilhelm Dilthey whose *Introduction to the Human Sciences* is now available in translation after more than a century during which this absolutely central and exemplary transdisciplinary discourse remained obscure to Anglo-American intellectual life.

It is not difficult to understand why Dilthey was untranslated until now. The appearance, more than a century ago, of this vigorous critique of positivism, especially of the effort of leading theorists such as Comte and Spencer to subsume the human sciences (corresponding to social sciences and the humanities) under the methods and the epistemological presuppositions of natural science, corresponded to the triumph within American universities of the ideal of positive sciences in the study of social relations and the marginalization of the humanities. Dilthey's was an unwelcome message in the era of segmentation, specialization, and natural-scientific hegemony over all intellectual knowledge. His argument for the incommensurability of the human and natural sciences or, more accurately, against the reduction of the former to the latter, relied on the shared inner experience of the investigator and her or his object, the social individual. This idea was dismissed by most social scientists as "idealism." Even more problematic from the perspective of social sciences that wished to emulate physics or biology were two of his more controversial claims: that aesthetics could not be separated from history; and that philosophical inquiry could not be separated from positive social and historical inquiry. Moreover, Dilthey has a surprisingly contemporary idea of knowledge:

Knowledge of a particular system is obtained through a complex of methodical operations conditioned by the position of that system within socio-historical reality. The resources for such knowledge are many: analyzing the system, comparing the particular forms contained in it and taking account of the relations in which this sphere of inquiry stands on the one hand, to psychological knowledge of the life-units [individuals] which are the elements of the interactions making up the system, on the other hand, to the socio-historical context from which it is isolated for investigation. *Still there is only one cognitive process.* The untenability of attempts to separate philosophical inquiry and the positive inquiry of particular sciences is due to the fact that only with the assistance of psychology can the concepts used in the inquiry be sufficiently established—e.g., the concepts of will and responsibility in the law, those of the imagination and the ideal in art.

Psychology, according to Dilthey, is the science of "inner experience" that, although individual in its starting point, is objective in the sense that it is socially and historically constituted.[2]

Dilthey's method is hermeneutic, although entirely empirical. One must examine the documents of history, but they must be *read* since there is no direct correspondence between experience and representations. Like Husserl, who influenced his later work, Dilthey adopts a hermeneutic method for uncovering the nature of historical processes, while crediting the facts of conscious experience for showing attention and interest. However, anticipating Freud, he insists that observation cannot fathom the contents of the unconscious. Thus, in concert with a long line of modern philosophic and psychological thought, Dilthey accepts the notion that investigation of conscious processes warrants the inference that there are unconscious contents or processes at work. In this sense, he shares an interest in the "irrational" in individual experience with the early theorists of sociology, among them Tonnies, Weber, and Simmel. Moreover, his program for a "descriptive psychology" became the occasion for commentary by both Husserl and Heidegger, each of whom sought to find the concordance and the distinction between their phenomenological epoche and Dilthey's attempt to found a rigorous human science that could challenge the mechanical causality of positivism.

The new interest in Dilthey and Wittgenstein, whose conception of language as a form of life interfaces with Dilthey's contextualization of knowledge, is, undoubtedly, part of the paradigm shift that is variously labeled postmodern. While it is Heidegger's call for a nonfoundational philosophy that has been the most immediately influential, Dilthey's insistence on the "unity" of the human sciences has proven to be one of those instances of prophecy whose realization awaited the crisis of modernity. The assertion that inner experience (a term appropriated later by, among other transgressors, George Bataille) is the key to the understanding of socio-historical life is by no means a psychological reductionism as some have alleged. Nor is it "personalistic" any more than Bergson's intersubjective notion of time is subjectivism. In both theorists, what is at stake is an attempt to overcome the dualism of western philosophy, which, despite its intentions, remains in all correspondence theory.

We are also witness to a renewed critique of the specializations that mark disciplinary boundary-keeping. It is not only that these boundaries are untenable at a time when what Dilthey called "socio-historical reality" overflows them; in addition, Dilthey's program for boundary restrictions between the human sciences and the natural sciences, erected to prevent reductionism from overcoming the former, has itself been overturned. For, as investigators have challenged the idea that the object of scientific investigation is external to the context of inquiry, the separation of "natural" from the human sciences seems increasingly problematic.

Whereas since the eighteenth century, the division of the labor in the production of knowledge has constituted a *principle* for both sides—one to preserve its hegemony, the other to preserve its specificity, that is, its capacity to represent the qualitative, the aesthetic, and the historical dimension of the life-world—we are on the verge of constituting a unified field that recognizes the aesthetic dimension of "natural" science, for already writers have shown, for example, that metaphors, tropes, and visualizations are as *indispensable* to microphysics as the system of mathematical inferences from imputed "observations," as well as the obvious but often resisted idea that humans are part of nature and that, as Dilthey insisted, their social and cultural interactions presuppose physical, biological, and physiological processes.

The question for contemporary inquiry is how to found a nonreductionist critical science in which the cultural-historical contexts are posited as the meeting ground for articulation, contexts rooted in everyday practices such as those proposed in the feminist critiques discussed in Chapter 7. To be sure, there are significant problems in such a project, among them whether craft may be considered an adequate tropology for the development of a new science. Further, Dilthey has discussed the aesthetic dimension in terms of the form of scientific discourse. As we have seen, in recent years there has been produced a body of work where writers have boldly shown the discursive, even ideological elements in scientific theory and research.

Yet the gulf remains between the power of the institutionalized disciplines to survive and the corrosive effects of theory. Given the inertial weight of tradition, even the boldest theorists, critics, and researchers are obliged to seek legitimacy *through* disciplines and the institutions that protect them that barely tolerate the new paradigm when they are not repressive. As we have seen, this often results in seeking refuge for intellectual work of a subaltern kind within the established disciplines. Of course, in their quest for survival, not to say hegemony, the disciplines choose and cultivate a few "stars" who appear to transcend the barriers that frustrate their less prominent colleagues.

However, the genie has wriggled out of the bottle. For the simple truth is that new agents have managed, despite compromise and exclusion, to get more than a single foot in the door. Even though the "war of position" may be prolonged, the disciplines are fighting a rear-guard action, a statement that could not have been made in the heyday of modernity. Judging by the ferocity of the counterattack by neoconservatives and liberal modernists, we are on the verge of a large-scale restructuring of legitimate intellectual knowledge. In this restructuring, the notion of "discipline" itself would yield to elective affinity.

In such a regime, faculty and students would develop courses of study on the assumption of their fundamentally transitory character. Thus, notions of "curriculum reform" would be replaced by a kind of "permanent revolution" because no regimen of learning could survive the elective affinities of the collaborative. Clearly, there would be room for those who wished to examine the traditional disciplinary canon but, as in any educational enterprise, it would no longer enjoy the status of received wisdom.

Here it must be noted that virtually any significant educational innovation already has a history somewhere in the annals of the American academic system. The point is to comb the archives to discover what has been done and what the fate of such programs was. I suspect that, like the Minnesota case, the experiment succeeded so the administration disbanded the program. However, given the broad challenges to the disciplines, and the palpable breakdown of many of the old certainties, there is no reason to infer from the current revanchism in universities that proponents of the new paradigm should conclude that the era of academic freedom is at an end. We are merely at the end of a beginning.

Notes

Introduction (pp. 1–19)

1. Benedict Anderson, *Imagined Communities* (rev. ed.), London, Verso Books, 1991.

2. Michael Novak, *The Rise of the Unmeltable Ethnics,* New York, Macmillan, 1971.

3. A recent front-page *New York Times* story reported that in New York City the street has become a major job market for casual labor especially among undocumented immigrants; see Alison Mitchell, "Wary Recruits: Immigrants Vie for Day Jobs," *New York Times,* May 21, 1992.

4. Jean-François Lyotard, *The Post Modern Condition: A Report on Knowledge,* Minneapolis, University of Minnesota Press, 1988.

5. Irving Kristol, "Comment" on Francis Fukuyama's "The End of History," *National Interest,* Summer 1989.

6. Arthur Schlesinger, Jr., "The Future of Socialism," *Partisan Review,* May–June 1947, p. 231.

7. Ibid.

8. Ibid., p. 230.

9. Talcott Parsons, *The Social System,* Glencoe Ill., Free Press, 1951.

10. This project was undertaken, most notably, by Raymond Williams; see Raymond Williams, *Politics and Letters,* London, New Left Books, 1979; *Problems of Materialism and Culture,* London, Verso Books, 1980.

11. George Lichtheim, "On David Reisman," *Partisan Review,* Fall 1964, p. 612.

12 Richard Lewontin, "The Human Genome Project," *New York Review of Books,* May 28, 1992, p. 31.

13. Ibid.

14. Daniel Kelves and Leroy Hood quoted in Lewontin, p. 31.

15. Ibid., p. 33.

16. Ibid., p. 34.

17. Sheldon Krimsky, *Genetic Alchemy,* Cambridge, MIT Press, 1982.

1. On the Politically Correct (pp. 20–62)

1. To be politically correct signified that one adhered to the line of whatever movement claimed to have a morally unimpeachable politics. It rapidly became an ironic comment among those who refused to join the rush toward revolutionary communist politics in the early 1970s. In conversation, it usually reminded an interlocutor that they were engaging in dubious moralism. Or, if you wished to say something that

was iconoclastic, you prefaced your remarks with "I know this may not be politically correct but. . . ."

2. Francis Fukuyama, "The End of History," *National Interest,* No. 16, Summer 1989.

3. Ibid., p. 3.

4. Ibid., p. 18.

5. Kristol, "Comment" in *National Interest* No. 16 , p. 28.

6. Sidney Hook, *Political Power and Personal Freedom,* New York, Collier Books, 1962, part 1.

7. Jurgen Habermas, *The Structural Transformation of the Public Sphere,* Cambridge, MIT Press, 1989; *Theory of Communicative Action,* vol. 2. Boston, Beacon Press, 1990.

8. Here I can only give representative works of an accelerating outpouring. For the best introduction, see Karen Knorr Cetina and Michael Mulkey, eds., *Science Observed,* London, Beverly Hills, and New Delhi, Sage Publications, 1983; Michael Mulkey, *Science and the Sociology of Knowledge,* London, George Allen and Unwin, 1979; David Bloor, *Knowledge and Social Imagery,* London, Routledge, 1976. In Chapter 7 I discuss feminist and philosophical critiques of science in connection with the debate concerning the authority of knowledge.

9. Thomas Kuhn, *The Structure of Scientific Revolutions,* 2nd ed. Chicago, University of Chicago Press, 1969.

10. Sandra Harding, *The Science Question in Feminism,* Ithaca, Cornell University Press, 1986, is clearly the most comprehensive feminist critique of scientific knowledge in the literature. It provides a thorough overview of the argument. See also Evelyn Fox Keller, *Reflections on Gender and Science,* New Haven, Yale University Press, 1985; Helen Longino, *Science as Social Knowledge,* Princeton, Princeton University Press, 1990.

11. Paul Forman, "Weimar Culture, Causality, and Quantum Theory 1918–1927: Adaptation by German Physicists and Mathematicians to a Hostile Intellectual Environment," in *Historical Studies in the Physical Sciences,* Third Annual Volume, 1971. This monograph may be taken as the exemplary work of the study of scientific knowledge as, in part, the outcome of the cultural context within which it is produced. While others have looked at "laboratory life" to find this context, Forman reaches to the complex influences on the intellectuals of art, philosophy, and the cultural consequences of cataclysmic events such as the Great War to discover the roots of physical knowledge.

12. Bruno Latour and Steve Woolgar, *Laboratory Life,* London and Los Angeles, Sage Publications, 1979; Ludvik Fleck, *Genesis and Development of a Scientific Fact,* ed. by Thomas Kuhn and Robert Merton, Chicago, University of Chicago Press, 1976.

13. For the best body of work about early twentieth-century American anarchism, see Paul Avrich's many historical writings. One neglected book is *The Modern School Movement,* Princeton, Princeton University Press, 1983; also see Emma Goldman, *Living My Life* (two volumes), New York, Dover, 1975.

14. The recent reclamation of the early years of the magazine *The Masses* has begun to revive the names of Max Eastman, Floyd Dell, John Sloan, Edward Carpenter, and Havelock Ellis who more or less vanished from public view about the time of World War II. For a start, one may consult William O'Neill, *The Last Romantic: A Life of Max Eastman,* New York, Oxford University Press, 1978; Rebecca Zurier, *Art for the Masses,* Philadelphia, Temple University Press, 1988; Leslie Fishbein, *Rebels in Bohemia: The Radicals of the Masses 1911–1917,* Chapel Hill, University of North Car-

olina Press, 1982; Christopher Lasch, *The New Radicalism in America 1889–1963: The Intellectual as a Social Type,* New York, Knopf, 1965.

15. Sidney Hook, "Failure of the Left," *Partisan Review,* March–April 1943, p. 167.

16. Ibid., p. 168.

17. Although virtually all of those associated with *PR* made, after 1945, their declaration "for the West" with greater or lesser enthusiasm (Hook's "Failure of the Left," which retains a broad "third camp" position, i.e., is still critical of the Roosevelt administration), the tilt is plainly toward an endorsement of liberal democracy as the best possible environment for the growth of democratic socialism, a perspective that had been formerly eschewed by all varieties of revolutionary socialists, except the Communists.

18. "Our Country and Our Culture," *Partisan Review,* May–June 1952, p. 283.

19. Daniel Bell, *Marxian Socialism in the United States,* Princeton, Princeton University Press, 1952.

20. "Editorial Statement to Our Country and Our Culture," p. 284.

21. Ibid., p. 319.

22. Ibid., p. 320.

23. Ibid., p. 323.

24. Howard Brick, *Daniel Bell and the End of Intellectual Radicalism,* Madison, University of Wisconsin Press, 1989.

25. In conversations with the author, 1982–1983.

26. Sidney Hook, "Failure of the Left," p. 166.

27. Phillip Rahv, "Testament of a Homeless Radical," *Partisan Review,* Summer 1945.

28. Irving Howe and B. J. Widick, *The UAW and Walter Reuther,* New York, Random House, 1949.

29. This year marks the demise of *Politics,* the remaining political journal of the independent intellectual left.

30. Sidney Hook, *Out of Step,* New York, Harper and Row, 1989; Lionel Trilling, "Appendix: Some Notes for an Autobiographical Lecture" (Spring 1971), in *The Last Decade: Essays and Reviews (1965–1975),* New York, Harcourt Brace Jovanovich, 1979.

31. Dwight Macdonald, *Against the American Grain,* New York, Da Capo Press, 1983.

32. Ibid., pp. 3–75.

33. Lionel Trilling, "Preface," *Beyond Culture,* New York, Harcourt Brace Jovanovich, 1965.

34. Loyalty to the war claimed such progressives as John Dewey, W. E. B. DuBois, and even some leading socialist intellectuals such as John Spargo, Charles Edward Russell, and William English Walling. However, most socialists followed Eugene Debs, the venerable party leader, and Morris Hillquit, its long-time chairman, in opposing the war. The progressive mobilization in favor of the war was highlighted by the defection of one of its major literary critics, Randolph Bourne.

35. Abraham Cahan, *The Education of Abraham Cahan,* vols. 1 and 2, translated by Leon Stein, Abraham P. Cohan, and Lynn Davidson, Philadelphia, Jewish Publication Society of America, 1969.

36. Sidney Hook, "On the Jewish Question," *Partisan Review,* May 1949.

37. Ibid., p. 480.

38. Ibid., p. 482.

39. C. Wright Mills, "Letter to the New Left," in *Power, Politics, and People,* edited by Irving Louis Horowitz, New York, Oxford University Press, 1963.

40. Sidney Hook, *Academic Freedom or Academic Anarchy,* New York, Delta Publishing Company, 1969.

41. Stanley Aronowitz and Henry Giroux, *Postmodern Education,* Minneapolis, University of Minnesota Press, 1991.

2. *Culture Between High and Low (pp. 63–84)*

1. Mikhail Bakhtin, *Rabelais and His World,* Bloomington, Indiana University Press, 1984.

2. It is interesting to note Bakhtin's understanding of this period: "We find this tight matrix of death with laughter, with food, with drink, with sexual indecencies in other representative figures of the Renaissance [besides Rabelais]; in Boccaccio (in the framing story itself, and in the material of the separate stories), in Pulci (the description of deaths and of paradise during the Battle of Roncevalles; in Margutte (a prototype for Panuge, who dies of laughter) and in Shakespeare (in the Falstaff scenes, the cheerful gravedigger of Hamlet, the cheerful drunk porter of Macbeth). The similarity among these scenes can be explained by the unity of the epoch and by the shared nature of the sources and traditions, the differences are in the breadth and fullness with which these materials are developed." Mikhail Bakhtin, "Forms of Time and Chronotope in the Novel," in *The Dialogic Imagination,* Austin, University of Texas Press, 1981, pp. 198–199.

3. Maynard Solomon, *Beethoven,* New York, Scribners, 1977.

4. Ludwig Wittgenstein, *Philosophical Investigations,* translated by G. E. M. Anscombe, New York, Macmillan, 1953, 1968, especially pp. 200–243 where, among other statements, Wittgenstein argues that there can be no private language and that meaning is produced by agreement of two or more speakers to observe the rules of the language game rather than possessing an intrinsic significance.

5. Compare Clement Greenberg, "Avant Garde and Kitsch" in *Art and Culture,* Boston, Beacon Press, 1961, and Theodor Adorno, *Philosophy of Modern Music,* New York, Continuum Books, 1972.

6. Greenberg, "Avant Garde and Kitsch."

7. Peter Berger, *Theory of the Avant Garde,* Minneapolis, University of Minnesota Press, 1984.

8. Alexis de Tocqueville, *Democracy in America,* New York, Vintage Books, 1990, vol. 2, p. 56.

9. Ibid., pp. 56–57.

10. Ortega y Gasset, *The Revolt of the Masses,* New York, W. W. Norton, 1932, p. 11.

11. Ibid., p. 12.

12. Ibid., p. 17.

13. Thorstein Veblen, *Theory of the Leisure Class,* New York, Penguin Books, 1979.

14. Thorstein Veblen, *The Instinct of Workmanship,* New York, Macmillan, 1914.

15. Walter Lippmann, *Public Opinion,* New York, Free Press, 1965, pp. 54–55.

16. Ibid., p. 195.

17. Plato, *The Republic,* quoted in Lippmann, *Public Opinion,* p. 258.

18. John Dewey, *The Public and Its Problems,* in *John Dewey's Later Works,* vol. 2, Carbondale, Southern Illinois University Press, 1984, p. 304.

19. Ibid., p. 306.

20. Ibid.

21. Henry Nash Smith, *Virgin Land,* Cambridge, Harvard University Press, 1950.

22. Dewey, *Public and Its Problems,* p. 306.

23. Here, of course, the question of who gets to vote is undiscussed by Dewey. We know the franchise in this "direct" democracy is reserved for white, male property owners. While the evidence for women's protest against their exclusion is scant, there has been considerable recent historical research showing that the "crowd" of tenants, wage laborers, and the unemployed who were typically denied the franchise in New England towns frequently responded with protests to town meeting decisions that affected them but over which they had no voice.

24. Dewey, *Public and Its Problems,* pp. 306–307.

25. Ibid., p. 308.

26. Ibid., p. 321.

27. John Dewey, *Freedom and Culture,* New York, G. P. Putnam Sons, 1939, p. 141.

28. *Freedom and Culture* is perhaps one of the best illustrations of the shift in Dewey's thought from an ethical-based scientific approach to human affairs to a social ethics strongly suffused with moral precepts.

29. Herbert Marcuse, "Some Social Implications of Modern Technology" in Andrew Arato and Eike Gebhardt, eds., *The Essential Frankfurt School Reader,* New York, Urizen Books, 1978.

30. Herbert Marcuse, *One Dimensional Man,* Boston, Beacon Press, 1964.

31. Wilheim Reich, *The Mass Psychology of Fascism,* 3rd ed., translated by Theodore Wolfe, New York, Orgone Press, 1946.

32. Max Horkheimer, *Critical Theory,* translated by Matthew Connell and others, New York, Herder and Herder, 1972.

33. Theodore Adorno, "On Popular Music" in *Studies in Philosophy and Social Science,* vol. 9, no. 1, p. 22; also "Popular Music," a chapter in Adorno's *Introduction to the Sociology of Music,* New York, Continuum Books, 1988; and Theodor Adorno, "On the Fetish Character of Music and the Repression of Listening" in Andrew Arato and Eike Gebhardt, eds., *The Essential Frankfurt School Reader,* New York, Urizen Books, 1978.

34. Leo Lowenthal, "Historical Perspectives of Popular Culture" in Bernard Rosenberg and David Manning White, eds., *Mass Culture,* Glencoe, Ill., Free Press, 1957, pp. 49–50.

35. Friedrich Nietzsche, *The Will to Power (Complete Works),* London, T. N. Foulis, 1910, volume 2, pp. 265–266, quoted in Lowenthal, ibid., p. 50.

36. Gilles Deleuze, *The Logic of Sense,* New York, Columbia University Press, 1990.

37. Theodor Adorno, *Introduction to the Sociology of Music.*

3. The Origins of Cultural Studies (pp. 85–108)

1. Some of the best explanations for the "new" Nietzsche in contemporary philosophy is provided by Gilles Deleuze, "Nomad Thought," and "Active and Reactive," in David B. Allison, ed., *The New Nietzsche,* New York, Delta Publishing Co., 1977.

2. The recent appearance of Lawrence Grossberg and Cary Nelson's mammoth collection *Cultural Studies* (New York, Routledge, 1992) confirms the persistence of the influence of the Centre for Contemporary Cultural Studies at Birmingham and its

key theorists—Edward Thompson, Richard Hoggart, and especially Stuart Hall and Raymond Williams. But if the theoretical framework of the articles in this collection remains, with the exception of some of the feminist, black, and "Third World" interventions, close to its British inspiration, the practices do not. Here, the focus remains, predominantly, on the American understanding of cultural studies as the critique of "representations," that is, of cultural artifacts in popular culture. The volume presents no reports of ethnographic work, American or otherwise, and Donna Haraway is virtually the only writer working on science and technology which is, as I argue below, among the most exciting of the new vistas for cultural studies. In sum, without regard to the value of the articles since, among other reasons, it arrived too late to permit of extensive comment, the volume is symptomatic, perhaps emblematic, of the general incorporation of U.S. cultural studies within English departments and other branches of the humanities.

3. Francis Mulhern, *The Moment of Scrutiny,* London, Verso Books, 1980.

4. Guy Debord, *The Society of the Spectacle,* Detroit, Black and Red, 1970.

5. Richard Hoggart, *Uses of Literacy,* Boston, Beacon Press, 1961, p. 31.

6. Ibid., p. 158.

7. Richard Hoggart, *An English Temper: Essays on Education, Culture and Communication,* London and New York, Oxford University Press, 1982.

8. Max Weber, "Class, Status, Party," in H. H. Gerth and C. Wright Mills, eds., *From Max Weber: Essays in Sociology,* London and New York, Oxford University Press, 1946.

9. The idea was crucial for the early theoretical orientation of the Centre. It was particularly important in perhaps the two most salient of the ethnographies produced during the Centre's twenty-five-year history: Paul Willis's *Learning to Labor: How Working Class Kids Get Working Class Jobs,* New York, Columbia University Press, 1981, first published in 1977; and Dick Hebdige's *Subculture: The Meaning of Style,* London and New York, Methuen, 1979; see also *Resistance through Rituals: Youth Subculture in Post-War Britain,* Stuart Hall and Tony Jefferson, eds., London, Allen and Unwin, 1979.

10. Hoggart, *Uses of Literacy,* p. 163.

11. Raymond Williams, *Politics and Letters,* London, New Left Books, 1979.

12. Hoggart, *Uses of Literacy,* p. 173.

13. Ibid., p. 184.

14. E. P. Thompson, *The Making of the English Working Class,* New York, Knopf, 1963, p. 12.

15. Ibid., p. 11.

16. Ibid.

17. Ibid., p. 802.

18. Ibid., p. 807.

19. James Gilbert, *Work Without Salvation: America's Intellectuals and Industrial Alienation, 1880–1910,* Baltimore, The Johns Hopkins University Press, 1977.

20. Stuart Hall, "Cultural Studies at the Centre," Stenciled Paper, Centre for Cultural Studies, 1979, p. 3.

21. Ralph Miliband, *Parliamentary Socialism,* London, Oxford University Press, 1964.

22. John and Barbara Hammond, *The Town Laborer,* London, Longmans Green, 1917.

23. E. P. Thompson, *The Poverty of Theory,* London, New Left Books, 1978; Louis Althusser, "Contradiction and Overdetermination," in *For Marx,* New York, Vintage Books, 1970.

24. George Dimitrov, "Report to the Seventh World Congress of the Communist International," published as *The United Front Against Fascism*, New York, New Century Publishers, 1943.

25. In the *Prison Notebooks* (New York, International Publishers, 1971) Gramsci suggested that the task of the communists was to work within the context of the "national-popular (see especially p. 406). Clearly, but not to many critics, this was meant as a cultural, not a nationalist political strategy. Its aim, discussed more fully in Chapter 5, was to contest the claim of conservatives and liberals to national traditions.

26. See Chapter 5 for a more extensive discussion of this point.

27. V. I. Lenin, "On the Right of Nations to Self-Determination," *Selected Works*, vol. 2, New York, International Publishers, 1947.

28. Thompson's work, especially *Making*, roughly articulates with this project.

29. Thompson, *Making*, p. 156.

30. Eric Hobsbawm, *Primitive Rebels*, New York, W. W. Norton, 1959; *Bandits*, New York, Delacorte Press, 1969.

31. Thompson, *Making*, pp. 551–552.

32. Bill Schwarz, "'The People' in History: The Communist Party Historians' Group," in Richard Johnson, Gregor McLennan, Bill Schwarz and David Sutton, eds., *Making Histories: Studies in History Writing and Politics*, Minneapolis, University of Minnesota Press, 1982, p. 87.

33. Ibid.

34. All of these in Gramsci, *Prison Notebooks*.

35. Thompson, *Making*, p. 732.

36. Raymond Williams, *Politics and Letters*, p. 135.

37. Raymond Williams, *Marxism and Literature*, New York, Oxford University Press, 1977, p. 7.

38. Louis Althusser, "Contradiction and Overdetermination," in *For Marx*.

39. Raymond Williams, "Base and Superstructure" in *Problems of Materialism and Culture*, London, Verso Books, 1980.

40. See especially Terry Eagleton, *Criticism and Ideology*, London, New Left Books, 1976.

41. Williams, *Politics and Letters*, pp. 18–19.

42. Ernesto Laclau and Chantal Mouffe, *Hegemony and Socialist Strategy*, London, Verso Books, 1985.

43. Williams, *Politics and Letters*, p. 139.

4. British Cultural Studies (pp. 109–130)

1. Stuart Hall, *Cultural Studies at the Centre*, p. 6.

2. Ibid., p. 27.

3. Ibid., p. 16.

4. Ibid., p. 19.

5. Ibid.

6. Ibid.

7. Althusser's use of the idea of epistemological break is borrowed from Gaston Bachelard's theory of scientific development. It signifies that science itself is constituted not, as in the incremental theory of scientific progress by the oscillation of observation, experiment, and generalization, but by critique that always involves a new way of seeing, particularly the reconstitution of the object of inquiry as well as a new con-

ception of the relation of inquiry to its object. See Althusser, *For Marx,* and Louis Althusser and Etienne Balibar, *Reading Capital,* London, New Left Books, 1970.

8. Hall, *Cultural Studies at the Centre,* p. 31.

9. Louis Althusser, "Ideology and Ideological State Apparatuses," in *Lenin and Philosophy,* New York, Monthly Review Press, 1971.

10. Gramsci, *Prison Notebooks.*

11. Nicos Poulantzas, *State, Power, Socialism,* London, New Left Books, 1979.

12. Wittgenstein, *Philosophical Investigations.*

13. Paul Gilroy, *There Ain't No Black in the Union Jack,* Chicago, University of Chicago Press, 1991, p. 12.

14. Stuart Hall and Tony Jefferson, eds., *Resistance Through Rituals: Youth Subcultures in Post-War Britain,* Unwin Hyman, 1990.

15. This is especially the case in many of the studies of working-class women conducted at the Centre. For a representative study, see Dorothy Hobson, "Housewife: Isolation and Oppression" in Women's Studies Group, *Women Take Issue: Aspects of Women's Subordination,* London, Hutchinson, 1982; also a historical study, Pam Taylor, "Daughters and Mothers, Maids and Mistresses: Domestic Service Between the Wars," in Stuart Hall, ed., *Culture, Media, Language,* London, Hutchinson, 1980; but a contemporary collection (A. McRobbie and Mica Nava, *Gender and Generation,* London, Macmillan, 1984) is notable for its theoretical orientation. The article by McRobbie, who had been associated with the Centre, is particularly noteworthy for its adoption of a feminist poststructuralist perspective associated with the work of Laura Mulvey and Teresa DiLauretis and its textual close reading of films. See Angela McRobbie, "Dance and Social Fantasy" in McRobbie and Nava, *Gender and Generation.*

16. J. Clarke et al., *Class and Subculture in Resistance Through Ritual,* pp. 47–48.

17. Dick Hebdidge, *Subculture: The Meaning of Style,* London, Methuen, 1979; Paul Willis, *Learning to Labor,* New York, Columbia University Press, 1981.

18. William Labov, *The Social Stratification of English in New York City,* Washington, Center for Applied Linguistics, 1966.

19. Clarke et al., *Class and Subculture,* p. 10.

20. Ibid., p. 39.

21. Stanley Aronowitz, *Crisis in Historical Materialism: Class, Politics and Culture in Marxist Theory,* Minneapolis, University of Minnesota Press, 1990.

22. See especially Richard Johnson and Gregor McLennan, eds., *Making Histories,* Minneapolis, University of Minnesota Press, 1983, and Richard Johnson, "What Is Cultural Studies, Anyway?" in *Social Text,* 1988, vol. 6, no. 3, p. 18.

23. Richard Hoggart, *An English Temper,* pp. 148–149.

24. Pierre Macherey, *A Theory of Literary Production,* London, New Left Books, 1976.

25. Stuart Hall, "Encoding and Decoding in the Television Discourse," Birmingham Centre for Cultural Studies, Stenciled Occasional Paper, 1973.

26. Ibid., p. 16.

27. Ibid., p. 19.

28. Janet Winship, "Sex for Sale," in Stuart Hall, ed., *Culture Media, Language,* London, Hutchinson, 1980; Judith Williamson, *Decoding Advertisements,* London, Marion Bogar, 1980.

29. Winship, *Sex for Sale.*

30. Ibid., p. 218.

31. Ibid.

32. David Bloor, *Knowledge and Social Imagery,* London, Routledge and Kegan Paul, 1976.

5. *Cultural Politics of the Popular Front (pp. 131–166)*

1. Robert Warshow, "The Legacy of the 30s," in *The Immediate Experience,* New York, Anchor Books, 1961, p. 3.

2. Ibid., p. 23.

3. Harvey Klehr, *The Heyday of American Communism,* New York, Basic Books, 1984.

4. George Charney, *Long Journey,* New York, Quadrangle Books, 1969.

5. See especially Harold Cruse, *The Crisis of the Negro Intellectual,* New York, William Morrow, 1967.

6. Gerald Meyer, *Vito Marcantonio,* Albany, State University of New York (SUNY) Press, 1989; Robin Kelley, *Hammer and Hoe,* Chapel Hill and London, University of North Carolina Press, 1990; Hosea Hudson, "A Negro Communist in the Deep South," *Radical America,* No. 11 (July–August 1977); Mark Naison, *Communists in Harlem during the Depression,* Urbana, University of Illinois Press, 1983.

7. James Robert Prickett, *Communism and the Communist Party in the American Labor Movement 1920–1950,* PhD diss., UCLA, 1975.

8. See especially Roger Keeran, *The Communist Party and the Auto Workers Union,* Bloomington, University of Indiana Press, 1980; also Frank Emspak, *The Breakup of the CIO (1945–1950),* PhD diss., University of Wisconsin, 1972.

9. Anthony Bimba, *History of the American Working Class,* New York, International Publishers, 1927, p. 9.

10. Gramsci, "Notes on the Southern Question," selections from the *Prison Notebooks.*

11. Gramsci, *Prison Notebooks,* p. 130.

12. For some of the more interesting novels, see Thomas Bell, *Out of This Furnace,* Pittsburgh, University of Pittsburgh Press, 1976, orig. Boston, Little Brown, 1941; Alexander Saxton, *The Great Midland,* Boston, Little Brown, 1948; Margaret Graham, *Swing Shift,* New York, Citadel Press, 1959.

13. Tom Bottomore, ed., *Austro-Marxism,* (Oxford, Clarendon Press, 1978) for a representative sample of Bauer's work on the national question.

14. In addition to Cruse's study of black intellectuals (see note 5), see also Ralph Ellison, *Invisible Man* (New York, Random House, 1947), and the lesser known novel by Chester Himes, *The Lonely Crusade* (New York, Thunder's Mouth Press, 1986) that deals with the relationships between the Communists in Los Angeles and blacks during World War II.

15. Francis Franklin, *The Rise of the American Nation,* New York, International Publishers, 1943; Jack Hardy, *The First American Revolution,* New York, International Publishers, 1938; Herbert Morais, *The Struggle for American Freedom,* New York, International Publishers, 1944; and especially Herbert Aptheker, *American Negro Slave Revolts,* New York, Columbia University Press, 1939. Aptheker and the black historian Carter Woodson pioneered in demonstrating that blacks in the antebellum period resisted their bondage in various ways, including armed insurrections.

16. Eugene Genovese, *Roll, Jordan Roll,* New York, Pantheon, 1974; Herbert Gutman, *The Black Family in Slavery and Freedom,* New York, Pantheon, 1976; Robert Fogel and Stanley Engerman, *Time on the Cross,* Boston, Little Brown, 1974. Gutman

wrote perhaps the most detailed and scathing review of *Time on the Cross*, published in the *New York Review of Books*. Fogel was National Student Director of the Communist party in the late 1940s and broke with the party sometime in the late 1950s; Genovese broke with the party at the same time, but not for the same reasons. He was associated, in the early 1960s, with a "left" critique of the Soviet Union and the American Communist party. He remained a self-professed Marxist until 1989 when, in the wake of the collapse of communist states, he declared socialism obsolete and that Marxism had "failed." Undoubtedly Thompson's leading American follower, Gutman was, characteristically, a consummate "professional" historian.

17. James Allen, *The Negro Question in the United States*, New York, International Publishers, 1928; Harry Haywood, *Negro Liberation*, New York, International Publishers, 1946.

18. David Montgomery, *Workers' Control in America*, Cambridge and New York, Cambridge University Press, 1981; *Fall of the House of Labor*, Cambridge, New York, Cambridge University Press, 1987.

19. George Rude, *The Crowd in the French Revolution*, Oxford and New York, Oxford University Press, 1959.

20. John Hope Franklin, *From Slavery to Freedom* (1961); Eric Foner, *Reconstruction: America's Unfinished Revolution 1863–1877*, New York, Harper and Row, 1988.

21. Kenneth Burke, *A Grammar of Motives and a Rhetoric of Motives*, New York, Meridian Books, 1961; *A Theory of Literary Form*, Baton Rouge, Louisiana University Press, 1941.

22. Perhaps the most widely read works of this group were Ruth Benedict, *Patterns of Culture*, Boston, Houghton Mifflin, 1934, and Ashley Montagu, *Man's Most Dangerous Myth: The Fallacy of Race*, New York, Columbia University Press, 1942.

23. Vernon Louis Parrington, *Main Currents of American Thought* (three volumes), New York, Harcourt, Brace and Co., 1924–1930.

24. Lionel Trilling, *The Liberal Imagination*, New York, Viking, 1950, p. 19.

25. Ibid., p. 23.

26. Ibid., p. 24.

27. Ibid.

28. Dwight Macdonald, "Masscult and Midcult" in *Against the American Grain*.

29. James T. Farrell, *Literature and Morality*, New York, Vanguard Press, 1947. Alan Wald observes that Farrell shared the antipathy of his fellow anti-Stalinist intellectuals to the philistinism of much of popular front culture, and defended modernism against this type of criticism, but was almost alone in recognizing the contribution of some of the exemplars of 1930s radical novels. See Alan Wald, *The New York Intellectuals*, Chapel Hill and London, The University of North Carolina Press, 1987.

30. For a critical perspective on the new social history, see Stanley Aronowitz, "New Introduction" to *False Promises: The Shaping of American Working Class Consciousness*, Durham, Duke University Press, 1992.

31. These were, of course, hits by one of the few postwar communist-oriented leftist folk groups that was able to break through to the mainstream charts, the Weavers.

6. *Cultural Study in Postmodern America (pp. 167–202)*

1. Marshall McLuhan, *Understanding Media*, New York, McGraw-Hill, 1964, pp. 3–4.

2. Ibid., p. 3.

3. Ibid., p. 8.

4. Ibid., p. 49.

5. Ibid., p. 9.

6. Arthur Kroker, *Technology and the Canadian Mind,* New York, St. Martin's Press, 1986.

7. Christian Metz, *Film Language: A Semiotics of Cinema,* Oxford, Oxford University Press, 1974.

8. Pauline Kael, "Trash, Art and the Movies" in *Going Steady,* New York, Atlantic Monthly Press, 1968, pp. 88–89.

9. Ibid., p. 91.

10. Ibid., p. 105.

11. Ibid., p. 106.

12. Ibid., p. 105.

13. Henry Nash Smith, *Virgin Land: The American West as Symbol and Myth,* Cambridge, Harvard University Press, 1950, p. 195.

14. Frederick Jackson Turner, *The Frontier in American History,* New York, Holt, Rinehart & Winston, 1962.

15. Particularly in John Dewey, *The Public and Its Problems* (1927) in *John Dewey's Later Works,* Vol. 2, Carbondale, Southern Illinois University Press, 1984; and John Dewey, *Freedom and Culture,* New York, G. P. Putnam Sons, 1939.

16. Robert Warshow, "Movie Chronicle the Westerner" in *The Immediate Experience,* New York, Anchor Books, 1964.

17. Robert Warshow, "The Movie Camera and the American," in *The Immediate Experience,* p. 125.

18. For a representative collection of essays in the "new" French cinema studies see Theresa Hak Kyung Cha, ed., *Apparatus,* New York, Tanam Press, 1980, particularly the essay by Jean Baudry, "The Apparatus," pp. 67–74.

19. Edmund Wilson, "Gilbert Seldes and the Popular Arts" in Edmund Wilson, *The Shores of Light: A Literary Chronicle of the Twenties and Thirties,* New York, Farrar Straus and Giroux, 1952, pp. 156–173.

20. Gilbert Seldes, *The 7 Lively Arts* (1924), New York, The Sagamore Press, 1957.

21. Ibid., pp. 207–219.

22. Ibid., p. 207.

23. Ibid.

24. Gilbert Seldes, "The One Man Show," in *The 7 Lively Arts,* p. 172.

25. Paul F. Lazarsfeld, "An Episode in the History of Social Research: A Memoir" in Donald Fleming and Bernard Bailyn, eds., *The Intellectual Migration,* Cambridge, Harvard University Press, 1969, p. 278.

26. Ibid., p. 299.

27. Ibid., p. 323.

28. Ibid., p. 324.

29. Theodor Adorno, "Memorandum to Lazarsfeld," quoted in Lazarsfeld, "An Episode," p. 324.

30. Clement Greenberg, "Avant Garde and Kitsch," *Partisan Review,* Fall 1939, pp. 34–49.

31. Tom Wolfe, *The Kandy Kolored Tangerine-Flake Streamlined Baby* (1965), New York, Farrar Straus and Giroux, 1987.

32. Ibid., "Introduction" pages in this edition unnumbered.

33. Ibid.

34. Ibid.

35. Wolfe, *Kandy Kolored,* p. 5.

36. Ibid., p. 7.
37. Greil Marcus, "Who Put the Bomp in the Bomp-Bomp de Bomp" in Greil Marcus, ed., *Rock and Roll Will Stand*, Boston, Beacon Press, 1969, p. 8.
38. Ibid., p. 15.
39. Greil Marcus, ed., *Stranded: Rock and Roll for a Desert Island*, New York, Knopf, 1979.
40. Robert Christgau, "New York Dolls," in Marcus, *Stranded*, p. 133.
41. Lester Bangs, "Astral Weeks," in Marcus, *Stranded*, p. 180.
42. Ellen Willis, "The Velvet Underground," in Marcus, *Stranded*, p. 74.
43. Ibid., p. 83.

7. The Authority of Knowledge (pp. 203–243)

1. Fritz Machlup, *The Production and Distribution of Knowledge in the United States*, New York, Columbia University Press, 1962, 1969.
2. Georges Canguilhem, *The Normal and the Pathological* (1943), New York, Zone Books, 1989, with an introduction by Michel Foucault. The appearance of this book in English helps put much of Foucault's work in historical perspective. Among other revelations, we can now see how much Foucault may be understood to be fundamentally indebted, not only to Canguilhem, but to the tradition of the critique of scientific knowledge as a crucial form of power in modern civilization.
3. But German universities harbored the most influential and legitimate bearers of intellectual knowledge; see Fritz Ringer, *The Decline of the German Mandarins*, Middletown, Wesleyan University Press, 1990.
4. Charles Sanders Peirce, "The Fixation of Belief," in Justus Buchler, ed., *Philosophical Writings of Peirce*, New York, Dover Books, 1958.
5. Alexis de Tocqueville, *Democracy in America*.
6. Ernst Mayr, *The Growth of Biological Thought*, Cambridge, Harvard University Press, 1982.
7. Andrew Pickering, *Constructing Quarks: A Social History of Particle Physics*, Chicago, University of Chicago Press, 1984.
8. See especially Murray Bookchin, *The Ecology of Freedom*, Palo Alto, Cheshire Books, 1982.
9. For a discussion of the concepts "critical" and "transformative" intellectuals, see Stanley Aronowitz and Henry Giroux, *Education Under Siege*, South Hadley, Bergin and Garvey, 1985.
10. Richard Rorty, *Philosophy and the Mirror of Nature*, Princeton, Princeton University Press, 1979; *Consequences of Pragmatism*, Minneapolis, University of Minnesota Press, 1981.
11. Clifford Geertz, *Interpretation of Cultures*, New York, Basic Books, 1973.
12. For representative works in this vein, see James Clifford and George E. Marcus, eds., *Writing Culture: The Poetics and Politics of Ethnography*, Berkeley and Los Angeles, University of California Press, 1986; James Clifford, *The Predicament of Culture*, Cambridge, Harvard University Press, 1988; George E. Marcus and Michael M. J. Fischer, *Anthropology as Cultural Critique: An Experimental Moment in the Human Sciences*, Chicago, University of Chicago Press, 1986. The term used here—"human sciences"—signifies a shift from the positivistic inclination of American social sciences to the methods and epistemological stance of contemporary literary theory to see the subjects and objects of knowledge as constituted by the social and political situation as well as the condition of writing.

13. Marcus and Fischer, *Anthropology,* p. 8.

14. Ibid., p. 35.

15. Marshall Sahlins, *Critique of Cultural Reason,* Chicago, University of Chicago Press, 1978.

16. Most recently by Richard Lewontin, "The Human Genome Project," *New York Review of Books,* May 14, 1992.

17. Stanley Aronowitz, *Science as Power: Discourse and Ideology in Modern Society,* Minneapolis, University of Minnesota Press, 1988.

18. Adam Smith, *The Wealth of Nations,* Chicago, University of Chicago Press, 1976, p. 18.

19. John Crowe Ransom, *Beating the Bushes: Selected Essays 1941–1970,* New York, New Directions Books, 1972, p. 174.

20. Frank Lentricchia, *After the New Criticism,* Chicago, University of Chicago Press, 1980; *Criticism and Social Change,* Chicago, University of Chicago Press, 1983.

21. Paul De Man, *Blindness and Insight,* Minneapolis, University of Minnesota Press, 1983.

22. See especially Paul Bové, *Intellectuals in Power,* New York, Columbia University Press, 1986; Bruce Robbine, ed., *Intellectuals,* Minneapolis, University of Minnesota Press, 1990.

23. Jeffrey Kittay and Wlad Godzich, *The Emergence of Prose,* Minneapolis, University of Minnesota Press, 1984; Samuel Weber, ed., *Demarcating the Disciplines,* Minneapolis, University of Minnesota Press, 1986.

24. For an influential attempt at theoretical articulation of this issue, see Gayatri Spivak, "Can the Subaltern Speak?" in Cary Nelson and Larry Grossberg, eds., *Marxism and the Interpretation of Cultures,* Champaign-Urbana, University of Illinois Press, 1988.

25. Rachel M. Brownstein, *Becoming a Heroine: Reading About Women in Novels,* Harmondsworth and New York, Penguin Books, 1982, p. 14.

26. Houston Baker, *Blues, Ideology and Afro-American Literature: A Vernacular Theory,* Chicago, University of Chicago Press, 1985.

27. Henry Louis Gates, "Canon Formation, Literary History and the Afro-American Tradition: From the Seen to the Told" in Houston Baker and Patrick Raymond, eds., *Afro-American Studies in the 1990s,* Chicago, University of Chicago Press, 1989.

28. Baker, *Blues,* p. 98.

29. Ibid., p. 103.

30. Henry Louis Gates, *The Signifying Monkey,* New York, Oxford University Press, 1988, p. 100.

31. Baker, *Blues,* p. 26.

32. Ibid., p. 2.

33. Ibid., p. 76.

34. Ibid., p. 77–78.

35. Ibid., pp. 9–10.

36. Moritz Schlick, *General Theory of Knowledge,* Vienna and New York, Springer Verlag, 1974, p. 2.

37. Ibid., p. 3.

38. Bruno Latour, *Science in Action,* Cambridge, Harvard University Press, 1987.

39. Merton's major essays on science have been collected in Robert Merton, *Sociology of Science,* Chicago, University of Chicago Press, 1973.

40. Ludwig Fleck, *Genesis of a Scientific Fact,* Thomas Kuhn and Robert Merton, eds., Chicago, University of Chicago Press, 1976.

41. Bruno Latour and Steve Woolgar, *Laboratory Life,* London and Los Angeles, Sage Publications, 1979.

42. Paul Feyerabend, *Against Method,* London, New Left Books, 1976.

43. Steven Shapin and Simon Schaeffer, *Leviathan and Air-Pumps: Hobbes, Boyle and the Experimental Life,* Princeton, Princeton University Press, 1985.

44. Donna Haraway Simians, *Cyborgs and Women,* New York, Routledge, 1991; Sandra Harding, *The Science Question in Feminism,* Ithaca, Cornell University Press, 1986; Evelyn Fox Keller, *Reflections on Gender and Science,* New Haven, Yale University Press, 1984.

45. Evelyn Fox Keller, *A Feeling for the Organism,* San Francisco, Freeman, 1983.

46. Barbara Katz Rothman, *Recreating Motherhood,* New York: W. W. Norton, 1989.

47. Cynthia Eagle Russett, *Sexual Science,* Cambridge, Harvard University Press, 1989.

48. Harding, p. 72.

8. The End of the Beginning? (pp. 244–253)

1. For four recent exceptions that, I hope, represent a powerful counterweight to banality, see Henry Giroux, *Border Crossings,* New York, Routledge, 1992; Emily Hicks Border, *Writing the Multidimensional Text,* Minneapolis, University of Minnesota Press, 1991; Mike Davis, *City of Quartz,* London and New York, Verso, 1991; Celeste Olalquiaga, *Megalopolis,* Minneapolis, University of Minnesota Press, 1992.

2. Wilhelm Dilthey, *Introduction to the Human Sciences,* translated and edited by Rudolph A. Makkreel and Fithjof Rodi, Princeton, Princeton University Press, 1989, p. 108.

3. Ibid.

Index

UNIVERSITY PRESS OF NEW ENGLAND

publishes books under its own imprint and is the publisher for Brandeis University Press, Brown University Press, University of Connecticut, Dartmouth College, Middlebury College Press, University of New Hampshire, University of Rhode Island, Tufts University, University of Vermont, and Wesleyan University Press.

ABOUT THE AUTHOR

Stanley Aronowitz is Professor of Sociology and Director of the Cultural Studies Program at the Graduate Center, City University of New York. Among his books are *The Politics of Identity* (1992), *Science as Power* (1988), *The Crisis in Historical Materialism* (1981), and, with Henry Giroux, *Postmodern Education* (1991).

Library of Congress Cataloging-in-Publication Data

Aronowitz, Stanley.
    Roll over Beethoven : the return of cultural strife /
Stanley Aronowitz.
      p.   cm.
    Includes bibliographical references (p.) and index.
    ISBN 0–8195–5255–0. — ISBN 0–8195–6262–9 (pbk.)
    1. United States—Cultural policy. 2. Politics and culture—
United States. 3. United States—Civilization—1970–   I. Title.
E169.12.A73   1993
973.928—dc20   92–56898